SOCIAL DIMENSIONS OF PRIVACY

Written by a select international group of leading privacy scholars, *Social Dimensions of Privacy* endorses and develops an innovative approach to privacy. By debating topical privacy cases in their specific research areas, the contributors explore the new privacy-sensitive areas: legal scholars and political theorists discuss the European and American approaches to privacy regulation; sociologists explore new forms of surveillance and privacy on social network sites; and philosophers revisit feminist critiques of privacy, discuss markets in personal data, issues of privacy in health care and democratic politics. The broad interdisciplinary character of the volume will be of interest to readers from a variety of scientific disciplines who are concerned with privacy and data protection issues.

BEATE ROESSLER is Professor of Philosophy at the University of Amsterdam, the Netherlands. She is co-director of the Philosophy and Public Affairs research programme.

DOROTA MOKROSINSKA is a research fellow in political theory at the Goethe University in Frankfurt am Main, Germany, where she is conducting research on the place of privacy in democratic politics.

SOCIAL DIMENSIONS OF PRIVACY

Interdisciplinary Perspectives

Edited by

BEATE ROESSLER

AND

DOROTA MOKROSINSKA

CAMBRIDGE
UNIVERSITY PRESS

CAMBRIDGE
UNIVERSITY PRESS

University Printing House, Cambridge CB2 8BS, United Kingdom

Cambridge University Press is part of the University of Cambridge.

It furthers the University's mission by disseminating knowledge in the pursuit of education, learning and research at the highest international levels of excellence.

www.cambridge.org
Information on this title: www.cambridge.org/9781107052376

First published 2015

A catalogue record for this publication is available from the British Library

Library of Congress Cataloguing in Publication data
Social dimensions of privacy : interdisciplinary perspectives / edited by Beate Roessler and Dorota Mokrosinska.
pages   cm
Includes bibliographical references and index.
ISBN 978-1-107-05237-6 (hbk)
1. Privacy, Right of – Social aspects.   I. Roessler, Beate,
1958– editor.   II. Mokrosinska, Dorota, 1967– editor.
JC596.S63 2015
323.44′8–dc23
2014049357

ISBN 978-1-107-05237-6 Hardback

CONTENTS

CONTRIBUTORS

ANITA L. ALLEN, Vice Provost for Faculty and Henry R. Silverman Professor of Law and Philosophy, University of Pennsylvania, Philadelphia, PA, USA

COLIN J. BENNETT, Professor at the Department of Political Science, University of Victoria, Victoria, BC, Canada

KOEN BRUYNSEELS, Research Fellow at the Section of Philosophy, Delft University of Technology, Delft, the Netherlands

ANDREAS BUSCH, Professor of Political Science and Chair in Comparative Politics and Political Economy at the Department of Social Sciences, Georg-August-Universität Göttingen, Göttingen, Germany

JUDITH WAGNER DECEW, Professor of Philosophy and Department Chair, Director of Ethics and Public Policy Concentration, Clark University, Worcester, MA, USA

KIRSTY HUGHES, University Lecturer in Public Law, University of Cambridge, Cambridge, United Kingdom

ANNABELLE LEVER, Associate Professor of Normative Political Theory, Department of Political Science and International Relations, University of Geneva, Geneva, Switzerland

GARY T. MARX, Professor Emeritus of Sociology at Massachusetts Institute of Technology (MIT), Cambridge, MA, USA

CHERYL A. METOYER, Associate Professor in American Indian Studies and Associate Dean for Research at the Information School, University of Washington, Seattle, WA, USA

DOROTA MOKROSINSKA, Postdoctoral Research Fellow at the Department of Political Science, Goethe University, Frankfurt am Main, Germany

ADAM MOLNAR, Lecturer at the Department of Criminology, Deakin University, Melbourne, Australia

ADAM D. MOORE, Associate Professor at the Information School, University of Washington, Seattle, WA, USA

BRYCE CLAYTON NEWELL, Research Fellow at the Tech Policy Lab and Ph.D. Candidate at the Information School, University of Washington, Seattle, WA, USA

HELEN NISSENBAUM, Professor, Media, Culture and Communication, Director, Information Law Institute, New York University, New York, NY, USA

CHRISTOPHER PARSONS, Postdoctoral Fellow and Managing Director of the Telecom Transparency Project in the Citizen Lab, Munk School of Global Affairs at the University of Toronto, Toronto, ON, Canada

PRISCILLA M. REGAN, Professor of Government and Politics, School of Policy, Government, and International Affairs, George Mason University, Fairfax, VA, USA

BEATE ROESSLER, Professor of Philosophy at the Philosophy Department, University of Amsterdam, Amsterdam, the Netherlands

JAMES B. RULE, Distinguished Affiliated Scholar in the Center for the Study of Law and Technology, at the Law School, University of California, Berkeley, CA, USA

PAUL M. SCHWARTZ, Jefferson E. Peyser Professor of Law, University of California, Berkeley Law School, Berkeley, CA, USA

DANIEL J. SOLOVE, John Marshall Harlan Research Professor of Law, George Washington University Law School, Washington DC, USA

VALERIE STEEVES, Associate Professor of Criminology at the Faculty of Social Sciences, University of Ottawa, Ottawa, ON, Canada

JEROEN VAN DEN HOVEN, Professor of Philosophy at the Philosophy Section, Delft University of Technology, the Netherlands

ACKNOWLEDGEMENTS

We gratefully acknowledge the funding received from the Netherlands Organization for Scientific Research (NWO) for the research project on "Social Dimensions of Privacy" (360-20-240), which provided us with the opportunity to conceive and realize the present volume. We are also very grateful for the support of the Netherlands Institute for Advanced Studies in the Humanities and Social Sciences (NIAS) and the Royal Netherlands Academy for Arts and Sciences (KNAW) for hosting the workshop that brought together many of the contributors to this volume prior to its publication in Wassenaar in January 2014. And we thank the Amsterdam School for Cultural Analysis (ASCA) and the Department of Philosophy at the University of Amsterdam for additional funding for this workshop.

We also want to thank a number of colleagues at the University of Amsterdam: the members of the Amsterdam Platform for Privacy Research and the participants of the Philosophy and Public Affairs Colloquium at the Department of Philosophy. We have benefited enormously from their advice and feedback and we are very grateful for their fruitful collaboration and for their support.

Our very greatest debt of gratitude is, of course, to the authors: for their immensely stimulating contributions, their enthusiasm and their willingness to engage with each other's ideas, which made this volume possible.

Kim Hughes, our editor at Cambridge University Press, has been extremely supportive and patient throughout and we are very grateful to her. Finally, we would like to express our warm thanks to Marijn Sax and Marjolein Lanzing for their editorial assistance.

Beate Roessler and Dorota Mokrosinska

ABBREVIATIONS

APEC	Asia-Pacific Economic Cooperation
BND	Bundesnachrichtendienst (Germany)
CAN-SPAM	Controlling the Assault of Non-Solicited Pornography and Marketing Act 2003 (USA)
CFR	Charter of Fundamental Rights (EU)
CPBR	Consumer Privacy Bill of Rights (USA)
CNIL	National Commission on Information Technology and Liberties (Commission Nationale des Informatiques et Libertés) (France)
COPPA	Children's Online Privacy Protection Act 2000 (USA)
DHS	Department of Homeland Security (USA)
ECHR	European Convention on Human Rights
EDPB	European Data Protection Board
EU	European Union
FACTA	Fair and Accurate Credit Transactions Act 2003 (USA)
FBI	Federal Bureau of Investigation (USA)
FCRA	Fair Credit Reporting Act 1970 (USA)
FIPPS	fair information practice principles
FTC	Federal Trade Commission (USA)
GCHQ	Government Communications Headquarters (UK)
GLBA	Gramm-Leach-Bliley Act 1999 (USA)
HIPAA	Health Insurance Portability and Accountability Act 1996 (USA)
HITECH Act	Health Information Technology for Economic and Clinical Health Act 2009 (USA)
IRS	Internal Revenue Service (USA)
NSA	National Security Agency (USA)
NTIA	National Telecommunications and Information Administration (USA)
OCR	Office for Civil Rights, Department of Health and Human Services (USA)
OECD	Organisation for Economic Co-operation and Development
PIPEDA	Personal Information Protection and Electronic Documents Act 2001 (Canada)

RFID	radio frequency identification
SNS	social networking sites/services
SSRC	Social Science Research Council (USA)
STS	science, technology and society
VPPA	Video Privacy Protection Act 1988

TABLE OF CASES

TABLE OF STATUTES

Introduction

DOROTA MOKROSINSKA AND BEATE ROESSLER

Challenges to personal privacy are among the most important challenges faced by contemporary modern societies. Developments in information and communication technology make it possible to gather, process, and analyze information about individuals that has traditionally been considered private. Biometrics, radio frequency identification, social media, smartphones, CCTV, web-based services, self-tracking devices, and search engines register personal data about individuals in ways and on scales that the individuals concerned do not notice or even imagine. More and more personal information is being collected, stored, and processed by private and public organizations such as online retailers, data companies, public transport services, employers, insurance companies, the secret services, and governments. While increased accessibility to personal data may have some important benefits, such as better service or attractive means of communication, control over access to information about oneself and how it is used has become a subject of serious concern.

These new technological developments have affected virtually every domain of life: Therefore, concerns about the influence that modern information and communication technologies have on our daily life as well as concerns about the question as to what happens with these data and with the personal information they carry is a common topic in contemporary theory and social criticism, and the dangers and risks have been pointed out in various ways. A lively debate on these issues is going on in the literature, discussing the consequences the Internet, the social media, and the big data market might have for individuals, their identity and anonymity (Kerr *et al.* 2009), for the individual self (Cohen 2012), for the transformation of social relationships (Marwick 2013; boyd 2014), for justice and equality (Turow 2011), for democratic political procedures (Lever 2012), and for society in general (Mayer-Schoenberger and Cukier 2013; Morozov 2013; Tanner 2014).

1

With our volume on the *Social Dimensions of Privacy: Interdisciplinary Perspectives* we want to contribute to this debate from a specific perspective, namely the perspective of privacy. This perspective is not just one among others. Rather, privacy plays a central role in all the issues mentioned above. We will see that it is through the lens of privacy – and especially through its social meaning – that the consequences of many of the problems of the digitalization of society become palpable. The concept of identity and autonomy, of equality and freedom, of the meaning of social relations, and of political relations, all play a distinct role in the contributions to this volume.

In contemporary privacy scholarship, the importance of privacy has mostly been justified by the individual interests and rights it protects, the most important of which are individual freedom and autonomy in liberal-democratic societies. From this perspective, it is the autonomy of individuals that is at stake in protecting the privacy of personal data and communication in the digital era. This perspective, however, seems insufficient to account for many other concerns raised in the debates on privacy-invasive technologies. With ever greater frequency, privacy-invasive technologies have been argued to endanger not only individual interests but also to affect society and social life more generally.

Privacy scholarship cannot address these broader societal concerns about privacy-invasive technologies, however, unless it moves beyond the traditional concept of privacy focused on the individual. The aim of the volume *Social Dimensions of Privacy: Interdisciplinary Perspectives* is to develop a conceptual framework capable of responding to this challenge: We aim to broaden and supplement the existing, individual-centered privacy paradigm by emphasizing privacy's social meaning and value. In the history of political and social philosophy, the complex distinction between the private and the public has been described and normatively conceptualized in various ways (Weintraub and Kumar 1997; Landes 1998; Geuss 2001; Roessler 2004). However, given that it is threats to informational privacy that have been in the foreground of privacy debates in the past decades, the essays collected in this volume mostly focus on the social dimension and value of *informational* privacy.

In recent years, a number of scholars have taken the first important steps towards developing a social approach to privacy. Arguing that an important aspect of the significance of informational privacy is that it goes beyond the interests of the individuals it protects, these scholars have emphasized the way in which privacy enables social and professional relationships, democratic decision-making processes, and political participation, and have stressed the necessary role of privacy for cooperation and trust within various associations, such as economic partnerships. Following this line of thought, Priscilla Regan classifies privacy as a common good (Regan 1995), Daniel Solove discusses privacy as a social value (Solove 2008), and Helen Nissenbaum argues that privacy is a norm that regulates and structures social life (Nissenbaum 2010). This volume draws on these insights and develops the social approach to privacy further. The volume's contributors engage, from different normative perspectives, with the conceptual aspects of the social understanding of privacy and employ this new perspective to reflect on the role of privacy in political and social practice, in law, in media and communication, in health care, and in the marketplace.

Reflection on the social dimensions of privacy is not only a theoretical exercise. It also has far reaching implications for the way in which conflicts between privacy and other interests can be handled in modern societies. The traditional view of privacy, in which protection of individual privacy is a means of protecting individual interests, has proved a weak basis for protection of privacy in political practice: When individual privacy conflicts with broader social interests such as law enforcement, public security, or the implementation of social justice, protecting individuals' interests seems to be a luxury that society can ill afford. It takes startling privacy invasions such as those involved in the National Security Agency surveillance programs to mobilize a political response. However, if it can be argued that the protection of individual privacy at the same time serves the interests of society, then the alleged conflict between privacy in terms of individual interest and the interests of society should be reconsidered. The contributors explore the implications of this perspective for recent privacy controversies as well as for existing privacy regulations and policies.

Important inspiration for the volume *Social Dimensions of Privacy* has come from the seminal work by Ferdinand Schoeman entitled *Philosophical Dimensions of Privacy: An Anthology* (1984). That landmark collection of articles on privacy reviewed the state of the art in privacy research at the time and became an important reference work for scholars engaging with the topic. Just like Schoeman's volume, this volume *Social Dimensions of Privacy* aspires to provide a synthetic analysis of the most recent developments at the forefront of the academic debate on privacy of its time. However, since the publication of Schoeman's anthology, the discussion of privacy has advanced in different, important ways, not only with respect to the development of the social dimension of privacy, but also with respect to the idea of *interdisciplinarity*: Privacy research has become broader in scope and more specialized in character. Therefore, next to foregrounding the social dimensions of privacy, our volume underlines its interdisciplinary nature. Nowadays, discussion on privacy addresses, among other things, issues in law, philosophy, political science, health sciences, engineering, and the media. Unlike Schoeman's volume, then, the present collection of essays engages multiple disciplines and the contributing authors represent a variety of disciplines: law, philosophy, sociology, media studies, political sciences, and information sciences.

Let us now turn to a brief overview of the following contributions. We have grouped the essays into three clusters. We open the volume with essays devoted to general analyses of the social meaning and value of privacy. The second group addresses recent controversies about privacy protection in different domains of social life and explores the way in which the emphasis on the social relevance of privacy helps resolve them. Finally, the third cluster of essays is devoted to issues in the regulation of privacy and the challenges of the social dimension for existing regulations.

The opening essay by James Rule calls for rethinking the place of privacy in social life in the face of increasing mass surveillance by large public and private organizations. Linking surveillance to demands for social control on the part of governments or corporations, he asks: How far are we prepared to allow such systems of control to reach? By way of a thought experiment, he invites us to think about what is lost from a privacy-free world. The subsequent essays in this volume, each in their own way, respond to this question.

Gary Marx develops a slightly different account and argues that surveillance, just like privacy, derives its social meaning and value from the role it plays in different institutional settings and social relationships and from the way it relates to their goals, rules, and expectations. Priscilla Regan revisits her claim of the social importance of privacy twenty years after she had first formulated it (Regan 1995), arguing that privacy relates importantly to its role in advancing the ends of democratic states: Privacy protection furthers the exercise of civil rights, constrains governmental power, and prevents fragmentation of the political public. Daniel Solove, who concludes this first group of essays, contends that a loss of privacy not only sets back individuals' interests such as personal reputation or autonomy, but the interests of society as a whole: If we are to better protect privacy interests, we should articulate its social value.

In the second cluster we have grouped together essays surrounding controversies about the protection of privacy in various domains of social life. The cluster opens with an essay by Judith Wagner DeCew, who revisits the feminist critique of the private–public distinction and explores how the endorsement of the social approach to privacy could address feminist concerns about privacy. Linked to these issues, although discussing them from a different angle, is the essay by Bryce Newell, Cheryl Metoyer and Adam Moore, who explore the private–public boundary within the family. Arguing that privacy conventions are crucial for human socialization and that the family is the primary socialization setting, the authors defend privacy rights among family members that should be set aside only in exceptional circumstances.

One of the most recent issues in privacy and technology concerns genetic data, and it is this topic that Koen Bruynseels and Jeroen van den Hoven address in their contribution. While collection of genetic data serves important social interests in contributing to improved health care and scientific progress, it carries high risks to individuals and their privacy, for instance concerning social classifications. Bruynseels and Van den Hoven postulate an attitude of moral restraint in interpretation of genetic data by users, which they call "epistemic modesty."

The next four essays are concerned with the social-political contexts of privacy issues: Beate Roessler discusses markets in personal data, arguing that the trade in personal data poses not only a problem for privacy, but also for a person's identity, the flourishing of social relations, and for social justice in a society more generally. Moving from social to political relations, the essays by Annabelle Lever and Dorota Mokrosinska present privacy as a political value and explore some of the most pervasive controversies surrounding privacy protection in political practice. Lever focuses on the conflict between the right to privacy and freedom of expression, exploring the constitutive role of privacy to democratic freedoms. Mokrosinska addresses the controversy about the scope of privacy owed to government officials.

The political meaning and value of privacy is also a key element in the contributions from Christopher Parsons, Colin Bennett, and Adam Molnar. They address the harms of multifaceted Internet surveillance to the democratic potential of social networking environments, arguing for the idea of deliberative democracy in conceptualizing the democratic role of privacy and social media, thereby criticizing individual theories of privacy as well as existing social approaches to privacy.

On the whole, the essays in the second cluster contend that privacy controversies may be better handled if privacy is understood from the perspective of social contexts and the role privacy plays in social as well as political relations. If this is the case, does it prompt a change in the existing privacy regulations? The third group of essays is devoted to answering this question.

The third cluster opens with Kirsty Hughes's examination of the jurisprudence of the European Court of Human Rights: Drawing on the Court's rulings in the areas of surveillance and media privacy, she argues that the Court remains within the traditional approach to privacy, associating it with individual autonomy or personhood. This is inconsistent with the way the Court presents other human rights such as the right to freedom of expression, which the Court associates with the values of democracy and tolerance. Therefore, in order to properly deal with future cases of surveillance and media privacy, the Court should include in its general principles an express statement of the importance of privacy to democracy. Valerie Steeves analyzes the Canadian privacy regulations with regard to the behavior on social media of young adults and argues that current legislation, rooted in the traditional approach to privacy, fails in its task because it does not correspond to the altered concept of the privacy of young adults. Steeves concludes that more suitable legislation would require a social approach to privacy, recognizing the role of privacy for social relationships.

Anita Allen discusses the limitations of existing information privacy law in the area of health care. She argues that the impact of these laws is impaired by gender and race prejudice: Violations of patients' privacy by health care providers affect disadvantaged social groups, and in particular women of color. Given that disregard for the privacy of female patients has its sources in entrenched social practices of discrimination and the subordination of women, we should address these. Helen Nissenbaum applies her theory of contextual integrity to discussing the "Principle of Respect for Context" included in the 2012 White House Consumer Privacy Bill of Rights. Nissenbaum argues that for the bill to advance the state of privacy protection in the USA, the principle should best be interpreted with reference to the theory of contextual integrity in order to guarantee the moral and political values and context-specific ends in the distinct social spheres.

In the concluding essays, both Schwartz and Busch take up the issue of privacy regulation in a more comparative perspective: Andreas

Busch reflects on the absence of harmonization in privacy regulation across states. While recognizing the advantages of global privacy regulation for economic development and growth, he raises doubts about its practicability and achievability. Paul Schwartz takes up the issue of privacy legislation bodies, arguing that the federal division of the privacy regulatory competencies, both at the level of states and at the level of supranational bodies, is of particular importance for the development of policies that advance the social interests at stake in privacy protection.

We trust that the contributions to this volume have achieved two things. First, the authors have taken privacy research an important step further and have demonstrated that the recognition of the social dimensions of privacy should play a central role in the way we understand privacy and approach current privacy controversies. Second, we hope – and we think – that the authors, from each of their different perspectives, have contributed to setting an agenda for future research on privacy.

References

boyd, d. 2014. *It's Complicated: The Social Lives of Networked Teens*. New Haven: Yale University Press.

Cohen, J. E. 2012. *Configuring the Networked Self: Law, Code, and the Play of Everyday Practice*. New Haven: Yale University Press.

Geuss, R. 2001. *Public Goods, Private Goods*. Princeton University Press.

Kerr, I., Steeves, V. and Lucock, C. 2009. *Lessons from the Identity Trail: Anonymity, Privacy and Identity in a Networked Society*. Oxford University Press.

Landes, J. (ed.) 1998. *Feminism, the Public and the Private*. Oxford Readings in Feminism. Oxford University Press.

Lever, A. 2012. *On Privacy*. New York: Routledge.

Marwick, A. E. 2013. *Status Update. Celebrity, Publicity, and Branding in the Social Media Age*. New Haven: Yale University Press.

Mayer-Schoenberger, V. and Cukier, K. 2013. *Big Data. A Revolution that will Transform How We Live, Work, and Think*. London: John Murray.

Morozov, E. 2013. *To Save Everything, Click Here. Technology, Solutionism, and the Urge to Fix Problems that Don't Exist*. New York: Penguin.

Nissenbaum, H. 2010. *Privacy in Context: Technology, Policy, and the Integrity of Social Life*. Stanford University Press.

Regan, P. 1995. *Legislating Privacy*. Chapel Hill: University of North Carolina Press.

Roessler, B. (ed.) 2004. *Privacies: Philosophical Evaluations*. Stanford University Press.

Schoeman, F. (ed.) 1984. *Philosophical Dimensions of Privacy: An Anthology.* Cambridge University Press.

Solove, D. 2008. *Understanding Privacy.* Cambridge, MA: Harvard University Press.

Tanner, A. 2014. *What Stays in Vegas.* New York: Public Affairs.

Turow, J. 2011. *The Daily You.* New Haven: Yale University Press.

Weintraub, J. and Kumar, K. 1997. *Public and Private in Thought and Practice. Perspectives on a Grand Dichotomy.* University of Chicago Press.

PART I

The social dimensions of privacy

PART II

Privacy: the *longue durée*

JAMES B. RULE

Introduction

This chapter is written for privacy-watchers. They comprise a diverse and diffuse community defined by their concern with the fate of personal information in the face of profound global change. Privacy-watchers – I count myself among them – include journalists, jurists, philosophers, social scientists, managers, lobbyists, government officials, grass-roots activists and miscellaneous policy specialists.

On matters of their shared interests, privacy-watchers disagree about nearly everything. They disagree about the nature of privacy "rights", for example – indeed, even over the existence of such rights. They disagree over whether privacy should be valued as an end in itself, or simply as a means toward other valued ends. They dispute whether government or private sector interests represent the more serious dangers to privacy. They debate what practices constitute the greatest threats to privacy today, and over what policies, institutions and legal mechanisms offer the best hope of countervailing against such threats. They argue over whether individual "consent" to sharing personal information represents a meaningful test of the acceptability of such sharing. Some privacy-watchers hold that the state of privacy today is so serious as to be hopeless. Others argue that it is hopeless, but perhaps not really serious.

But on one point privacy-watchers agree. All acknowledge that the social role of personal information is in the midst of far-reaching – and unfinished – change. The state of privacy today is far from what it was just a few decades ago, and at least as far from where it will be in another generation, let alone another century.

Many privacy-watchers appear so absorbed in the day-to-day controversies surrounding these changes as to disavow speculation as to their long-term directions. This is unfortunate. True, the seemingly discontinuous, disruptive character of innovation in the uses of personal data may appear to defy prediction as to what to expect next. And indeed, predicting the "next big thing" in exploitation of personal information is a trick that few can claim to master. Yet my concern here is not with identifying the next start-up success or technological breakthrough. Instead, I seek in the following pages to anticipate the *broad categories of demands* for personal information likely to arise over the coming generation or more – and hence, the pressures on privacy that our children, and theirs, can expect to confront. What areas of life, what forms of conduct, what social relationships will be subjected to institutional surveillance in fifty years, or a century? Borrowing a term from the *Annales* historians, I am seeking to anticipate the history of privacy in the *longue durée*.

In fact, we have many resources for building such judgments. One hundred years ago – even in the world's most prosperous countries – centralized institutions of the state or private organizations collected very few details of most individuals' lives. By the mid twentieth century, this picture had begun to change profoundly. Governments had adopted social insurance systems, income taxation, driver and vehicle registration and the like. Corporations were beginning to track individual consumers' credit use and consumption habits. By the early 2000s, citizens and consumers reflexively expect their dealings with big institutions of all kinds – from credit card companies and public utilities to tax authorities and law enforcement agencies – to be mediated by their "records". We take it as axiomatic that the role of such records will be immensely consequential. They spell the difference between access or denial to medical care or consumer credit; between the ability to board an air flight and exclusion based on a "no-fly" list; between the ability to find employment versus roadblocks stemming from a criminal record or prejudicial data from the Internet. And we know, on reflection, that the institutions implementing these discriminations are actively at work to refine and extend their powers.

So indeed, we cannot say which specific innovations will fuel the next new forms of institutional surveillance – the next equivalent of mobile telephony or biometric identification. But we can take note of the kinds of *social situations* that have nurtured developments like these in the past and the *claims* made by organizations to implement consequent demands for more personal information. We know, in broad fashion, what areas of life or conduct on the part of the governed states have long sought to track and to shape – and we can anticipate where such interests will lead in the future. We know where corporations have aimed to track and direct consumers' behavior in the past – and here, too, we can make intelligent judgments on what the future has in store.

True, not all emerging pressures on privacy involve demands from big organizations, either governmental or corporate. The twenty-first century has also served up all sorts of new opportunities for privacy outrages perpetrated by individuals – dissemination of sexually compromising photos or videos that humiliate former spouses or lovers, for example. Critics also point to the rise of seemingly self-inflicted privacy wounds via the new social media, as participants post photos and other personal information that they later come to regret. These trends are anything but trivial in their effects on human welfare.

Nevertheless, my story here focuses on the pressure by large bureaucracies to appropriate personal information and to exploit such data for decision-making on the persons concerned. These, I hold, have driven the most extensive and most consequential demands for personal data that have hypertrophied over the last half-century, and the ones most likely to bulk large in the evolution of privacy over the *longue durée*.

Social control

Why is it that both governments and corporations, over the last century, have exerted themselves to compile and use such vast amounts of personal information? What generalizations can we make about the "needs" that have driven their widespread and forceful efforts to track ever more closely the lives of those they deal with?

This upwelling in bureaucratic tracking of individual lives aims to extend what sociologists would call *social control*. By social control I do not necessarily mean application of force or compulsion. Social control refers simply to the array of processes that encourage the "right" kinds of behavior and statuses, and discourage their opposites. These processes run the gamut from benign to repressive – everything from delivering medical care and promoting public health to identifying and hunting down would-be terrorists. They include processes that identify and reward those who have played by the rules in the past, and those that sanction or constrain those whose "records" point to them as likely sources of future trouble. Social control, in this broad sense, requires surveillance. It is impossible to encourage "good" behavior and discourage the opposite without knowing how those from whom compliance is sought have acted in the past. This leads to the thirst of public and private organizations to create, analyze, share and store data on the people they deal with.

Throughout the world's "advanced" societies, the twentieth century saw a vast mobilization of efforts by state and private organizations to establish and maintain new systems of social control. Many of these replaced informal, local processes with centralized systems running on formal bureaucratic rules. Law enforcement surveillance took on national and supranational forms of organization. Control over drivers and the use of vehicles followed the same patterns. Business interests seeking control over consumption behavior – through advertising and marketing – developed their own centralized national surveillance systems, as did the insurance industry in its efforts to insure those least likely to make claims, and to exclude those likely to be unprofitable customers. The consumer credit industries – credit cards companies, banks, retailers and others – have perhaps outdone all other private sector organizations in developing close surveillance and quick responses aimed at encouraging credit use by "good" customers, and constraining access to credit by potentially troublesome users.

It will not do to portray this extension of surveillance and control as some sort of Manichaean struggle between goodness and evil. These are basic and pervasive social processes – as fundamental in the intensive care ward of any hospital as in efforts to track and apprehend criminals. What is beyond dispute is that in the last century these processes have grown more centralized, more formal and more massive in scale. While the monitoring and sanctioning powers of family, local community and other face-to-face social parties have widely waned, the scope and consequence of bureaucratic and centralized surveillance have hypertrophied. And however one reckons the balance between benefits and losses stemming from these changes, one thing is clear: they fuel major pressures on privacy. By the beginning of the new millennium, we moderns must assume that our finances, our consumption habits, our movements, our communication patterns, our health care access and countless other realms of everyday life are being tracked by distant organizations – the ones known to us and others.

My question here is simply *how far should we expect these extensions and intensifications of bureaucratic surveillance to reach*? How much of an ordinary life will be tracked and influenced by such systems a generation or a century from now? Is there any "natural limit" to people's tolerance for such close monitoring by state agencies and corporate actors? Can one envisage any social force or countervailing process that would block the indefinite extension of centralized surveillance into the fine interstices of everyone's everyday life?

My concern is best illustrated with an analogy: will the transformations of privacy in the face of institutional demands over the next century ultimately resemble a chemical reaction that *runs to completion*? I am thinking of processes that continue until all the original constituents are transformed into new compounds – as when sugars break down into carbon dioxide, alcohol and water.

Some real-world social processes, unfolding over long periods, involve virtually such complete transformations. Think of the enclosure movement in England. From the Middle Ages, much of the country's arable land was in the form of commons – spaces open to use by any local resident, for the growing of produce, the pasturing of cattle, the foraging of pigs or geese, and so on. Small-scale agriculture on these lands sustained many rural families, without their holding individual title to the lands they worked. But with the rise of the market economy, large landlords could profit by appropriating bits of common land for their exclusive, commercial use – above all, for producing wool for sale to the nascent textile industry. The result, over centuries, was to deprive many peasants and small farmers of their livelihoods, driving many into the newly rising population of landless workers. It was, in one commentator's epithet, "the age when sheep ate men." By the end of the nineteenth century, enclosure had mostly run its course. One can still find morsels of common land here and there throughout England – village greens, for example. But common land as a source of livelihood is all but finished.

Could private information suffer a similar historical fate – incrementally devoured by organizations determined to turn it to the purposes of social control? For most of us, this is a profoundly disturbing prospect. Yet it would be rash to dismiss it.

Social and political conditions of mass surveillance

For some observers, the fate of privacy lies in the hands of the arbitrary gods of Technology – imagined with a capital T. Speculation about the future of privacy or of efforts to protect it are epiphenomenal, in this view. The unfolding dictates of technological change will settle human affairs regardless of human wishes and interests in the matter.

One hears versions of this view even from sophisticated observers who should know better. And obviously, the possibilities afforded by prevailing information technology have much to do with pressures on privacy. But not all uses of personal data that are technologically feasible – or efficient, or profitable – have any chance of adoption. Civic life in the USA would benefit vastly, many of us believe, from close tracking of the activities of high-stakes lobbyists – noting their whereabouts and movements, their expenditures, their clients and the "metadata" generated by their communications. The logs of such monitoring, similar to what is now collected for suspected terrorists, would be marvelously useful to journalists, researchers, political campaigners and ordinary concerned citizens seeking to understand how their government works. The reasons why we are unlikely to see such beneficent forms of surveillance any time soon have nothing to do with technological feasibility – and everything to do with the social and political standing of lobbyists and the interests that they serve.

In short, assessments of current and future pressures on privacy need to take account of both technological possibilities and the social and political chemistry that makes some forms of surveillance publicly acceptable, and rules out others. Let me sketch three of the social and political conditions that appear indispensable to the rise of systems of mass surveillance.

1. Identification of "disorderly" social states. Organizations develop large-scale tracking of individuals' lives to address domains of human affairs where things are not as they should be. Mass surveillance, in other words, aims at "straightening out" or *rationalizing* one or another realm of social life, to render it more acceptable, more satisfactory or more efficient – these criteria are always being reckoned by the organizations' own standards. Thus governments may seek to establish "safety nets" to ensure, say, children's well-being. Such a classic welfare state aim, however benevolent, triggers requirements for surveillance – to identify children eligible for such subsidies, for example, and to ensure that benefits go only to those eligible for them. At a minimum, such basic surveillance requirements will likely include demand for birth certificates, school registration documents and the like, to ensure that benefit claims are valid.

The history of mass surveillance consists of successive social constructions of new realms of social life as susceptible to social control in this way. The twentieth century brought the targeting of consumer behavior and consumer credit, for example; or personal income as a basis for income taxation; or people's sympathies and connections with militant extremism as a basis for domestic security surveillance. Each new definition of this kind requires significant public persuasion, as sponsors of surveillance seek their mandate to establish control over new realms of social experience.

Often these campaigns benefit from the drama of public events. Every American knows how the 9/11 attacks gave impetus and license to significantly extended state surveillance over once-private domains of life.

Similarly, public consciousness of the losses – in dollars and cents, as well as in needless suffering and loss of life – attributed to haphazard medical record-keeping has helped sell the idea of centralized monitoring of all Americans' medical encounters. Aggressive organizational entrepreneurs – government or corporate – understand that they have much to gain by establishing surveillance and social control over new realms of social life: tracking and controlling crime, for example; or thwarting would-be terrorists and their supporters; or identifying which consumers represent the best prospects for further selling. Potentially fabulous rewards for success in extending the reach of bureaucratic monitoring make it clear that we have embarked on a long and consequential journey.

2. Availability of actionable information. A second key condition for establishment and extension of mass surveillance is access to what I term "actionable" personal information. Obviously any form of tracing and monitoring human lives is impossible without processes that furnish relevant data – who people are, where they are, what they have done, what resources they have at their disposal, and so on. Conditions shaping availability of such data certainly include the state of information technology. But they also include a variety of social and institutional circumstances – for example, bureaucratic systems for reliably documenting births, marriages, deaths and other vital life junctures. Creation of such institutions is normally a long and laborious process: public registration of vital events in the United States was not complete until well into the early decades of the twentieth century. But once such sources of personal information come into existence, bases for new relationships and processes becomes available. The recent extension of biometric identification to much of the population of India, for example, has reportedly enabled many poor Indians to access banking services – for example, the ability to send and receive payments – that were previously impossible for them to use.

Not all personal information theoretically available to surveillance organizations is *actionable* in this sense. Strictly social factors determine when personal data can be deemed sufficiently reliable to trigger decisions on the people concerned – decisions to make an arrest, to pitch specific products or services, to allocate social insurance payments, and so on. When surveillance organizations achieve a mandate to act on their sole discretion, mere suspicion may be all that is required to designate someone for corrective action. Today in the United States, the organizations operating the country's "no-fly" listings of potential terrorists forbidden to board commercial air flights seem to enjoy something close to this total discretion. On the other hand, social and legal barriers enacted in the interests of privacy may block appropriation of personal information for surveillance deemed excessively intrusive – as in legislation placing people's genetic data off-limits for decision-making governing access to jobs and insurance.

3. Default Legitimacy. Endemic tensions between the interests of privacy and surveillance often turn on what forms and sources of personal data can properly be considered *actionable* in this sense. Are personal data collected from website visits actionable for targeting advertising, or for identifying terrorist sympathizers? Are location data derived from cell phone use actionable for these purposes? What about the contents of email, text messages and telephone conversations?

No surveillance system can maintain itself, let alone expand, without some claim to what I call default legitimacy. By this I mean public acceptance of the means and ends of the project as at least minimally consistent with prevailing values. Such default legitimacy need not entail enthusiastic moral support or deep personal conviction on the part of the public. It may simply entail grudging public acquiescence – enough to forestall challenge to surveillance practices on moral grounds. Today many such practices seem to exist just above that minimal threshold – for example, the intrusive security checking practiced at American airports and at points of entry to the United States from abroad.

One can imagine surveillance systems that are feasible, yet certain to fail this criterion for existence. For example, a system aimed at identifying and tracking under-age sexual partners for adults seeking to contact them. No doubt a system of this kind could be highly efficient and immensely profitable. But it would fail to reach the threshold of default legitimacy in the United States today. Any such system would be illegal, given the status of the activities that it would support. More decisively, it would go against the grain of public sentiment on what most Americans regard as a basic principle.

Default legitimacy is powerful, but not immutable. The 9/11 attacks on the United States obviously led to broadened legitimacy for a variety of surveillance practices, including those embodied in the Patriot Act, that had previously faced effective resistance on grounds of principle. And at the time of this writing, other American surveillance practices – notably the National Security Agency (NSA) monitoring of telecommunications data of an entire population – appear subject to challenge in terms of its acceptability to the public conscience. As we weigh the future directions of surveillance, and their impacts on privacy, we need to consider what changes in residual legitimacy the *longue durée* may hold.

Mass surveillance in the *long durée*

Let us imagine that the growth and intensification of surveillance does, indeed, come to resemble a chemical reaction that runs to completion. Imagine, in other words, that the three conditions cited above are amply fulfilled, and institutional monitoring of once-private life eventually approaches something like saturation. What concrete form would such changes take? What public rationales and justifications might plausibly uphold their legitimacy?

In this section, I seek to put flesh on this abstract possibility by projecting the evolution of surveillance in three areas: health and health-related conduct; financial affairs and consumption; and the whereabouts and movements of the governed. In each of these sketches, I treat the triumph of mass surveillance as though it were a fait accompli and its public legitimacy established. Conjuring up these possibilities hardly amounts to predicting that they will come to pass. Instead, I mean to invoke them as what sociologists in the tradition of Max Weber call *ideal types* – abstract models more extreme than one would expect to encounter in the real world. Once these possibilities are clear, it will be possible to weigh the forces countervailing against them.

Health and Health-Related Conduct. By the early twenty-first century, educated publics have come to understand that health is anything but a strictly private matter. Both the costs of ill-health and the benefits of well-being are felt by all members of society – through the shared costs of medical care, for example, and through the shared benefits of greater productivity and economic growth afforded by a healthier labor force. More people now realize that what we may experience as the most intimate and personal details relating to our bodily well-being are also matters of vital public concern. Thus, aggressive exploitation of once-private health-related data represents a major opportunity for all.

Creation of truly comprehensive and centralized systems of health-related personal data is essential to any such efforts. The first steps in this direction are already well advanced. In the United States, both the George W. Bush and Barak Obama administrations have backed creation of a single national repository for *all* medical data. In this effort, every examination, every test, every diagnosis, every prescription, every treatment, every known outcome will be coded and recorded in a centralized database. These efforts have already triggered major corporate investments – for example, in software development aimed at managing the vast troves of resulting data.

The benefits of such a comprehensive system are so obvious that one wonders why no such program was attempted before. Medical care providers today are constantly called upon to diagnose and treat illnesses with only the most fragmentary medical histories available to them. In emergencies, the patient may not even be able to cooperate in providing such information. By creating a truly comprehensive compendium of everyone's medical history, and by ensuring positive identification of every patient with his or her complete record, the new system will vastly reduce inappropriate or counterproductive treatments and even deaths. Perhaps even more important are the stunning analytical possibilities of trawling the records of a system like this – the biggest of "big data". All sorts of investigations about origins and determinants of good and ill health will be vastly simplified. With data on virtually the entire US population, many cause–effect relationships now hidden from investigators will emerge – for instance, complex but rare drug interactions with genetic inheritance or past treatment history.

But to fulfill the logic of its promise, a system like this must not stop at medical information, narrowly understood. Many other life circumstances besides one's medical history impinge on health and well-being – diet and nutrition, most notably. Here, too, surveillance capabilities now in embryonic form await aggressive development. Supermarkets and other retailers already track consumption patterns of food, drink and medication for their own marketing purposes. Expansion of these capabilities will afford more comprehensive views of the determinants of every person's health status. To realize this potential, all consumers should be furnished with some form of smartcard ID, whose use would be required for the purchase of any substance to be ingested. All resulting data, collected at check-out counters, would be forwarded to the same central repository of medical and health data described above. Restaurants and other vendors of food – now already required in some places to list the nutritional breakdown of their offerings – would come under the same requirement. Analyses of these inputs would obviously add vast power to understanding of both individuals' medical states and determinants of health for everyone.

To be sure, some consumers and citizens will initially resist requirements to register their every purchase of food and other items taken into the body. To encourage everyone to fulfill their civic obligation of comprehensive reporting in this connection, strict legislation would be needed to back the requirement of presenting one's smartcard to register every such purchase. Everyone would come to recognize that attempts to acquire comestibles without registration are tantamount to admission of having something to hide. Anti-social personalities found deliberately flouting their civic obligations in this respect – for example, by off-the-record binging on junk food – would be subject to stiff penalties.

Perfection of these extended forms of surveillance will help focus attention on other health-related activities that require monitoring. It has long been understood that lifestyle variations – in exercise and other leisure time activities – have major bearings on health outcomes. Thus every ID device issued in this connection should include monitoring equipment to record participants' daily exercise levels. Ultimately, more sophisticated devices could record such matters as vital signs and blood alcohol content. No less relevant than exercise levels are sexual habits and indulgence in other risky leisure activities such as skydiving and rock climbing. Casual, unprotected sex is a particular danger; one can hope and expect that technological progress will afford ways of identifying sexual partners and linking their medical histories to those of the subject.

All participants in the system – which is to say, all citizens and legal residents – will receive a quarterly health and nutrition report detailing strengths and defects of their recorded lifestyles. These will build on the synergistic use of all data available to the system, to suggest further room for improvement in diet and health habits. In extreme cases of self-neglect, warning mechanisms can be designed into the health smartcard that will sound an unmistakable alarm at particularly unfortunate choices registered at the supermarket checkout or pizza parlor.

Personal Finance and Consumption. Another disorderly realm of social life now ripe for central coordination is personal finance and consumption. I am referring to all consumers' financial resources and spending patterns. As with health and medical care, sophisticated opinion now recognizes that this supposedly "private" area of life holds major and legitimate interests for other parties. State agencies of course have many legitimate concerns with the financial affairs of the governed – in connection with taxation; prevention and prosecution of crime; financial planning and projections, and so on. Private sector parties are no less interested. Fuller access to the internal finances and consumption patterns of consumers can vastly enhance the efficiency and profitability of businesses – for purposes of marketing, consumer credit control and projection of future demands for products and services. Comprehensive and centralized monitoring of personal finance and consumption can also benefit consumers themselves. For example, discreet and timely warnings from central authorities could serve to deter people from

expenditures revealed by algorithms to be beyond their means, or otherwise inappropriate.

Again as in health-related affairs, many fragmentary and partial systems of tracking already await merger into a single, comprehensive system. Credit reporting has grown vastly in sophistication to afford tracking
of the great majority of American consumers. Advertising and marketing
interests have created vast databases for tracking individuals' consumption habits and buying power. Law enforcement agencies – from local
police to the Internal Revenue Service, Federal Bureau of Investigation
(FBI) and federal agencies – already enjoy almost-unquestioned access to
consumers' account data with banks, credit card companies and virtually
all other account-holding bodies. But vast though these institutions and
practices are, they remain uncentralized and uncoordinated. They also
fall far short of the total coverage of personal data required to realize the
fullest benefits of this form of surveillance.

The next step ahead is creation of a centralized and comprehensive
repository of all personal finance and consumption data, comparable to
the health data center described above. Here, too, participation by all consumers would be a legal requirement. The finance and consumption center would track all consumers' assets, liabilities and expected future needs
such as impending college expenses for offspring and retirement – along
with their past histories of meeting financial obligations. It would thus
function as an advanced, comprehensive credit reporting agency serving all parties with legitimate interests in individuals' personal finances,
including consumers themselves.

But purely quantitative tracking will not suffice here. To fulfill its full
promise, this surveillance operation will need to track qualitative dimensions of consumers' conduct as well. This will entail amassing data on the
details of taste and consumption habits – products and services chosen,
website browsing habits, recreation and leisure time use, and projected
change in these things, as revealed by analysis of all relevant data. The utility of these data, for purposes ranging from marketing and advertising to
enforcement of tax obligations, need hardly be emphasized. Proponents
will point out that commercial exploitation of these new resources will
actually enhance privacy – by making commercial appeals based on each
consumer's full record more precisely targeted, thereby reducing or eliminating useless and annoying advertising for things that people are in fact
unwilling or unable to purchase.

Clearly special steps will be necessary to ensure full participation in the
new system. Some alienated consumers will initially seek to evade their

obligations to share access to their affairs in the public interest. As with health monitoring, this system will necessarily require all participants – which is to say, every citizen and legal resident – to record all relevant events on some form of smartcard ID or the like. A crucial step in this direction will be elimination of cash and all other anonymous financial transactions, so that all personal finance events – purchases, payments, income and expenditure – pass through the system and are recorded in it. It will necessarily become impossible to consummate any transaction except by use of one's smartcard ID. Once it is understood that the system is essential to civic morality and economic growth, attempts to resort to cash, barter or other anachronistic payment methods will be understood as admissions that one has something to hide, and accordingly condemned.

As results of compliance with the new system come fully to light, support will surely build. Under the system described here, tax evasion will become so difficult as hardly to be worth the effort. The savings to law-abiding taxpayers of full compliance will inexorably contribute to support for the system. Moreover, the vast proportion of crimes associated with money will become much riskier for perpetrators, so that law-abiding behavior grows commensurately. "Big data" analyses of expenditure patterns and other data from the system will generate countless leads for investigators of crime and other forms of wrongdoing. At the same time, products and services of all kinds will become cheaper and more accessible, as sellers exploit opportunities for marketing to precisely those consumers most willing and able to pay for what is being sold. These successes will be so dramatic in the public eye as to discredit any dead-end resistance to the new system from antisocial parties.

Population Whereabouts and Movements. A third major domain of social behavior overdue for centralized monitoring and coordination is people's whereabouts and movements. Both to ensure good governance and to foster maximum economic growth and productivity, much more needs to be known about where citizens and consumers are and where they are heading at any given moment. Meeting these responsibilities will require steps that parallel those to be taken in matters of public health and personal finance.

Here, too, embryonic elements of a truly comprehensive system are in place at the time of this writing. Government agencies widely require positive ID for access to sites and activities – train and air travel, for example, or entry to government buildings. The ease of tracking increasingly ubiquitous cell phones has led law enforcement and anti-terrorist agencies to experiment with this means of monitoring persons of interest. Likewise, both government and corporate parties have exploited GPS-based systems for tracking vehicles and their drivers. Retailers and other corporations have experimented with cell phone tracking and face recognition technologies to track the movements of would-be customers within establishments and, in one case, on the streets of affluent parts of London.

Obviously these forays fall far short of their potential because they lack comprehensiveness. Most subjects requiring attention, most of the time, evade the scrutiny that they deserve. To bring all data together on all the people, all the time, government and industry need total contact with everyone. This can be accomplished by issuing a dedicated smartphone to every citizen and legal resident, a device that would remain on at all times. These special phones would uniquely identify each user, through linkage to his or her DNA or other biometric characteristics, and would be operable only by that user. Such a phone could also provide the crucial contact points for collection of health and financial data as envisaged above. The constant need to engage one's phone to purchase food and medication, or to complete financial transactions, will underline the life-giving civic importance of keeping in touch with the authorities. The resulting constant contact between government and the governed will in turn foster more efficient, more competent state services in all respects.

Here, too, some initial resistance can be expected. Some users will attempt to discard their assigned smartphones – though this will be difficult, given the impossibility of making any economic transactions without them. Others will seek to abandon their phones for long periods, no doubt to cover up illegal or antisocial activity. Technologies yet to be developed will make it possible to combat such smartphone abuse by signaling the central monitoring agency the moment contact is broken between the phone and its assigned user. The real-time connection will enable authorities to assume that the assigned user must still be in close proximity to the abused phone.

The extreme sensitivity of the resulting data – precise intelligence on where everyone is located at every moment, and on the paths taken by their travels – will of course require the strongest measures to protect privacy. A highly secure center will be necessary to monitor and archive the location data, with the strongest guarantees against its abuse or improper release. Only government officials with authentic needs to know will be permitted to access intelligence on people's whereabouts – including members of law enforcement and counterterrorist agencies, immigration authorities, offices concerned with taxation and administration of government benefits, social welfare and educational services, those involved in the war on drugs and other bodies with enforcement or investigative powers.

But the most dramatic gains for public welfare afforded by this system would be in the realm of governance. It could hold out for government planners the appeal of building moral support for government in general. A system like this could deter or pre-empt many crimes, while yielding quick arrests in the remaining instances. Once the authorities know who is present at every point at every moment, crime investigation will virtually take care of itself. Even crimes that go unnoticed for months or years – for example, molestation of minors – would be easily investigated and closed once complaints were filed. Given near-certainty of detection, most would-be perpetrators would be deterred. A few crimes of passion would no doubt still occur, but they would become open and shut cases for the authorities.

Missing person cases would virtually be a thing of the past. Responses to emergencies and disasters would become vastly more efficient, as the whereabouts of affected people would be known instantly. The state would finally be able to fulfill the most basic expectation held out for it by citizens – its role of ensuring public safety and freedom from fear of lawlessness. At the same time, the "big data" generated by a system like this would be vastly suggestive in *predicting* crime and antisocial behavior *before these things could occur.* Thus, if analysis of the movements and whereabouts of known child pornographers – or terrorist sympathizers, or tax evaders – show distinctive patterns, it would be irresponsible of the authorities not to apply the closest attention to all citizens showing the same patterns.

A state that mastered capabilities like these could assure compliance with obligations of all kinds. Tax bills, environmental protection requirements, compliance with court orders – virtually all legal obligations – would be all but self-enforcing, particularly in conjunction with enhanced surveillance over public health and financial affairs as discussed above. At the same time, the vast social costs entailed in everyday personal vigilance against crime would be vastly reduced, as people grew more confident in the ability of the state to uphold community expectations.

Everything that rises must converge

The domains of social life discussed above – personal health, personal finance, and persons' movements and whereabouts – are simply three of many logical targets for extension of mass surveillance and social control. One could entertain similar scenarios for many other forms of human activity. Examples include ecological responsibility (how careful are people not to waste scarce energy?); or parenting (are parents sending their children to school each day with their homework complete?); or civic engagement (how faithfully do people vote, and how well do they inform themselves in doing so?). Countless realms of social life cry out for systematic improvement – that is, measures to bring the conduct of people's lives into conformity with accepted standards. And as more sources of actionable information on the details of human conduct continually become available, enterprising state and private organizations will propose surveillance to support the new forms of social control.

As these three examples show, systems of mass surveillance grow to resemble one another. But even more important, systems of mass surveillance *reinforce and support one another.* Virtually every such system has capabilities and assets that similar systems need; and nearly all need crucial support from others. Both systems already familiar to us and – I am convinced – systems yet to be born tend to join forces with other systems, to reinforce their influence over those they seek to influence.

Accordingly, we can expect systems like those sketched above that monitor individuals' health, finances and whereabouts to multiply their strengths through close symbiosis with similar systems. Information will be readily shared among such systems – and not only information, but also enforcement capabilities. Thus, if universal smartphones become necessary media for financial transactions and health care access, for example, these same now-indispensable amenities can be expected to sound urgent alarms when their holders' driver's licenses have expired or have been suspended, or when their consumption habits or movements threaten to trigger increases in their insurance rates. This mutual reinforcement, cumulated over long development of mass surveillance, is bound to play a tremendous role in shaping privacy in the *longue durée.*

Conclusion: which *long durée*?

Almost any privacy-watcher will recoil at the future sketched above. Of course, this vision of an array of privacy-destroying processes that "run to completion" is not intended as prophecy, but as an extreme model of one set of possibilities. Such models challenge us to identify how the real world of empirically manifest processes, events and institutions may or may not approximate the model's "textbook case." What forces can be expected to deter or countervail against the full-blown triumph of mass surveillance envisaged here? Can we point to plausible competing forces – popular indignation from below, for example, or enlightened action by policy elites – that would impose meaningful limits on the movement to pervasive and unrestricted mass surveillance?

The troubling point here is that, *qualitatively*, most of the principles underlying privacy-eroding innovations like those described above have already been accepted in practice. In nearly every sector of life, default legitimacy has upheld the notion that collective interests in efficiency, economic growth and "innovation," state security or crime prevention may trump privacy claims. No one has proposed a bright conceptual line between *inherently* private personal data and information legitimately targeted for institutional surveillance. Indeed, I believe that there is no such line to be drawn, in any ethical tradition commanding wide currency. And given these facts, aren't privacy-watchers and everyone else basically disputing the *extent* of further renunciation, rather than the underlying principle?

Thus we can imagine the public outrage – today – at a system that would require us to record every purchase of food in a centralized databank devoted to tracking the health habits of the population. Yet qualitatively similar requirements on a smaller scale have long gained acceptance. In the United States, more and more employers expect their employees to report lifestyle information relating to their medical needs. And these demands often come with the threat of penalties for those who fail to take steps to control their weight, their diet and their exercise in the interests of healthier living – and of reducing medical insurance payouts. In the USA, such penalties have come under fire as intrusions on privacy. But the identical policies should enjoy more success if packaged as *extra rewards* to employees who obligingly report their lifestyle data and adjust their habits as requested.

Similarly, we may suppose that populations would never support requirements to carry government-issued smartphones engineered to track everyone's whereabouts and movements. That idea actually goes beyond Orwell's *1984* in the intensity of surveillance; in that dystopia, at least, one's presence could go unnoticed so long as one remained outside the view of telescreens. But haven't citizens of the world's prosperous liberal societies recently come to accept forms of tracking involving the same qualitative principles? Most of us have grown accustomed to having to identify ourselves for such ordinary activities as entering government buildings. Most Americans have probably forgotten that less than twenty years ago one could board a domestic air flight without providing positive identification. If the same smartphone-like device used to identify persons at crucial junctures in their life movements were also necessary to access any form of medical care, or to complete any significant financial transaction, the inclination to resist the system would be much reduced.

And if such surveillance could convincingly promise radical reductions in crime and other forms of deviance, the appeal would be enormous. Consider the amount of time, money and human energy devoted to avoiding lawless activity – ranging from women's avoidance of settings where sexual assault appears possible to the needs for safes, burglar alarms and other forms of "security." If promoters of mass surveillance could convince the public of their ability to eliminate even a small proportion of those costs, many privacy objections would surely be set aside.

Truly consequential roadblocks in the evolution toward a privacy-free future like the one sketched above require a more profound qualitative change in public mindset. They would require trading the blanket default legitimacy accorded to mass surveillance in the post-9/11 era for some form of blanket skepticism. Such historic shifts do occur. In the United States, the Watergate era entailed such a shift. At that point, public suspicion of all forms of authority was already at a historic low, just at the point when dramatic revelations of abuse of power by the Nixon administration confirmed many Americans' worst suspicions. It did not go unnoticed that many Nixonian abuses – both actual and planned – involved recourse to government sources of personal information to torment political enemies.

One result was America's Privacy Act of 1974. Still the country's most comprehensive national privacy legislation, it remains weak and limited by comparison to other national privacy laws. Dominant political interests in the USA successfully resisted enactment of omnibus privacy rights and a national privacy ombudsman – basic features of the privacy landscape in today's EU and other countries with strong privacy laws. But clearly even the flawed Privacy Act of 1974 would never have existed, short of that high-water mark in public skepticism of institutional use of personal data. By contrast, the recent revelations of NSA surveillance came at a much different moment in Americans' public mood. The fact that many Americans remained convinced of imminent danger from foreign-inspired terrorism has helped partially to defuse indignation that would otherwise be directed at a government evidently engaged in spying on its own citizens.

A volume of studies on the history of privacy as a public issue in some seven countries documented similar moments in many of those settings (Rule and Greenleaf 2008). Some of the strongest privacy measures described there had been erected in countries that had recently thrown off authoritarian governments: Hungary (Szekeley 2008) and South Korea (Park 2008). Szekeley describes the abolition in 1991 of Hungary's universal ID system following the collapse of the Communist regime, despite "fierce criticism among the entire government apparatus" (2008: 181). Both authors, however, allow that strong privacy measures in their countries have lost support, or at least salience in public opinion, as memories of repression under the previous regimes wane. Such decay, in the context of everyday realities of privacy erosion in all countries, poses an enduring challenge in the *longue durée*.

I have sought to show how organizations of all kinds are constantly finding ways to bring more and more areas of social life under institutional scrutiny and management. These processes create a relentless drip–drip–drip of devolution in privacy that could plausibly "run to completion." Often the incremental steps are seductive, in terms of convenience and economic rewards – as in innovations such as mobile telephony and the ease of purchasing, paying and communicating that it has afforded its users. Elsewhere surveillance interests profit from public climates of fear and anxiety – as in currently prevailing deference to security needs. And once instated, the capital-intensive systems created in response to these surveillance victories are rarely dismantled. Strictures against sharing of data among systems, for example, may not outlast the political climate in which they are framed – *vide* the circumvention of privacy restrictions under the draconian American Patriot Act 2001 passed in the wake of 9/11.

On these latter points, perhaps most privacy-watchers would agree. My own conclusion – certainly *not* shared by all privacy-watchers – is the best hope for privacy values to escape the fate of English commons is to avoid creation of personal data, and of mechanisms for using and sharing such data, in the first place. Concomitant of this strategy is the need to preserve the right to negotiate the maximum number of life-junctures – travel, for example, or access to websites, or financial transactions – anonymously, so that one's actions leave no data trail that might subsequently become fodder for future surveillance operations.

Such an approach would involve simply refusing to develop databases of people's telecommunications connections; or their air travel or other movements; or their financial situations. It will not do to ignore the fact that such data uses may actually be useful and beneficial to the people concerned or others at some point. Privacy advocates must insist that even many potentially beneficial surveillance systems must sometimes be counted too threatening to be worth having. Otherwise, if any surveillance system that can show itself arguably *useful* is held worth developing, it is hard to see any limit to the ever-extending reach of such systems.

But let us admit that such positions represent hard sell these days. In contrast to the post-Watergate era, American public opinion in the early twenty-first century seems often in the thrall of new systems for knowing and analyzing human affairs, and for reaching out to reshape people's lives in light of such knowledge. The alleged dictates of Technology (always with a capital T) in this view not only offer the fruits of scientific and technological thinking for their users. They also provide the prospect of an ever-flowing cornucopia of economic growth that supposedly benefits users and non-users alike.

As so often is the case, fiction and poetry are canaries in the coal mine of our information culture. Dave Eggers' dystopian novel *The Circle* (2013), set in a fabulously successful information company in Silicon Valley, portrays the missionary vision and mindset of that enterprise, bent on disclosing everything that is hidden. The main character, Mae Holland, has the good fortune to be hired by The Circle – which sounds very much like any or all of several familiar giants of the information economy – where she rides a wave of triumphs that propel her quickly toward the top. At a climactic staff meeting, she achieves something close to sainthood within the company by formulating what quickly becomes a corporate mantra:

SECRETS ARE LIES
SHARING IS CARING
PRIVACY IS THEFT

In a world where exploitation of personal information promises to be fabulously valuable – both in ways apparent today, and in now-unknown but infinitely enticing future possibilities – privacy does look a lot like theft. Those who insist on it resemble the hold-outs resisting transformations of their downtown neighborhoods to accommodate superhighways or big box retailers. Seen as stuck on outmoded values blocking the way of a better world for everyone, they appear as spoilers, at best. Often their prospects look about as promising as those of peasants seeking to eke a living from shrinking common lands.

The one thing we can know with certainty about the *longue durée* in the evolution of informational privacy is that there will be one. We are clearly in the midst of profound and unfinished change in the institutional treatment of personal information. Fifty years or a century from now, we can be sure that this crucial element of life will look much different from the way it looks now. I have tried to demonstrate that forces now at work could well open nearly all areas of everyday life to institutional scrutiny and influence. Indeed, such forces thus far appear ascendant. If they are not ultimately to dominate, we need a compelling alternative vision of a world where efficiency, convenience and even personal safety must sometimes give way to the interests of privacy.

We should realize that we often stand to gain or lose from widely experienced gains or losses to privacy, regardless of what happens to information about ourselves individually. If nearly everyone around me feels and acts as though all conversations were being overheard, then something crucial is lost from public life – even if I am convinced that my own conversations are secure. Thus, as with freedom of expression, losses to privacy may not only be experienced by those whose information is appropriated. We all suffer when those around us sense that anything they do, or perhaps even any inclination to act in the future, is subject to monitoring and corrective action.

References

Eggers, D. 2013. *The Circle*. New York: Knopf.

Park, W. 2008. "Republic of Korea," in Rule and Greenleaf (eds.), pp. 207–29.

Rule, J. B. and Greenleaf, G. (eds.) 2008. *Global Privacy Protection: The First Generation*. Cheltenham: Edward Elgar.

Szekely, I. 2008. "Hungary," in Rule and Greenleaf (eds.), pp. 174–206.

2

Coming to terms: the kaleidoscope of privacy and surveillance

GARY T. MARX

The test of a first-rate intelligence is the ability to hold two opposed ideas in the mind at the same time and still retain the ability to function.

F. Scott Fitzgerald, 1945, *The Crack-up* (New York: New Directions)

This chapter considers privacy and surveillance filtered through the specification of some individual and social dimensions of information control. The two can be related in a variety of empirical and ethical configurations. In both academic and popular discussion privacy is too often *justified* as a value because of what it is presumed to do for individuals. But as this volume shows, it can also be a positive social value because of what it does for the group. An additional point (neglected by some of privacy's more strident supporters) is that it can also be an anti-social value tied to private property and modernization.[1]

In contrast, surveillance is too often *criticized* for what it is presumed to do for more powerful groups (whether government or corporations) relative to the individual. But it can also be a pro-social value. Just as privacy can support the dignity and freedom to act of the person, surveillance can protect the integrity and independence of groups vital to a pluralistic democratic society and it can offer protection to individuals, whether for the dependent such as children and the sick, or to those who like clean water and industrial safety and do not want their precious liberties destroyed by enemies. Surveillance, like privacy, can be good for

---

This chapter draws from Marx 2015 and various articles at www.garymarx.net.

[1] Privacy as a fundamental right protecting the borders of the individual and as a necessary condition of a democratic society is of recent historical origin and not found in the same form in societies lacking the Western concept of individualism. It can be seen as divisive and destructive of community and as a way of protecting dastardly deeds – from the abuses that can go on in families behind closed doors to those seen in some presidential use of executive privilege and organizational cover-ups.

the individual and for society, but like privacy it can also have negative consequences for both.

As with most interesting questions, "it all depends." But what does it depend on? To begin with we must come to terms with the meaning of some basic terms for information control. A map and a common language are required to explain and evaluate fundamental properties, contexts and behaviors involving personal information. The empirical richness of information protection and revelation needs to be disentangled and parsed into basic categories and dimensions. Some of the confusion and debate about privacy and surveillance is caused by the failure to consider different types of these and the dimensions that may crosscut and divide them. Varying time periods, the particular groups and individuals in question and the variety of positive and negative consequences (and ways of measuring and weighing these) must be noted.

Little can (or better should) be universally said about the topic apart from such specification. Terms must be defined and connections noted. What we see and conclude depends on how we turn the conceptual kaleidoscope. In broadening and turning the kaleidoscope, this chapter considers some connections between surveillance, privacy and publicity, elaborates on some meanings of surveillance and privacy and then considers contexts and goals (and conflicts between goals) that inform the normative questions and make them so challenging.

Related but distinct: surveillance and privacy, privacy and publicity

How do surveillance and privacy relate? Before considering their logical, empirical and ethical connections, they need to be seen as elements within a broader sociology of information control framework. They both are about the control of information – in one case as discovery, in the other as protection. At the most basic level, surveillance is a way of accessing data. Surveillance implies an *agent* who *accesses* (whether through discovery tools, rules or physical/logistical settings) personal data. Privacy, in contrast, involves a *subject* who *restricts access* to personal data through the same means.[2]

In popular and academic dialogue surveillance is often wrongly seen to be the opposite of privacy and, in simplistic dramaturgy, the former is seen as bad and the latter good. For example, social psychologist Kelvin

---

[2] Subjects can of course surveil themselves, as with home health tests and glancing at car speedometers, and agents may simultaneously video themselves and others and may watch themselves in order to stay within the law.

(1973) emphasized privacy as a nullification mechanism for surveillance. But Kelvin's assertion needs to be seen as only one of the four basic empirical connections between privacy and surveillance. Surveillance is not necessarily the dark side of the social dimension of privacy.

1. Yes, privacy (or better actions taken to restrict access to all or only to insiders) may serve to nullify surveillance. Familiar examples are encryption, whispering and disguises.
2. But surveillance may serve to protect privacy. Examples include biometric identification and audit trails.
3. Privacy may serve to protect surveillance. Consider undercover police who use various fronts and false identification to protect their real identity and activities.
4. Surveillance may serve to nullify privacy (big data, night vision video cameras, drugs tests break through protective borders).

Privacy may be easier to think about than surveillance because it has opposites. Consider:

Privacy–publicity (nouns)
Privatization–publicization (action nouns)
Privatize–publicize (verbs)

The noun surveillance and the verb to surveil are the same figures of speech as privacy and privatization. The latter, however, have their opposites in publicity and publicization. But where are the equivalent opposites for surveillance as a noun and a verb? If privacy and publicity are opposites, can we say that privacy and surveillance are also opposites? They can certainly be in opposition. But it does not then follow that to surveil and to publicize are automatically joined, although, as the next paragraph suggests, they can be linked.

In English there is no easy term for the action that is the opposite of surveillance. The verb form *to surveil* suggests active surveying by an agent, just as the verb form *to privatize* suggests active protection (although the more common usage involves property rights as with privatization). While publicize is the opposite of privatize, the best worst term we have for a potential surveillance agent who doesn't act is that he or she demonstrates anti- or non-surveillance.[3] The agent chooses not to act. He or she doesn't want to know (as with the proverbial three monkeys who

---

[3] But not counter-surveillance – an action of some subjects of surveillance as with sous-surveillance (Mann *et al.* 2003).

were capable of surveilling but did not). One form here is *minimization* in which a surveillance agent engages in self-restraint given laws or policies (e.g. wiretap restrictions in a search warrant). In contrast, with privatization, the subject who has the data chooses to act to protect-restrict its being known by unspecified others. But the subject could also take actions of publicization in efforts to broadcast it.[4]

The distinct activities covered by the umbrella term surveillance do not have equivalent implications for privacy. The most common meaning refers to an act of data discovery-collection, but these occur within a broader system of connected activities. Seven kinds of activity conceived as *surveillance strips* can be noted: tool selection; subject selection; collection; processing/analysis; interpretation; uses/action; and data fate. Considered together these strips constitute the *surveillance occasion* and offer a way to bind a given application. Privacy is most likely to be at issue with respect to data collection and uses that involve the communication of results.

The discovery of information and its communication are sequentially linked. Surveillance involves the ferreting-out (or at least reception) of data. It thus has an element of publicization – at least to the surveillant who finds it. In this sense, to make public is to make it available to at least some persons beyond those whose initially have the data. The public (or better audience) for results may be minimal, as with surveillance data classified as top secret, proprietary or confidential. Here the results of surveillance are "private" (even in the act of their becoming "public" to some, although the agent may not share it). Yet this involves an act of restricting information rather than an offering or broadcasting to "the public" as the term is usually understood (e.g. in the form of a newspaper story, a posting on a webpage, or Freedom of Information Act results).

Privacy and publicity

Privacy, like surveillance, is a multidimensional concept whose contours are often ill-defined, contested, negotiated and fluid, and dependent on the context and culture. Consideration needs to be given to how the different forms of privacy and surveillance relate beyond considering these as generic forms. Among some major forms are *informational* (Westin 1967), *aesthetic* (Rule *et al.* 1983), *decisional* (DeCew 1997) and *proprietary* (Allen 2007) privacy.

---

[4] Although this is done passively by not protecting it, there is a parallel to the failure of the surveillance agent to act, bringing us to the challenging ethical issues of commission and omission.

Informational privacy is the most significant and contested contemporary form and involves the rules and conditions around personal information. Violations of aesthetic privacy, while usually carrying minimal implications for life chances, are often the most shocking (as with a hidden video camera in a girl's locker room). Breaches of decisional or proprietary privacy involve application or use of private information rather than information discovery, which is the core of surveillance. However, if individuals can nullify surveillance (e.g. hiding their use of contraceptives when that was illegal; blocking paparazzi from taking pictures; encryption) then they need not worry about that information being used.

Brief mention can be made of the term "public" in relation to the term "private" and they can be linked within the same framework. Both involve rules about the protection and revelation of information. Privacy norms are discretionary in generally giving individuals the right to control their personal information and restrict surveillance agents. Publicity norms require that information not be restricted – that is that it be made public, in effect legitimating the surveillant's discovery actions.[5]

When the rules specify that a surveillance agent is not to ask certain questions of (or about) a person and the subject has discretion about what to reveal, we can speak of *privacy norms*. When the rules specify that the subject must reveal the information or the agent must seek it, we can speak of *publicity norms* (or, better perhaps, disclosure norms). With publicity norms the subject has an obligation to reveal and/or the agent to discover (Marx 2011).[6]

---

[5] While sharing elements, for policy purposes there are major differences between the privacy of individuals and the secrecy of organizations. The standards for the latter should not automatically be applied to the former given the more negative societal-wide implications of potential organizational misuse. Nor should privacy be automatically equated with secrecy. Privacy norms give the individual discretion regarding whether or not to reveal, while secrecy norms generally do not give the holder of the secret the discretion to reveal.

[6] Beyond rules, privacy and publicity can be thought of in literal and metaphorical spatial terms involving invisibility–visibility and inaccessibility–accessibility. The privacy offered by a closed door or a wall and an encrypted email message share information restriction, even as they differ in many other ways. Internet forums are not geographically localized, but in their accessibility can be usefully thought of as public places, not unlike the traditional public square where exchanges with others are possible, or where others are visible as with open architecture. Erving Goffman (1971), in writing of "relations in public" and "public life," attends to the elements and possibilities within the immediacy of physical co-presence. This is the strand of "publicness" as visibility. It suggests the "public" as known to at least one other person rather than to any rules about the status of information – for example, that the information must be revealed or concealed. Nor does public as used here refer to a legally defined place such as a private golf course. So we can paradoxically speak of "public order in private places" (Goffman 1971, XIV). We can also speak about expectations of the private even within the public (Nissenbaum 1998; Marx

As with surveillance, there are a multiplicity of legitimate goals for privacy and publicity and the social consequences depend on the context, the time period and the particular interests involved. In and of themselves and viewed abstractly, as will be argued with surveillance, they are neither good nor bad. There is often an optimal point and going too far in either direction may have negative consequences. No one wants to live in a fish bowl or spotlight all the time, and privacy can protect the ability to act strategically and can protect the individual against discrimination and other forms of unfair treatment. Privacy can aid in presenting a positive sense of self and give a feeling of being in control. Selectively sharing information can be a resource for intimacy and trust. The contribution of information control to autonomous group action is central for a democracy and a free market. Yet privacy can also protect illegality, and hiding information is a central feature of deception and can be destructive of community. A rich mixture of consequences can also be seen for publicity – as visibility, it can bring accountability and fairness, but in violating legitimate privacy it can be invasive and can make it difficult for groups to pursue their goals. The last section considers some goal and value conflicts. Let us next turn to some further elements of surveillance.

What is surveillance?

The English noun *surveillance* comes from the French verb *surveillir*. It is related to the Latin term *vigilare* with its hint that something vaguely sinister or threatening lurks beyond the watchtower and town walls. Still, the threat might be successfully warded off by the vigilant. This ancient meaning is reflected in the association many persons still make of surveillance with the activities of police and national security agencies. Yet in contemporary society the term has a far wider meaning.

The dictionary, thesaurus and popular usage suggest a set of related activities: look, observe, watch, supervise, control, gaze, stare, view, scrutinize, examine, check out, scan, screen, inspect, survey, glean, scope, monitor, track, follow, spy, eavesdrop, test, guard. While some of these are more inclusive than others and can be logically linked (e.g. moving from look to monitor), and while we might tease out subtle and distinctive meanings for each involving a particular sense, activity or function,

---

2001). In the latter case, the information is available (as with someone's appearance or a conversation overheard in a restaurant). But limits remain, as can be seen in expectations about not staring or listening too closely to what others nearby are saying.

they all reflect what the philosopher Ludwig Wittgenstein calls a family of meanings within the broader concept (Wittgenstein 1958).

At the most general level surveillance of humans (which is often, but need not be, synonymous with human surveillance) can be defined *as regard or attendance to others (whether a person, a group or an aggregate as with a national census) or to factors presumed to be associated with these.* A central feature is gathering some form of data connectable to individuals (whether as uniquely identified or as a member of a category). This may or may not involve revealing what was "private" as in not knowing and/or supporting or violating a norm about how a subject's information is to be responded to.

A verb such as "observe" is not included in the definition because the nature of the means (or the senses involved) suggests subtypes and issues for analysis and ought not to be foreclosed by a definition (e.g. how do visual, auditory, text and other forms of surveillance compare with respect to factors such as intrusiveness, validity and the perception of a privacy invasion?). If such a verb is needed, to "scrutinize," "regard" or "attend to" is preferable to observe, with its tilt toward the visual.

The multiplicity of surveillance goals

Many contemporary theorists offer a narrower definition tied to the goal of control (e.g. Rule *et al.* 1983; Dandecker 1990; Lyon 2001; Manning 2008; Monahan 2010) – a factor that contributes to surveillance being viewed as on the dark side. Taking a cue from Foucault's earlier writings, control as domination is emphasized (whether explicitly or implicitly) rather than as a more positive direction or neutral discipline. Yet as Lianos (2003) observes, the modern role of surveillance as control must be placed in perspective alongside its fundamental importance in enhancing institutional efficiency and services and also in offering protection to individuals and societies.

Surveillance, particularly as it involves the state and organizations, but also in role relationships as in the family, commonly involves power differences and on balance favors the more powerful. Understanding of this is furthered with comparisons to settings where control and domination are not central, as with other goals such as surveillance for protection, entertainment or contractual relations; where surveillance is reciprocal; and where it does not only, or necessarily, flow downward or serves to disadvantage the subject.

Authority and power relations are closely related to the ability to collect and use data. The conditions for accessing and using information are elements of a democratic society (Haggerty and Samatas 2010). The greater the equality in subject–agent settings, the more likely it is that surveillance will be bilateral. Given the nature of social interaction and a resource-rich society with civil liberties, there is appreciable data collection from below as well as from above and also across settings. Reciprocal surveillance can also be seen in many hierarchal settings. Mann *et al.* (2003) refers to watchful vigilance from below as *sousveillance*.

The historical changes Foucault observed in *Discipline and Punish* (Foucault 1977) are central for the analysis of contemporary events, even if in that book he does not go beyond 1836 (no examples of computer dossiers or biometric analysis bolster his case). Yet one unfortunate legacy of his work is to call attention away from the pro-social aspects of surveillance and technology more broadly. Foucault's empirical documentation is illustrative rather than systematic and tends to exclude important surveillance topics beyond the control of superordinates in hierarchical organizations. His tone and examples give a subversive, even conspiratorial, twist to the hallowed ideals of the Renaissance and the Enlightenment regarding the consequences of seeking truth and social betterment. Rather than ensuring freedom and universal benefits, knowledge serves the more powerful. However, he does not offer an adequate theory of why hierarchy is necessarily undesirable.

With respect to categories I suggest elsewhere (Marx 2015), Foucault focuses on the watchers who are directly carrying out internal-constituency, non-reciprocated, rule-based, organizational surveillance of individuals on behalf of the organization's goals. The hope behind such watching is that subjects' fear of possible discovery will lead to self-surveillance and that rational analysis will improve outcomes desired by agents. The social significance of these forms is clear.

Yet other forms neglected by Foucault – for example, organizational surveillance for more benign ends, inter-organizational surveillance, and the non-organizational surveillance of individuals of each other – also need consideration. His analysis, as with that of many contemporary observers, does not give sufficient attention to the multiplicity and fluidity of surveillance goals and the conflicts between them. Surveillance may serve parallel or shared goals of the individual as well as the organization. It may be initiated by the individual and used against an organization. It may focus on rule-based standards involving kinds of behavior or it may involve social, psychological and physiological characteristics used to classify persons – whether to favor or disfavor them. Again we see there is no simple relationship or evaluation possible when considering surveillance–privacy connections.

Foucault, and many of those in the surveillance essay and dystopian novelist tradition, collapse or reduce the more general process or activity of surveillance to just one context – the organizational – and to one goal, which is control, a term often used interchangeably with domination and repression. This needs to be seen along with other goals that can be more illustrative of the pro-social aspects of surveillance. The list below identifies twelve major goals for the collection of information on persons. This list is hardly exhaustive. Additional goals that may cut across these or fit within them include kinds of control (whether involving coercion or care), categorization, determination of accountability, and inclusion or exclusion involving access to the person and the person's access (whether to resources, identities or physical and social egress and exit).

Surveillance goals for collecting personal information

A Compliance
  – behavioral rules
  – certification standards
  – subjective rules (correct inner attitudes and feelings)
B Verification
C Discovery
D Documentation
E Prevention and protection
F Strategic advantage (influence)
G Profit
H Symbolism
I Publicity
J Organizational functioning (or governance/administration/management)
K Curiosity
L Self-knowledge

The concepts in the above list were developed using an inductive method, sifting hundreds of examples to answer the question: "what is use of the tool intended to accomplish?" I added categories until any new example fitted within the existing categories. I do not argue that any given application will necessarily fit into only one category (although one may be dominant), that goals should only be studied statically, nor that observers would all necessarily agree on how to categorize what agents say about goals. For example, the point of view of the respondent may differ from that of the analyst; that is, a respondent might categorize surveillance of children as being for protection, while an analyst might code it as a form of control. The private and the public may be present as expectations stemming from formal rules or from manners and may exist as conditions regarding the visibility of the information independent of the rules.

Rather than being seen as bimodal dimensions with values at the ends of a continuum (such as whether a technology requires a power source or can be invisible), here each goal is an end point (although it could be treated as bimodal if scored as present or absent). The goals may occur together (e.g. compliance and documentation) and some are broader than others. For example, the goals of organizational functioning and documentation are perhaps the broadest and most content-neutral of those in the list, potentially touching most of the others.

The temporal patterns of some natural clusters of goals tend to be associated with specific contexts. Yet there may also be tension between goals (e.g. prevent vs. document). Goals A–J are disproportionately associated with organizations, while K and L are more likely to involve individuals acting in a personal rather than an organizational capacity (although individuals may also seek many of the other goals such as documentation, influence and prevention).

The definition of surveillance as hierarchical watching-over or social control is inadequate. The broader definition offered here is based on the generic activity of surveilling (the taking-in of data). It does not build in the goal of control, nor specify directionality. In considering current forms we need to appreciate bidirectionality and horizontal as well as vertical directions. Control needs to be viewed as only one of many possible goals and/or outcomes of surveillance.

Contexts, goals and conflicts

Goals along with rules are a central factor for contextual analysis. Attention to the appropriateness of goals and of means for a given setting illustrate a central argument of this chapter – that surveillance and privacy must in general be judged according to the legitimate expectations of the institution or organization in question (Marx 1988; Nissenbaum 2010). To articulate a goal and apply a surveillance or privacy protection–revelation tool brings questions of empirical and ethical judgment. That is, how well does the tactic achieve both immediate and broader goals appropriate for the context? How does it compare to other means for achieving the goal or doing nothing? Is the goal desirable and if so, by what standard? The clarity and consequences of publicly stated goals along with the appropriateness of means are central to understanding surveillance.

The surveillance–privacy relationship will vary depending on the kind of surveillance with respect to contexts and goals, as well as the kind of privacy. One element here is the distinction between *non-strategic* and *strategic surveillance*. In his analysis of "The Look," Sartre (1993) describes a situation in which an observer is listening from behind a closed door while peeking through a keyhole, when "all of a sudden I hear footsteps in the hall." He becomes aware that he himself will now be observed. In both cases he is involved in acts of surveillance, but these are very different forms. In the latter case he simply responds and draws a conclusion from a state of awareness. Only the former where he has taken the initiative, actively and purposively using his senses to collect data on others, raises important privacy issues.

Non-strategic surveillance refers to the routine, auto-pilot, semi-conscious, often even instinctual awareness in which our sense receptors are at the ready, constantly receiving inputs from whatever is in perceptual range. Smelling smoke or hearing a noise that might or might not be a car's backfire are examples. In contrast, strategic surveillance involves a conscious strategy to gather information. This may be in a cooperative or adversarial setting – contrast parents watching a toddler with corporations intercepting each other's telecommunications. Much non-strategic surveillance involves data that is publicly available to an observer (in not being protected) and as such is freely (if not necessarily voluntarily in a purposive sense) offered.

Within the strategic form – which to varying degrees ferrets out what is not freely offered – we can identify two mechanisms intended to create (or prohibit) conditions of visibility and legibility – material *tools* that enhance (or block) the senses and *rules* about the surveillance itself. While these are independent of each other, they show common linkages, as with rules requiring reporting when there are no available tools for discovery or rules about the conditions of use for tools that are available. A stellar example are the "Lantern Laws," which prohibited slaves from being out at night unless they carried a lantern (Browne 2012). Here the emphasis is on requiring the subject to make him or herself visible given the limitations brought by darkness. But note also efforts to alter environments to make them more visible, as with the creation of "defensible space" via taking down shrubs or using glass walls (Newman 1972) or less visible à la architecture of bathrooms.

Within the strategic form we can distinguish the *traditional* from the *new surveillance*. Examples of the new surveillance include computer matching and profiling, big data sets, video cameras, DNA analysis, GPS, electronic work monitoring, drug testing and the monitoring made possible by social media and cell phones. The new surveillance tends to be more intensive, extensive, extends the senses, is based on aggregates and big data, has lower visibility and involves involuntary (often categorical) compliance of which the subject may be unaware, decreased cost and remote locations. While the historical trend here is clear, it is more difficult to generalize about other characteristics, such as whether or not surveillance has become more deceptive or more difficult to defeat. Many forms are more omnipresent and often presumed to be omnipotent.

The new surveillance may be defined as *scrutiny of individuals, groups and contexts through the use of technical means to extract or create information*. In this definition the use of "technical means" to extract and create the information implies the ability to go beyond what is naturally offered to the senses and minds unsupported by technology, or what is voluntarily reported. Many of the examples extend the senses and cognitive abilities by using material artifacts, software and automated processes, but the technical means for rooting out can also involve sophisticated forms of manipulation, seduction, coercion, deception, infiltrators, informers and special observational skills. The new surveillance is at the core of contemporary privacy concerns.

Including "extract and create" in the definition calls attention to the new surveillance's interest in overcoming the strategic or logistical borders that inhibit access to personal information. These inhibitors may involve willful hiding and deception on the part of subjects or limits of the natural world, senses and cognitive powers. "Create" also suggests that data reflect the output of a measurement tool. The tool itself reflects a decision about what to focus on and the results are an artifact of the way they were constructed. Of course constructions vary in their usefulness, validity and reliability. Our perceptions of the empirical world are conditioned by where and how we look and these may vary in their fidelity to that world. It is this powerful, border-busting quality that raises profound implications for privacy.

The use of "contexts" along with "individuals" recognizes that much modern surveillance attends to settings, or patterns of relationships and groups, beyond focusing on a given, previously identified individual. Meaning may reside in cross-classifying discrete sources of data (as with computer matching and profiling) that, when considered separately, are not revealing. Systems as well as persons are of interest. The collection of group data or the aggregation of individual into group data offers parameters against which inferences about individuals are drawn for purposes of classification, prediction and response. Depending on the parameters, this may bring rationality and efficiency, but there is always an inferential leap in going from *group* characteristics based on *past events* to *future* predictions about a given *individual.* Here is another factor that can confuse the issue – while there may seem to be no privacy concern in collecting group rather than individually identified data, we need to think about whether identity groups should have rules protecting the privacy or at least image of the group (Alpert 2003). Group surveillance raises a new privacy question and one that may become more important in an age of big data collections and mergings. Should some groups have a right to privacy just as individuals do? With respect to that, consider the possible stigmatizing effect of public information on disease or crime data by ethnic or religious groups.

Neither dark nor light

Context directly involves the normative questions. The discussion above suggested some of the ways that privacy and surveillance can be approached and illustrates the variety of empirical connections that can be seen depending on the types and dimensions of interest. Let us now turn more directly to normative issues and a central argument: surveillance and privacy as such are "neither good nor bad, but context and comportment make it so" (Marx 2015). Context refers to the type of institution and organization in question and to the goals, rules and expectations they are associated with (Marx 1988, 2015; Nissenbaum 2010). *Comportment* refers to the kind of behavior actually shown by those in various surveillance roles relative to what is expected.

Snaking through these are expectations about the means and ends of information collection, communication, use and protection. Apart from the specifics of empirical settings, we can say little about our topics. Privacy for whom, of what, why and under what conditions, and surveillance of whom, of what, by whom, why and under what conditions need to be specified. This yields a rich array of information control games and calls attention to the myriad desirable and undesirable empirical consequences for the individual and society.

While sharing some elements, differences in four basic surveillance and privacy contexts involving coercion (government), care (parents and children), contracts (work and consumption) and free-floating accessible personal data (the personal and private within the public) will lead to different normative conclusions for the same privacy-invading or protecting behavior on the part of agents and subjects. Informational privacy and its surveillance must be judged in light of the institutional contexts and physical–logistical settings (e.g. financial, educational, health, welfare, employment, criminal justice, national security, voting, census); places (a street, a bathroom) and times (dinner time, day or night); the kind of data involved, such as about religion or health; participant roles; and aspects of technology and media, such as audio or visual, wire or wireless, print, phone, computer, radio or TV. Considerations of setting, location, time, data type and means offer the contingencies for righteousness or righteous indignation and are central to legislation and regulation. They are, however, rich in anomalies and cross-cultural differences.

It is one thing to defer to context and the rules and goals and broader values underlying them as the Rosetta Stone for deciding about the ethics of the social control of information. Applying them to reach judgments is another matter. Even if we can agree on what a goal and related legitimating values associated with it mean, the further nettlesome issue of prioritizing values and resolving conflicts between them remains. For many purposes (at least for persons and organizations of good will) the struggle is often between the good and the good.

Goal and value conflicts

Value conflicts are everywhere. Thus we seek privacy and often in the form of anonymity, but we also know that secrecy can hide dastardly deeds and that visibility can bring accountability. On the other hand, too much visibility may inhibit experimentation, creativity and risk-taking. And while we value disclosure and "permanent records" in the name of fairness and just deserts, we also believe in redemption. New beginnings after individuals have been sanctioned, or after they have otherwise overcome limitations or disadvantages, are fundamental to the American reverie.

In our democratic, media-saturated, impression-management societies, many of us want to both see and be seen (e.g. social media) even as we also want to look the other way and be left alone. We may want to know but also be shielded from knowing. We value freedom of expression and a free press but do not wish to see individuals defamed, harassed or unduly humiliated (whether by their own actions or those of others). Also as ideals, we desire honesty in communication and also civility and diplomacy. In interpersonal relations (in contrast to the abrasive talk shows) we may work hard to avoid embarrassing others by not seeking certain information or by holding back on what we know. We value the right to know, but also the right to control personal information. The absence of surveillance may bring freedom from censorship, but also open the door to the worst demagogues, liars and self-deluded snoops. Yet undue surveillance chills non-conforming communication and is the companion of repression.

Individuals expect organizations to treat them in a fair, accurate and efficient manner, and to judge them as unique, not as undifferentiated members of a general category, while at the same time they hesitate to reveal personal information and desire to have their privacy and confidentiality protected. Meeting the first set of goals necessarily requires giving up personal data, and up to some point the more one gives up, the more accurate and distinctly reflective it will be of the unique person. Yet the more data one reveals, the greater the risk of manipulation, misuse and privacy violation. At the same time, knowing more can bring new questions and less certainty to surveillance agents. Depending on their role and social location, individuals and groups differ in the relative importance they give to privacy as compared to accuracy.

The individual's expectation to be assayed in his or her full uniqueness may conflict with an organization's preference for responding to persons as part of broad common aggregates – something seen as more rational, effective and even efficient. The idea of due process and fairness to be determined in each individual case can radically conflict with an organization's utilitarian goals and bottom line. In the criminal justice context, for example, civil liberties sometimes conflict with the goal of effective enforcement. The case for *categorical surveillance* (without cause) versus *particularized surveillance* (only with cause) and for prevention versus after-the-violation responses can be well argued either way.

Culture sends contradictory messages. On the one hand, individuals are expected to submit to surveillance as members of a community that supports the common good and fairness (e.g. the required census or social security number that apply to all), or that allows one to participate in certain behaviors such as traveling, buying on credit or obtaining an entitlement. Yet fairness apart, when such surveillance goes beyond minimal verification and is done in a coercive manner, it may conflict with the expectation that before personal information borders are crossed, there needs to be some grounds for suspicion. If agents have to wait to do surveillance until they have cause in situations where there is evidence of preparatory actions or where violations are of low visibility or hidden outright, many violators get a free ride. This limitation protects the innocent against unnecessary searches. Yet it can also mean failing to prevent terrible events – for example, in the case of 9/11, where well-intentioned policies from another era as well as many informal factors blocked the FBI and CIA from exchanging information about the perpetrators.

If your tools work and if you search them all, you will likely get the guilty, not to mention the innocent. Profiling as a surveillance tool permeates society far beyond ethnicity, religion or national origin. In contemporary society, with its emphasis on prevention, the push is toward broader and deeper searching absent cause. The dilemma can be identified but not solved because observers differ in judging the trade-offs between equality, fairness, grounds for suspicion, invasiveness, prevention and effectiveness, and the likelihood and seriousness of risks.

The above discussion involves conflicts between abstract values. But more concrete conflicts may also appear in applying the tools. The intrinsic properties of a device may work against the agent's desire for secrecy. While much contemporary surveillance is defined by its ability to root out the unseen and unknown, it also paradoxically may reveal itself through electrical and chemical and other forms of data. That which silently gathers the emanations of others, if not exactly a mirror image, nonetheless emanates itself, offering discovery possibilities and means of neutralization to technically competent adversaries. The watchers may also be watched by the means they apply to others. Also, if an agency publicizes a surveillance system that has as one goal making citizens feel more secure, it may in addition have the opposite effect because it sends the message that dangers are so great as to warrant the need for such a system. Or this same publicity may alert committed malefactors to the presence of surveillance, triggering evasive, blocking or displacement means – a kind of unfair (at least to the law-abiding public) warning. Thus, advertising the means versus keeping them secret highlights the potential conflict of goals between deterrence and apprehension so apparent with undercover work. The existence of practices with a good potential for abuse traditionally leads to demands for regulation. A bureaucratic and legalistic response may lessen problems, but ironically it can also lead to expanded use of potentially troubling means. In contrast, without a formal mandate legitimating and acknowledging the tactic, agents may hesitate to use it because of uncertainty about where to draw the lines.

In sum, this chapter has sought to illustrate the complexity of the information control relationships between privacy and surveillance. It argues that little useful can be said in general terms apart from specifying types of privacy and surveillance and the dimensions that may cut across or unite them. Judgments must define the context and comportment of concern. Surveillance, like privacy, can be good for the individual and for society, but like privacy it can also have negative consequences for both. Appreciation of this complexity hardly solves any problem, but it might bring a little light and less heat to issues of great importance.

References

Allen, A. 2007. *Privacy, Law and Society.* St. Paul: Thomson/West.

Alpert, S. 2003. "Protecting medical privacy challenges in the age of genetic information." *Journal of Social Issues* 59: 301–11.

Browne, S. 2012. "'Everybody's got a little light under the sun': Black luminosity and the visual culture of surveillance." *Cultural Studies* 26: 542–64.

Dandeker, C. 1990. *Surveillance, Power, and Modernity: Bureaucracy and Discipline from 1700 to the Present Day.* Cambridge: Polity Press.

DeCew, J. Wagner 1997. *In Pursuit of Privacy: Law, Ethics, and the Rise Of Technology.* Ithaca, NY: Cornell University Press.

Foucault, M. 1977. *Discipline and Punish: The Birth of the Prison.* New York: Vintage.

Goffman, E. 1971. *Relations in Public. Micro Studies of the Public Order.* New York: Basic Books.

Haggerty, K. and Samatas, M. 2010. *Surveillance and Democracy.* London: Routledge.

Kelvin, P. 1973. "A social-psychological examination of privacy." *British Journal of Clinical Psychology* 12: 248–61.

Lianos, M. 2003. "Social Control After Foucault." *Surveillance & Society* 1: 412–30.

Lyon, D. 2001. *Surveillance and Society: Monitoring Everyday Life.* Buckingham and Philadelphia: Open University Press.

Mann, S., Nolan, J. and Barry Wellman, B. 2003. "Sousveillance: Inventing and using wearable computing devices for data collection in surveillance environments." *Surveillance & Society* 1: 331–55.

Manning, P. K. 2008. "A View of Surveillance," in S. Leman-Langlois (ed.) *Technocrime: Technology, Crime, and Social Control.* Cullompton: Willan Publishing, pp. 209–42.

Monahan, T. 2010. *Surveillance in the Time of Insecurity.* New Brunswick: Rutgers University Press.

Marx, G. T. 1988. *Undercover: Police Surveillance in America*. Berkeley: University of California Press.

2001. "Murky conceptual waters: the public and the private." *Ethics and Informational Technology* 3: 157–69.

2011. "Turtles, Firewalls, Scarlet Letters, and Vacuum Cleaners: Rules about Personal Information," in W. Aspray and P. Doty (eds.) *Privacy in America: Interdisciplinary Perspectives*. Lanham: Scarecrow Press, pp. 271–94.

2015. *Windows into the Soul: Surveillance and Society in an Age of High Technology*. University of Chicago Press (forthcoming).

Newman, O. 1972. *Defensible Space*. New York: MacMillan.

Nissenbaum, H. 1998. "Protecting privacy in an information age: the problem of privacy in public." *Law and Philosophy* 17: 559–96.

2010. *Privacy in Context: Technology, Policy, and the Integrity of Social Life*. Palo Alto: Stanford University Press.

Rule, J. B., McAdam, D., Stearns, L. and Uglow, D. 1983. "Documentary identification and mass surveillance in the United States." *Social Problems* 31: 222–34.

Sartre, J.-P. 1993. *Being and Nothingness*. New York: Washington Square Press.

Westin, A. 1967. *Privacy and Freedom*. New York: Columbia University Press.

Wittgenstein, L. 1958. *Philosophical Investigations* (trans. G. E. M. Anscombe), Oxford: Basil Blackwell.

3

Privacy and the common good: revisited

PRISCILLA M. REGAN

In *Legislating Privacy: Technology, Social Values, and Public Policy* (Regan 1995), I argued that privacy is not only of value to the individual but also to society in general and I suggested three bases for the social importance of privacy. First, privacy is a common value in that all individuals appreciate some degree of privacy and have some shared perceptions about privacy. Second, privacy is a public value in that it has worth broadly to all aspects of the democratic political process. And third, privacy is a collective value in that technology and market forces are making it hard for any one person to have privacy without all persons having a similar minimum level of privacy.

In this chapter I will first reflect briefly on the major developments that have affected public policy and philosophical thinking about privacy over the last fifteen plus years. Most prominently, these include: (1) the rather dramatic technological changes in online activities including social networking, powerful online search engines, and the quality of the merging of video/data/voice applications; (2) the rise of surveillance activities in the post-9/11 world; and (3) the rapid globalization of cultural, political and economic activities. As our everyday activities become more interconnected and seemingly similar across national boundaries, interests in privacy and information policies more generally tend also to cross these boundaries and provide a shared more global public and philosophical bond.

Then I will turn attention to each of the three bases for the social importance of privacy, reviewing the new literature that has furthered philosophical thinking on this topic, including works by Helen Nissenbaum, Daniel Solove, Julie Cohen, Beate Roessler and Valerie Steeves. The nuanced and various approaches taken by these scholars have enriched the theoretical thinking about the social value of privacy. Finally, I will revisit my thinking on each of the three philosophical bases for privacy – expanding and refining what I mean by each, examining how each has fared over the last twenty years, analyzing whether each is still a legitimate and solid basis for the social importance of privacy, and considering whether new bases for privacy's social importance have emerged today. In this section, I am particularly interested in developing more fully both the logic behind privacy as a collective value and the implications for viewing privacy from that perspective.

A more complex society?

The transition from the late twentieth century to the early twenty-first century has been accompanied by profound changes in the ways in which we conduct our personal, business, community, political and professional lives – and which have affected our ability to protect privacy, as well as our conceptions of the value of privacy. Literally everything we do is mediated or facilitated – or can be mediated or facilitated in some way – by systems operated and organized by enormous private sector companies. Facebook, for example, was launched in 2004 – and founded by someone born in 1984. Google began in 1996 as a research project, registered its domain of google.com in 1997, incorporated and had an index of about 60 million pages in 1998, first sold adverts in 2000 and issued an initial public offering in 2004, at which time it handled about 85 percent of Internet search requests. During this same time period newspapers, universities, charities, health care providers, banks and retail stores have all moved parts or all of their operations online. Virtually every "bricks and mortar" entity has an online presence as well. And those that don't, often fail.

It is now rather generally acknowledged that these systems are not merely corporate enterprises but are "socio-technical" systems (Johnson and Regan 2014). This phrase reflects the understanding that these systems are not simply technological information systems but are also complex interdependent systems of technical artifacts, cultural practices, social actors and situated meanings. Such an understanding derives from scholarship in the "science, technology and society" (STS) field that argues that technology is constructed, or constituted, by society – and that society is constructed by technology (Winner 1986; Bijker and Law 1992; Latour 1992). There is, in effect, a mutual or co-construction process between technology and society – not two independent logics and processes.

The expansion of these socio-technical systems has been accompanied by the changes wrought by 9/11, which validated and expanded the surveillance capabilities embedded in systems such as Facebook and Google, inflated the activities and reach of security systems such as Secure Flight, and established new entities such as Fusion Centers (Regan and Monahan 2014). The recent Snowden revelations regarding the breadth and detail of the National Security Agency (NSA) surveillance activities in the USA and abroad underscore the scope and unchecked nature of such surveillance. In all these cases, the focus is on perfecting information-gathering, processing, searching and retrieval – all in the name of enhancing security. The emphasis on security can be seen in cameras throughout cities recording the everyday comings and goings of ordinary people; in long lines, personal disrobing and technological checkpoints at airports; in careful tracking of disease patterns within and between countries; in GPS systems that monitor real-time movements of cell phone users and vehicles; and in archiving and search capabilities affixed to all online activities.

Focus on the prevention and detection of suspicious activities that could threaten the well-being of communities and nations has justified the augmentation and more fine calibration of security systems – often at the perceived loss of liberty and privacy. This has set up a debate framed in "either–or" terms – security or privacy, and security or liberty. This dichotomous framing has forced public debate into two opposite sides and has foreclosed more "common sense" discussion of how best to achieve both security and privacy/liberty.

Finally, globalization – a trend that began in the twentieth century – has become the conventional way of talking about and viewing the twenty-first century world. The interconnections among countries work on all levels and in all spheres of modern life and include economic, political, social, religious, cultural, educational and recreational activities. Communications and transportation infrastructures, in particular, have facilitated the globalization trends, which now have become the backdrop of twenty-first century life. With globalization has come a push to "harmonize," to use the language of the European Union, laws and policies so that individuals and businesses can move between and among countries without needing to alter their legal and administrative frameworks. Moreover, the ubiquity of systems like Facebook and Google, as well as of music, film and literature, have facilitated somewhat more common orientations towards and ways of viewing cultural values – such as privacy.

Early thinking on social value of privacy

As society moved into the twentieth century, thinking about the importance of privacy was profoundly shaped by Warren and Brandeis' 1890 *Harvard Law Review* article defining privacy as the "right to be let alone" (Warren and Brandeis 1890). This mantra was modified by Alan Westin in his seminal book *Privacy and Freedom* in 1967, in which he defined privacy as the right "of the individual to control information about himself" (Westin 1967). Both the focus on the individual right and the emphasis on individual control dominated much of liberal legal and philosophical thinking about privacy during late 1960s and through the 1980s – a time when information and communication technologies transformed the ways that businesses, governments and individuals collected, retained, analyzed and transferred information about individuals.

During the same time an alternative, but quite complementary line of thinking about privacy was beginning to develop, but was less well recognized – at least among philosophers and legal scholars. Sociologists in particular identified privacy as a component of a well-functioning society. Robert Merton in *Social Theory and Social Structure* (1967: 375) states that " 'Privacy' is not merely a personal predilection; it is an important functional requirement for the effective operation of social structure." Although this passage is quoted by Westin in *Privacy and Freedom*, Merton's thinking does not get picked up by legal scholars or by philosophers writing at the time. Other social thinkers do develop along the paths identified by Merton with Erving Goffman, a sociologist, in *The Presentation of Self in Everyday Life* (1959) and Irwin Altman (1975), a social psychologist, both writing about privacy as a social phenomenon. Goffman and Altman both distinguish privacy as important not just for individual self-development and freedom but also as important to society more generally.

Although the dominant thinking in the legal and philosophical communities' writing about privacy focused on the liberal and individual rights nature of privacy, there was a group of philosophical thinkers who began to consider a broader social value of privacy. In a 1971 compendium of essays published by the American Society for Political and Legal Philosophy (Pennock and Chapman 1971), Carl Friedrich and Arnold Simmel both acknowledge that privacy has some broader social importance. Friedrich wrote that he was "not concerned ... with the private aspect of this privacy, individualistic and libertarian, but with the political interest that may be involved. Has it a distinctive function in particular political orders?" (Friedrich 1971: 115). Although he raises this question, his analysis still roots the functionality of privacy in its importance to the individual. Simmel more fundamentally argues that privacy is "part and parcel of the system of values that regulates action in society" (Simmel 1971: 71), but then ultimately defines the drawing of boundaries of self, family and social organization as involving "conflicts over the rights of individuals" (1971: 87). A series of articles in *Philosophy and Public Affairs* in 1975 also opens up the possibilities of a social value, or the social importance, of privacy. Judith Jarvis Thomson (1975), Thomas Scanlon (1975) and James Rachels (1975) each grapple with how to broaden the interest in privacy beyond traditional liberal thinking and in a way that would both be consistent with liberalism but also expand and revitalize its importance in light of the complexities of modern organizational and technological changes.

In an anthology on privacy (1984) and a later book (1992), Ferdinand Schoeman begins a more serious and broader scholarly discussion about the social importance of privacy. Drawing upon Goffman's (1959) notions of "audience segregation," "role" and "role credibility," Schoeman argues "that respect for privacy enriches social and personal interaction by providing contexts for the development of varied kinds of relationships and multiple dimensions of personality" (Schoeman 1984: 413). He concludes: "it is important in a society for there to be institutions in which people can experience some of what they are without excessive scrutiny. Privacy is such an institution" (Schoeman 1984: 415–16). In his 1992 book, Schoeman further develops his thinking about the importance of privacy in our social encounters, "situates privacy in a social process" (Schoeman 1992: 2), and argues for "the form and function of privacy in promoting *social* thinking" (1992: 2, emphasis in original). He goes on to state: "the practice of privacy, not as a right but as a system of nuanced social norms, modulates the effectiveness of social control over an individual" (1992: 6). He believes privacy is important as it "facilitates association with people, not independence from people" (1992: 8).

Schoeman's book tracked closely to the writings and thinking of other privacy scholars of that time – all of whom recognized that a narrow individual rights justification for and basis of privacy was inadequate to the actual importance that privacy played in modern life. Spiros Simitis argued that privacy should not be regarded as a "tolerant contradiction" but as a "constitutive element of a democratic society" (Simitis 1987: 732). Richard Hixson suggests that personal privacy thrives in a community where there is mutual self-regard, not in isolation (Hixson 1987: 130).

Legal scholars, such as Robert Post (1989), began to shape arguments that privacy's value to society could be found in tort law's recognition of the importance of both the community and the individual. In 1995 I argued, as noted above, that privacy is not only of value to the individual but also to society in general and I suggested three bases for the social importance of privacy: privacy as a common, a public and a collective value.

The early 2000s witnessed a burgeoning of interest in the social value, role and importance of privacy. Daniel Solove (2008) emphasized a pragmatic value of privacy based on the common good and on the value of privacy in specific situations. Valerie Steeves (2009) drew upon the earlier writings of Westin, Altman and George Herbert Mead to recapture the social aspects of privacy; she argues that privacy is "a social construction that we create as we negotiate our relationships with others on a daily basis" (2009: 193). Provoked by a concern about "privacy in public" (Nissenbaum 1997) and the fact that much of our modern lives occur in more public places, and drawing upon the earlier philosophical thinking of Schoeman and the sociological thinking of Goffman, Helen Nissenbaum (2010) argues that different social contexts are governed by different social norms that govern the flow of information within and outside of that context. Protecting privacy entails ensuring appropriate flows of information between and among contexts. Key to Nissenbaum's framework is the construct of "context-relative informational norms" (Nissenbaum 2010: 129), which express "entrenched expectations" regarding flows of information.

Interest in fully understanding and articulating in a meaningful way the social importance of privacy continues. Among legal scholars, philosophers and social scientists interested in privacy, there is an unmistakable sense that situating privacy as a social value is appropriate, intellectually defensible and vital given the trajectory of current surveillance activities, whether taken in the name of national security, public safety or consumer choice.

Rethinking the social value of privacy

In this section I revisit my development of the three bases for the social importance of privacy – common, public and collective – and consider how the changes identified earlier – the ubiquity of socio-technical systems, the post-9/11 focus on security and globalization of economic, social and political life – affect each basis. Do the changes we have witnessed in the past twenty years provide a stronger or weaker case for the

social value of privacy? Do these changes require tweaking of our thinking in a way that compromises or fortifies the social value of privacy? Do
the changes reveal a need for other bases upon which to construct the
social value of privacy? In my rethinking I will draw upon not only my
own initial insights but also the valuable work of other scholars who have
been grappling with this question over the last several years.

Common value

I based my earlier thinking on the common value of privacy on the notion
that all individuals value some degree of privacy and have some common
perceptions about privacy. Although individuals may indeed have different definitions of privacy and may draw dissimilar boundaries about what
they regard as private and public, they all recognize privacy as important.
I drew upon both theoretical and empirical arguments to support privacy
as a common value.

Theoretically, my analogy was to freedom of conscience – individuals
may believe in different religions or no religion, but they similarly acknowledge the importance of freedom of conscience. In the same way that one
need not agree on the particulars of religious beliefs, one need not agree
on the particulars of privacy beliefs to accept that privacy is essential to
one's individual and social existence. Going back to John Stuart Mill and
Ruth Gavison, I argued that privacy is important for the development of a
type of individual that forms the basis for the contours of society that we
share in common. Mill's concern was echoed by John Dewey in his claim
that the perception of the "public" arises from the perception of broader
consequences – "concern on the part of each in the joint action and in the
contribution of each of its members to it" (Dewey 1927: 181).

Empirically, I turned to public opinion data for support of common
perceptions. Public opinion surveys from the 1970s to the 1990s provided
support that people were concerned about their privacy, that they shared
such concern in rather large numbers and that their perceptions of privacy issues were quite similar. The data supported the notion that people
had a shared meaning regarding the value, importance and meaning of
privacy – even if they applied that meaning somewhat differently in their
own lives. Respondents to a series of Louis Harris and Alan Westin surveys during this time, as well as a 1994 American Civil Liberties Union
survey, reported that they did care about privacy in a number of social,
political and economic contexts and that generally they supported more
government action to protect privacy (see Regan 1995: 50–68).

On a theoretical level, the idea that privacy is of common value would appear to hold true in the twenty-first century, as privacy continues to be important for individual development in today's society. The traditional liberal view of privacy as important for self-development and for the particular kind of society liberal theory values is only strengthened when joined by the sociological arguments of Goffman and Altman. Their theoretical arguments about the common value of privacy have only become more important in privacy thinking as the contours of the twenty-first century evolve. Drawing upon Westin's emphasis on information control and social withdrawal, Altman's focus on privacy as a dynamic process of setting interpersonal boundaries, and George Herbert Mead's insights regarding privacy as a boundary between different roles that individuals adopt and adapt, Valerie Steeves reclaims the social value of privacy by focusing on the social interactions individuals undertake to negotiate the personal boundaries in their relationships (Steeves 2009: 191–208).

My ongoing research with Valerie Steeves, Jane Bailey and Jacquelyn Burkell (Regan and Steeves 2010; Bailey *et al.* 2013), as well as others researching young people and privacy (Livingstone 2005, 2008; boyd and Marwick 2011), underscores the value of privacy in self-development, in giving young people the space to try on different roles and personal approaches. Julie Cohen identifies a "dynamic theory of individual autonomy" where the individual is valued "as an agent of self-determination and community-building" and where "productive expression and development ... have room to flourish" (Cohen 2000: 1377).

Without the space in which to engage in the "conscious construction of the self" (Cohen 2000: 1424) that privacy protects, individuals' beliefs and desires are more likely to track with the mainstream and expected. The concept of the self as "socially constructed" provides substantial support for the social importance of privacy. As Cohen more directly elaborates in her 2012 book, the modern individual is widely recognized as a socially constructed, "situated, embodied being" (Cohen 2012: 6), and privacy plays an important role in protecting against the tyranny of the majority and allowing individuality and creativity to flourish (2012: 110–11).

Acceptance of the self as "socially constructed" provides what may be considered as macro-level confirmation for the social value of privacy. Helen Nissenbaum's emphasis on "social context" provides support for the social value of privacy at the mid and micro levels. Nissenbaum views privacy as a social norm that specifies what information is appropriate to reveal and how that information should move in different social contexts with the understanding that, as members of society, we share certain understandings of the normative values that govern different social contexts. Privacy has a social value because it serves to maintain different social contexts and the values of these different contexts. The social context of education is different than that of health care; the privacy norms in each context help administrators evaluate what information-sharing practices are appropriate and, at the same time, maintain the somewhat unique boundaries of that context and the comfort level of individuals in that context. For Nissenbaum, privacy is a "shared collective value of a community" and a "legitimate reason for accepting or rejecting a given socio-technical system" (Nissenbaum 2010: 66).

Public opinion surveys and, perhaps more unambiguously, the actions that people take provide continued support for privacy as we move into the twenty-first century. Although the 1999 statement of Scott McNealy, Sun Microsystems Chief Executive Officer, that "You have zero privacy anyway. Get over it." (Sprenger 1999) received a great deal of press attention, most commentators now recognize it as hyperbole. People have not accepted "zero privacy" but indeed have taken numerous public and private actions to carve out and protect privacy in ways that demonstrate common views about privacy's meaning and importance. We see evidence for this on many fronts – continued recognition of the sensitivity of medical information as we move health files into electronic systems that give medical providers and patients timely access; continued recognition of the need to protect financial records as security breach notification laws are passed by most states and as tax information is carefully protected by both state and federal governments; growing concern with tracking online transactions of individuals as they move around electronically in the online world, as they move around physically in GPS-monitored physical space, and as the online and physical spaces continually converge and blend.

The behavior and actions of individuals with respect to privacy in two areas of modern life – social networking sites and national security surveillance – provide empirical support that privacy is viewed in common terms and as similarly important. Debates over privacy on social networking sites, especially Facebook, present concrete empirical evidence that privacy is viewed as similarly important among users. Typically Facebook members are not quiescent when the company appears to have altered the terms of contract or privacy notices, and initiates practices to which members object. The pull and tug between Facebook the company, in its quest for more information and transparency of users' activities, and Facebook users, who realize they value privacy once they concretely see or experience changes in the flow of information, is continual and at times very heated. For example, in early September 2006 Facebook decided to add two new features, News Feeds and Mini-Feed, which tracked and published changes that users made to their pages, including notifying users when friends posted new photos. The user community protested, finding the new features to be "stalker-esque," "creepy" and denying the community control over the content. E. J. Westlake reported that some users felt monitored in a way that made them uncomfortable and others were annoyed at the amount of insignificant information they were receiving (Westlake 2008: 22). Michael Calore (2006) commented: "The outcry suggests the exhibitionism and voyeurism implied by participation in social networking sites has ill-defined but nonetheless real limits, and expectations of privacy have somehow survived the publishing free-for-all." In December 2009 Facebook changed its default privacy settings to make text, photo and video updates publicly visible to everyone rather than to friends only – again provoking online protests, as well as broader media criticism (Kirkpatrick 2010; Perez 2010). The "Beacon" program, in which users' activities on other sites (partnered with Facebook) were transmitted into a users' news feed also provoked protest and in 2009 Facebook settled a class-action lawsuit that resulted from objections to the program (McCarthy 2009).

Debates about privacy and national security follow a somewhat different path. At first, there was broad public acceptance of the need for enhanced surveillance capabilities following 9/11. But with time that support became somewhat tempered by concern over the intrusiveness of some techniques, debate over their effectiveness and questions over accountability and due process – all of which sprung in part from shared perceptions that the "national security state" had intruded too far into the kind of privacy protections society valued and needed to be pulled back into a less aggressive and more carefully regulated stance. Protests over increased and more technologically sophisticated screening of airline passengers are one obvious example. The visual of ordinary people standing still with their legs spread and arms in the air while an image of their body is captured and screened by Transportation Security Administration officials provoked a common reaction that security may have gone a bit too far. The Snowden revelations provoked heated public debate, not only in the USA but also throughout the world, about the value of privacy – and drew renewed attention to the oversimplification of debate about "either" national security "or" privacy, as well as about "if I have nothing to hide, I have nothing to be concerned about." In both cases, debunking of these generalizations seems to have provided a more nuanced understanding of the common value of privacy among large segments of the public.

Public value

I based my original thinking about the public value of privacy on the argument that privacy was important to the democratic political system and the workings of the democratic political process. In most of the legal and constitutional writing about privacy and democracy in the US literature, privacy is seen as an instrumental right that is particularly important in two respects – furthering the exercise of First Amendment rights and providing constraints on the use of government power, especially in Fourth Amendment terms. In 1995 I argued that privacy was also independently important to the democratic process as the development of commonality, essential to the construction of a "public" or Arendt's "community of one's peers," required privacy so that people were not over-differentiated (Regan 1995: 226–7). I claimed that the use of personal information for targeting political messages, for example, violates the integrity of the electoral process because they fragment the body politic.

The philosophical and legal scholarship since 1995 support the public value of privacy, both as supporting democratic processes and as crucial to the forming of a body politic or public. This is reflected in the writings of Paul Ohm, Paul Schwartz and Daniel Solove on the legal side and Beate Roessler on the philosophical side. Roessler refers to how the "public realm is turned into an 'Arendtian nightmare' that no longer has anything to do with civic commitment to public welfare, or indeed with any notion of 'public'" (Roessler 2005: 170).

Theoretical support for the public value of privacy is also revealed in recent Supreme Court decisions regarding the Fourth Amendment, where the Court continues to use the Fourth Amendment as a means of restricting the use of government power. In *US* v. *Knotts* (1983) the Court permitted the use of a tracking device on a vehicle as it moved in public, but emphasized that this was permissible because it merely enhanced what could be seen in public; in *US* v. *Karo* (1984) the Court restricted the use of tracking devices inside a home. And in *Kyllo* v. *US* (2001) the Court looked at the generalized acceptance of a tracking device to determine the legitimacy of a search. The most recent Supreme Court decision in this area is *United States* v. *Jones* (2012) in which the Court decided that a GPS device placed by law enforcement officers on a car required a warrant. The Court decided this case based on the physical trespass involved and did not directly address the question of whether warrantless tracking more generally violates the Fourth Amendment, although five justices in concurring opinions suggest that long-term GPS monitoring impinges on expectations of privacy. This distinction is similar to that identified by the DC Circuit Court, which in *United States* v. *Maynard* (2010) developed what has become known as the "mosaic theory" of the Fourth Amendment, noting that prolonged surveillance

> can reveal more about a person than does any individual trip viewed in isolation ... A person who knows all of another's travels can deduce he is a weekly church goer, a heavy drinker, a regular at the gym, an unfaithful husband, an outpatient receiving medical treatment, an associate of particular individuals or political groups – and not just one fact about a person but all such facts.
>
> (*United States* v. *Maynard* (2010): 562)

Justice Sotomayor further elaborated this point in *US* v. *Jones*, arguing that: "The net result is that GPS monitoring – by making available at a relatively low cost such a substantial quantum of intimate information about any person whom the Government, in its unfettered discretion chooses to track – may alter the relationship between the citizen and government in a way that is *inimical to democratic society*" (*US* v. *Jones* (2012): 956, emphasis added).

The Court, however, has held privacy as less important regarding the First Amendment. The Court's seminal ruling in *Buckley* v. *Valeo* (1976) enshrined that "free speech" should not be compromised and that disclosure of donor information serves public purposes in deterring corruption and in aiding enforcement of anti-corruption laws, as well as providing useful information to voters. With the widespread availability of this information on the Internet, as well as the ability to data mine public records and other information, scholars are beginning to question whether the original goals of "public records" and "public disclosure" are being served (Solove 2002; Johnson *et al.* 2011). Interestingly the Court's more recent decisions in *Citizens United* v. *FEC* (2010) and *McCutcheon* v. *FEC* (2013) have further exacerbated debates about the public value of information about campaign contributions by permitting rather unfettered corporate and non-profit campaign spending without public disclosure.

Perhaps the most telling evidence for the public value of privacy can be found in how candidates, political parties and interest groups are collecting, analyzing and using personal information to foster the polarization and partisanship in today's electorate in the USA (Solove 2002; Johnson *et al.* 2011). This has been lamented by many and I will not repeat their arguments. The empirical effect, though, is seen in the reapportionment of congressional seats into safe districts where votes are predetermined by the demographics and likely voting patterns. It is similarly illustrated in Senate and gubernatorial races where candidates carefully couch their messages and positions to particular segments of the electorate rather than to the electorate as a whole. The Supreme Court's decision in *Citizens United* and the influx of huge amounts of private money into political races at all levels buttress this trend and further obliterate any meaning of the "public."

The current polarization and gridlock in Washington DC provide evidence for the effects of what such segmentation and targeting messaging means for democracy generally and the public in specific. Following the 2012 tragic shooting of school children in Newtown, Connecticut, over 90 percent of the "public" supported background checks for gun purchases (Drake 2013). Yet the political will to act in the "public" interest was undermined by special interests and by fear of partisan challenges and loss of campaign dollars – both of which have been fueled by private money and targeting of voters that is made possible by refined techniques to divide the "public." Recognition of a public value of privacy as justification for restricting collection and disclosure of voters' specific views on an issue would inhibit the reach and specificity of targeted political messages, enable the development of a more unified sense of the public, and quite possibly reduce political polarization.

Collective value

I based my earlier thinking about the collective value of privacy on the belief that technology and market forces were making it harder for any one person to have privacy without all persons having a similar minimum level of privacy. I argued that privacy was in effect a "collective or public good," as used in economics (Coase 1974), for three reasons. First, I maintained that privacy was not a "private good" in that one could not effectively buy back or establish a desired level of privacy because of the non-voluntary nature of many record-keeping relationships. Second, I contended that the market will not produce an optimal supply of the good. As with clean air and national defense, the market is an inefficient mechanism for supplying privacy. And third, I held that the complexity and interrelatedness of the computer and communication infrastructure make it more difficult to divide privacy. This claim that privacy is a collective value may be seen as counterintuitive, so I will briefly review each of my reasons before proceeding further.

It is somewhat difficult to regard privacy as "good" in economic terms, but in 1995 it was fairly obvious that it was becoming harder to disengage in larger societal relationships that might impinge on one's privacy. The list of record-generating relationships that were regarded as necessary parts of modern life – including, for example, banking, credit and health care – was growing. If individuals exited these relationships in order to protect their privacy, not only would they make their own lives more complicated to live, they would also make the functioning of a modern economy and society more complicated and less efficient. These developments arguably make privacy less of a "private good," where one could buy back or establish a desired level of privacy, and more of a "collective good," where one's level of privacy affects not only others' level of privacy but also the functioning of the institutions whose activities might implicate privacy.

The contention that the market will produce a suboptimal supply of privacy is an easier one to understand. It is widely recognized, and borne out by experience, that the calculus of any organization – private, public or non-profit – will be to collect as much information as possible about individuals to reduce any risk of decision-making about that individual. An organization will rationally be privacy-invasive in its information-gathering and use. But for individuals, the rational calculus is often to not see the privacy implications of their decisions. Privacy choices are often hidden transaction costs; the individual is focused on the purchase or service being negotiated – not on the opportunity or need to make a decision about privacy. Both the organizational calculus and the individual calculus thus result in less privacy – a suboptimal supply both because the quality of the information flowing within the system may be degraded and because trust in the system may be compromised. Left to its own devices, privacy invasions are the result of market failures.

The idea that the complexity and interrelatedness of the communication infrastructure made it more difficult to divide privacy was supported by the agreement that the design of the overall system determines what is possible. As Lawrence Lessig noted, "code is law" (Lessig 1999: 3–8) and defaults built into the system architecture establish the floor for what is possible in the system.

In a 2002 article I again tried to grapple and refine this idea of privacy as a collective value, arguing that personal information can be viewed as an overused "common pool resource" (Hardin 1968; Ostrom 1990) whose value to any one user is curtailed by other users. I claimed that the common pool resource system for personal information was *overloaded* in that the collection of more personal information was driving up the costs to subjects and users, was *polluted* in that inaccurate, irrelevant and out-of-date information contaminated the resource pool, and was *over-harvested* in that more users take similar pieces of information from the pool, reducing the unique value of that information for any one user (Regan 2002: 400). Viewed from this perspective, privacy becomes a collective value that protects the common pool resource of personal information.

The collective value of privacy seems even more profoundly evident in 2014 – especially as a result both of the ubiquity and complexity of the communications systems on which much of modern life occurs and of the "big data" that results from and fuels those systems. The idea that one can individually set one's own privacy level unaffected by others is undermined by social networking sites (SNS) in which others may, knowingly or unknowingly, reveal information that implicates the privacy of others. Barocas and Nissenbaum refer to this as the "tyranny of the minority," whereby "the volunteered information of the few can unlock the same information about the many" (Barocas and Nissenbaum 2014: 61).

Moreover, the methods of collecting, analyzing and using "big data" have become far removed from the point at which an individual consciously provides information about herself and similarly obviate the possibility of setting one's privacy level. Paul Ohm points out that the correlations that result from big data techniques make it "difficult to know that we are in the presence of risky data, the kind of data that will likely lead to privacy harm" (Ohm 2014: 101).

Indeed, the record-generating relationships of the late twentieth century have evolved into networks of computerized databases, sophisticated algorithms and high-speed global communications systems. The concept of "record" is somewhat anachronistic – as are concepts of individual privacy harms or invasions. For example, the data breach that a US chain store experienced during November and December 2013 involved the personal data of about 110 million customers – a number more characteristic of a collective harm than discrete individual harms. Dennis Hirsch likens the effects of such data breaches to oil spills, causing broad, widespread harm to the social environment – not a greenhouse effect but a *glass house effect*, conveying the sense of living in a glass house (Hirsch 2014). Greenwood *et al.* point out that when data are accessible over networks, "the traditional container of an institution makes less and less sense" and the complex ways in which data travel between services has "become too complex for the user to handle and manage" (Greenwood *et al.* 2014: 200).

There is also growing recognition that the complex organizational systems in which we run our lives are not only technological systems – but that they are also more fundamentally socio-technical systems and in some cases, such as Google and Facebook, these systems are exhibiting attributes of public infrastructures (Johnson and Regan 2014). There appears to be a demonstrable paradigm shift in the ways in which we characterize and talk about these systems. Koonin and Holland refer to the "instrumenting of society" as "big data" technologies are "producing data streams of unprecedented granularity, coverage and timeliness" (Koonin and Holland 2014: 137). Marwick and boyd (2015) view these technological shifts in the information and cultural landscape as creating "networked publics" and necessitating a conceptualization of privacy that moves "from an individualistic frame to one that is networked." As we move towards a "networked public," it becomes much more difficult for any one person to set her own privacy standards and to monitor the flow of information about her. In a networked public, it is hard for any one person to have a level of privacy without all other persons in that network having a similar level of privacy. Instead, privacy is established as part of the network and the various databases and interconnections that compose the network, and is shared collectively by those in the network.

Indeed, Facebook and Google are "poster children," supporting both the socio-technical systems in which modern life takes place and the increasingly collective nature of privacy. The complexity of their architectures and business models, the scale and reach of their operations, and the huge number of people worldwide who use these systems underscore their embedded infrastructural characteristic. Facebook, for example, has over 500 million users, is a global operation, and sits at the center of third-party applications, business partners and advertisers. Its scale is perhaps best captured in a statement that Marc Rotenberg made in congressional testimony in 2010: "If Facebook were a country, it would be larger than the United States, Germany and Japan combined" (Rotenberg 2010). Given such scale, it is difficult to think of one individual carving out a level of privacy that suits his or her individual preferences – without the cooperation of both Facebook's socio-technical system and also other Facebook users.

Conclusion

Both the privacy scholarship over the last twenty years and the empirical transformations of modern life reinforce and strengthen the earlier arguments that privacy should be viewed as a social value – with common, public and collective characteristics.

The current common nature of the value of privacy seems relatively similar to that of 1995 in that the public reactions to over-reaching on the part of companies and governments are supportive of common perceptions of the contours of privacy, as well as its importance. There is a similar sense of the shared value that privacy has for the kind of society in which people wish to live. In this sense, the basic culture of society has not changed dramatically despite technological advances and increased complexity – privacy is still understood in fairly similar terms. The normative underpinnings of the value of privacy are still largely shared among members of society, although their exact manifestations may be evolving as technology, culture and generations change.

Most recently the public nature of privacy seems very much threatened by the increasing fragmentation, polarization and partisanship of the body politic and the increasing surveillance of activities in public and private. Both political polarization and increased surveillance have a similar effect in generating a concomitant increase in public distrust of government – underscoring the importance of privacy as a public value that is important for maintaining the integrity and legitimacy of a democratic political system. At the same time, the increased surveillance activities of public and private organizations and individuals within those organizations have exposed people in ways that were unforeseen in the mid-twentieth century – and have magnified the effect of fragmenting people in their public life. There may now be a growing realization of the negative implications of targeting, monitoring and fragmenting individuals, based on analyses of their personal information and transactions, that is leading to renewed focus on privacy's importance as a public value.

Finally, the collective value of privacy is more obvious today than it has been previously. The technological advances in computer and communications technologies that have occurred since 1995 have dramatically changed the ways in which individuals conduct their daily lives, corporations conduct their businesses and governments govern. The result is a more data-intensive, higher speed and interconnected environment in which the notion of an isolated individual in control of her life is harder to fathom. Instead the norm has become socially constructed selves living in a networked public – with all the richness of experiences and opportunities that it provides while also rendering privacy part of that social construction and social network. In such a setting the collective value of privacy is evident – although finding a way to secure that value remains a challenge.

References

Altman, I. 1975. *The Environment and Social Behavior*. Monterey: Brooks/Cole.

Bailey, J., Steeves, V., Burkell, J. and Regan, P. 2013. "From 'bicycle face' to Facebook: Negotiating with gender stereotypes on social networking sites," *Journal of Communication Inquiry* 37(2): 91–112.

Barocas, S. and Nissenbaum, H. 2014. "Big Data's End Run around Anonymity and Consent," in Lane, J., Stodden, V., Bender, S. and Nissenbaum, H. (eds.), *Privacy, Big Data, and the Public Good*. New York: Cambridge University Press, pp. 44–75.

Bijker, W. and Law, J. (eds.) 1992. *Shaping Technology*. Cambridge, MA: MIT Press.

boyd, d. and Marwick, A. 2011. Social Privacy in Networked Publics: Teens Attitudes, Practices and Strategies. SSRN, online: http://papers.ssrn.com/sol3/papers.cfm?abstract_id=1925128.

Calore, M. 2006. "Privacy Fears Shock Facebook," *Wired News* (September 6). Accessed from: www.wired.com/news/culture/1,71739-0.html.

Coase, R. 1974. "The lighthouse in economics," *Journal of Law and Economics* 17(2): 357–76.

Cohen, J. 2000. "Examined lives: informational privacy and the subject as object," *Stanford Law Review* 52(5): 1373–438.

2012. *Configuring the Networked Self: Law, Code, and the Play of Everyday Practice*. New Haven: Yale University Press.

Dewey, J. 1927. *The Public and its Problems*. Chicago: Swallow Press.

Drake, B. 2013. "A Year After Newtown, Little Change in Public Opinion on Guns," Pew Research Center (December 12). Accessed from: www.pewresearch.org/fact-tank/2013/12/12/a-year-after-newtown-little-change-in-public-opinion-on-guns/.

Friedrich, C. J. 1971. "Secrecy versus Privacy," in Pennock, J. R. and Chapman, J. W. (eds.), *Privacy*, Nomos Series 13, Yearbook of the American Society for Political and Legal Philosophy. New York: Atherton Press, pp. 105–20.

Goffman, E. 1959. *The Presentation of Self in Everyday Life*. Garden City: Doubleday.

Greenwood, D., Stopczynski, A., Sweatt, B., Hardjono, T., and Pentland, A. 2014. "The New Deal on Data: A Framework for Institutional Controls," in Lane, J., Stodden, V., Bender, S. and Nissenbaum, H. (eds.), *Privacy, Big Data, and the Public Good*. New York: Cambridge University Press, pp. 192–210.

Hardin, G. 1968. "The tragedy of the commons," *Science* 162: 1243–8.

Hirsch, D. D. 2014. "The glass house effect: Big data, the new oil, and the power of analogy," *Maine Law Review* 66: 373–96.

Hixson, R. F. 1987. *Privacy in a Public Society: Human Rights in Conflict.* New York: Oxford University Press.

Johnson, D. G., Regan, P. M. and Wayland, K. 2011. "Campaign disclosure, privacy and transparency," *William and Mary Bill of Rights Journal* 19(4): 959–82.

Johnson, D. G. and Regan P. M. (eds.) 2014. *Transparency and Surveillance as Sociotechnical Accountability: A House of Mirrors.* New York: Routledge.

Kirkpatrick, D. 2010. *The Facebook Effect.* New York: Simon & Schuster.

Koonin, S. E. and Holland, M. J. 2014. "The Value of Big Data for Urban Science," in Lane, J., Stodden, V., Bender, S. and Nissenbaum, H. (eds.), *Privacy, Big Data, and the Public Good.* New York: Cambridge University Press, pp. 137–52.

Latour, B. 1992. "Where Are the Missing Masses? The Sociology of a Few Mundane Artifacts," in Bijker, W. and Law, J. (eds.), *Shaping Technology/Building Society: Studies in Sociotechnical Change.* Cambridge, MA: MIT Press, pp. 225–58.

Lessig, L. 1999. *Code and Other Laws of Cyberspace.* New York: Basic Books.

Livingstone, S. 2005. "Mediating the public/private boundary at home: Children's use of the internet for privacy and participation," *Journal of Media Practice* 6(1): 41–51.

2008. "Taking risky opportunities in youthful content creation: Teenagers' use of social networking sites for intimacy, privacy and self-expression," *New Media and Society* 10(3): 393–411.

Marwick, A. and boyd, d. 2015. "Theorizing Networked Privacy," *New Media and Society*, 10th Anniversary of Facebook special issue (forthcoming).

McCarthy, C. 2009. "Facebook Beacon Has Poked its Last" *The Social* (September 18). Accessed from: http://news.cnet.com/the-social/?keyword=Beacon.

Merton, R. 1957. *Social Theory and Social Structure.* Glencoe: Free Press.

Nissenbaum, H. 1997. "Toward an approach to privacy in public: The challenges of information technology," *Ethics and Behavior* 7(3): 207–19.

2010. *Privacy in Context: Technology, Policy and the Integrity of Social Life.* Stanford University Press.

Ohm, P. 2014. "Changing the Rules: General Principles for Data Use and Analysis," in Lane, J., Stodden, V., Bender, S. and Nissenbaum, H. (eds.), *Privacy, Big Data, and the Public Good.* New York: Cambridge University Press, pp. 96–111.

Ostrom, E. 1990. *Governing the Commons: The Evolution of Institutions for Collective Action.* Cambridge University Press.

Pennock, J. R. and Chapman, J. W. (eds.) 1971. *Privacy*, Nomos Series 13, Yearbook of the American Society for Political and Legal Philosophy. New York: Atherton Press.

Perez, S. 2010. "The 3 Facebook Settings Every User Should Check Now." *New York Times*. January 20. Accessed from: www.readwriteweb.com/archives/the_3_facebook_settings_every_user_should_check_now.php.

Post, R. 1989. "The social foundations of privacy: Community and self in the common law tort," *California Law Review* 77(5): 957–1010.

Rachels, J. 1975. "Why privacy is important," *Philosophy and Public Affairs* 4: 323–33.

Regan, P. M. 1995. *Legislating Privacy: Technology, Social Values, and Public Policy*. Chapel Hill: University of North Carolina Press.

2002. "Privacy as a common good," *Information, Communication and Society* 5(3): 382–405.

Regan, P. M. and Monahan, T. 2014. "Fusion center accountability and intergovernmental information sharing," *Publius: The Journal of Federalism* (Summer/Annual Review) 44(3): 475–98.

Regan, P. M. and Steeves, V. 2010. "Kids R Us: Online social networking and the potential for empowerment," *Surveillance and Society* 8(2): 151–65.

Roessler, B. 2005. *The Value of Privacy*. Cambridge: Polity Press.

Rotenberg, M. 2010. Testimony for Hearing on Online Privacy, Social Networking and Crime Victimization, before the Subcommittee on Crime, Terrorism and Homeland Security of the House Committee on the Judiciary. July 28.

Scanlon, T. 1975. "Thomson on privacy," *Philosophy and Public Affairs* 4: 315–22.

Schoeman, F. 1984. "Privacy and Intimate Information," in Schoeman, F. (ed.), *Philosophical Dimensions of Privacy*. Cambridge University Press, pp. 403–18.

1992. *Privacy and Social Freedom*. Cambridge University Press.

Simitis, S. 1987. "Reviewing privacy in an information society," *University of Pennsylvania Law Review* 135: 707–46.

Simmel, A. 1971. "Privacy Is Not an Isolated Freedom," in Pennock, J. R. and Chapman, J. W. (eds.), *Privacy*, Nomos Series 13, Yearbook of the American Society for Political and Legal Philosophy. New York: Atherton Press, pp. 71–87.

Solove, D. 2002. "Access and aggregation: Public records, privacy and the Constitution," *Minnesota Law Review* 86: 1137.

2008. *Understanding Privacy*. Cambridge, MA: Harvard University Press.

Sprenger, P. 1999. "Sun on Privacy: 'Get Over It'," *Wired* (January 26). Accessed at: http://archive.wired.com/politics/law/news/1999/01/17538.

Steeves, V. 2009. "Reclaiming the Social Value of Privacy," in Kerr, I., Steeves, V. and Lucock, C. (eds.), *Lessons from the Identity Trail: Anonymity, Privacy, and Identity in a Networked Society*. New York: Oxford University Press, pp. 191–208.

Thomson, J. J. 1975. "The right to privacy," *Philosophy and Public Affairs* 4: 295–314.

Warren, S. D. and Brandeis, L. D. 1890. "The right to privacy," *Harvard Law Review*, 4(5): 193–220.

Westin, A. 1967. *Privacy and Freedom*. New York: Atheneum.

Westlake, E. J. 2008. "Friend me if you Facebook: Generation Y and performative surveillance," *TDR: The Drama Review* 52(4): 21–40.

Winner, L. 1986. "Do Artifacts Have Politics?" in Winner, L. (ed.), *The Whale and the Reactor: A Search for Limits in an Age of High Technology*. University of Chicago Press, pp. 19–39.

The meaning and value of privacy

DANIEL J. SOLOVE

Our privacy is under assault. Businesses are collecting an unprecedented amount of personal data, recording the items we buy at the supermarket, the books we buy online, our web-surfing activity, our financial transactions, the movies we watch, the videos we rent, and much more. Nearly every organization and company we interact with now has tons of personal data about us. Companies we have never heard of also possess our profiles. Digital dossiers about our lives and personalities are being assembled in distant databases, and they are being meticulously studied and analyzed to make judgments about us: What products are we likely to buy? Are we a good credit risk? What price would we be willing to pay for certain items? How good a customer are we? Are we likely to be cooperative and not likely to return items or complain or call customer service?

Today, government has an unprecedented hunger for personal data. It is tapping into the data possessed by businesses and other organizations, including libraries. Many businesses readily comply with government requests for data. Government agencies are mining this personal data, trying to determine whether a person might likely engage in criminal or terrorist activity in the future based on patterns of behavior, purchases, and interest (O'Harrow 2005). If a government computer decides that you are a likely threat, then you might find yourself on a watch list, you might have difficulty flying, and there might be further negative consequences in the future.

The threat to privacy involves more than just records. Surveillance cameras are popping up everywhere. It is getting increasingly harder to have an unrecorded moment in public. In the United States, the National Security Agency is engaging in massive telephone surveillance. In the United Kingdom, millions of CCTV cameras monitor nearly every nook

This chapter adapts and discusses the ideas in my book, *Understanding Privacy* (Solove 2008); it was published previously in *OPEN Magazine* on October 19, 2009.

and cranny of public space (Rosen 2004). At work, many employers monitor nearly everything – every call their employees make, every keystroke they type, every website they visit.

Beyond the government and businesses, we are increasingly invading each other's privacy – and exposing our own personal information. The generation of young people growing up today is using blogs and social network websites at an unprecedented rate, spilling intimate details about their personal lives online that are available for anybody anywhere in the world to read (Solove 2007). The gossip that circulates in high school and college is no longer ephemeral and fleeting – it is now permanently available on the Internet, and it can readily be accessed by doing a Google search under a person's name.

With all these developments, many are asking whether privacy is still alive. With so much information being gathered, with so much surveillance, with so much disclosure, how can people expect privacy anymore? If we can't expect privacy, is it possible to protect it? Many contend that fighting for privacy is a losing battle, so we might as well just grin and bear it.

Do people expect privacy anymore?

These attitudes, however, represent a failure to understand what privacy is all about. The law often focuses on whether we expect privacy or not – and it refuses to protect privacy in situations where we do not expect it. But expectations are the wrong thing to look at. The law is not merely about preserving the existing state of affairs – it is about shaping the future. The law should protect privacy not because we expect it, but because we desire it.

Privacy is often understood narrowly, and these restrictive concepts lead to people neglecting to recognize privacy harms (for example Westin 1967; Gavison 1980; Posner 1981; Etzioni 1999). For example, it may be true that many businesses hold a lot of personal data about you. Does this mean you lack a privacy interest in that data? Those who view privacy narrowly as keeping information totally secret might say that you no longer have privacy in information that others possess.

But privacy is about much more than keeping secrets. It is also about confidentiality – data can be known by others, yet we have social norms about maintaining that information in confidence. For example, although librarians know information about the books we read, they understand that they have an obligation to keep the information confidential.

Doctors know our medical information, but they, too, are under a duty of confidentiality.

Privacy also involves maintaining data security. Those who possess data should have an obligation to keep it secure and out of the hands of identity thieves and fraudsters. They should have an obligation to prevent data leaks.

Another dimension of privacy is having control over our information (Westin 1967; Fried 1968; Miller 1971). Just because companies and the government have data about you does not mean that they should be allowed to use it however they desire. We can readily agree that they should not be able to use personal information to engage in discrimination. The law can and should impose many other limits on the kinds of decisions that can be made using personal data.

Those that use data about us should have the responsibility of notifying us about the data they have and how they plan to use it. People should have some say in how their information is used. There needs to be better "data due process." Currently, innocent people are finding themselves on terrorist watch lists and with no recourse to challenge their inclusion on the list. Financial and employment decisions are made about people based on profiles and information they do not even know about.

Privacy thus involves more than keeping secrets – it is about how we regulate information flow, how we ensure that others use our information responsibly, how we exercise control over our information, how we should limit the way others can use our data.

Some argue that it is impossible for the law to limit how others use our data, but this is false. Copyright law is a clear example of the law regulating the way information is used and providing control over that data. I am not suggesting that copyright law is the answer to privacy, but it illustrates that it is possible for the law to restrict uses of data if it wants to.

We can protect privacy, even in light of all the collection, dissemination, and use of our information. And it is something we must do if we want to protect our freedom and intellectual activity in the future.

But how? The first steps involve rethinking the concept and value of privacy.

Rethinking the concept of privacy

Privacy is a concept in disarray. Commentators have lamented that the concept of privacy is so vague that it is practically useless. When we speak of privacy invasions, we often fail to clearly explain why such an infringement is harmful. The interests on the other side – free speech, efficient consumer transactions, and security – are often much more readily comprehended. The result is that privacy frequently loses in the balance. Even worse, courts and policymakers often fail to recognize privacy interests at all.

Many attempts to conceptualize privacy do so by attempting to locate the common denominator for all things we view as private (for example Fried 1968; Miller 1971; Gavison 1980; Inness 1992). This method of conceptualizing privacy, however, faces a difficult dilemma. If we choose a common denominator that is broad enough to encompass nearly everything, then the conception risks the danger of being over-inclusive or too vague. If we choose a narrower common denominator, then the risk is that the conception is too restrictive.

There is a way out of this dilemma: We can conceptualize privacy in a different way. The philosopher Ludwig Wittgenstein argued that some concepts are best understood as family resemblances – they include things that "are *related* to one another in many different ways" (Wittgenstein 1958: § 65, original emphasis). Some things share a network of similarities without one particular thing in common. They are related in the way family members are related. You might have your mother's eyes, your brother's hair, your sister's nose – but you all might not have one common feature. There is no common denominator. Nevertheless, you bear a resemblance to each other.[1] We should understand privacy in this way. Privacy is not one thing, but a plurality of many distinct yet related things.

One of the key issues in developing a theory of privacy is how to deal with the variability of attitudes and beliefs about privacy. Privacy is a product of norms, activities, and legal protections. As a result, it is culturally and historically contingent. For example, it is widely accepted today that the naked body is private in the sense that it is generally concealed. But that was far from the case in ancient Greece and Rome. At the gymnasium in ancient Greece, people exercised in the nude. In ancient Rome, men and women would bathe naked together (Goldhill 2004: 15, 19). In the Middle Ages, people bathed in front of others and during social gatherings (Rybczynski 1986: 28, 30). Norms about nudity, bathing, and concealing bodily functions have varied throughout history and in different cultures. Likewise, although the home has long been viewed as a private

---

[1] As Wittgenstein observes, instead of being related by a common denominator, some things share "a complicated network of similarities overlapping and crisscrossing: sometimes overall similarities, sometimes similarities of detail" (Wittgenstein 1958: § 66).

space, in the past it was private in a different way than it is now. Until the seventeenth century, many homes merely consisted of one large room where there was scant seclusion for "private" activities such as sex and intimacy. A married couple would often sleep in the same bed as their children, and would share it with houseguests (Flaherty 1972: 45). Like the body, the home is not inherently private – at least not in the same way we view it as private today.

Many theories of privacy focus on the nature of the information or matter involved. They seek to identify various types of information and matters that are private. But as I illustrated with the body and the home, no particular kind of information or matter is inherently private. Others contend that we should define privacy with the reasonable expectation of privacy test. This method defines privacy based on expectations that society considers reasonable. This is the prevailing method that American courts, as well as courts in many other countries and the European Court of Human Rights, use to identify privacy interests protected by the Fourth Amendment as well as other areas of law (Tomás Gómez-Arostegui 2005: 153).

But how are reasonable expectations of privacy to be determined? The US Supreme Court has never engaged in giving empirical evidence when applying the reasonable expectation of privacy test. It merely guesses at what society expects. One way of determining societal expectations is to take polls. But people's stated views about privacy often differ dramatically from their actions. A person might say she values privacy greatly, but then she will trade away her personal data for tiny discounts or minor increases in convenience. For this reason, others contend that we should examine behavioral data rather than polls. There are several factors, however, that make people's behavior unreliable as a measure for their views on privacy. In many circumstances, people relinquish personal information to businesses because they do not have much of a choice or because they lack knowledge about how the information will be used in the future.

Even with a reliable way of measuring societal expectations of privacy, such expectations only inform us about existing privacy norms. Privacy law and policy depend on more than merely preserving current expectations. The history of communications privacy best illustrates this point. In colonial America, mail was often insecure. Letters, sealed only with wax, left many people concerned that they were far from secure. For example, Thomas Jefferson, Alexander Hamilton, and George Washington all complained about the lack of confidentiality in their correspondence (Solove 2004: 225). Despite the expectation that mail was not very private, the law evolved to provide strong protection of the privacy of letters. Benjamin Franklin, the colonial postmaster general before the Revolution, made postal workers take an oath not to open mail (Solove 2004: 225). After the Revolution, the US Congress passed several statutes to protect the privacy of letters. In 1877 the US Supreme Court held that the Fourth Amendment protected sealed parcels despite the fact that people handed them to the government for delivery (*Ex Parte Jackson* 1877: 727, 733). The extensive protection of the privacy of written correspondence stemmed from a public desire to keep them private, not from an expectation that they were already private.

A similar story can be told with electronic communications in the USA. Concerns over telegraph privacy were legion in its early days during the mid nineteenth century. Laws in almost every state ensured that telegraph employees could not improperly disclose telegrams. State laws also prohibited the interception of telegraph communications. During the telephone's early days, calls were far from private. Until well into the twentieth century many people had party lines – telephone lines that were shared among a number of households. There were rampant concerns about eavesdropping and wiretapping. Legislatures responded by passing laws to protect the privacy of phone communications. More than half the states had made wiretapping a crime by the early twentieth century.

The moral of the story is that communications *became* private because people wanted them to be private. Privacy is not just about what people *expect* but about what they *desire*. Privacy is something we construct through norms and the law. Thus we call upon the law to protect privacy *because* we experience a lack of privacy and desire to rectify that situation, not because we already expect privacy.

What, then, should we focus on when seeking to understand privacy? I contend that the focal point for a theory of privacy should be on the problems we want the law to address. According to John Dewey, philosophical inquiry begins with problems in experience, not with abstract universal principles. A theory of privacy should focus on the problems that create a desire for privacy. Privacy problems arise when the activities of the government, businesses, organizations, and other people disrupt the activities of others. Real problems exist, yet they are often ignored because they do not fit into a particular conception of privacy. Many problems are not even recognized because courts or policymakers cannot identify a "privacy" interest involved. Instead of pondering the nature of privacy in the abstract, we should begin with concrete problems and then use theory as a way to better understand and resolve these problems. In my book

Understanding Privacy (2008) I develop a framework for recognizing privacy problems, and I identify and examine sixteen such problems.

There are four basic groups of harmful activities: (1) information collection, (2) information processing, (3) information dissemination, and (4) invasion. Each of these groups consists of different related subgroups of harmful activities.

I have arranged these groups around a model that begins with the data subject – the individual whose life is most directly affected by the activities classified in the taxonomy. From that individual, various entities (other people, businesses, and the government) collect information. The collection of this information itself can constitute a harmful activity, though not all information collection is harmful. Those that collect the data (the "data holders") then process it – that is, they store, combine, manipulate, search, and use it. I label these activities "information processing." The next step is "information dissemination," in which the data holders transfer the information to others or release the information. The general progression from information collection to processing to dissemination is the data moving further away from the individual's control. The last grouping of activities is "invasions," which involve impingements directly on the individual. Instead of the progression away from the individual, invasions progress toward the individual and do not necessarily involve information.

The first group of activities that affect privacy is information collection. *Surveillance* is the watching, listening to, or recording of an individual's activities. *Interrogation* consists of various forms of questioning or probing for information.

A second group of activities involves the way information is stored, manipulated, and used – what I refer to collectively as "information processing." *Aggregation* involves the combination of various pieces of data about a person. *Identification* is linking information to particular individuals. *Insecurity* involves carelessness in protecting stored information from leaks and improper access. *Secondary use* is the use of collected information for a purpose different from the use for which it was collected without the data subject's consent. *Exclusion* concerns the failure to allow the data subject to know about the data that others have about her and participate in its handling and use. These activities do not involve the gathering of data because it has already been collected. Instead, these activities involve the way data is maintained and used.

The third group of activities involves the dissemination of information. *Breach of confidentiality* is breaking a promise to keep a person's information confidential. *Disclosure* involves the revelation of truthful information about a person that affects the way others judge her reputation. *Exposure* involves revealing another's nudity, grief, or bodily functions. *Increased accessibility* is amplifying the accessibility of information. *Blackmail* is the threat to disclose personal information. *Appropriation* involves the use of the data subject's identity to serve another's aims and interests. *Distortion* consists of disseminating false or misleading information about individuals. Information dissemination activities all involve the spreading or transfer of personal data or the threat to do so.

The fourth and final group of activities involves invasions into people's private affairs. Invasion, unlike the other groupings, need not involve personal information (although in numerous instances, it does). *Intrusion* concerns invasive acts that disturb one's tranquility or solitude. *Decisional interference* involves incursion into the data subject's decisions regarding her private affairs.

Privacy is not one thing, but many distinct but related things. For too long, policymakers and others have viewed privacy too myopically and narrowly, failing to recognize many important privacy problems. Understanding privacy in a more pluralistic manner will hopefully improve the way privacy problems are recognized and addressed.

The social value of privacy

Another problem with the way privacy is often conceptualized involves how its value is assessed. Traditional liberalism often views privacy as a right possessed by individuals. For example, legal theorist Thomas Emerson declares that privacy "is based upon premises of individualism, that the society exists to promote the worth and dignity of the individual ... The right of privacy ... is essentially the right not to participate in the collective life – the right to shut out the community" (Emerson 1970: 545, 549). In the words of one court: "Privacy is inherently personal. The right to privacy recognizes the sovereignty of the individual" (*Smith* v. *City of Artesia* 1989).

Framing privacy exclusively in individualistic terms often results in privacy being undervalued in utilitarian balancing, which is the predominant way policymakers resolve conflicts between various interests. When individual interests are pitted against the common good, the latter often wins out. The interests often in tension with privacy – free speech, efficient consumer transactions, or security – are frequently understood as valuable for all of society. Privacy, in contrast, is seen as a zone of respite for the sake of the individual.

There is a way, however, to justify privacy from a utilitarian basis. Pragmatist philosopher John Dewey has articulated the most coherent theory of how protecting individual rights furthers the common good. For Dewey, there is no strict dichotomy between individual and society. The individual is shaped by society, and the good of both the individual and society are often interrelated rather than antagonistic: "We cannot think of ourselves save as to some extent *social* beings. Hence we cannot separate the idea of ourselves and our own good from our idea of others and of their good" (Dewey 1908: 268, original emphasis). Dewey contended that the value of protecting individual rights emerges from their contribution to society. In other words, individual rights are not trumps, but are protections by society from its intrusiveness. Society makes space for the individual because of the social benefits this space provides. Therefore, Dewey argues, rights should be valued based on "the contribution they make to the welfare of the community" (Dewey 1936: 374). Otherwise, in any kind of utilitarian calculus, individual rights would not be valuable enough to outweigh most social interests, and it would be impossible to justify individual rights. As such, Dewey argued, we must insist upon a "social basis and social justification" for civil liberties (Dewey 1936: 375).

I contend, like Dewey, that the value of protecting the individual is a social one. Society involves a great deal of friction, and we are constantly clashing with each other. Part of what makes a society a good place in which to live is the extent to which it allows people freedom from the intrusiveness of others. A society without privacy protection would be suffocating, and it might not be a place in which most would want to live. When protecting individual rights, we as a society decide to hold back in order to receive the benefits of creating the kinds of free zones for individuals to flourish.

As Spiros Simitis declares, "privacy considerations no longer arise out of particular individual problems; rather, they express conflicts affecting everyone" (Simitis 1987: 707, 709).[2] Privacy, then, is not the trumpeting of the individual against society's interests but the protection of the individual based on society's own norms and practices. Privacy is not simply

---

[2] In analyzing the problems of federal legislative policymaking on privacy, Priscilla Regan demonstrates the need for understanding privacy in terms of its social benefits. See Regan 1995: xiv ("[A]nalysis of congressional policy making reveals that little attention was given to the possibility of a broader social importance of privacy").

a way to extricate individuals from social control, as it is itself a form of social control that emerges from the norms and values of society.

We protect individual privacy as a society because we recognize that a good society protects against excessive intrusion and nosiness into people's lives. Norms exist not to peek into our neighbor's windows or sneak into people's houses. Privacy is thus not an external restraint on society but is in fact an internal dimension of society (Post 1989: 957, 968, arguing that privacy is society's attempt to promote norms of civility). Therefore, privacy has a social value. Even when it protects the individual, it does so for the sake of society. It thus should not be weighed as an individual right against the greater social good. Privacy issues involve balancing societal interests on both sides of the scale.

Because privacy involves protecting against a plurality of different harms or problems, the value of privacy is different depending upon which particular problem or harm is being protected. Not all privacy problems are equal; some are more harmful than others. Therefore, we cannot ascribe an abstract value to privacy. Its value will differ substantially depending upon the kind of problem or harm we are safeguarding against. Thus to understand privacy, we must conceptualize it and its value more pluralistically. Privacy is a set of protections against a related set of problems. These problems are not all related in the same way, but they resemble each other. There is a social value in protecting against each problem, and that value differs depending upon the nature of each problem.

Clearing away the confusion

Understanding privacy as a pluralistic concept with social value will hopefully help add clarity and concreteness to a concept that has been shrouded in a fog of confusion for far too long. This conceptual confusion has caused policymakers to struggle to respond to the myriad emerging threats technology poses for privacy, from the rise of surveillance cameras to the extensive data trails created by the Internet and electronic commerce. With greater conceptual clarity in understanding the meaning and value of privacy, we can better tackle the difficult task of protecting privacy in the Information Age.

References

Dewey, J. 1978 (1908). "Ethics," in Boydston, J. A. (ed.) *The Middle Works of John Dewey*. Carbondale: Southern Illinois University Press, pp. 31–50.

1991 (1936). "Liberalism and Civil Liberties," in Boydston, J. A. (ed.) *The Later Works of John Dewey*. Carbondale: Southern Illinois University Press, pp. 372–75.

Emerson, T. I. 1970. *The System of Freedom of Expression*. New York: Random House.

Etzioni, A. 1999. *The Limits of Privacy*. New York: Basic Books.

Flaherty, D. H. 1972. *Privacy in Colonial New England*. Charlottesville: University Press of Virginia.

Fried, Ch. 1968. "Privacy. A moral analysis," *Yale Law Journal* 77: 475–93.

Gavison, R. 1980. "Privacy and the limits of law," *Yale Law Journal* 89: 421–71.

Goldhill, S. 2004. *Love, Sex, and Tragedy: How the Ancient World Shapes Our Lives*. University of Chicago Press.

Inness, J. 1992. *Privacy, Intimacy and Isolation*. Oxford University Press.

Miller, A. 1971. *The Assault on Privacy: Computers, Data Banks, and Dossiers*. Ann Arbor: University of Michigan Press.

O'Harrow, R. 2005. *No Place to Hide*, New York: Free Press.

Posner, R. 1981. *The Economics of Justice*. Cambridge, MA: Harvard University Press.

Post, R. C. 1989. "The social foundations of privacy: Community and self in the common law. Tort," 77 *California Law Review*: 957–1010.

Regan, P. M. 1995. *Legislating Privacy*. Chapel Hill: University of North Carolina Press.

Rosen, J. 2004. *The Naked Crowd: Reclaiming Security and Freedom in an Anxious Age*. New York: Random House.

Rybczynski, W. 1986. *Home: A Short History of an Idea*. New York: Penguin Books.

Simitis, S. 1987. "Reviewing privacy in an information society," 135 *University of Pennsylvania Law Review*: 707–46.

Solove, D. J. 2004. *The Digital Person: Technology and Privacy in the Information Age*. New York University Press.

2007. *The Future of Reputation: Gossip, Rumor, and Privacy on the Internet*. New Haven: Yale University Press.

2008. *Understanding Privacy*. Cambridge, MA: Harvard University Press.

Tomás Gómez-Arostegui, H. 2005. "Defining private life under the European Convention on Human Rights by referring to reasonable expectations," *California Western International Law Journal* 35: 153–202.

Westin, A. 1967. *Privacy and Freedom*. New York: Atheneum.

Wittgenstein, L. 1958. *Philosophical Investigations* (trans. G. E. M. Anscombe). Oxford: Basil Blackwell.

PART II

Privacy: practical controversies

PART III

5

The feminist critique of privacy: past arguments and new social understandings

JUDITH WAGNER DECEW

Introduction

In the last two decades of privacy debates, much of the emphasis has come to focus not merely on the individual, but also on the social dimensions of privacy. This new perspective has changed and broadened the earlier understanding of privacy that centered on the meaning and value of privacy for individuals and for individual rights. There has been consensus that the significance of privacy is almost always justified for the individual interests it protects, most importantly protections of freedom and autonomy in a liberal democratic society. Most of the authors writing on various social dimensions of privacy retain their belief in the value of privacy for individuals defended in the past to control information about oneself (Fried 1968; Parent 1983); to enhance personhood including an individual's inviolate personality, integrity and human dignity (Bloustein 1964; Reiman 2004), as well as human flourishing and well-being (Roessler 2005; Moore 2010); to allow for human intimacy (Gerety 1977; Gerstein 1978; Cohen 1992; Inness 1992); as the essential context for fundamental relations of respect, love, friendship and trust to give one the ability to mediate various social relationships (Fried 1968; Rachels 1975; Schoeman 1984); and to protect an individual's ability to restrict or allow others' access (Gavison 1980; Bok 1983; Allen 1988). Others see and defend privacy as a cluster concept allowing individuals to control information about themselves, to control access to them and their physical selves, and to preserve their ability to make personal decisions about themselves and their families, their activities and lifestyles (Allen 1988; Schoeman 1992; DeCew 1997).[1] Defenders of the

---

[1] For more details see DeCew (2013); portions of this chapter are drawn from DeCew (1997).

social value of privacy, however, are now drawing attention to the additional value of social understandings of privacy. The general discussion of privacy has advanced as questions are being asked about the social dimension of privacy. Concerns over the accessibility and retention of electronic communications and the expansion of camera surveillance have led commentators to focus attention on loss of individual privacy as well as on privacy protection with respect to the state and society (Regan 1995; Reiman 2004; Nissenbaum 2010).

According to Daniel Solove, "[b]y understanding privacy as shaped by the norms of society, we can better see why privacy should not be understood solely as an individual right ... Instead, privacy protects the individual because of the benefits it confers on society" (Solove 2008: 98). Moreover, "the value of privacy should be understood in terms of its contribution to society" (Solove 2008: 98, 171 fn.). Solove believes privacy fosters and encourages the moral autonomy of citizens, a central requirement of governance in a democracy. These views on the instrumental value of privacy to society develop from the earlier philosophical writings on the value of privacy – that it heightens respect for individual autonomy, individual integrity and human dignity, but also enhances the value of privacy in various social roles and relationships that contribute to a functioning society. According to this contemporary scholarship, privacy norms help regulate social relationships such as intimate relations, family relationships, professional relationships including those between a physician and a patient, a teacher and a student, a lawyer and a client, and so on. Thus privacy enhances social interaction on a variety of levels, and in this way enhances intimacy, self-development and the ability to present ourselves in public as we wish. According to Solove, a society without respect for privacy for oneself and others becomes a "suffocating society" (Solove 2007: 15).

A moving account of understanding privacy as a necessary and also indispensable condition for individual freedom as well as for a democratic society comes from a literary quotation from Milan Kundera:

> But one day in 1970 or 1971, with the intent to discredit Prochazka, the police began to broadcast these conversations [with Professor Vaclav Cerny, with whom he liked to drink and talk] as a radio serial. For the police it was an audacious, unprecedented act. And, surprisingly: it nearly succeeded; instantly Prochazka *was* discredited: because in private, a person says all sorts of things, slurs friends, uses coarse language, acts silly, tells dirty jokes, repeats himself, makes a companion laugh by shocking him with outrageous talk, floats heretical ideas he'd never admit in public, and so forth. Of course, we all act like Prochazka, in private we

bad-mouth our friends and use coarse language; that we act different in private than in public is everyone's most conspicuous experience, it is the very ground of the life of the individual; curiously, this obvious fact remains unconscious, unacknowledged, forever obscured by lyrical dreams of the transparent glass house, it is rarely understood to be the value one must defend beyond all others. Thus only gradually did people realize (though their rage was all the greater) that the real scandal was not Prochazka's daring talk but the rape of his life; they realized (as if by electric shock) that private and public are two essentially different worlds and that respect for that difference is the indispensable condition, the sine qua non, for a man to live free; that the curtain separating these two worlds is not to be tampered with, and that curtain-rippers are criminals. And because the curtain-rippers were serving a hated regime, they were unanimously held to be particularly contemptible criminals.

(Kundera 1995: 261, original emphasis)

The analogies between Kundera's scenario and electronic surveillance and street cameras common in society today are clear. Kundera helps us see the interconnections between privacy as a value for individuals as well as for a flourishing and free society that is not suffocating.

What I am interested in is what this shift from individual to social dimensions of privacy means for the feminist critique of privacy. If we understand privacy in a more social way, does this have any consequences for the feminist perspective? Are there societal contexts, for instance, which show that a social understanding of privacy can more plausibly address the feminist critique? Thus, in addition to a history of the feminist discussions, I shall focus on the more systematic implications of the social dimensions of privacy for a feminist perspective. In particular, I shall argue that we can and should retain a fundamental concept of privacy, but may understand social considerations of context in a way that justifies appropriate invasions of privacy to enhance the public and collective value of privacy and social well-being.

One problem has been trying to articulate what exactly are the interests protected by privacy concerns, and what is the current and appropriate scope of privacy protection. Many have found this a serious and intransigent difficulty. It has been difficult for philosophers and others to provide clear guidelines for understanding what privacy protects and why it is important, and this is true for defenders of privacy as a value for individuals as well as those writing on the social importance of privacy.

It may be messy and difficult to find adequate words to express just what privacy governs, and it is understandable that some still believe the term "privacy" is too vague and not well enough articulated. But concepts like privacy, and equality, for example, are crucial for understanding our role as social beings and for protecting values fundamental to living lives free from unacceptable individual and governmental intrusions and surveillance.

The public/private distinction and the feminist critique

Nevertheless, the concern about just what privacy protects, and an understanding of privacy's value for individuals as well as society, lead to additional difficulties about understanding the boundaries between the private and the public in problematic cases, and in particular the darker side of privacy raised by feminist critiques of privacy. There may be ways in which the more recent discussions of the social dimensions of privacy may help advance feminist ideas on the interconnectedness of privacy and the public sphere and may provide some guidance about how to approach and respond to the feminist critique of privacy. In the following, I first want to present important positions in the feminist debate on the public and the private, before I turn in the next section to a discussion of the social meaning of privacy and, in the conclusion, to the idea that this discussion can shed new light on the feminist position.

Early versions of the feminist critique of privacy relied heavily on Aristotle's distinction in *The Politics* (1941) between the *polis*, or political realm, and the *oikos*, or domestic realm. The political realm of governing, open to men only, was deemed by Aristotle to be a public arena, whereas the domestic realm of home and family was viewed by him to be a private arena. John Locke provides another well-known example of a historical reference to a public/private distinction. Locke invokes the distinction discussing property in his *Second Treatise on Government* (1690). In the state of nature, he argues, one owns one's own body and yet other property is held in common, or deemed public. When one mixes one's labor with property – harvesting grain or catching fish, for example – that which was held in common becomes one's private property. Although individuals are cautioned to leave "enough and as good" for others, private property acquisition is heralded by Locke as an appropriate goal. The distinction between public and private spheres of life has continued to influence and dominate much of the scholarship on privacy, perhaps to the detriment of an adequate understanding of privacy.

The feminist critique of privacy has been discussed by philosophers and legal theorists from the 1960s through the 1990s, citing privacy's potential to shield domination, repression, degradation and physical harm to women and others. The most famous version of this critique was advanced by Catharine MacKinnon in 1989. She observes that the law of privacy fails to recognize and take into account the pre-existing oppression and inequality of women. For MacKinnon, privacy represents yet another domain where women are deprived of power, all on the suspect theory that "the government best promotes freedom when it stays out of existing social relationships" (MacKinnon 1989: 164–5).

> For women the measure of the intimacy has been the measure of the oppression. This is why feminism has had to explode the private. This is why feminism has seen the personal as the political. The private is public for those for whom the personal is political. In this sense, for women there is no private, either normatively or empirically. Feminism confronts the fact that women have no privacy to lose or to guarantee. Women are not inviolable. Women's sexuality is not only violable, it is – hence women are – seen in and as their violation. To confront the fact that women have no privacy is to confront the intimate degradation of women as the public order. The doctrinal choice of privacy in the abortion context thus reaffirms and reinforces what the feminist critique of sexuality criticizes: the public/private split.
>
> (MacKinnon 1989: 191)

MacKinnon is making two distinct but related claims here. The first is that women have no privacy, and hence protecting privacy provides no benefit to women. Privacy protection may even be a detriment to women, giving men the legal right to treat their wives and partners (and children) unequally or even brutally. The old rape shield laws, for example, made it impossible for women to claim their husbands raped them. The second claim is that feminism has demonstrated the importance of criticizing the split between public and private domains, and thus "has had to explode the private." Consider each in turn.

Why is it that women have no privacy to lose or guarantee? MacKinnon's answer appears to be that because women are violable and violated, they have no zone of autonomy within which to control their destinies. In particular, in the realm of sexuality, often viewed as a paradigm of the private, women do not have control. Men can and often do maintain their power over women in such intimate circumstances. Although sexual intimacy, and activities within the home and family, may be private in the sense of being withheld from public view and shielded from governmental intrusion, they are not private in the sense of being areas where women have control over their decision-making. That women are in fact violated in private contexts, however, implies nothing about the worth and value of protecting a zone within which they can have the power to limit intrusions and violations. In short, descriptive facts about actual limitations on privacy fail to imply anything about the normative value of seeking privacy protection for women.

MacKinnon's second point in this passage underscores the importance of rejecting the public/private split. The public/private distinction has captured the imagination of many feminist scholars. In fact a substantial portion of feminist theory and political struggle over the past 200 years has been concerned with deconstructing the traditional notion, going back as far as Aristotle, of a public (male) political realm and a private (female) domestic realm. Some of the most influential work in feminist political theory, philosophy and legal theory takes this paradigm as its starting point in analyzing women's oppression. Carol Pateman goes so far as to claim that the "public/private dichotomy is, ultimately, what the feminist movement is about" (Pateman 1989: 188). Despite this emphasis on the public/private distinction, it is difficult to clarify what the feminist critique of it entails. Feminist scholars such as Ruth Gavison and Carole Pateman have made clear that there is no single or privileged version of the feminist critique of privacy. There is a multiplicity of interwoven ways of understanding attacks on the public/private dichotomy. MacKinnon says we must "explode" the private, so appears to believe there is no distinction between public and private because there is no private realm for women at all. But this hardly establishes that there *should* be no public/private distinction and that there *should* be no private realm for women.

In part MacKinnon is, like other prominent feminists, drawing attention to the degree to which sexual and physical violence in the family has been a degrading and life-altering experience for so many women (and children and some men). She is surely correct that abusive relationships in those traditionally private contexts are pervasive. To the extent that the private or domestic sphere is held unavailable for public scrutiny, abuse and degradation can continue unchecked. When there are legal avenues for women to combat abuse, the system often does not or cannot enforce them effectively. Moreover, on MacKinnon's view, both the public and private spheres exhibit the social power of sexism. The subordination of women to men is evident in public, and in private it is mirrored and allowed to run its course, "inaccessible to, unaccountable to ... anything beyond itself" (MacKinnon 1989: 190).

We can clearly agree with MacKinnon that the distinction *can* work to the detriment of women. But what is the alternative? If the line between public and private is sometimes indeterminate, does it follow that nothing is or should be private? If there is no distinction between public and private, is everything public? One interpretation of MacKinnon's view is that we must completely reject the realm of the private and conclude that everything is public. Susan Moller Okin writes: "The protection of the privacy of a domestic sphere in which inequality exists is the protection of the right of the strong to exploit and abuse the weak" (Okin 1989: 174). The rejection of the dichotomy is accomplished by collapsing the private into the public. Others have viewed this as a plausible reading of the feminist critique of privacy, for instance Jean Bethke Elshtain (1995: 43), and a similar understanding of the feminist critique is echoed by Ruth Gavison, who observes: "Usually when the dichotomy between public and private is challenged, the argument is that all is (or should be) public" (Gavison 1992: 28). Yet Gavison quickly notes that feminists often equivocate when confronted with the implications of this rejection of the public/private split:

> But once we look at particular questions, it is rare to find feminists who argue consistently either that everything should be regulated by the state, or that the family and all other forms of intimate relationships should disappear in favor of public communities that ... police the different ways in which members interact. When pushed, feminists explicitly deny this is their ideal ... [I]t is hard to specify even one context or dimension of the distinction in which the claim is that the whole category of the private is useless.
>
> (Gavison 1992: 28–9)

Thus, even if women are often vulnerable and exploited in the private, domestic sphere, we may ask whether there are *no* contexts in which women wish to keep the state out of their lives. MacKinnon appears to say yes; nevertheless, I believe the answer must be no. Anita Allen has suggested that an analogy between privacy and liberty is helpful here. Just as the harm that results from the exercise of individual liberty does not lead to the rejection of liberty, similarly there is inadequate reason to reject privacy completely based on harm done in private (Allen 1988: 40).

Feminists have correctly identified the ways in which the public/private distinction can be dangerous if it is used to devalue the work of women in domestic roles, to silence them politically by categorizing them as having no voice or value, and to allow the continuation of abuse and degradation under the cover of a private sphere unavailable for public censure. Thus feminists are right to urge that the distinction not be used to justify differential social and legal treatment of women.

But we need not reject the concept of privacy altogether. Some feminist authors who have wanted to rescue privacy, including Allen (1988), DeCew (1997) and Roessler (2005), have continued to focus on a concept of individual privacy. While defenders of privacy may have underestimated the emphasis on *individual* male power and domestic abuse, critics may underestimate the implications of *state-sponsored* expressions of control over women. Consider, for example, intrusions such as government sterilization programs and interventions involved in state control over welfare programs, including the withdrawal of benefits from women upon the birth of additional children. Consequently rejecting the public/private distinction by eliminating privacy obscures the difference between individual and institutional expressions of (male) power.

Thus, arguing for the rejection of privacy, according to its defenders, fails to address the need to differentiate between justified and unjustified uses of state power over individuals. Governmental regulation might refer to reasonable laws regarding family matters, such as giving women the right to charge husbands with rape. But it might, on the other hand, mean that the state will reveal and regulate all the embarrassing details. Evaluating the justifiability of state intervention may be exceedingly difficult, and exploitation and abuse should be matters of public concern. But even if we agree with feminist insights about the oppression and inequality of women, the reality and pervasiveness of abuse, and the dangers of distinguishing a private domestic realm immune from public scrutiny that preserves the status quo, there may still be value in making a distinction between public and private.

This value is what the second feminist interpretation of privacy seeks to defend.[2] On this alternative interpretation, rejecting the public/private divide by collapsing the private side onto the public is neither the feminist point nor an implication of the feminist position. According to this second feminist account (for instance Allen (1988), Roessler (2005) and DeCew (1997), but also Pateman (1989) and Olsen (1983), see below), the boundaries between public and private need to be redrawn. They would not jettison privacy but recognize that what happens in the family is not always beyond scrutiny. An alternative understanding of the feminist critique of privacy, therefore, is that feminists merely want to reject the public/private distinction *as it has been understood in the past*, from Aristotle on. These feminists are emphasizing that the state must stop ignoring the unbelievable abuses that have been protected in the name of privacy; this

---

[2] I am grateful to Joan Callahan for helping me understand this alternative interpretation.

is, they believe, a position that is not captured by the public/private distinction as it has been known and used in pre-feminist times and theories. On this account, feminists are talking about a position that bypasses the public/private distinction in a different way.

For example, Frances Olsen discusses the radical separation of two spheres of activity – the (public) market and (private) family – and their relationship to two other dichotomies, between state and civil society and between male and female. Olsen describes strategies for improving the status of women, in part because of the unequal bargaining power of women compared to men. She insists:

> as long as we view market and family as a dichotomy, our ideal images of market and family will remain incomplete and unsatisfactory ... The reforms that make the family more like the market and the market more like the family likewise do not overcome the dichotomy between market and family but presuppose it. Although these reforms might appear to be a step toward transcending the market/family dichotomy, experience with such reforms suggests a persistent tendency simply to reproduce in each sphere the failures as well as the successes of the other.
>
> (Olsen 1983: 68)

Olsen urges that the public/private and market/family dichotomies are a way of thinking, a human creation; they are a prism through which we have come to see our lives. It is not enough to recognize the crippling effects of such dichotomies.

Olsen worries that rejection of the public/private split will lead to an alternative system "in which the state controls every aspect of human life and nothing is personal and private" (Olsen 1983: 83), and she emphatically rejects this implication, saying she does not advocate replacing the present dichotomies with an all-powerful state. Instead, Olsen urges that we neither reject the humanization and connectedness of the family nor the efficient production of goods and services in the market. It is their separation and polarization that reinforces the status quo and limits possibilities of human association. On her view, "[w]e cannot choose between the two sides of the dualism because we need both" (Olsen 1983: 88). The preferable alternative is to transcend the dichotomies in some yet-to-be articulated way, preserving a meaningful role for an important concept of privacy.

Carole Pateman reiterates the feminist challenge to the separation and opposition between public and private spheres as central categories of political liberalism, where domestic family life is paradigmatically private. Pateman believes that "the dichotomy between the private and the public obscures the subjection of women to men within an apparently universal, egalitarian and individualist order" (Pateman 1989: 20). But she emphasizes that feminists reject the claim that a public/private dichotomy is inevitable:

> They [feminists] argue that a proper understanding of liberal social life is possible only when it is accepted that the two spheres, the domestic (private) and civil society (public) held to be separate and opposed, are inextricably interrelated; they are the two sides of the single coin of liberal-patriarchialism ... [Furthermore,] feminist critiques insist that an alternative to the liberal conception must also encompass the relationship between public and domestic life.

> (Pateman 1989: 121–2, 123)

What is needed, on Pateman's view, is a feminist theoretical perspective that takes account of *social* relationships between men and women within the context of interpretations of both the public and the private. Work by political theorists as well as practical experience from the feminist movement, has shown that women's place in the private sphere cannot simply be augmented by extending to women a role in the public sphere. The spheres are not additive, but integrally related. In sum, Pateman views the feminist critique of privacy as stressing rejection of the dichotomy *as it has been understood*, but she concludes that the "separate" worlds of private and public are closely interrelated and that both are necessary dimensions of a future, democratic feminist social order. An adequate account will develop a *social* theory in which these categories are distinct but interrelated, rather than totally separate or opposed.

Clearly the feminist critique of privacy is multifaceted. Quite a few feminists – among them Allen, DeCew, Roessler, but also Olsen and Pateman – acknowledge the difficulties of the public/private dichotomy and the damaging effects of accepting it as it has been defended in the past. Feminists articulating this strand of the feminist critique maintain that the public/private dichotomy is misleading when it fails to recognize the *interconnections* between private and public life. The challenge for those unwilling to jettison privacy completely – given the lingering influence, in our culture and law, of the separate spheres analysis that women belong in the home and men in public positions – is to *preserve* some understanding of the two spheres while extricating them from their gendered past and connotations.

Social understandings of privacy

At this point the feminist critique connects to recent debates about the value of privacy for society and the social dimension of privacy. Drawing on Pateman's emphasis on accounting for *social* relationships between men and women within the context of interpretations of both public and private, makes it clear that feminists should be interested in new social approaches for understanding privacy and hopefully addressing the feminist critique. Regan (1995), Solove (2008) and Nissenbaum (2010) defend social understandings of privacy and it is promising to link this approach with the feminist ideas on the interconnectedness of privacy, public and social relationships.

Priscilla Regan began to take account of the social value of privacy, noting that Westin and others saw privacy and social participation as competing desires that an individual would need to balance. Rejecting this conflict, Regan argues that threats to privacy can be individual concerns as well as social problems. "Most privacy scholars emphasize that the individual is better off if privacy exists; I argue that society is better off as well when privacy exists" (Regan 1995: 221). Regan argues that privacy is a *common value*, a *public value* and a *collective value* (Regan 1995: 213). She echoes others who have argued that privacy is valuable for a democracy by creating a place for deliberation, bolstering the voting process and helping to develop people who are capable of the kind of participation that democracy requires. Ultimately Regan's argument is: "Privacy is becoming less an attribute of individuals and records and more an attribute of social relationships and information systems or communication systems" (Regan 1995: 230).

Daniel Solove expands on this social understanding of privacy, worrying about the concept of privacy being in disarray, but he argues that privacy is important across the globe, and recognized explicitly by the United States, countries in the European Union, Asia-Pacific and elsewhere. Discussing examples of privacy violations leads him to note that responses that treat them as one kind of violation are not as nuanced as they should be, and he urges that being aware of *context* in privacy violations needs to be supplemented so that the concept of privacy is not overstretched to become an empty concept. Solove addresses different conceptions of privacy developed by legal scholars, philosophers and social scientists and argues that many of these views also fail to explain why the way in which issues deemed private are often formed within a social context.

Solove defends his own conception of privacy, understood as various kinds of good that have similar characteristics, that can be found in particular contexts and are flexible enough to be understood in different cultures and times. He writes: "Therefore, my approach to conceptualizing privacy understands it pluralistically rather than as having a unitary common denominator. In focusing on privacy problems, my approach seeks to be contextual without being overly tied to specific contexts, flexible enough to accommodate changing attitudes toward privacy, yet firm enough to remain stable and useful" (Solove 2008: 9, Allen 2003). His emphasis on the social dimension of privacy is based in part on his argument that the value of privacy should be rooted in its utility for society, not individual rights, because its value is determined by the social importance of the activities privacy makes possible.

Solove focuses on a pragmatic approach embracing a focus on specific situations, and thus sensitive to contextual situations. He cites Nissenbaum's framework of the "contextual integrity" of privacy in arguing for the importance of context, but he also believes that context is not enough. Anita Allen's insight into the role of accountability is also important: people are held, or feel, accountable within relationships, not "across the board" (Solove 2008: 48). What counts as private is not accidental on Solove's view. To the contrary, issues are private because people want them to be.[3]

Solove does not find feminist critiques persuasive enough to lead to rejecting privacy, and he points out that privacy can liberate women as well (see Allen, DeCew, Gavison), thus in my view setting the stage for how his view that privacy is instrumentally valuable for specific problems and contexts deemed important in society can be helpful in replying to the feminist critique of privacy. "Privacy should be weighed against contrasting values, and it should win when it produces the best outcome for society" (Solove 2008: 87). The value of privacy is social because it leads to benefits to society, not simply the individual. One such benefit may be in addressing domestic abuse in private contexts.

Although Solove recognizes privacy's importance for information, I applaud the expansion of his view to be about a broader concept covering invasions including physical intrusion and decisional interference. In his conclusion Solove also addresses cultural differences in approaches to privacy. On his view different cultures, when balancing privacy problems against other values, may come to different conclusions, with some

---

[3] See Roessler on preferences, though Solove does not endorse her view.

cultures putting little value on some privacy problems while protecting against others, because these privacy problems can be weighed differently depending on the historical and situational context. As we shall see, this may help address the feminist critique of privacy, but may raise other difficulties as well.

Let us next have a look at a second approach to the social dimensions of privacy. Helen Nissenbaum's position is narrower than Solove's work in that it focuses solely on informational privacy. She writes: "What people care most about is not simply *restricting* the flow of information but ensuring that it flows *appropriately*, and an account of appropriate flow is given here through the framework of contextual integrity" (Nissenbaum 2010: 2, original emphasis). Thus I believe she fleshes out the idea of contextual integrity in ways that may provide more specific details about how to use a social understanding of privacy to reply to the feminist critique of privacy. Several of her key concepts can be adapted to be useful in a broader way that could include domestic and family life.

Nissenbaum notes that the public/private distinction has been a common source of our conception of privacy, bringing both a positive aspect of private space and a negative aspect of over-inclusiveness in the ways we use the concept of privacy. Citing DeCew, she agrees that the public/private division can be difficult to define and is used in different ways depending on the discipline or author, but can be defined in a useful way to use privacy as a protective barrier between individuals and government or others, as well as a line between the domestic and political realms. Yet she concludes: "The framework of contextual integrity ... does not take sides in these controversial line-drawing exercises; rather, it reveals them to be symptoms of the deeper problem of invoking the private/public dichotomy to inform our understanding of privacy" (Nissenbaum 2010: 102). Therefore, the public/private dichotomy is not necessarily problematic, but is not useful as a normative conception of privacy. On her view privacy standards have not changed, but threats to privacy have. She concludes that the private/public dichotomy leaves too many theoretical gaps to be used as a justification for privacy, yet she does not reject it outright. And she stresses that her own contextual integrity view is neutral with regard to alternative theories of privacy's value.

What is more important, according to Nissenbaum, is to focus on context, because privacy expectations are "systematically related to characteristics of the background social situation" (Nissenbaum 2010: 129) and "Contexts are structured social settings characterized by canonical activities, roles, relationships, power structures, norms (or rules), and internal values (goals, ends, purposes)" (Nissenbaum 2010: 132). Contexts will be determined by different roles, such as teacher or physician, activities conducted by people in those roles, norms specifying acceptable actions and practices guiding behavior, and values which are the goals and purposes of a given context. These attributes are a way of understanding a "snapshot" of a particular context, where the latter – values, goals and purposes – are clearly the most important. Nissenbaum urges that contexts may have both formal norms and values as well as tacit and general ones, and this can generate disagreements about privacy. Norms may work in unity or may conflict. There may be no general solution to the conflicts, but we navigate our way through such conflicts often in daily life. Contexts such as health care or the workplace will have a background of goals such as the health of patients in medical care, as well as norms, and norms may differ for different actors (one's physician or employer) and they can change. Her point is to have norms that give *appropriate* guidelines of behavior, for example, for the transmission of medical information, and these may differ for one's physician and one's employer. But "contextual integrity is a proposed benchmark for privacy" (Nissenbaum 2010: 140). Nissenbaum believes there are entrenched norms on information-gathering and sharing in many contexts, but those may change with new technologies.

My suggestion is that contextual integrity may be a useful framework for explaining appropriate and inappropriate informational transmission, as proposed by Nissenbaum, but may also serve as a useful framework for explaining appropriate and inappropriate behavior in the context of the domestic realm. Clearly there are formal and explicit laws and rules against domestic violence, incest, wife-battering and child abuse in the USA and multiple other countries. Moreover, in the domestic realm there are actors in roles such as mother, father, parent, child, extended family, and so on, as well as activities performed within the family in the domestic context. There are entrenched norms about appropriate parental caretaking, meeting children's basic needs as well as enrichment and enhancement for child development and preserving respect for partners, all set within the goals and purposes of the context, for example that the family unit is, in general, meant to provide a safe space where parents and children can thrive without abuse. It seems to me that we need not reject the domestic realm as a private realm, nor reject privacy as being normatively valuable due to its protection of freedom, equality and the good life, but can recognize that spousal abuse, battering, rape, as well as child abuse violate explicit laws and entrenched norms of appropriate behavior in the family that justify external intervention from government or other public agencies including social services. The *default* is that privacy protection is fundamental, but considerations of contextual integrity can provide a secondary set of considerations to justify appropriate intervention.

While I use several of Nissenbaum's concepts, there are differences between our views. My claim is that the understanding of privacy has to be consistent with the appropriate norms governing our lives (private and public). There may be a wide range of agreement about which norms are appropriate, but there will be some disagreements as well. Nissenbaum, however, seems to imply that the appropriateness of privacy contexts is inherent to the privacy norms themselves (but see Nissenbaum 2010: 182). I believe there are more fundamental underlying norms that can be used to criticize certain privacy contexts and can explain when privacy can be overridden. While it is not completely clear what makes norms or behavior appropriate or not, I believe that we can make some determinations about appropriate norms based on the connection between privacy and its use in defending equality and freedom.

Nissenbaum's framework allows that even entrenched norms may change to allow for progress, as she notes that for her focus on information technology there have been recent shifts in what is viewed as normal. For example, new technologies such as body screening at airports and video surveillance are now viewed as normal. "The approach I recommend here is to compare entrenched normative practices against novel alternatives or competing practices on the basis of how effective each is in supporting, achieving or promoting contextual values" (Nissenbaum 2010: 166). Similarly, in the domestic realm of the family, a historical understanding of the "traditional" heterosexual family is now evolving to recognize and validate same sex partnerships, without altering norms about appropriate respectful and non-abusive behavior between partners. Contextual integrity looks at the purpose of the context of domestic family life, for example to see if a new practice such as same sex marriage helps or hinders that purpose. Clearly new social understandings of same sex marriage indicate that most now view it as reasonable and not abnormal, and believe it does not hinder the goal of providing a caring space and unit where all members can be supported and thrive without harm. Looking at the big picture and not just single privacy decisions, as Nissenbaum apparently recommends, can be an important way of evaluating and prescribing appropriate behavior in the domestic realm.

This approach need not lead us to totally jettison the public/private dichotomy and the fundamental value of privacy, nor to view privacy as a relativistic notion as Solove appears to do, but to understand that within private contexts there will in addition be contextual purposes and goals, norms for actors and appropriate activities and behavior within those contexts, leading to insightful ways of prescribing *appropriate* behavior and justifying external intervention when those norms are violated. We can recognize individual violations against women in the domestic realm but judge them as inexcusable and inappropriate in the domestic context to achieve Solove's goal of creating the best outcome for society.

Nissenbaum believes that use of her contextual integrity framework for information access and transmission is primary, and will mean that changes over time and culture may no longer be an issue, and this will be a benefit in the domestic realm where changes in social views on consenting adult homosexuality and same sex marriage can be understood and embraced. Nevertheless, I treat privacy as fundamental with the contextual integrity framework as a secondary way to determine when invasions into a private realm can be justified. However, I do not feel that even this useful though secondary contextual integrity framework will solve all the difficult issues of privacy protection across religions and cultures. There is clearly the difficulty of determining which norms are appropriate guidelines for behavior – also a problem for Nissenbaum's work on information technology – and there will be particularly thorny issues in the context of the domestic realm. For example, one may wonder whether parents should have the power to withhold cancer or other medical treatments from children – for religious or other reasons – when such treatments are medically sound and have been shown to increase survival rates. While some may view this as a completely private family decision, it seems extremely difficult to justify in the face of clear harm to the children. As a family decision it may be viewed as presumptively private, but it may be that explicit and entrenched norms prohibiting harm to others and norms defending some degree of paternalism in certain cases may conflict with deeply entrenched religious beliefs. Contextual integrity does not resolve the conflict on its own, but at least clarifies which norms are in conflict, and suggests that considerations of the goals and purposes of the domestic family, including how to enhance children's abilities to thrive, are clearly important goals for society.

Consider another example. Deeply entrenched cultural beliefs, in favor of female genital mutilation, for example, seem to lead to the conclusion that even with "consent" the state should not necessarily remain out of the affairs of individuals. Otherwise it would seem that a physician must honor a woman's rational yet culturally entrenched decision that the physician must perform genital mutilation surgery on her. Thus it seems there must be some constraints on what counts as significant and meaningful consent. Here, norms about a physician's health care role in enhancing patient health and doing no harm may help support his refusal to accede to the patient's request. Yet questions in such a conflict may remain.

Conclusion

So where do we stand? In the first part of this chapter I have given an outline of two interpretations of the feminist critique of privacy and the private/public distinction, one that rejects privacy and collapses it into the public realm, and one that preserves the distinction while recognizing that it has to be understood in a new way. In the second part I have presented two approaches to the social understanding of privacy and have tried to show ways they connect and help address the feminist critique. Acknowledging that there will be some extremely difficult cases, it nevertheless seems to me that recognizing the important social dimensions of privacy explained by Regan and the emphasis on context rather than individual privacy claims defended by Solove and Nissenbaum, and endorsing Solove's broad conception of privacy extending to decisional contexts along with Nissenbaum's contextual integrity approach, help us see ways in which a fundamentally private context such as the domestic realm can be viewed through a lens of appropriate norms of behavior and important social goals for enhancing security, personal excellence and well-being in society. Public and social goals may be intertwined in addressing violence against women and domestic abuse. As not only Allen, DeCew and Jean Cohen, but also Pateman and Olsen have argued, we need not reject important uses of the term "privacy" and its fundamental value, and we need not be chained to the ancient public/private dichotomy. Theories of privacy will need to say more about how to determine which norms are appropriate or inappropriate, and will need to move forward on the discussion of cultural differences in perspective on privacy and social norms. However, we may have found a theoretical perspective that can be endorsed by feminists that embraces the importance of privacy, yet allows privacy invasions when taking account of social relationships between men and women within the context of various areas of daily life.

References

Allen, A. L. 1988. *Uneasy Access: Privacy for Women in a Free Society.* Totowa: Rowman & Littlefield.

2003. *Why Privacy Isn't Everything: Feminist Reflections on Personal Accountability.* Totowa, NJ: Rowman & Littlefield.

Aristotle. *The Politics,* trans. Benjamin Jowett, in *The Basic Works of Aristotle.* Richard McKeon (ed.) 1941. New York: Random House, 1127–324.

Bloustein, E. J. 1964. "Privacy as an aspect of human dignity: An answer to Dean Prosser," *New York University Law Review* 39: 962–1007.

Bok, S. 1983. *Secrets: On the Ethics of Concealment and Revelation.* New York: Random House, Vintage Books.

Cohen, J. L. 1992. "Redescribing privacy: Identity, difference and the abortion controversy," *Columbia Journal of Gender and Law* 3: 43–117.

DeCew, J. Wagner 1997. *In Pursuit of Privacy: Law, Ethics and the Rise of Technology.* Ithaca, NY: Cornell University Press.

2013. "Privacy," *Stanford Encyclopedia of Philosophy* (Fall 2013 Edition), edited by Edward N. Zalta. Available at http://plato.stanford.edu/archives/fall2013/entries/privacy/.

Elshtain, J. B. 1995. *Democracy on Trial.* New York: Basic Books.

Fried, C. 1968. "Privacy," *Yale Law Journal* 77: 475–93.

Gavison, R. 1980. "Privacy and the limits of law," *Yale Law Journal* 89: 421–71.

Gavison, R. 1992. "Feminism and the public/private distinction," *Stanford Law Review* 45: 1–46.

Gerety, T. 1977. "Redefining privacy," 12 *Harvard Civil Rights–Civil Liberties Law Review* 12: 233–96.

Gerstein, R. 1978. "Intimacy and privacy," *Ethics* 89: 76–81.

Inness, J. 1992. *Privacy, Intimacy and Isolation.* Oxford University Press.

Kundera, M. 1995. *Testaments Betrayed: An Essay in Nine Parts.* New York: Harper Collins.

Locke, J. 1690. *Second Treatise on Government,* Thomas P. Reardon (ed.) Reprinted: New York: Macmillan, Library of Liberal Arts.

MacKinnon, C. 1989. *Toward a Feminist Theory of the State.* Cambridge, MA: Harvard University Press.

Moore, A. D. 2010. *Privacy Rights: Moral and Legal Foundations.* Penn State University Press.

Nissenbaum, H. 2010. *Privacy in Context: Technology, Policy, and the Integrity of Social Life.* Stanford University Press.

Okin, S. M. 1989. *Justice, Gender, and the Family.* New York: Basic Books.

Olsen, F. E. 1983. "The Family and the market: A study of ideology and legal reform," *Harvard Law Review* 96: 1497–578.

Parent, W. 1983. "Privacy, morality and the law," *Philosophy & Public Affairs* 12: 269–88.

Pateman, C. 1989. "Feminist Critiques of the Public/Private Dichotomy," in Pateman. C. *The Disorder of Women: Democracy, Feminism, and Political Theory*. Stanford University Press.

Rachels, J. 1975. "Why privacy is important," *Philosophy & Public Affairs* 4: 323–33.

Regan, P. 1995. *Legislating Privacy*. Chapel Hill: University of North Carolina Press.

Reiman, J. 2004. "Driving to the Panopticon: A Philosophical Exploration of the Risks to Privacy Posed by the Information Technology of the Future," in Roessler, B. (ed.) *Privacies: Philosophical Evaluations*. Stanford University Press, pp. 194–214.

Roessler, B. 2005. *The Value of Privacy*. Cambridge, MA: Polity Press.

Schoeman, F. (ed.) 1984. *Philosophical Dimensions of Privacy: An Anthology*. Cambridge University Press.

1992. *Privacy and Social Freedom*. Cambridge University Press.

Solove, D. J. 2008. *Understanding Privacy*. Cambridge, MA: Harvard University Press.

2007. "'I've Got Nothing to Hide' and Other Misunderstandings of Privacy," accessed at: http://tehlug.org/files/solove.pdf.

6

Privacy in the family

BRYCE CLAYTON NEWELL, CHERYL A. METOYER,
ADAM D. MOORE

Introduction

While the balance between individual privacy and government monitoring or corporate surveillance has been a frequent topic across numerous
disciplines, the issue of privacy within the family has been largely ignored
in recent privacy debates. Yet privacy intrusions between parents and children or between adult partners or spouses can be just as profound as those
found in the more "public spheres" of life. Popular access to increasingly
sophisticated forms of electronic surveillance technologies has altered the
dynamics of family relationships. Monitoring, mediated and facilitated
by practices of both covert and overt electronic surveillance, has changed
the nature of privacy within the family. Parents are tracking children via
GPS-enabled cell phone tracking software and are monitoring the Internet
use of family members. Parents, siblings, and children are also posting
information about their family members online, often without consent,
and are creating social media profiles for others online. Prior scholarly
work in philosophy and law has primarily addressed the privacy of children from third parties, usually commercial entities, and in the context of
making medical decisions.[1] Less attention has been directed at exploring
a more general right of privacy of one family member against parents, siblings, children, or spouses. In this chapter we do just that. In the pages that
follow we consider several moral rules that determine appropriate privacy boundaries within the family. More specifically, we will consider when

---

[1] For example, the USA's Children's Online Privacy Protection Act (COPPA, 2000) gives
parents a veto over the "further use" of information collected from a child but it also
requires security and confidentiality of this information. 15 USC §§ 6501–6506.

overt or covert surveillance of a child, spouse, or partner by a family member is morally permitted.[2]

Our discussion proceeds within the conceptual framework developed in prior work. In the next section we define privacy as the right to control access to, and uses of, places, bodies, and personal information and discuss prior empirical and theoretical work establishing the moral value of privacy. While admittedly contentious, we adopt an essentialist or objective account of moral value tied directly to human well-being or flourishing. For example, practices that cause disease or ill health are, on our account, morally disvaluable. Alternatively, practices that promote human health and well-being are morally valuable. The third section considers several studies that analyze the effects of different sorts of monitoring on adolescents. An established claim of child development theory is that children who are not monitored have a greater risk of engaging in problematic behavior – including drug, tobacco, and alcohol use, dropping out of school, and early pregnancy. Interestingly, children who are subject to covert spying, as well as other forms of surveillance both overt and covert, are subject to the same increased risks as adolescents who are virtually abandoned by their parents. Two-way information-sharing based on respect and caring, on the other hand, is connected to decreased risky or problematic behavior. In the final section we argue that privacy, understood as a moral and social mechanism that ensures the proper development and functioning of individuals, is essential for trust and provides the foundation for intimate family relationships.

Included in our discussion is a critique of Anita Allen's defense of spying on one's children, spouse, or partner. We conclude by arguing for two rules. A rule of "two-way communication" establishes a practice of trust, respect, and caring. Such a standard would help preserve private spaces within family life – spaces where children, spouses, or partners can appropriately withdraw for purposes of self-development without fear of unjustified monitoring. If in a specific instance or as a practice the two-way sharing rule fails, we retreat to a probable cause standard to determine the appropriateness of parental or other intra-familial surveillance. Probable cause is established when a parent, spouse, or partner has discovered information through logical inquiry that would lead a reasonably intelligent and prudent person to believe that their child, spouse, or

---

[2] We will not consider overt or covert spying between siblings. Nevertheless, the principles defended in the sections to follow could be extended to such cases.

partner is subject to, or the cause of, a specific and serious threat to safety or well-being. If we are correct, covert or overt surveillance would only be justified in a narrow range of cases.

Privacy: its meaning and value

While privacy has been defined in many ways over the last century, we favor what has been called a "control"-based definition of privacy (see Warren and Brandeis 1890; Westin 1967; Gross 1971; Parker 1974; Gavison 1983; Parent 1983; Allen 2003). A right to privacy is a right to control access to, and uses of, places, bodies, and personal information (Moore 2003, 2008, 2010). For example, suppose that Smith wears a glove because he is ashamed of a scar on his hand. If you were to snatch the glove away, you would not only be violating Smith's right to property, since the glove is his to control, but you would also be violating his right to privacy – a right to restrict access to information about the scar on his hand. Similarly, if you were to focus your X-ray camera on Smith's hand, take a picture of the scar through the glove, and then publish the photograph widely, you would violate a right to privacy. While your X-ray camera may diminish Smith's ability to control the information in question, it does not undermine his right to control access (Moore 2007).

Privacy also includes a right over the use of bodies, locations, and personal information. If access is granted accidentally or otherwise, it does not follow that any subsequent use, manipulation, or sale of the good in question is justified. In this way privacy is both a shield that affords control over access or inaccessibility, and a kind of use and control-based right that yields justified authority over specific items – such as a room or personal information (Moore 2007). For example, by appearing in public and leaving biological matter behind, someone may grant access to specific sorts of personal information. We should not conclude, however, that by granting access this individual has also waived all control over any and all future uses of the biological matter or the information found within.

To get a sense of the importance of privacy and separation, it is helpful to consider similar interests shared by many non-human animals. While privacy rights may entail obligations and claims against others – obligations and claims that are beyond the capacities of most non-human animals – a case can still be offered in support of the claim that separation is valuable for animals. Alan Westin in *Privacy and Freedom* notes:

> One basic finding of animal studies is that virtually all animals seek periods of individual seclusion of small-group intimacy. This is usually

described as the tendency toward territoriality, in which an organism lays private claim to an area of land, water, or air and defends it against intrusion by members of its own species.

(Westin 1967: 8)

More important for our purposes are the ecological studies demonstrating that a lack of private space, due to overpopulation and the like, will threaten survival. In such conditions animals may kill each other or engage in suicidal reductions of the population.

Given the similarities between humans and many non-human animals, it is plausible to think that we share many of the same traits. For example, Lewis Mumford notes similarities between rat overcrowding and human overcrowding. "No small part of this ugly urban barbarization has been due to sheer physical congestion: a diagnosis now partly confirmed by scientific experiments with rats – for when they are placed in equally congested quarters, they exhibit the same symptoms of stress, alienation, hostility, sexual perversion, parental incompetence, and rabid violence that we now find in large cities" (Mumford 1961: 210). These results are supported by numerous more recent studies. Household overcrowding and overcrowding in prisons has been linked to violence, depression, suicide, psychological disorders, and recidivism (see Morgan 1972; Baum and Koman 1976; Edwards and Booth 1977; Megargee 1977; Paulus *et al.* 1978; Cox *et al.* 1980; Farrington and Nuttal 1980; McCain *et al.* 1984; Porporino and Dudley 1984; Ruback and Carr 1984; Clauson-Kaas *et al.* 1996; Fuller *et al.* 1996).

Cultural universals have been found in every society that has been systematically studied (see Murdock 1955; Nussbaum 2000). Based on the Human Relations Area Files at Yale University, Alan Westin has argued that there are aspects of privacy found in every society – privacy *is* a cultural universal (see Westin 1967; Roberts and Gregor 1971). While privacy may be a cultural universal necessary for the proper functioning of human beings, its form – the actual rules of association and disengagement – is culturally dependent (see Spiro 1971). The kinds of privacy rules found in different cultures will be dependent on a host of variables including climate, religion, technological advancement, and political arrangements. Nevertheless, we think it is important to note that relativism about the forms of privacy – the rules of coming together and leave-taking – does not undermine our claim regarding the objective need for these rules. There is strong evidence that the ability to regulate access to our bodies, capacities, and powers and to sensitive personal information is an essential part of human flourishing or well-being.

Barry Schwartz, in an important article dealing with the social psychology of privacy, provides interesting clues as to why privacy is universal (Schwartz 1968; see also Mill 1859; Rachels 1975). According to Schwartz, privacy is group-preserving, maintains status divisions, allows for deviation, and sustains social establishments (Schwartz 1968: 741). Privacy also preserves groups by providing rules of engagement and disassociation. Without privacy or what may be called a dissociation ritual, there could be no stable social relation. As social animals we seek the company of our fellows, but at some point interaction becomes bothersome and there is a mutual agreement to separate. Thus, having "good fences" would be necessary for having "good neighbors" (Rachels 1975: 331).

Schwartz also notes that privacy helps maintain status divisions within groups. A mark of status is a heightened level of access control. Enlisted men in the armed services have less privacy when compared to commissioned officers. Line level employees work without doors or secretaries who screen access to them. By protecting status divisions and determining association and disassociation rules, privacy has a stabilizing effect on groups or social orders (see McGinley 1959: 56). Privacy also protects and leaves room for deviation within groups. As J. S. Mill noted in *On Liberty* (1859, Chapter 2), when individuals engage in different forms of living, protected by the walls of privacy, new ideas are produced and, if good, are adopted.

Growing up can be understood as the building of a series of walls – the walls of privacy.[3] Infants are without privacy. As infants grow into toddlers and begin to communicate with language, they express wishes for separation at times. This process continues as children grow into adults.[4] Toddlers and small children begin requesting privacy as they start the process of self-initiated development. More robust patterns of disassociation continue as children enter puberty. Finally, as young adults emerge, the walls of privacy have hardened and access points are maintained vigorously.

As an example of the universal yet relational aspects of privacy, consider the following set of cases. Privacy in Native American communities is best understood within the context of a philosophy that includes two critical values: relationality and the sacred. According to Wilson: "Rather than

---

[3] "Both animals and humans require, at critical stages of life, specific amounts of space in order to act out the dialogues that lead to the consummation of most of the important acts of life" (Spitz 1964: 752).

[4] "The door of openness closes perhaps halfway as a recognition of self-development during childhood, it shuts but is left ajar at pre-puberty, and closes entirely – and perhaps even locks – at the pubertal and adolescent stages when meditation, grooming, and body examination become imperative" (Schwartz 1968: 749; see also Erikson 1963 and Kessler 1966).

viewing ourselves as being in right relationship with other people or things, we are the relationships that we hold or are part of" (Wilson 2008: 80).

Relationality means that matters of place, people, and community are inextricably intertwined. In addition, Native American knowledge systems and ways of life see the mental, physical, social, and spiritual domains of existence flowing into and informing one another. For Native people, this value system governs proper behavior in relation to people and the spaces in which they interact. As to place, "home" in this context is a sacred space, encompassing more than house. Recall that, until relatively recently, many indigenous dwellings consisted of one or two rooms that contributed to communal living practices.

There are numerous daily ceremonies and rituals that underscore the reverence that is essential to the concept of "home." Marisa Duarte (2013) expresses this relationship in the Yaqui community in the following statement:

> The sacred private space of the home is for the family who lives there, and is maintained with respect for the elders and children and women (in that order) who live in that home. Even good friends of the family and distant relatives are expected to enter the yard around the house by the front, and wait by the white cross in the front of the house to be greeted. Children are not allowed to participate in conversations among adults, and are expected to play outside, or sit quietly.
>
> (Duarte 2013)

In comparison to the Mexican American side of her family, she recognizes a critical difference: "Where [on] the Mexican American side, children are allowed to close and lock their doors, not report their daily comings and goings, and not introduce their friends to the family. It is considered rude, but not inappropriate. When those things happen in Yaqui families, the child is considered spiritually unwell and in danger" (Duarte 2013).

Privacy exists in Native American communities to ensure the dignity and respect of persons. Nevertheless, proper behavior, in reference to physical contact, varies by tribal community. Duarte notes that:

> adult women – the mother – can go into any place in the house, including the adolescent child's room. Usually children share rooms until adulthood. The father can, too, although past a certain age, fathers maintain a respectful distance for adolescent daughters as young women. Women's spaces are particularly sacred. Elders' spaces may be filled with ancestors and other spiritual forces that can be overwhelming to children, and especially spiritually sick (anxious/depressed/ill) children. These places need to be prayed through, candles lit, and cleaned frequently, for the health of vulnerable young people.
>
> (Duarte 2013)

The impact of technology, mobile phones, and tracking devices on the behavior of Native children in reservation communities is difficult to assess, primarily because no comprehensive assessment of technology in Indian Country has been conducted. However, in contemporary reservation communities families rely on neighbors and other family members to keep track of their children's whereabouts. People know the kids in the neighborhoods/sections of the reservations. They know where the kids hang out or go to play. They know the place. It is important to recall that families have often lived in these places for hundreds of years.

Privacy and surveillance in the family

As mentioned above, the starting point for our discussion begins with a conceptualization of the role of privacy in human development and the place for surveillance in familial relationships. Scholars in a variety of fields, including developmental and clinical science, have investigated the impact of parental monitoring in a variety of settings. Ann Crouter and Melissa Head (2002) distinguish between two concepts that have historically been confused and under-conceptualized in the relevant literature, leading to disconnects between theoretical concepts and empirical measurement: parental monitoring and parental knowledge (see also Crouter *et al.* 2006). Traditionally, parental monitoring has been defined as "a set of correlated parenting behaviors involving attention to and tracking of the child's whereabouts, activities, and adaptations" (Dishion and McMahon 1998). Crouter and Head argue that empirical measures used to investigate parental monitoring have often actually measured parental *knowledge*, while much less research has focused on the *practice* of parental surveillance (the activities and technological tools employed to keep track of children) (Crouter and Head 2002: 461).

Additionally, recent research has begun to identify that a high level of parental knowledge is much more closely related to "trusting parent–child relationship[s]" and a "child's willingness to confide" in a parent than it is to the actual practice of parental surveillance. Thus parental knowledge can be described as "a relationship property" and speaks more to the importance of establishing trusting relationships than it does to the virtues (or practical benefits) of spying on family members. A "good monitor" is not a spy, but rather a parent who has made an effort to build trust with his or her child – although a child must also willingly disclose honestly (Crouter and Head 2002: 461; see also Stattin and Kerr 2000a).

As children grow and begin to communicate effectively with language, they express wishes for separation. More robust patterns of disassociation continue as children enter puberty. Finally, as these children become young adults, walls of privacy have become rigid and access points are secured – although the formulation of these access points may be determined partly by the level of trust they maintain with parents and/or siblings. Thus, as parental knowledge depends, to some significant extent, on trust and two-way relationships, activities that damage trust, or have the potential to do so, are inherently risky and suspect, both ethically and for practical purposes. Spying, especially covert surveillance between family members that invades established boundaries or evades walls of expected privacy, bears a substantial risk to trusting relationships (Crouter *et al.* 1990: 656).

Empirical investigation of the impact of actual parental surveillance practices may be limited, but some do exist. In a study conducted by Czeskis *et al.* (2010), interviews were conducted with nine parent–child pairs. They were primarily concerned with understanding how technologically aided parental surveillance trends involving mobile phone monitoring impacted children and their parents. Cellular phones and other technologies allow family members to track each other's geographic locations, record content, activate cameras and microphones on mobile devices, initiate automatic alarms when entering areas deemed unsafe or off-limits, detect and report on devices that happen to be nearby, or even measure emotions (Czeskis *et al.* 2010: 1).

Czeskis *et al.* asked questions about possible mobile phone systems that could transmit information from the child to the parent under various conditions. The researchers found that eight of the nine teens would choose to limit the disclosure of certain information to their parents, and that most parents expressed support for these decisions, especially when they involved personal information about friends or significant others. Teens also expressed interest in the ability to disclose information and to write things to friends on Facebook that they would be uncomfortable having their parents read. Six of nine teens studied had lied to their parents about where they were on at least one occasion. Claiming laziness and changing locations as primary reasons – rather than pure intent to deceive – these teens deceived their parents, who were generally unaware of these misleading disclosures (Czeskis *et al.* 2010: 7).

In an important article by Stattin and Kerr (2000a) we find compelling support for the claim that certain sorts of monitoring are harmful. Moreover, Stattin and Kerr conclude that two-way parent–child communication and sharing – not monitoring or spying – is beneficial in promoting appropriate behavior. Surprisingly, children who are monitored by parental solicitation or with the use of rule sets (you have to be home by 7 p.m.; no playing with this or that kid; etc.) have the same rate of problematic behavior as those children who are not monitored at all. "[C]ross-sectional and longitudinal studies show that poorly monitored adolescents tend to be antisocial, delinquent, or criminal … [they] also tend to use illegal substances … tobacco … do worse in school … and engage in more risky sexual activity" (Stattin and Kerr 2000b: 1072). Where there is two-way communication between parents and children, when all are actively participating, including the voluntary sharing of information, there is an associated drop in the behaviors mentioned above. In a follow-up article, Kerr and Stattin conclude: "[I]t appears that the less effective strategy, and the one that has the potential of backfiring, is to try to prevent adolescents from getting into trouble by rigorously controlling their activities and associations" (Kerr and Stattin 2000b: 378; see also Kafka and London 1991; Barnes, Farrell, and Banerjee 1994; Eaton et al. 2009; Hare et al. 2011).

Covert monitoring by parents is first perceived as non-engagement by the child. Thus, if successful and never disclosed to the child, all of the risks of parental non-involvement are present. If covert monitoring is discovered, many of these adolescents will take countermeasures (keeping two diaries, secret email accounts, etc.) and resist or defeat parental surveillance. Citing Livingstone and Bober (2006), Kay Mathiesen notes: "in a survey of children 9–17 years old in Great Britain, 69% said that they mind their parents restricting or monitoring their Internet use; 63% of 12–19 year olds said that they took some action to protect … privacy" (Mathiesen 2013: 264). Moreover, there is now the issue of trust that must be considered by the child – discovered covert monitoring will likely undermine the practice of two-way information sharing.

If correct, there are obvious and strong connections between flourishing or well-being and privacy for adolescents. Furthermore, problematic behavior or "poor adjustment," including depression, violent outbursts, engaging in risky sexual behavior, and the like, increase with loss of privacy and control. Kerr and Stattin put the point succinctly:

> [T]here are both theoretical and empirical reasons to believe that vigilant tracking and surveillance might be linked to some forms of poor adjustment. Research has shown that the perception of personal control is important to people's physical and psychological health and well-being.
>
> (Kerr and Stattin 2000a: 366)

We conclude that, as with adults, privacy – defined as the right to control access to and uses of locations and personal information – is morally valuable for children. In the following section we will consider when these privacy norms may be justifiably set aside, or trumped, by other important values.

Two-way sharing, probable cause, and Allen's case for justified parental paternalism

Family life is not only an important setting for individual development, it is also a primary site for social development and socialization. The norms of coming together and leave-taking that occur within the family provide an important backdrop for meaningful and continuing social interactions. Thus privacy arrangements within the family have an important social function. We employ this argument to take issue with Anita Allen's (2008) defense of the virtues of spying. After an analysis and critique of Allen's position, we will defend the view that individuals within families have privacy rights that should only be set aside once specific conditions are met. While contextually dependent, the rules for setting aside privacy rights within the family will parallel the "probable cause" and "sunlight" provisions found in the legal traditions of developed societies.

Anita Allen is widely known for arguing that spying on one's children or spouse is morally justified when specific conditions obtain. She begins with what she calls the anti-spying principle: "spying on other(s) ... is prima facie unethical. Spying ought always to be approached with caution and circumspection. Regardless of its motive, spying carries an ethical cloud" (Allen 2008: 3). Allen goes on to argue that the anti-spying principle can be overridden in a range of cases. Among others, Allen argues that obligations of caretaking and self-defense may allow for or perhaps require spying. Allen notes: "Sometimes, for limited purposes, responsible moral agents should be willing to make themselves the invisible monitors of others" (Allen 2008: 6). When used to protect one's children from "seriously unsafe behavior," spying is a matter of responsible parenting. Allen would go so far as to covertly monitor one's children, read private diaries, and search bedrooms to look for signs of trouble. Surprisingly, even protecting one's children from poor eating habits justifies spying in Allen's view. Allen considers McCloskey's position that adults who target children have no privacy claims. McCloskey writes:

> Child Predators: People are thought to have a right to privacy in respect of the affaires [sic] they have ... Yet I suggest that if the girl involved in the affaire [sic] is a minor, a father who spied on the pair could not be charged with an improper invasion of their privacy; and if the man involved knew she was a minor, he could not complain that he had suffered a loss of privacy as a result of the father's spying, because by his actions he had put that area of his life outside the area of privacy.
>
> (McCloskey 1971: 313–14)

Allen notes that parents should spy to stop statutory rape and child abuse, but not by any means necessary. She writes: "I think a better view is that the sexual offender has legitimate privacy expectations and interests, but that not all of them would be wrongly breached by spying" (Allen, 2008: 9–10). In a related case Allen drives this point home.

> Plaxico: Glenn Michael filed for custody of his six-year-old daughter, who lived with his ex-wife and her friend, Rita Plaxico. Mr. Michael came to believe living with him was in the girl's best interest after he heard that his ex-wife was having a lesbian affair with her roommate. He surmised that the family court would view a heterosexual father as the better parent if he could produce strong evidence of his ex-wife's homosexual affair. One night Michael drove to the home shared by his ex-wife and Plaxico, sneaked up to a bedroom window, and observed the two women unclothed and having sex. Pleased by his good luck, Michael grabbed a camera from his car and snapped some semi-nude images. After presenting the photographs to the court, Michael won custody of his daughter. Ms. Plaxico, who had not been a party to the child custody matter, sued Mr. Michael for invasion of her privacy, but lost.
>
> (Allen 2008: 10)

The court found that Glenn Michael, the father in the *Plaxico* case, had a compelling and overriding interest in protecting his child that was weightier than Plaxico's right to privacy. Allen contends that Michael's actions went too far – good motives, such as trying to protect one's children from harm do not justify the magnitude of the intrusion in this case. Moreover, there were other, less invasive ways to determine the facts surrounding his ex-wife's relationship status. A general form of Allen's safety argument proceeds as follows:

P1.   Parents are obligated to protect their children from harm.
P2.   Information about children and their activities is needed to protect them from harm.
P3.   Overt and covert monitoring are good ways to gather this information.
P4.   Overt and covert monitoring are most plausible when coupled with a "least harmful/invasive means" rule.
C5.   So it follows that parents ought to overtly and covertly monitor their children.

Given the plausibility of the premises, the argument appears strong. But if we take the results of the prior section seriously, most if not all forms of covert and overt monitoring would be ruled out. The harm prevented by spying, unannounced room searches, or coercive questioning would likely lead to further systemic harms, including the use of countermeasures, and loss of trust. Adopting a policy of two-way sharing avoids these risks and is much less invasive. We can imagine cases where parents have cause to spy, but this is only after failing to establish the sort of open relationship with a child that would render such spying unnecessary.

This is also true of McCloskey's child predator case. A practice of two-way information-sharing between parents and children would likely yield the requisite information to determine if further inquiry or action was needed. In instances where the sharing rule fails, we employ a probable cause rule. To examine this second rule, we consider another case provided by Anita Allen – the case of Jeanine and Albert Pirro.

> Cheating Spouse: Albert Pirro was not a very nice man when it came to his wife of many years, Jeanine. He was a classic louse. He was guilty of dating-while-married. He was unfaithful ... cheated on the family taxes ... and was convicted of a felony ... Ms. Pirro became a Republican candidate for the Attorney General of New York in 2006. She believed she had a shot at becoming the first woman in history to hold the post ... Pirro felt she had had to consider spying to find out if her husband was having an extramarital affair with one her friends. She knew Albert was dishonest about such things and that she could not trust his denials. Her hope was to make any such affair public before someone else did, catching her unawares on the eve of Election Day, ruining her chances for victory.
>
> (Allen 2008: 14)

Allen claims that spying in this case would be justified. Her only complaint was that Jeanine Pirro made poor decisions about who to hire as a spy and what methods to use. It seems that Jeanine hired a less than honorable private detective who used questionable surveillance methods. Had Jeanine Pirro used different methods, Allen would have defended the surveillance on grounds of self-defense. A more formal version of Allen's argument proceeds as follows:

P1. Out of self-interest or self-defense adults are justified in spying on their spouses.
P2. Information about one's spouse and his/her activities is needed to protect oneself from harm.
P3. Overt and covert monitoring are good ways to gather this information.
P4. Overt and covert monitoring are most plausible when coupled with a "least harmful/invasive means" rule.
C5. So it follows that spouses ought to overtly and covertly monitor their wives/husbands/boyfriends/girlfriends.

As with Allen's argument from child safety, the self-defense or self-protection argument in favor of spying on one's spouse or partner seems strong. Who would deny that, when life or limb is at stake, covert and overt surveillance may be justified when less invasive means are unavailable. The problem is that these conditions will almost never obtain. First, establishing a relationship and practice of two-way information-sharing would be less invasive while at the same time preserving trust, love, and respect. While it is true that the Pirro's are well beyond such a relationship, and thus two-way sharing may not be an option, there are other options that could have been used.

In our view, probable cause coupled with a two-way sharing rule yields an appropriate balance in specific cases and as a general practice. Probable cause is established when a parent or other family member has discovered information through logical inquiry that would lead a reasonably intelligent and prudent person to believe that further monitoring is warranted on grounds of safety or self-protection. This basic standard is, of course, drawn from the criminal law, and generally applies to restrict state surveillance, search, or seizure. In American Fourth Amendment law, this standard outlines the boundaries of acceptable state intrusion into the private affairs of individual citizens. It prevents the state from engaging in "fishing expeditions," by limiting state action to situations where officers have a reasonable and articulable basis to believe criminal conduct has occurred. We argue that this standard also serves a valuable purpose in governing legitimate surveillance within the family. In concert with two-way information-sharing practice, such a standard would help preserve the ability to appropriately withdraw for purposes of self-development without fear of unjustified monitoring.

Intra-familial surveillance, especially covert surveillance, is only justified when it results from failed attempts to engage in two-way sharing or when such attempts are not feasible, and is then based on evidence reasonably amounting to probable cause. Additionally, if these conditions exist, the surveillance ought to be practically implemented in a minimally intrusive fashion. In any case, making determinations about the appropriateness of possible conduct is essential if we want a theory that can be used, practically, to guide moral behavior as it occurs.

Let's re-examine the *Plaxico* scenario presented above. First, in the *Plaxico* example, Allen contended that Mr. Michael was not justified in taking photographs of his ex-wife's lesbian encounter in her own bedroom because the privacy intrusion was overly severe, given the assumed security threat. We agree with Allen that being raised by a same-sex couple does not, and should not, constitute a "serious risk of harm." Nevertheless, assume there was such a worry present in this case. As a father Michael may justifiably inquire about the status of his daughter. Suppose while he is told that everything is fine and there are no safety concerns, he notices bruising on his daughter's arms and a change in behavior. Suppose further that his daughter withdraws and refuses to share any information about what occurs at her mother's home. After talking with teachers, neighborhood friends, and exhausting other information sources, Michael may well appeal to probable cause in justifying the use of technology to attain the requisite information. But this hardly sanctions becoming a covert peeping Tom or adopting a strategy to acquire total information awareness about his daughter, her mother, and the activities occurring when he is not present. Using probable cause along with a "least invasive means" rule promotes the values of safety, privacy, and trust.

Consider the case where a parent or spouse claims to "have a right to know everything" about a partner or child. A different way to focus on the inappropriateness of such a view and the forms of surveillance it implies is to ask if someone from an unbiased vantage point would have consented to monitoring in similar circumstances. Knowing about privacy and trust, would a rational and prudent individual unrelated to the case at hand agree that privacy should be waived on grounds of safety or self-defense? It may be true that we all want to know more about others while keeping our own secrets, but we should resist this impulse on grounds of privacy and respect.

Imagine upon returning home one day you find your partner (or child) searching through the trash, painstakingly putting your shredded notes and documents back together. In response to your stunned silence your family member proclaims: "I have a right to know everything about you – there is no reason to hide is there?" An appropriate reply to this sort of "fishing expedition" would be to highlight that privacy rights exist even within families, privacy is morally valuable and connected to human health, and that the principles of respect or trust would demand different sorts of behavior between loved ones.

The primary difference between our view and Allen's is that we are more restrained when it comes to spying on family members. While we agree with Allen's "least intrusive method" rule, we also employ a two-way information-sharing rule and a probable cause rule. Overt or covert spying on a family member is only justified in cases where a parent or partner has compelling evidence that safety or well-being is threatened. Allen writes: "Columbine and similar incidents around the country point to why parents are justified in inspecting teenagers' rooms for signs of trouble ... even poor eating habits can be grounds for monitoring (Allen 2008: 7). We have argued against this view. Without good reasons, prying into the private lives of a child or partner is a violation that undermines trust and respect. As noted earlier, we can imagine cases where parents or partners have justified cause to spy, but this is only after failing to establish the sort of open relationship that would render such spying unnecessary.

Moreover, as citizens we certainly would not think that intrusions into private areas are justified because of relatively rare acts of terrorism at home and abroad. The remote threat of such travesties would not sanction governmental fishing expeditions into private lives of citizens in violation of the Fourth Amendment. Additionally, such remote threats should not be used to sanction privacy violations within the family.

Conclusion

Privacy, defined as the right to control access to and uses of locations and personal information, is morally valuable for children, adults, and within families. Moreover, privacy preserves groups, maintains status divisions, allows for deviation and personal growth, and sustains social establishments. Childhood problematic behavior or "poor adjustment," including depression, violent outbursts, engaging in risky sexual behavior, and the like, increase with loss of privacy and control.

To outline the proper balance between various privacy and safety interests within a family, we have argued for three rules. First, a rule of "two-way communication" establishes a practice of trust, respect, and caring. Such a standard would help preserve private spaces within family life – spaces where children, spouses, or partners can appropriately withdraw for purposes of self-development without fear of unjustified monitoring. Second, if in a specific instance or as a practice the two-way sharing rule fails, we retreat to a probable cause standard to determine the appropriateness of surveillance. Probable cause is established when a parent, spouse, or partner has discovered information through logical inquiry that would lead a reasonably intelligent and prudent person to believe that their child, spouse, or partner is subject to, or the cause of, a specific and serious threat to safety or well-being. Third, in cases where monitoring is justified, a "least invasive means" rule should be employed. If correct, covert or overt surveillance within the family would only be justified in a narrow range of cases.

References

Allen, A. 2003. *Why Privacy Isn't Everything: Feminist Reflections on Personal Accountability.* Lanham: Rowman & Littlefield.

2008. "The virtuous spy: Privacy as an ethical limit," *The Monist* 91: 3–22.

Barnes, G. M., Farrell, M. P. and Banerjee, S. 1994. "Family influences on alcohol abuse and other problem behaviors among Black and White adolescents in a general population sample," *Journal of Research on Adolescence* 4: 183–201.

Baum, A. and Koman, S. 1976. "Differential response to anticipated crowding: Psychological effects of social and spatial density," *Journal of Personality and Social Psychology* 34: 526–36.

Clauson-Kaas, J., Dzikus, A., Stephens, C., Hojlyng, N. and Aaby, P. 1996. "Urban health: Human settlement indicators of crowding," *Third World Planning Review* 18: 349–63.

Cox, V., Paulus, P. and McCain, G. 1984. "Prison crowding research: The relevance of prison housing standards and a general approach regarding crowding phenomena," *American Psychologist* 39: 1148–60.

Crouter, A. C. and Head, M. R. 2002. "Parental Monitoring and Knowledge of Children," in Bornstein, M. H. (ed.) *Handbook of Parenting, Vol. III: Being and Becoming a Parent.* Mahwah: Lawrence Erlbaum, pp. 461–84.

Crouter, A. C., MacDermid, S. M., McHale, S. M. and Perry-Jenkins, M. 1990. "Parental monitoring and perceptions of children's school performance and conduct in dual- and single-earner families," *Developmental Psychology* 26: 649–57.

Crouter, A. C., Bumpus, M. F., Davis, K. D. and McHale, S. M. 2006. "How do parents learn about adolescents' experiences? Implications for parental knowledge and adolescent risky behavior," *Child Development* 76: 869–82.

Czeskis, A., Dermendjieva, I., Yapit, H., Borning, A., Friedman, B., Gill, B. and Kohno, T. 2010. "Parenting from the pocket: Value tensions and technical directions for secure and private parent-teen mobile safety," *Proceedings of the Symposium on Usable Privacy and Security,* 1–15.

Dishion, T. and McMahon, R. 1998. "Parental Monitoring and the Prevention of Problem Behavior: A Conceptual and Empirical Reformulation," in Ashery, R. S., Robertson, E. B. and Kumpfer, K. L. (eds.) *Drug Abuse Prevention through Family Interventions,* NIDA Research Monograph 177, pp. 229–59.

Duarte, M. 2013. Unpublished interview with Marisa Elena Duarte, Ph.D., on file with authors.

Eaton, N., Kruger, R., Johnson, W., McGue, M. and Incono, W. 2009. "Parental monitoring, personality, and delinquency: Further support for a reconceptualization of monitoring," *Journal of Research in Personality* 43: 49–59.

Edwards, J. N. and Booth, A. 1977. "Crowding and human sexual behavior," *Social Forces* 55: 791–808.

Erikson, E. 1963. *Childhood and Society.* New York: Norton.

Farrington, D. and Nuttal, C. 1980. "Prison size, overcrowding, prison violence and recidivism," *Journal of Criminal Justice* 8: 221–31.

Fuller, T. D., Edwards, N. J., Vorakitphokatorn, S. and Sermsri, S. 1996. "Chronic stress and psychological well-being: Evidence from Thailand on household crowding," *Social Science Medicine* 42: 265–80.

Gavison, R. 1983. "Information Control: Availability and Control," in Benn, S. I. and Gaus, G. F. (eds.) *Public and Private in Social Life.* London: St Martin's Press, pp. 113–34.

Gross, H. 1971. "Privacy and Autonomy," in Pennock, J. R., and Chapman, J. (eds.) *Privacy: Nomos XIII.* New York: Atherton Press, pp. 169–81.

Hare, A., Marston, E. and Allen, J. 2011. "Maternal acceptance and adolescents' emotional communication: A longitudinal study," *Journal of Youth and Adolescence* 40: 744–51.

Kafka, R. and London, P. 1991. "Communication in relationships and adolescent substance use: The influence of parents and friends," *Adolescence* 26: 587–98.

Kerr, M. and Stattin, H. 2000. "What parents know, how they know it, and several forms of adolescent adjustment: Further support for a reinterpretation of monitoring," *Journal of Developmental Psychology* 36: 366–80.

Kessler, J. 1966. *Psychopathology of Childhood.* Englewood Cliffs: Prentice-Hall.

Livingstone, S. and Bober, M. 2006. "Regulating the Internet at Home: Contrasting the Perspectives of Children and Parents," in Buckingham, D., and Willett, R. (eds.) *Digital Generations: Children, Young People, and New Media.* Mahwah: Lawrence Erlbaum Associates, pp. 93–113.

McCain, G., Cox, V. and Paulus, P. 1980. "The effect of prison crowding on inmate behavior," Washington DC: US Department of Justice.

McCloskey, H. J. 1971. "The political ideal of privacy," *The Philosophical Quarterly* 21: 301–14.

McGinley, P. 1959. "A Lost Privilege," *Province of the Heart.* New York: Viking Press.

Mathiesen, K. 2013. "The Internet, children, and privacy: The case against parental monitoring," *Ethics of Information Technology* 15: 263–74.

Megargee, E. I. 1977. "The association of population density reduced space and uncomfortable temperatures with misconduct in a prison community," *The American Journal of Community Psychology* 5: 289–98.

Mill, J. S. 1859. *On Liberty.* London: Longman, Roberts & Green.

Moore, A. D. 2003. "Privacy: Its meaning and value," *American Philosophical Quarterly* 40: 215–27.

2007. "Toward informational privacy rights," *San Diego Law Review* 44: 809–45.

2008. "Defining privacy," *Journal of Social Philosophy* 39: 411–28.

2010. *Privacy Rights: Moral and Legal Foundations.* University Park, PA: Penn State University Press.

Morgan, G. 1972. "Mental and social health and population density," *Journal of Human Relations* 20: 196–204.

Mumford, L. 1961. *The City in History*. New York: Harcourt, Brace & World.

Murdock, G. 1955. "The Universals of Culture," in Hoebel, E. A., Jennings, J. D., and Smith, E. R. (eds.) *Readings in Anthropology*. New York: McGraw-Hill.

Nussbaum, M. 2000. *Woman and Human Development: The Capabilities Approach*. Cambridge University Press.

Parent, W. A. 1983. "Privacy, morality, and the law," *Philosophy and Public Affairs* 12: 269–88.

Parker, R. 1974. "A definition of privacy," *Rutgers Law Review* 27: 275–96.

Paulus, P., Cox, V. and McCain, G., 1978. "Death rates, psychiatric commitments, blood pressure and perceived crowding as a function of institutional crowding," *Environmental Psychology and Nonverbal Behavior* 3: 107–16.

Porporino, F. and Dudley, K. 1984. *An Analysis of the Effects of Overcrowding in Canadian Penitentiaries*. Ottawa: Research Division, Programs Branch, Solicitor General of Canada.

Rachels, J. 1975. "Why privacy is important," *Philosophy and Public Affairs* 4: 323–33.

Roberts, J. and Gregor, T. 1971. "Privacy: A Cultural View," in Pennock, J. R., and Chapman, J. (eds.) *Privacy: Nomos XIII*. New York: Atherton Press, pp. 199–225.

Ruback, B. and Carr, T. 1984. "Crowding in a woman's prison," *Journal of Applied Social Psychology* 14: 57–68.

Schwartz, B. 1968. "The social psychology of privacy," *American Journal of Sociology* 73: 741–52.

Spiro, H. 1971. "Privacy in Comparative Perspective," in Pennock, J. R., and Chapman, J. (eds.) *Privacy: Nomos XIII*. New York: Atherton Press, pp. 121–48.

Spitz, R. 1964. "The derailment of dialogue," *Journal of the American Psychoanalytic Association* 12: 752–75.

Stattin, H. and Kerr, M. 2000a. "Parental monitoring: A reinterpretation," *Child Development* 71: 1072–85.

2000b. "What parents know, how they know it, and several forms of adolescent adjustment: further support for a reinterpretation of monitoring." *Journal of Developmental Psychology* 36: 366–80.

Warren, S. and Brandeis, L. 1890. "The right to privacy," *The Harvard Law Review* 4: 193–220.

Westin, A. 1967. *Privacy and Freedom*. New York: Atheneum.

Wilson, S. 2008. *Research Is Ceremony: Indigenous Research Methods*. Black Point: Fernwood Publishing.

7

How to do things with personal big biodata

KOEN BRUYNSEELS, JEROEN VAN DEN HOVEN

Genetic privacy is increasingly hard to guarantee due to the growing volume of personal health care data stored in databases. Although attempts are made to make the data anonymous or unlinkable, it was shown that individuals are at risk of being identified and reidentified. Anonymous DNA data was demonstrated to be linkable to individuals on the basis of publicly available information on the Internet. Utilization of linkable data can result in harm, inequities and discrimination since these data potentially reveal intimate personal, medical and family details. The increasing availability of genomic data – and more generally 'personal big biodata'[1] (which comprises a wide variety of medical and health care data covering both medical images and a panoply of biomarkers) – combined with the computational power and analytical tools of bioinformatics calls for a rethinking of privacy. In this chapter we argue that in the age of personal big biodata, privacy implies first and foremost the responsible appraisal of the limits of what data allow us to know about individuals, and we suggest furthermore that respect for human persons and their dignity implies an acknowledgement of the fact that there is always more to know about them than even the most comprehensive set of data may offer in terms of knowledge. We refer to the ideal of acknowledging the limits of our knowledge of persons as "epistemic modesty." We offer the epistemic modesty account of what privacy entails in the age of advanced genomics as a partial explication of the fundamental principle of the International Declaration on Human Genetic Data adopted by UNESCO in 2003: "to ensure the respect of human dignity" (UNESCO 2003). Personal big biodata carry the risk of epistemic immodesty. We argue that privacy is instrumental in ensuring a person's ability for self-determination in view of personal big

---

[1] The term 'genomic data' in this chapter refers to whole genome sequence data or to genotyping data. 'Genetics data' refers to data on a set of markers in the genome. 'Big biodata' also includes other types of molecular data (e.g. transcriptomics, metabolomics, proteomics) and phenotype data (e.g. fMRI images).

biodata and the acts of epistemic immodesty of others. In addition to *ex ante* approaches to data protection such as privacy-enhancing technologies, we also draw attention to the potential of *ex post* approaches.

A call for rethinking genomic privacy

Biomedical sciences currently witness a flood of data on research subjects. Techniques such as personal genome sequencing, RNAseq expression profiling, metabolic profiling and medical imaging provide large volumes of personal biological data. These data potentially contain sensitive information, especially when they are combined with other types of health care data and lifestyle data, now often voluntarily collected by individuals with the help of smart wearable devices. The "Baseline Study" initiated by Google is indicative of the increased interest and ability to execute combined analyses on a multitude of biological and other datasets. Google is collecting genetic and molecular data from 175 participants and aims to scale this up to thousands. Smart algorithms will be applied to pinpoint how a healthy human being should look from a data point of view. This baseline will be used to identify biomarkers for disease states.

Currently, deidentification of electronic records is commonly used as a measure to protect the privacy of research participants and patients. This, however, does not provide an absolute guarantee of privacy. Privacy regulations such as the US HIPAA (Health Insurance Portability and Accountability Act) Privacy Rule therefore request measures that minimize the probability of information disclosure, rather than demanding absolute guarantees of privacy, since the latter cannot be guaranteed. According to the HIPAA Privacy Rule, a record is considered deidentified if either an expert assesses the remaining risk of deidentification to be "very small," or if a fixed set of identifiers is removed (HIPAA Privacy Rule 2007). However, the probability that deidentified records can be reidentified is bound to sharply increase, as personal biological data are becoming ubiquitous and more easily accessible (Malin *et al.* 2011). Genomic data in particular prove to be prone to reidentification (El Emam 2011). Small sets of genomic features can already function as a unique identifier for a person. Moreover, a growing number of people have personal genotype data and even whole genome data stored in databases. In a research setting, the Thousand Genomes Project Consortium (2012) reported on the sequencing of the whole genomes of 1,092 individuals. The Personal Genomes Project aims at sequencing 100,000 individuals (Lunshof *et al.* 2010). Public health care is also shifting its interest from genetic profiling towards full genome sequencing. The Faroe Islands started the FarGen initiative, an endeavor to sequence all 50,000 citizens (details available at www.fargen.fo/en/). The results will be stored in a database that is linked to the Genetic Biobank, which contains samples from island inhabitants and medical and genealogical records. The UK Biobank is collecting samples and medical data from half a million Britons (Gottweis *et al.* 2012), and the UK 100,000 genomes initiative aims at sequencing that many patients and their close relatives. In addition to the traditional realm of research and health care, commercial companies are building proprietary databases with consumer genetics data. Companies such as 23andMe, Navigenics and DeCode genetics experimented with genotyping services directed towards consumers. As a result of these and related activities, genetic and genomic data are accumulating in a multitude of databases.

This new data situation can lead to an increased risk of reidentification. Gymrek *et al.* (2013) traced the identity of participants in genomic studies based on public data. Sweeney *et al.* (2013) used previously published methods to reidentify volunteers from the Personal Genome Project. The authors were able to identify about 40 percent of the individuals out of 579 anonymous records that contained postal code, birth date and gender. Algorithms that link deidentified family relations to named people have already been developed (Malin 2006). Homer *et al.* (2008) demonstrated that genotyping data provides a very strong identifier, by using it to determine whether the DNA of a person is present in a DNA mixture of up to 200 individuals.

This evolution towards a ubiquitous production of personal biological data, and the related risk of reidentification demands a rethinking of genomic privacy and big biodata privacy. There is a long-standing intuition that storing and sharing genetic information deserves special caution. "Genetic privacy" is the term that is most often used to refer to a cluster of rights associated with this point of view (Roche and Annas 2001). Central is the right to protection from non-voluntary disclosure of genetic information (Lunshof *et al.* 2008). This right has been embedded in legislation in many countries around the world. Measures to guarantee genetic privacy range from protective (Soini 2012) to more liberal. The frameworks were developed for a setting where genetic information is mainly used for research purposes or clinical testing. This context changes now that genetic data are frequently used beyond research. Moreover, the sheer amounts of data that are produced shift practices to whole genome analysis and other types of big biological data processing. This radically new situation calls for a careful revision of the existing practices and technologies that are used to store, mine and communicate personal genomic data (Erlich and Narayanan 2014) and big biological datasets in general (Choudhury *et al.* 2014; Sarwate *et al.* 2014).

Rationales for the special status of genomic data

The privacy concerns regarding genomic data have always been prominent in public debates. This prominence can be explained by the fact that they are accorded a very special status, an idea sometimes referred to as *genetic exceptionalism*. Genetic exceptionalism is the thesis that genomic data are different from other types of biological and medical data, and therefore require a special status and special protection. In this view, genomic data are seen as being *extraordinarily* informative. Green and Botkin observe, for example, that "Right or wrong, genetic information is believed to reveal who we 'really' are, so information from genetic testing is often seen as more consequential than that from other sources" (Green and Botkin 2003: 572). Article 1 of the Universal Declaration on the Human Genome and Human Rights (United Nations 1998) proclaims: "The human genome underlies the fundamental unity of all members of the human family, as well as the recognition of their inherent dignity and diversity. In a symbolic sense, it is the heritage of humanity." A large body of literature focused on the question whether genomic data are indeed exceptional. The special biological roles of the DNA molecule were often put forward as a main argument. Such special roles are the immutable nature of the genome base sequence, the fact that it uniquely identifies an individual, the informational nature of DNA, and the fact that parts are shared among family members and ethnic communities (Green and Thomas 1998; Sarata 2008; Ilkilic 2009). DNA is the central information carrier in biology and therefore potentially can reveal information about future illness or genetic defects, or unknown facts about familial relationships. Genomic sequences not only reveal information about a particular individual, but also about her or his relatives and the ethnic group the person belongs to. Taken on their own, these features do not uniquely distinguish genetic information from other types of medical data (Green and Botkin 2003). One can argue that not one unique property in itself, but rather the *combination* of properties distinguishes genetic data from other types of medical data (Sarata 2008). It is implied in the general definition of a category that it is associated with a unique combination of properties that sets it apart from other categories. The fact that DNA-based data is characterized by a specific set of properties therefore does not provide a rationale for a special status of the data; it just implies that it is different from other categories of data. Moreover, deducing a special moral status from scientific facts about a molecule can be regarded as committing the naturalistic fallacy (Ilkilic 2009). Nevertheless, there is a persistent intuition that genetic data is special. Surveys show there is a belief that genetic information needs special consideration (Sarata 2008). This belief has been explained in different ways. One explanation is that the scientific discoveries in molecular biology gave rise to an aura of power when it came to DNA. Such sociological explanations leave open the question of whether there are more fundamental reasons for a special status of DNA-based data that remain overlooked, and that warrant genetic and genomic privacy.

A different set of rationales can be provided to account for the status and salience of genomic data as revealing "who we really are." These rationales are based on (i) the information content of genetic information; (ii) the naturalistic connotation or "naturalistic load" genetic information carries, that is the fact that it is construed as a veridical and direct representation of what the world is really like; and (iii) the unique identification of individuals that genetic information makes possible, which depends in turn on the immutability and the uniqueness of the information. The first two arguments – in varying degree – not only apply to genomic data but also to other types of big biodata.

Rationales based on information content

Genomic data and big biodata can contain sensitive information. Genomic sequences, for instance, are related to how a person physically develops, to what extent she or he is prone to develop certain diseases, reacts to certain medication, is likely to display certain physical characteristics such as muscle strength or longevity, and so on. Behavioral traits can also have a hereditary component, for example verbal and numerical intelligence, susceptibility to addiction and to certain mental diseases, and certain character traits. Many of these characteristics are morally salient, and the derived claims are not restricted to an individual but also to relatives and ethnic groups. It also needs to be noted that genomic data are bound to contain more information than current methods are able to extract from them. For example, about 80 percent of the variation in height in a human population can be attributed to heritability, but the loci currently known to relate to height are only able to explain about 10 percent (GIANT consortium 2010).

Intelligence also has a hereditary component, but even with very large samples of individuals, no common genetic variants related to intelligence can be identified (Le Hellard and Steen 2014). This problem of missing heritability makes it plausible that more information will be derived as insights are gained into how to interpret genomic data. For other types of big biodata, the sensitive nature of the information can even be more prominent. Brain scans provide more direct information about a person's mental health and gene expression studies can provide information about disease states. Nevertheless, the sensitivity of the information that currently can be derived only partially explains the exceptional weight that is attributed to big biodata, since usage is currently limited. Translating personal genomic data into concrete medical advice, for instance, proves to be challenging (Ashley *et al.* 2010). Health claims based on genetic data can be conflicting as they depend on the specific subset of genomic features that is probed, the specific genome-wide association studies that are used in the interpretation, and so on.

Rationales based on naturalistic connotations

Big biodata are derived from biological molecules or structures. These data are therefore perceived to reflect structures inherent in nature itself. Big biodata are derived from molecules (DNA, mRNA, proteins, metabolites, etc.), that is from entities in a physicalist realm. These molecules take part in complex networks of biochemical interactions, which are the result of billions of years of evolutionary processes. Statements that are derived from big biodata are therefore perceived to carry a naturalistic load, which provides an additional rationale for attributing a special status to big biodata.

On the other hand, big biodata are also part of the world of language and meaning. One can try to interpret the information that is embedded in these molecules and networks, and use this information to build theories and in discussions and assessments. Gilbert Hottois (1996) highlighted the fundamental difference between this "naturalistic" and "symbolic" realm in his analysis of technosciences. Hottois characterizes the naturalistic realm as "operational": it concerns physical and chemical processes that bring about or produce reality. The symbolic realm is the area of language and meaning, of culture and values. One can try to represent the operational reality by making use of symbolic systems, as in scientific theories or in common language. But there is a limit to this. Both realms are fundamentally different and therefore have different dynamics. Following this distinction, we can state that big biodata have a unique position at the interface between the physicalist and the symbolic realm. This can be illustrated with genomic data. DNA is a molecule that is the result of evolutionary processes: it "works" by bringing about organisms via its interactions with other molecules, but it is clearly not designed to be "read." On the other hand, DNA has the character of a text, with modularity, structure and compositionality that can be read and interpreted. The sequence of the bases in the molecule constitutes a quaternary code that can be represented in a computer. Notwithstanding the limited ability to interpret genomic data, it is clear that the DNA carries crucial information for the development and functioning of the person. It is an information carrier and thus also part of the symbolic realm. For these reasons, genomic data have been referred to as the "genetic blueprint," the "genetic code" or the "genetic program" of a person.

Other big biodata types similarly reside at the interface between nature and culture. fMRI measurements of brain activation patterns, for instance, reflect biological processes in the brain via imaging software that implements models, but can eventually be translated into claims about mental states. This particular position of big biodata – at the interface between the physical and the symbolic levels – affects the weight that is attributed to the derived symbolic statements.

The fact that this impact is assigned can be accounted for by looking at the way the relation between big biodata and natural kinds is conceived. In a realist interpretation of the world, certain groupings of entities are not merely man-made distinctions but reflect the way nature itself is structured. When organizing a collection of stones, one can, for instance, group them by shape: round stones, square stones, heart-shaped stones, or by the role they play in religious ceremonies, or by their color and patina (and other so-called secondary properties, etc.). The stones can also be grouped based on their inner atomic structure, crystal lattice structure, chemical composition, which is tightly linked to their geological formation: igneous stones, sedimentary stones, metamorphic stones. A realist will state that the latter classification is a better reflection of the way nature itself is structured (Wilkerson 1995). The hidden inner structure of the stones determines their membership of a natural kind. In chemistry, natural kinds seem to be unproblematic. For instance water is defined by the chemical structure H_2O. Realists hold that this is the case in every possible universe. Even if a person lacks the epistemic means to uncover the hidden structure, membership of the class "water" will depend on whether a sample X and the reference "water" sample have the same hidden structure. The underpinning idea is that natural classes exist independent of human interests. This notion of hidden structures and natural classes is central to physicalist accounts of the universe. Natural kinds supposedly "carve nature at its joints." They underpin a categorization that is not arbitrary, but reflects the way nature is structured (Wilkerson 1995). For many centuries, biology delivered the archetypical examples and paradigm cases of natural kinds. Species were believed to be natural kinds, and the essence of an organism determined its membership of a species. Extrapolating this essentialist worldview to the genomic era puts a heavy metaphysical weight on genomic data, since claims based on genomic data will acquire the authority of reflecting the "hidden structure" or the essence of a person, analogous to the chemical structure of a water sample that determines its membership of the natural kind "water." Distinctions that are based on genomic data are strong, since they have the appearance of not being the result of a cultural and social convention, nor being an accidental attribute or secondary property of a person. They are easily equated to epistemic claims about the "very essence" of a person and easily give rise to essentialism about persons and their properties.

Rationales based on the role of genomic data as unique identifier

In addition to the information content and the naturalist load, there is another factor that supports the claim that genomic data are special, to the extent that they may be called "exceptional and unlike any other information about a person." The reason can be found in the unique identifying power of genomic data. Genomic data uniquely identify a person. They are given at birth and, epigenetic modifications and mutations aside, they are probably one of the most constant characteristics of a person. This unbreakable link between a person and her or his genomic data adds to the reification of claims based on a person's genome. An essentialist interpretation of personal genomic data reifies the symbolic claims that are derived from it (Barnes and Dupré 2008). The strength of the identification between a person and his or her genomic data is carried over to value-laden claims that are made based on these data.

Big biological data as a substrate for social classification

Because of this widely shared conception of the special status and salience of genomic data, genomics has also inserted itself into our thinking about the social classification and categorization of persons.

At this point a distinction should be made between the use of genomic data (i) in *forensic practices* as evidence for (re)identifications of individuals, (ii) as a basis for classifications in *clinical and clinical research practices* and (iii) as a basis for categorizations *in social and institutional practices*. The use of DNA in forensics has been widely accepted as a highly reliable technique of establishing or confirming the identity of both criminals and victims. Genetic material is in both cases a great help in finding out "who is who." Statistics and Bayesian probability theory have been applied to increase the reliability of our reasoning with genetic evidence in criminal justice procedures so as to prevent errors in inferences in these contexts. Genetic evidence is one of the strongest, unique identifiers of individuals in a forensic sense.

Second, the use of genomic data in clinical diagnosis, therapy and research is ubiquitous. Our knowledge of diseases and health problems has benefited tremendously from our study and understanding of the human genome. But it also became obvious that the picture is far more complex than initially anticipated. The complexity of the information embedded in DNA proved to go far beyond the approximately 20,000 protein coding genes. Studies over big populations show that phenotypic traits are often associated with large sets of genomic features. The non-protein coding part of the genome plays a significant role, as highlighted by the ENCODE project (ENCODE Project Consortium 2012). In most cases a complex network of multiple genes, gene control elements and so on contribute to the phenotype. The secrets of epigenetics and proteomics are being unraveled and add to the complexities. For many diseases with a genetic component it is anything but clear that genetic material allows for easy and quick clinical diagnosis with high reliability. Reasoning from genomic data implies feature selection: out of the 3.2 billion base pairs of the human genome, characterizing features and discrete categories need to be extracted. For instance, in the case of personal genomic information, the process starts with a biological sample taken from an individual. The DNA in the biological sample is extracted, prepared and run through a sequencing machine, which will generate a series of signals that correspond to the sequence of bases in the DNA fragments. The signals are recorded, stored in a computer system and assembled via bioinformatics tools into a genomic sequence. The end result is a series of character strings on a computer hard drive. The features in this personal genomic sequence can then be analyzed in order to derive personal genomic information: statements about disease susceptibilities or character traits, for example. This process of interpretation often relies on the output of statistical inferences like Genome Wide Association Studies (GWAS). At the highest level of abstraction, interpretation of a personal genome sequence results in *symbolic* statements. For example: "Person A belongs to the group of people that has a higher risk of developing disease D." This statement divides the population in two groups: the group non-D that has a low risk of developing the disease, and the group D that has a high risk. Given the complexity of biological systems and the underlying probabilistic nature of the inferred relations, this statement is a simplification of a complex molecular and biochemical reality. Interpretation of genomic data often renders probabilities, rather than deterministic certainties or memberships of clearly distinguishable classes. A classical example is the presence of the ApoE4 allele that relates to an increased risk of developing Alzheimer's disease. The information needs to be interpreted as probabilistic: one can be carrier of the allele and nevertheless grow old without developing the disease. The same mechanism holds true for other types of personal big biodata. For metabolite data or brain images, for example, features also need to be extracted in order to put these data to use. Reduction of big biological datasets to symbolic statements allows for talking in a common language – closer to ordinary language – about what these complex datasets can mean for us. It is a necessary process if we want to use these data in everyday assessments, comparisons or categorizations. We need to keep in mind, though, that such statements are always simplifications of an underlying complex biological reality.

Third, as far as the evidentiary role of genetic information in *social classifications* (e.g. entrepreneurial, leadership, impulse control, alcoholism) is concerned, the story is even less straightforward and the following considerations need to be taken into account. As indicated, interpretation of big biological datasets implies a data reduction, in which complex characteristics are used to classify individuals in terms of membership of discrete social or clinical categories. Some of these categories represent naturalistic properties in a natural population; others, however, are social constructs that may be socially controversial and contested, categories such as "Attention Deficit Disorder," "homosexuality," "weak impulse control" and "alcoholism." In social, institutional and non-scientific discourse the certainty and special evidentiary role that genomic data can play in forensic identification and in a clinical context, as discussed above, cannot be assumed to carry over to social classification practices. Simply because genomic data can help to identify a person uniquely with high degrees of certainty, or may help to underpin statistical inferences in clinical research, we cannot infer that symbolic interpretations and the corresponding social labels attach with the same degree of certainty to a given individual. This process implies jumping beyond the evidence and endorsing claims that often cannot be justified. Nevertheless, social categorization and classifications based on a person's genomic data may give rise to entrenched perceptions or "frames" of a person's social identity and may eventually constrain an individual's ability to choose how he or she presents and defines himself or herself in social contexts. The genetic basis of novelty-seeking behavior can be taken as an example. Some allelic variants of the dopamine receptor genes were associated with differences in dopamine binding and with phenotypes related to novelty-seeking behavior (Padmanabhan and Luna 2013). A genetic test can thus in principle be designed to label individuals as either carrying this allele or not carrying this allele. However, genetic evidence will not warrant tagging individuals with the labels "novelty-seeking" or "not novelty-seeking." The presence of the allele does not say much about the novelty-seeking tendencies of a particular individual. At best, it may indicate a statistically higher likelihood of displaying such behavior. Without caution, the information on whether an individual carries the allele could get translated into a claim about how a person is *really*, namely being eager or not eager to engage in novel experiences.

We refer to this cognitive attitude as *epistemic immodesty*. Epistemic immodesty (Van den Hoven 2008) is defined as the making of knowledge claims about persons that are not fully supported by the evidence available, with potentially significant cost or negative moral consequences to the target person while ignoring how the person involved would like to be identified. In epistemic immodest judgments one draws conclusions about who a person is, or one claims to be acquainted with one or more of his or her properties on the basis of limited or irrelevant evidence. Because of the reasons mentioned before, big biodata inherently carry the risk of giving rise to immodest claims on what one knows or can know about a given person. Classification of people based on biological characteristics transforms statistical claims into symbolic claims about who a person is. These claims are strengthened by the naturalistic load of the classifications and by the unique identifying power of genomic data. Moreover, genomic studies often concern morally salient characteristics, increasing the proneness to epistemic immodesty. As an example, a study on patients with bipolar disease revealed a genomic region that was indicative of an increased proneness to suicide attempts (Willour *et al.* 2012). Epistemic immodest claims can arise when such probabilistic findings are put to use beyond the field of science. When applied by a future employer or to customers in a consumer genetics setting, for instance, the focus is not on identifying generalizations out of the data of many research subjects. In this different pragmatic context, the focus shifts towards the labeling of particular individuals by putting the generalized data to use. It can be foreseen that the claim to know that person will give rise to moral judgments that may negatively affect the person. The immodesty is constituted by the fact that the judgment fails to take into account the subjective experience of individuals and the way they want to be identified.

Genomic privacy and the right to self-determination

The question then is how to deal with personal big biodata and how to respect and protect them so as to prevent making data subjects vulnerable in the light of the availability of the data. Personal big biodata need to be protected to prevent harms, inequities and discriminatory practices of which patients and data subjects may become victims (for a taxonomy of moral reasons for data protection see Van den Hoven (2008)). It is obvious that individuals can be harmed, wronged, disadvantaged, targeted and exploited in numerous ways on the basis of the access that others have to their genetic information. With respect to the right to control access to one's own big biodata, the requirement of informed consent is still the central point of all existing data protection legislation. There are four types of moral reason for this: 1. Prevention of (information-based) harm, 2. Equality of opportunity and fair treatment in markets for commodified personal data, 3. Informational justice and discrimination and 4. Moral autonomy (Van den Hoven 2008).

First of all, it is clear from the discussions above that personal big biodata can potentially be the cause of information-based harm. Information-based harm is here defined as harm that could not have been (easily) inflicted if particular information had not been available. Second, another type of moral wronging may occur when big biodata are commercially exploited without proper benefits to the data subject, or without him or her even knowing about this. Third, a form of moral wrongdoing occurs when the data are produced in a research or clinical context, but become available in a very different social sphere, such as the world of insurance or potential employers (market) or police or criminal courts (criminal justice). The use of information about a person at a time and place where it is deemed inappropriate or is irrelevant is a form of discrimination. The prevention of discrimination calls for controlling the boundaries of social spheres in which the big biodatasets are produced and used. Also the different practices (forensic, clinical research, social or institutional), their different associated standards of care in reasoning and methodology, the governance and their norms for the fair allocation of access ought to be observed and separated.

Autonomy is the fourth moral reason to be concerned with the protection of personal big biodata. Some types of personal big biodata such as genomic data and brain structures are largely immutable during a person's lifetime. Such immutable data that is intimately linked to a person vastly increases the impact when releasing this data, since it can impair a person's ability to determine how he or she presents himself or herself to others. The focus of privacy concerns in this case is to prevent one specific form of wronging moral persons, namely the fact that they are made subject to social sorting, categorization and classification, on the basis of personal genomic data or personal big biodata in general. When people are classified in this way and given the perceived reality of genetic exceptionalism, there is a *lack of plausible deniability* of the evidence for these classifications on the part of an individual (assuming he or she is not an expert in genetics). This interferes with the moral autonomy of persons, the moral right of persons to define themselves and shape their own identity, present themselves and have their chosen public persona recognized and respected by others. Controlling the way one presents oneself provides the necessary space for self-determination. To be recognized as a being who is able to conceal information is fundamental to being perceived as a "self-representing being," as argued by Velleman (2001). Norms of privacy dictate that certain things should be allowed to be concealed. If the ability for self-presentation is impaired, one is naked in the sense that one is exposed in a way that fundamentally impacts one's standing as a social agent.

In the case of personal big biodata that are immutable, change in a person's profile can only occur at the level of the interpretation of these data. It is thus important to instill mechanisms to control the process of the inscription of meaning to the data. However, this process is largely outside the control of the person. A first reason for this lack of control lies in the fact that new interpretations emerge as technologies and insights evolve. This fact is acknowledged, for instance, in the informed consent form of the Personal Genome Project: "because the science in this area is evolving, and data will be collected on an on-going basis by the PGP, the risks involved due to your participation in this study, as well as the likelihood and severity of such risks, will change over time" (Personal Genome Project 2014). Second, information systems that are used to store personal data can constrain the freedom of a person to manage his or her own identity (Manders-Huits and Van den Hoven 2008; Manders-Huits 2010) irrespective of the type of personal data that are stored and processed. In the case of personal big biodata, these systems represent a person via a digital record, which can contain the person's genomic sequence, medical record and so on. Digital representations reduce a person to his or her representation in the system, and allow for the creation of "types" of people by clustering such representations. Together with the fact that data in these systems tend to persist, digital identities result in a reduced ability to reshape one's identity. Central to this moral autonomy, reason for data protection (Van den Hoven 2008) is Bernard William's proposition that respect for persons *implies attempts at moral identification*, namely the identification of a person as someone who is engaging in self-identification and who ought to be identified as such. This is an important aspect of what it means to respect someone: we owe the other an attempt at identification (not clinical or forensic) as the person who he wants to be identified with. The object of knowledge claims therefore becomes a more complex one, namely an objective physical human being who is characterized in terms of a panoply of biomarkers and a genome, but who has a subjective conception of him- or herself. Self-identification encompasses the ability and freedom to determine and reorient oneself. In databases this ability can be constrained when a person's identity is reduced to a digital record. Defining one's course of life can be hampered when the person has no ability to control this digital information.

Epistemic modesty is thus a moral source of restraint in the process of the inscription of meaning when this process of inscription of meaning is out of the control of the subject. In addition to the avoidance of information-based harm and the prevention of inequity and discrimination, genomic privacy provides a person with the freedom to shape his or her own social and moral identity, and to relativize or completely undo previous and external determinations made by others and actively engage in self-presentation in a range of social contexts. The epistemic or immodesty that is so easily produced by practices associated with collection and utilization of personal big biodata should be counteracted by instilling and institutionalizing forms of epistemic modesty about claims that we know "who someone really is" if we know this person's genomic blueprint.

Ensuring privacy as a property right in one's own biological data, and creating markets for personal biological data, may not work to ensure a fair processing of these data. Markets where people sell and buy personal biological data are highly problematic, as is the case, for example, in markets for organs. The items changing hands are unique and in a relevant sense belong to the individual, or can be seen to be co-constitutive of the individual. And the transfer is irreversible, since once the data is out, it is practically impossible to get control over it again. The idea of a market also implies freedom, informed consent and full information, which are all precisely what is at stake. Genetic data protection by means of data markets and transferable property rights therefore seems a bad idea. An alternative to a market is the "information altruism" as highlighted by Lunshof *et al.* (2008). In this setting, the individual shares his or her genomic data in order to support scientific progress, aiming at generating benefits for many. Information altruism is a peculiar form of altruism since the audience to whom one provides the information is unknown and global, and so are the potential beneficiaries. By subscribing to the open consent form, the research subject allows the storage of his or her personal genomic data in publicly accessible databases without any guarantee of anonymity, privacy or confidentiality. Withdrawal from a study is possible at any time, but the research subjects need to acknowledge that their data might not be completely removable. They also need to acknowledge that the information release might not be to their benefit and can even harm them. An information-altruistic policy can therefore lead to the vulnerability of research subjects.

The tension between personal and societal interests is bound to be a central topic in big biodata privacy debates (Knoppens 2009). The individual benefits from a strong protection of his or her big biodata. The community benefits from improved health care that is the result of a better understanding of biological data. Inaccessibility of personal genomic data for the research community can hamper scientific progress and the related societal benefits. There is a need for solutions that ensure protection of the individual, while allowing researchers to mine the data. Whether technical solutions can dissolve this moral dilemma is being investigated (Ayday 2013). For instance, Baldi *et al.* (2011) applied encryption technologies to full personal genome sequences. Such technologies allow for the *in silico* execution of genome tests, without disclosing the information outside of the intended audience. In this setting, a person can have personal genomic data available on an electronic carrier in an encrypted way. The person then can consent to let a service provider run an algorithm on his or her genomic data, without having to disclose the data to this service provider. Such encryption strategies can provide the basis for innovations in health care and consumer genetics that ensure genetic privacy, while providing researchers proper access to analyze the data.

In any setting, it will be crucial to create room for self-determination, and for mitigating the effects of epistemic immodesty, by giving persons more means to control not only the access to their big biodata, but also by giving society the means to ensure proper interpretation and usage of these data. Such means imply pluriformity in available models, frameworks and rival theories, and access to countervailing interpretations, checks and balances in actions based on interpretations of genomic data. Good governance of personal genomic data is a way to instill epistemic modesty in users. Practices should also extend to training and support for genetic counselors, in systematic reviews of the interpretations offered by genetic services, the required indication of probabilities in claims, creation of modes of contesting available categorizations and the dissemination of scientific information in society.

References

Ashley, E. A., Butte, A. J., Wheeler, M. T., Chen, R., Klein, T. E., Dewey, F. E., Dudley, J. T., Ormond, K. E., Pavlovic, A., Morgan, A. A., Pushkarev, D., Neff, N. F., Hudgins, L., Gong, L., Hodges, L. M., Berlin, D. S., Thorn, C. F., Sangkuhl, K., Hebert, J. M., Woon, M., Sagreiya, H., Whaley, R., Knowles, J. W., Chou, M. F., Thakuria, J. V., Rosenbaum, A. M., Zaranek, A. W., Church, G. M., Greely, H. T., Quake, S. R. and Altman, R. B. 2010. "Clinical assessment incorporating a personal genome," *The Lancet* 375 (9725): 1525–35.

Ayday, E., De Cristofaro, E., Hubaux, J.-P. and Tsudik, G. 2013. "The chills and thrills of whole genome sequencing," IEEE Computer Society Digital Library, eprint arXiv:1306.1264 http://doi.ieeecomputersociety.org/10.1109/MC.2013.333.

Baldi, P., Baronio, R., De Cristofaro, E., Gasti, P. and Tsudik, G. 2011. "Countering GATTACA: Efficient and secure testing of fully-sequenced human genomes," CCS 11 *Proceedings of the 18th ACM conference on Computer and communications security*, arXiv:1110.2478.

Barnes, B. and Dupré, J. 2008. *Genomes and What to Make of Them*. University of Chicago Press.

Choudhury, S., Fishman, J. R., McGowan, M. L. and Juengst, E. T. 2014. "Big data, open science and the brain: lessons learned from genomics," *Frontiers in Human Neuroscience* 8: 239.

El Emam, K. 2011. "Methods for the de-identification of electronic health records for genomic research," *Genome Medicine* 3: 25.

ENCODE Project Consortium, 2012. "An integrated encyclopedia of DNA elements in the human genome," *Nature* 489: 57–74.

Erlich, Y. and Narayanan, A. 2014. "Routes for breaching and protecting genetic privacy," *Nature Reviews Genetics* 15(6): 409–21.

GIANT (Genetic Investigation of Anthropocentric Traits) Consortium 2010. "Hundreds of variants clustered in genomic loci and biological pathways affect human height," *Nature* 467: 832–8.

Gottweis, H., Kaye, J., Bignami, F., Rial-Sebbag, E., Lattanzi, R. and Macek, M. Jr., 2012. "Biobanks for Europe, a challenge for governance," European Commission (report from the expert group on dealing with ethical and regulatory challenges of international biobank research).

Green, M. J. and Botkin, J. R. 2003. "'Genetic exceptionalism' in medicine: clarifying the differences between genetic and nongenetic tests," *Annals of Internal Medicine* 138 (7): 571–5.

Green R. M. and Thomas, A. M. 1998. "DNA: five distinguishing features for policy analysis," *Harvard Journal of Law & Technology* 11(3): 571–91.

Gymrek, M., McGuire, A. L., Golan, D., Halperin, E. and Erlich, Y. 2013. "Identifying personal genomes by surname inference," *Science* 339 (6117): 321–4.

HIPAA Privacy Rule, 2002. http://privacyruleandresearch.nih.gov/.

Homer, N., Szelinger, S., Redman, M., Duggan, D., Tembe, W., Muehling, J., Pearson, J. V., Stephan, D. A., Nelson, S. F. and Craig, D. W. 2008. "Resolving individuals contributing trace amounts of DNA to highly complex mixtures using high-density SNP genotyping microarrays," *PLoS Genetics* 4(8): e1000167.

Hottois, G. 1996. *Symbool en techniek. Over de technowetenschappelijke mutatie in de westerse cultuur.* Original: *Philosophie et technosciences.* 1995. Translated by Maarten van der Marel. Kampen: Kok Agora.

Ilkilic, I. 2009. "Coming to grips with genetic exceptionalism: roots and reach of an explanatory model," *Medicine Studies* 1: 131–42.

Knoppens, B. M. 2009. "Genomics and policymaking: from static models to complex systems?" *Human Genetics* 125: 375–9.

Kupferschmidt, K. 2011. "Danish archipelago launches mass sequencing plan," http://news.sciencemag.org/europe/2011/10/danish-archipelago-launches-mass-sequencing-plan.

Le Hellard, S. and Steen, V. M. 2014. "Genetic architecture of cognitive traits," *Scandinavian Journal of Psychology* 55(3): 255–62.

Lunshof, J. E., Chadwick, R., Vorhaus, D. B. and Church, G. M. 2008. "From genetic privacy to open consent," *Nature* 9: 406–11.

Lunshof, J. E., Bobe, J., Aach, J., Angrist, M., Thakuria, J. V., Vorhaus, D. B., Hoehe, M. R. and Church, G. M. 2010. "Personal genomes in progress: from the

Human Genome Project to the Personal Genome Project," *Dialogues in Clinical NeuroSciences* 12(1): 47–60.

Malin, B. 2006. "Re-identification of familial database records," *AMIA Annual Symposium Proceedings*: 524–8.

Malin, B., Loukides, G., Benitez, K. and Clayton, E. W., 2011. "Identifiability in biobanks: models, measures, and mitigation strategies," *Human Genetics* 130(3): 383–92.

Manders-Huits, N. 2010. "Practical versus moral identities in identity management," *Ethics and Information Technology* 12: 43–55.

Manders-Huits, N. and van den Hoven, J. 2008. "Moral Identification in Identity Management Systems," in Fischer-Hübner, S., Duquenoy, P., Zuccato, A., Martucci, L. (eds.) *The Future of Identity in the Information Society*, Boston: IFIP International Federation for Information Processing, Springer, Vol. 262: 77–91.

Padmanabhan, A. and Luna, B. 2013. "Developmental imaging genetics: linking dopamine function to adolescent behavior," *Brain and Cognition* 89: 27–38. Available at www.sciencedirect.com/science/article/pii/S0278262613001462.

Personal Genome Project 2014. "PGP Consent Form," www.personalgenomes.org/harvard/sign-up.

Roche, P. A. and Annas, G. J., 2001. "Protecting genetic privacy, *Nature Review Genetics* 2: 392–6.

Sarata, A. K. 2008. "CRS Report for Congress. Genetic exceptionalism: genetic information and public policy," *Congressional Research Service*, www.hsdl.org/?view&did=707472.

Sarwate, A. D., Plis, S. M., Turner, J. A., Arbabshirani, M. R. and Calhoun, V. D. 2014. "Sharing privacy-sensitive access to neuroimaging and genetics data: a review and preliminary validation," *Frontiers in Neuroinformatics* 8: 35.

Soini, S. 2012. "Genetic testing legislation in Western Europe – a fluctuating regulatory target," *Journal of Community Genetics* 3(2): 143–53.

Sweeney, L., Abu, A. and Winn, J. 2013. "Identifying participants in the personal genome project by name," *Harvard University Data Privacy Lab.* arXiv:1304.7605: 1021–1.

The Thousand Genomes Project Consortium. 2012. "An integrated map of genetic variation from 1,092 human genomes," *Nature* 491: 56–65.

United Nations, 1998. Universal Declaration on the Human Genome and Human Rights, www.ohchr.org/EN/ProfessionalInterest/Pages/HumanGenomeAndHumanRights.aspx.

UNESCO, 2003. International Declaration on Human Genetic Data, http://portal.unesco.org/en/ev.php-URL_ID=17720&URL_DO=DO_TOPIC&URL_SECTION=201.html.

Van den Hoven, J. 2008. "Information Technology, Privacy, and the Protection of Personal Data", in Van den Hoven, J. and Weckert, J. (eds.) *Information Technology and Moral Philosophy*, Cambridge Studies in Philosophy and Public Policy. Cambridge University Press, pp. 301–21.

Velleman, D. 2001. "The genesis of shame," *Philosophy & Public Affairs* 30(1): 27–52.

Wilkerson, T. E. 1995. *Natural Kinds*, Avebury: Ashgate Publishing.

Willour, V. L., Seifuddin, F., Mahon, P. B., Jancic, D., Pirooznia, M., Steele, J., Schweizer, B., Goes, F. S., Mondimore, F. M., Mackinnon, D. F., The Bipolar Genome Study (BiGS) Consortium, Perlis, R. H., Lee, P. H., Huang, J., Kelsoe, J. R., Shilling, P. D., Rietschel, M., Nöthen, M., Cichon, S., Gurling, H., Purcell, S., Smoller, J. W., Craddock, N., DePaulo J. R. Jr., Schulze, T. G., McMahon, F. J., Zandi P. P. and Potash J. B. 2012. "A genome-wide association study of attempted suicide," *Molecular Psychiatry* 17: 433–44.

8

Should personal data be a tradable good? On the moral limits of markets in privacy

BEATE ROESSLER

Behavioral targeting is valuable: a survey of nine of the top fifteen advertising networks "found that behaviourally-targeted advertising accounted for around 18% of total advertising revenue during 2009 (USD 595 million), cost 2.68 times as much as run-of-network advertising and was more than twice as effective at converting users who click on the advertisements into buyers – a 6.8% conversion versus the 2.8% conversion from run-of-network advertisements" (OECD 2013: 14). Examples like this abound and demonstrate that markets in personal data form one of the most lucrative markets in the world: the data concern every aspect of and every bit of information about personal lives, from health, shopping, news preferences, geographic data – this list could be continued almost endlessly. The Internet, and the market in private personal data, has become an essential part of our lives.

Concerns about what happens with these data and with the personal information they carry is a much discussed topic in contemporary theory and social criticism, and the dangers and risks have been pointed out in various ways: the consequences that the big data market might have for individuals and their privacy, their freedom and identity, but also for social relations and for the transformation of society in general (Turow 2011; Halpern 2013; Marwick 2013, Mayer-Schoenberger and Cukier 2013; Tanner 2014). Although the concept of privacy, its protection and its transformations stands central in many of these analyses, their concern can also focus on the transformation of social relationships (Marwick 2013; boyd 2014), on the idea of identity (Cohen 2012), on issues

I am very grateful to Robin Celikates, Susan James, Andrew Roberts, Valerie Steeves and to the participants at the NIAS workshop in January 2014 on the Social Dimensions of Privacy for comments and discussions. I am also deeply indebted to the detailed, critical and constructive comments by Christopher Parsons that helped me enormously to sharpen my arguments.

of justice and equality (Turow 2011), and on democratic political procedures (Lever 2012).

It is these analyses of the different invasions of our lives through the Internet that form the background for this contribution. I shall take up these criticisms, though I wish to pursue a slightly different direction. My starting point is that the trade in personal data poses not only a problem for individual privacy in its different social contexts, but is also a problem that concerns the possible transformation of social relations through the influence of markets more generally. These further-reaching consequences seem to have more to do with the marketization of personal data, and less to do with surveillance and other forms of invasion of privacy: that is why I approach the problem of the protection of privacy or personal data in the digital age through the question of what the market in personal data could mean to persons and their identities, to the flourishing of social relations as well as to social justice in a society. Personal data are collected, processed, mined, disseminated and sold, and are, thereby, treated as tradable goods. Therefore, my question is whether the ethical debate on the moral limits of markets can contribute to an understanding of the social and cultural consequences of markets in personal data. Why should there be limits to the commodification of information about our private lives?

Note that I do not think that this approach has to be understood as an alternative to existing approaches: in law, for instance, we have the idea that we need the informed consent of persons to what is happening to their data. We also have the rules – amongst others – of use and purpose limitation to what can be done with collected data, which already help to limit the market in data (Zuiderveen Borgesius 2014). In theories of privacy, we have critical approaches on the basis of personal control of access to data and the protection of autonomy and freedom (Allen 1988; Roessler 2005); or on the basis of the protection of the integrity of contexts (Nissenbaum 2010). Both the law and philosophical approaches to privacy provide us with good arguments for limiting the market in personal data. However, I want to argue for taking up the social-critical perspective of the moral limits of markets: only in this way, by drawing on the resources of this theoretical discourse, can we get into view the more general transformations and possible social pathologies that might follow from an unlimited market in personal data.

My assumption is that, as Sandel puts it, "the more markets extend their reach into noneconomic spheres of life, the more entangled they become with moral questions" (Sandel 2012: 88) and that it is worthwhile investigating this entanglement when dealing with markets in personal data. Therefore, I shall draw on literature dealing not primarily with privacy problems but with the question of universal commodification, of turning every aspect of human life into a commodity. I shall do this by taking up three questions: the question of commodification more generally and what commodification of personal data could mean for persons and their agency; the moral question of social injustices as a consequence of markets; and, third, the ethical question of possible transformations of social relations through the logic of the market, thus of the possible consequences of these markets for our individual and social good life. It will become clear, I hope, that these three questions comprise the whole problematic of the possible moral limits of markets in personal data.[1]

In what follows, I first discuss some problems regarding the notion of personal data and the idea of the neutrality of the market. In a second step, I explore in greater detail the critique of the neutrality of the market and theories of the moral limits of markets, with the three previously mentioned guiding perspectives: universal commodification and its consequences for individual agency; the market as (re)producing discrimination and inequality; and the consequences of universal marketization for our social and individual good lives, under the aspect of the possible alienation and reification of social relations. In my last step, I specify and deepen the understanding of the possible harmful consequences of market-based relations for our social life, as well as for the subjects themselves.

The idea I argue for in this contribution is that the consequences of the commodification of personal data and the market in these data can be detrimental for a society and for social relationships, and that the arguments that we find in debates on the moral limits of markets can be helpful in understanding this. I do not want to deny, though, the obvious positive effects this market has: it is convenient, helps people in their searches and in their purchases, enormously simplifies communication, and can generally help enrich people's lives. This is certainly right: but I am concerned here only with the negative effects these markets can have if they take possession of realms and contexts that are devalued by the very logic of the

---

[1] Note, however, that when I am discussing the moral limits of data *markets*, I am not at the same time writing about the moral limits for *governments* to collect and process data. I believe that the reasons for setting limits to data markets are different from the ones we have for setting limits to government surveillance – although one could make the case that collecting and trading personal data also constitutes a form of (consumer) surveillance (Cohen 2013; Richards 2013).

market. We shall see, though, that this does not necessarily mean that we could not consider ideas of "incomplete commodification" (Radin 1996; O'Callaghan 2013): personal data could play a meaningful role within friendships and other non-market relations, and yet, within limits, be treated as a commodity in a data market. This will become clearer in what follows.

Privacy, personal data and the neutrality of the market

"Personal data" can mean any information concerning the "personal or material circumstances" of an identified or identifiable individual, or a "data subject" in the discourse of law (see Wacks 1989, 2010: 110ff; Wacks).[2] Let me quote the definition given recently by the OECD Privacy guidelines:

> [P]ersonal data ... is a broad concept, which includes, by way of example, the following types of personal data: User generated content, including blogs and commentary, photos and videos, etc. – Activity or behavioural data, including what people search for and look at on the Internet, what people buy online, how much and how they pay, etc. – Social data, including contacts and friends on social networking sites; – Locational data, including residential addresses, GPS and geo-location (e.g. from cellular mobile phones), IP address, etc. – Demographic data, including age, gender, race, income, sexual preferences, political affiliation, etc. – Identifying data of an official nature, including name, financial information and account numbers, health information, national health or social security numbers, police records, etc.
>
> (OECD 2013: 7)

Thus, what we call personal data can originate from very different sources, and these may be data that are more or less "private" or sensitive from the point of view of the individual person herself. This sensitivity can vary depending on the contexts in which it is used as well as on the distance it has to what a person would call her personality (Wacks 2010: 111ff, 118). As we know, however, the question of whether there is something like a "biographical core" of data and the question of how one objectively determines sensitive data is contested (Millar 2009: 104ff; see also Nissenbaum 2010: 120ff). So, no matter whether the sensitivity of personal data should be dependent on contexts or conceptualized around a non-contextualized "core," the idea of sensitivity illustrates the normative

---

[2] See also the Data Protection Directive 95/46/EC. Online: http://eur-lex.europa.eu/LexUriServ/LexUriServ.do?uri=CELEX:31995L0046:EN:HTML.

dimension of personal data and their protection comprising both a legal and a moral dimension. Yet from the perspective of the market, these differences are important only insofar as they put possible legal limits on data collection, analysis and trade. Apart from that, the market is largely interested in what it can learn about the person as a consumer and as a possibly interesting object of advertising.

When I speak of personal data as a tradable good, I mean exactly this sort of digitalized information, which is produced through the Internet and is collected, processed and so on by interested parties. During the last decade or so, personal data have been harnessed in order to develop a gigantic – "big" – data market: the amount of data stored in databases and the possibility of processing them through increasingly sophisticated means is almost incomprehensible, and the market in databases is one of the most profitable (Craig and Ludloff 2011; OECD 2013; for many examples see Marwick 2014; Tanner 2014). As Meyer-Schoenberger and Cukier explain, the value of such data is constantly rising as the cost of digital storage falls, as the means of processing become more precise and as targeting becomes increasingly specific and, therefore, increasingly profitable (Mayer-Schoenberger and Cukier 2013: 98ff). Accordingly, the economic value of personal data cannot be overestimated, and the quantification and monetization of personal information constitutes an economic value that will only increase in the future.

Now the question is, of course: what is wrong with a market in personal data? A market arranges the exchange of goods or services on the basis of self-interest and supply and demand, which determine the value/money for the goods in question. Markets are convenient and efficient, they coordinate behavior and a society without markets is hardly imaginable. However, doubts concerning the perfect neutrality of markets have been raised since their inception (Herzog 2013). Over the past few years, such doubts have been accentuated following the global financial crisis of 2008, which led even conservative critics to express some skepticism about the workings of financial markets. Of course, such concerns and broader concerns addressing the very idea of the neutrality of markets have prominently been taken up in the debates of moral philosophy for a long time. So what can we say about the harm that such markets can cause?

Three problems with markets in everything

One of the classic positions arguing for constraining the market sphere is that of Michael Walzer. In his book *Spheres of Justice* from 1983, he developed the idea of complex equality based on different societal spheres as distributional realms that should be maintained and limited if justice is to be done. The meaning of the different societal goods – education, hard work, money, leisure time and so on– placed in the different spheres, is essential for the respective criteria of their distribution, and since the meanings vary widely, so too do the criteria for distribution. Walzer's theory forms the background for many contemporary critics of the market because of the idea of spheres – compartments – that should not be succumbed to the logic of markets, and because of the idea that goods might lose their meaning and significance for us, if they were commodified.[3] However, as has been argued frequently, the mere reference to different spheres and alleged common understanding of meanings cannot explain precisely on which reasons the separation between the spheres should be grounded (Dworkin 1985; Radin 1996: 46ff; Satz 2010: 80f).

So let us look more closely at the limits of marketization with the help of the three questions I sketched earlier: the first one on the very idea of what commodification of personal data means for persons and their agency; the second question concerning the moral problem as to the possible *injustice* of markets; and the third one concerning the ethical problem of the possible consequences of markets in personal data for the individual and social good life.

Commodification, identity and agency

It does not seem wrong to diagnose a certain discontent in people when they are made aware of the fact that big companies such as Amazon, Facebook, Google and, of course, Acxiom not only collect their data, store and mine them but can also trade them or make them accessible to other firms. This form of collection and trade in personal data causes uneasiness and seems to constitute a harm that is not easy to analyze. This discontent does not seem to be reducible to violations of privacy; neither does it seem to be analyzable as a violation of property rights; and nor simply as an aversion to consumer surveillance. The discontent seems to be stronger than that and seems to be directed quite generally against the idea of a market in personal data: therefore, it appears reasonable to turn to theories of commodification in seeking explanations.

---

[3] Walzer's position has been used not only in debates on the moral limits of markets, but also in privacy debates: Nissenbaum follows Walzer in her theory of informational contexts and (in)appropriate flows of personal information (Nissenbaum 2010: 166ff).

So the first question about markets in everything concerns the very idea of a commodity and of commodification. Commodification means turning something into a commodity in order to exchange it on a market, where that "something" is usually regarded as an object that should not be so commodified (Ertman and Williams 2005). One of the most influential theories of commodification is Radin's. She sets out four criteria ("indicia", Radin 1996: 118) to define commodification (see also Lukes 2004: 62f): in order for something to count as a commodity, it has to be objectified, functional, fully interchangeable with other commodities and obtain a value ascription on a value scale, on the scale of money. Objects can be commodified, but so can relations – when we try to "buy" a friend – and, more generally, practices such as donating blood (Titmuss 1971, Singer 1973: 314; Sandel 2012: 126).

This is still a rather general concept of commodification, but it can already serve to clarify a first critical step. According to critics of the market, not everything people value qualifies as saleable: part of the reason why we do value some things and relationships is precisely, as was already made clear by Walzer, that they are not fit to be traded in a market, or to be assigned a value in terms of money. As an object to be bought or traded for money, they lose their value, they become "corrupted" for us (Lukes 2004: 63; Sandel 2012: 93ff, following Walzer).

But what sort of commodity is personal data? First, in order to be understood as a commodity, the data has to be seen as a set of independent objects, independent of the person and her social relations, as Radin argues (Radin 1996: 6; Satz 2010: 189ff; A. Phillips 2013: 107f). No matter how "personal" they are (information about your shopping or your postings on social media), the data have to be commodified as separate from the person and have to be, following Radin, objectified, functional, fully interchangeable and, of course, purchasable for money. However, personal data seem to be an odd good: while money is made with personal data, the person whose data are sold is not the one who receives the money (Morozov 2014), unlike the person who puts on sale her kidney. Although prima facie personal data ("belonging to a person") seem to have structural analogies with organs, which also "belong" to a person (Satz 2010: 189ff; A. Phillips 2013: 97ff), it does not really help here to refer to the debate on organ selling that figures so prominently in the debates on the moral limits of markets. The person who has bought my kidney is no longer interested in my whereabouts, whereas the company that has my personal data in its possession is at least interested in me as reidentifiable, traceable, as a bundle of data, as a potential buyer of something.

Of course, not all personal data qualify to be traded in a market. The rationale under which the data is collected is also important, insofar as the degree of identification can vary, significantly, between me as an individual person, as an individual cookie number, as a member of a specific population, and so forth. Moreover, data are not necessarily collected to sell – they can be purchased, for instance, for research purposes, the intention of which is not advertising. However, even in these more benevolent situations, the data are purchased as some kind of a commodity, since to have these data made available to us, even for research purposes, we must buy them (as, for instance, if we want to do research on the Internet behavior of young people). In this context, the data is a commodity, but in a much weaker sense than when companies buy the data in order to make more money. This is where the idea of incomplete commodification comes in (Radin 1996: 102ff): the data in the social context of research is far less "completely" commodified than the data a network company buys in order to perfect their behavioral targeting. I shall come back to this point.

Furthermore – to move on in the discussion of why personal data are an odd commodity – I do not think that it helps to refer to the question of property and to maintain that personal data are owned by the person, as supposedly (as some theories suggest) kidneys are owned by a person. If we look at the debate concerning the possessability of data, which focuses on whether the corresponding rights have to be seen as property rights, or whether data protection rights have to be construed as civil rights (Zwick and Dholakia 2001; O'Callaghan 2013: 25ff), we can see that it does not really shed any light on the question of commodification and tradability as such. Even if they were my property, there could still be arguments for moral limits to markets in these data – just as there are moral norms to limit the market in organs, even though organs could be seen as being "owned" by the person they come from. I do not think it is reasonable to want to decide the question of tradability of personal data by defining them as property; moreover, I do not think it is very coherent to conceptualize data as property in the first place, but this is another matter.

It is helpful here to make a difference between sets of data, as we have seen above in the definition of personal data. Let us take the sets of data that are in a broad sense connected to the intentions and self-chosen activities of the persons concerned:

> user generated content including blogs and commentary, photos and videos, etc. – Activity or behavioural data, including what people search

for and look at on the Internet, what people buy online, how much and
how they pay, etc. – Social data, including contacts and friends on social
networking sites; – Locational data, including residential addresses, GPS
and geo-location (e.g. from cellular mobile phones), IP address.

(OECD 2013: 7)

In thinking about commodification, starting with only these sets of data
makes sense because it is these data that people probably think most
clearly "belong to the person," and in a different sense than, for instance,
the color of their eyes, or identifying data of an official nature. We could
then say that personal data are to be understood as belonging to a person
in the specific sense that they – voluntarily or non-voluntarily – express
her identity and personality rather directly, in different contexts and
dimensions of her life, and in different ways. Other sets of data – which
are conceived of as more remote from what the person would consider her
identity – could then be seen to be commodified in a less problematic way.
When data from the more identity-related sets are taken into a completely
different context from the one in which they were communicated, when
they are commodified and commercialized, when they are strategically
used to invite me or entice me to make purchases, then the discontent
with commodification seems to have good reasons.

Critique of this commodification of personal data should therefore be
linked to the most fundamental arguments against universal commodification. Walzer is right in pointing out the detrimental consequences the
transgression of spheres can have – and the discontent I mentioned in the
beginning is certainly at least partly explained by this illegitimate change
of spheres. But we can say even more than that. The reason why commodifying and commercializing data that were supposed to belong to and
stay in the sphere of social relations is harmful is because it ultimately
hinders and distorts my autonomy and identity: by being manipulated
into a certain commercialized behavior, being forced to adopt a view on
myself and on my social relations that is motivated not by friendship but
by the market, and therefore not self-determined, or determined through
the norms of the social context.

For Radin, the argument against total commodification ultimately rests on anthropological considerations, since commodifying or
commercializing friendship or family relations, for instance, would
"do violence to our deepest understanding of what it is to be human"
(Radin 1996: 56). We can apply this to commodifying personal data,
although it might be even more plausible to articulate the critique of

commodification in terms of social freedom, autonomy or individual agency in different social contexts. In both approaches, however, the commodification of personal data can affect the constitution of identity and personality of people in a most fundamental way. I shall return to these problems and to the consequences this form of commodification can have for the subject's agency, identity and her social relations in more detail in the following sections.

Markets discriminate and are unfair

Let us now have a look at the second question, the moral problem of the possible unjust consequences of markets. Theories of market neutrality argue typically that markets are neutral because everybody enters the market as equal and if the market works as it should, no instance of *unfair* inequality can result from the exchanges. However, this has been disputed from different perspectives, some of which are central to the critique of a market in personal data. Let me first review some of the arguments (Radin and Sunder 2005; Satz 2010: 15–38).

Markets are a potential source for inequality and discrimination; therefore some markets – "noxious markets" – are harmful and unjust: this is what Satz argues in her seminal study of the moral limits of markets (Satz 2010: 81, 91ff). She develops four parameters to evaluate markets: if market participants have "very weak or highly asymmetric knowledge and agency", and/or if the market "reflect[s] the underlying extreme vulnerabilities of one of the transacting parties", and/or if the markets produce "extremely harmful outcomes," for either the individual or the society, then, Satz argues, the market has to be criticized as being damaging and morally wrong. She is primarily interested in the effects of markets on the equal standing of the participants in the market and in society at large, in the impact of markets on justice and equality in a society.

Satz describes and analyzes many examples of markets *producing* inequality through exploiting weak agency and through exploiting the vulnerability of the parties involved (Satz 2010: 115ff). These markets have noxious results because they produce and consequently reinforce detrimental forms of inequality and power imparities. However, markets also *reproduce* inequalities and discrimination against persons or groups of persons: people do not enter the market as equals and the inequality is exacerbated through market transfers. Lukes, too, cites a large number of examples of cases where market forces aggravate the position of the poorer market participants, who enter the market with fewer resources

(Lukes 2004: 71f) and are pushed into an increasingly bad social situation by market forces.

If we apply these arguments to the market in personal data, we can see that this market can easily produce detrimental inequalities: it is precisely one of the goals of online advertisers to treat people differently in order to get more "hits" and make more profit. Turow discusses many instances of social sorting and discrimination in the market of personal data on the basis of age, gender and income. Roberts, too, provides examples that demonstrate that the trade in personal data can have discriminatory and unjust consequences for the data subjects (Turow 2011: 88ff; Cohen 2013; Richards 2013; Marwick 2014; Roberts 2015). We know that companies generate customer's profiles on the basis of their former purchases, and also, far more precisely, on the basis of information purchased through big data companies, hence on the basis of the person's all-round Internet behavior. In this way it is possible to mine the data for patterns and to use the patterns for predictive analytics, producing more and more precisely personalized customer profiles. Because of these profiles, customers receive, for instance, very different and differently attractive offers from companies without their being aware that the offers are personalized to their overall financial, social, private situation. As Turow argues in an interview:

> I'm concerned about ... social discrimination ... In an everyday world where companies are deciding [how] I'm targeted, making up pictures about me, I'm getting different ads and different discounts and different maps of even where I might sit in an airplane based on what they think about me. In the future ... you might be placed into "reputation silos" by advertisers, who will then market products to you accordingly.
>
> (Turow 2012)

In the same line, Marwick characterizes the practice of Acxiom: "An Acxiom presentation ... in 2013 placed customers into 'customer value segments' and noted while the top 30 percent of customers add 500 percent of value, the bottom 20 percent actually cost 400 percent of the value. In other words, it behooves companies to shower their top customers with attention while ignoring the bottom 20 percent" (Marwick 2014: 24). Promising clients are "targets"; consumers with a financially and socially less attractive profile are "waste" (Turow 2011).

Even apart from the manipulative aspects that this form of targeting, profiling and predicting consumer's behavior manifests (and to which I will return below), what interests me in this section is the discriminatory effects these markets can have for people and social groups on the basis of their overall social situation. We know from history and experience that increasing social injustices can have destabilizing effects on societies; therefore, to trace out this line a little, the market in personal data can not only have detrimental consequences for individual persons, but also for society at large (see Satz 2010: 95).

Different forms of social action: system and lifeworld

Let us now have a look at the third question: the possible consequences of a market in personal data and its non-neutrality as an ethical problem, as a problem for the way we live together well. A powerful argument against the neutrality of markets can be found in Habermas' theory of communicative action: it is in this *opus magnum* where Habermas develops the distinction between system and lifeworld. He argues that a society can only reasonably be said to be integrated – to keep up its social order in a reasoned and democratic way – and to reproduce itself in ways that are constitutive of a rational, democratic society and flourishing individual personalities, if it comprises these two very different "action orientations" of system and lifeworld and upholds the difference between the two (Habermas 1987: 113ff; Celikates and Pollmann 2006; Cooke and Juetten 2013). Let me briefly illustrate again why it can be helpful to refer to Habermas:

> Websites, advertisers, and a panoply of other companies are continuously assessing the activities, intentions, and backgrounds of virtually everyone online; even our social relationships and comments are being carefully and continuously analyzed ... *Over the next few decades, the business logic that drives these tailored activities will transform the way we see ourselves, those around us, and the world at large.*
>
> (Turow 2011: 3, my emphasis)

The business logic driving activities where no business logic should be working – this is precisely Habermas' point in the idea of the colonization of the lifeworld through the system.

Lifeworld is the concept for the realm of actions oriented toward understanding: it forms the background for agents who are always already situated and contextualized in a lifeworld's culture and tradition (Habermas 1987: 113ff). Essential for the lifeworld is the first person perspective: the hermeneutic participants' perspective that subjects take up and share, communicating with one another with the shared goal of mutual understanding. Thus the lifeworld comprises those realms of modern societies that cannot be reduced in their modes of interaction to instrumental rationality and to strategic, instrumental action oriented towards goals, success and/or profits. The constitutive task of the life-world is the "symbolic reproduction" – the socialization of individual personalities, the cultural transmission between the generations and the social integration. It is these aspects of human life that are grounded in and expressed through communicative action (Habermas 1987: 141ff). Without these characteristic modes of action, a society cannot preserve its culture, socialize healthy personalities or take care of the different forms of social integration.

System, on the other hand, refers to those mechanisms of a society that comprise their material reproduction: in modern capitalist societies these are basically the systems of economy and of the state bureaucracy, with their steering mechanisms of money and power. The system ena-bles a purely functional coordination between agents through influen-cing the consequences of their actions, uncoupled from the orientations and intentions of the individual agents. The system thus operates in its action-coordination purely instrumentally and is not dependent on the understanding of the first person perspective. But it is important to real-ize that the functioning of the system is itself dependent on the "always already" of the communicative background conditions of the lifeworld and its different forms of symbolic reproduction.

In itself, Habermas argues, nothing is wrong with the separation: the system and the lifeworld each fulfill different tasks within a society and each is necessary for societal integration. Furthermore, of course, in the lifeworld we are always also involved in strategic (system-)action: in work, for instance, or in our role as consumers, we necessarily have to have two different action orientations. However, this does not preclude the lifeworld from fulfilling its central tasks, which are built around communicative action. So we should not see the lifeworld and the sys-tem as two completely different separate spheres, but rather as two dif-ferent action orientations, oriented towards different goals and forms of understanding.

Habermas argues not so much for the moral limits of the market as for the possibility of properly functioning social integration, of cul-tural reproduction and of the enabling conditions of socializations of healthy personalities. However, these conditions – and this is one of his central arguments – are violated or damaged when the market tries to take over the action coordination of social relations in the life-world: think, for instance, of universities following exclusively economic imperatives, thereby endangering the very idea of education. In this way, Habermas analyzes different forms of crisis and pathologies that are generated by various forms of "border violations" between system and lifeworld (Habermas 1987: 374ff). Problems arise when the system and its logic encroaches upon the communicative aspects of the lifeworld: the system-imperatives of the economy and the administration infiltrate and permeate dimensions and areas of the lifeworld that previously had been integrated through communicative action. The imperatives of material reproduction force the subjects to replace their communicative action orientation with the use of only their strategic reason: the communicative practices of the lifeworld run the risk of being replaced by strategic behavior. So even if we need strategic actions in contexts of the lifeworld, its core tasks, if they are to be preserved, will still have to be fulfilled as communicative actions.

Let me focus on the question of how Habermas' theory could be made fruitful for the problem of the tradability of personal data. Habermas uses the concept "colonization of the lifeworld" to analyze and interpret the phenomenon of markets taking over important functions in and of the lifeworld, thereby not only influencing, but possibly transforming culture, social relations and personal identities. It is the notion of the colonization of the lifeworld that can be used to analyze the encroachment of the market in personal data, of the market of advertisements on the social relations of private life. The subjects are encouraged to see each other as "customer," each getting (different) adverts, each being attracted into different purchases, but all of them forced to be oriented – maybe involuntarily – towards profit, instead of being oriented to mutual understanding between friends. Habermas' distinction between societal integration through systems on the one hand and through norms and values on the other hand enables us to conceptualize harmful and damaging commodifications as the "reification of relations," as leading to alienation (Habermas 1987: 118). For Habermas, reification threatens when "strategic, 'observing' (beobachtende) modes of behaviour" take over precisely those social spheres or contexts for which communicative orientations are constitutive (Honneth 2005: 55). What we lose in losing these functions of the lifeworld is an ethical loss, a way of living well: if we are forced to act strategically in those contexts of the lifeworld that are meant only for communicative understanding, then the very function of the lifeworld is endangered, with the social life and social relations losing their power of cultural reproduction and socializing healthy personalities (Habermas 1987: 332ff; Celikates and Pollmann 2006).

This is, therefore, how Turow's thesis should be argued for: the concerns that the market in personal data is transforming our social world, that business logic is taking over from the logic of mutual understanding, is a worry about the system forcing its logic on the lifeworld. Marketization contradicts the form and function of the social relationships in the lifeworld, thereby running the risk of drying up the very sources necessary for the integration of societies.

Quantified relations and quantified selves

In the previous section I reviewed three different perspectives on the limitation of markets in general and specifically of markets in personal data: the question of the commodification of everything, the question of social injustices as a consequence of markets and the question of possible transformations of social relations through the logic of markets. In the following, I shall come back to these arguments and reasons against the neutrality of markets in order to further deepen the understanding of the effect of markets on our social life.

It is usually the predictable consumer as object that serves as the point of reference for market transactions. In this sense, the industry of data-based marketing endangers and threatens individual agency – subjects are not understood as agents but as perfectly predictable data objects. Of course, consumers' data can be mined with very different goals, not solely for improving behavioral targeting. But when we focus on the goal of using a profile to entice a person to purchase specific goods, then it is probable that the more precise the profiles, based on millions of personal data, the more predictable and susceptible to manipulation the subject becomes. Let me come back in more detail to the question of friendships and social relations on the social media: of course we should allow for the fact that people have very different relationships called "friends" on social media. But at least a section of these relationships are conceived of by the subject as friendships or intimate relationships, such as families, belonging, as Habermas puts it, to the lifeworld. I have already argued in the previous section that these relations can change when the subjects are pushed to see themselves primarily as data objects and no longer as subjects in relations: since personal data that are collected through social media are useful and valuable for any data broker and are thus commodified, the relationship between the subject and her friends on social media might be transformed. As Steeves argues, we have to "better understand how commercial mining of the social world restructures social relationships and restricts the kinds of identity performances available to young people online ... The detailed individual profiles that result enable marketers to integrate mediatized messages into children's social environment, through behavioural targeting and "natural" or immersive advertising" (Steeves 2015). This analysis obviously applies not only to children and young adults. From the perspective of the interests of the data market, I am driven to view the information I share with my friends no longer as intimate communication "oriented towards understanding" but as yet another item to be used by companies to send yet another advert to, to strategically suggest to me to go for yet another "hit." This is a change in perspective from the first person participant to the third person perspective of the observer and precisely the shift from communicative to strategic action that we saw being analyzed and criticized in Habermas' theory. Of course, this does not always have to happen: persons will not always understand one another through this third-party lens; they might even engage in subversive practices, trying to undermine market logics. However, the possibility of the transformation of these social practices has to be diagnosed as such if we want to take seriously what I referred to earlier on as "discontent."

Thus one aspect here is the change in the meaning of the relationship if it is predominantly seen as a relation between data subjects; as Marwick has also pointed out, the sheer struggle for "status" on social media can entail the commodification of personal information, thus changing and harming the meaning of the relationship (Marwick 2013; see also Kennett and Matthews 2008; Fuchs *et al.* 2012). Again, I want to point out that we do not have to assume that these pieces of personal information are completely commodified: even incomplete commodification can form a threat to the communicative functions of these social relations. That this process and development should have consequences for a person's own idea of differences in self-presentations in different relations, and therefore for a person's identity and personality, is not surprising. I therefore want to go one step further and have a look at what the market in personal data could mean for the identity and self-relation of the subject.

"Self-knowledge through numbers" is the advertising motto of the Quantifiedself-movement. On their website (http://quantifiedself.com) you find everything about self-tracking: measuring, noting, registering and putting down all of your activities 24/7. The Apps[4] you are supposed to use are mostly available free of charge and the data you collect can not

---

[4] For many examples of Apps, see Lupton 2014; Till 2014.

only be shared with the group of friends in your quantified self group, but also with companies and data brokers. As Laura Phillips writes:

> Fitbit, for example, allows us to record and monitor our physical activity as part of a health and wellness regime, in the process collecting contextual information about calories expended and food consumed. This allows Fitbit to create new business models, selling this information to insurance companies to help them better understand the actual and potential behaviour of their customers and thus better calculate risks.
>
> (L. Phillips 2014)

On the one hand, this form of self-observation stands in the long and venerable tradition of diaries and self-observation (Passig 2012). Not every tracking of one's own personal data constitutes the distancing of the subjects from themselves in a harmful or inimical, damaging way. Self-observation, we know, can have very positive effects, individually and in social contexts, and not every self-tracker shares her data with the companies, or even with friends. However, the reasons why we could understand the self-tracking and objectification of the self as possibly having alienating effects and as yet another form of commodification is, first, that the perspective on the person herself can be changing because she is turning into an observer of her own behavior, and is not any longer the acting subject as the first person (Lupton 2013, 2014). The idea of self-knowledge, then, is prone to degenerate from the imperative "know thyself" into knowledge of numbers about oneself as a moving object: "self-knowledge through numbers."

Second, the collection of data about oneself can go hand in hand with the data being collected, mined and sold (prominently in the case of health data), as we have seen in the Fitbit example and can observe in many more examples (Lupton 2013, 2014). Honneth, in his theory of reification, characterizes reified social relations as violating ethical principles in not respecting the other person in her individuality. Instead, the other persons are seen "as 'things' or 'commodities'" (Honneth 2005: 19). He subsequently applies this idea to the relation of the subject to herself, the self-reification (*Selbstverdinglichung*) which the subject cannot escape if and because the social relations in which she finds herself are commodified in the way described (Honneth 2005: 78ff). Marwick, who also criticizes "self-commodification," suggests a similar argument in her chapter on *Lifestreaming* (Marwick 2013: 117, 205ff): the digital self assumes that everything she does is translatable into data that consequently demonstrate to her who she "really" is. This supports my argument that a market in these data can have detrimental effects in changing the perspective on ourselves, the meaning we give to self-knowledge and, therefore, to agency and autonomy. Even if we should be cautious not to exaggerate the threats that lie in the as yet incomplete commodification of our personal data, it certainly is right to point out wrong directions.

Let me conclude: my intention in this contribution was to approach the problem of the protection of privacy or personal data in the digital age through the question of what the market in personal data could mean to persons and their identities, to the flourishing of social relations as well as to social justice in a society. And I hope to have demonstrated that reference to debates on the neutrality of markets and their moral limits provide us with substantial arguments that help to protect the personal data of individuals in their different social contexts. I have already pointed out in the introduction that the critique of the commodification of personal data does not necessarily mean that we could not consider ideas of "incomplete commodification" (Radin 1996; O'Callaghan 2013): personal data could play a meaningful role in friendships and other non-market practices and relations, and yet, within limits, be treated as a commodity in a data market. Other examples of incomplete commodification demonstrate the possibility of having both, an object or relationship that is commodified while at the same time being meaningful. Consider work: work is a commodity, but can also be meaningful and autonomous for the person herself, and as a practice (Radin 1996: 105). Consider books: they clearly are a commodity, but they are perfectly meaningful objects at the same time. Radin suggests viewing commodification on a continuum between two endpoints: the complete commodification of an object and its complete non-commodification. Incomplete commodification of personal data would then take up a middle position on this continuum.

Note, however, that we have different ways to conceptualize this incompleteness: in Radin, the commodified and non-commodified meaning of an object can peacefully coexist, making its meaning incompletely commodified (think of work, again). With personal data, we should conceive of incomplete commodification in a different way: we should conceive of some data being easily commodified, with other sets of data resisting commodification (as I in fact have argued in the above sections). We could also make a difference between contexts: in some contexts, for instance on social media, commodification or commercialization is clearly more tenuous than in other contexts.

So what can we learn from the debate on the moral limits of markets? The perspective from the market in personal data demonstrates the need for moral norms that are not primarily based on individual consent and control of privacy violations, or, for that matter, on the idea of contextual integrity of information flows, but that take into account how the market in personal data can transform our social lives in ways that are harmful, detrimental or injurious. This moral and ethical dimension of the consequences of the marketization of personal data can only be captured when we take up the perspective of the moral limits of markets. Personal or private data are de facto a tradable good; and even if these norms do not tell us where precisely to stop with commodification, the task for ethics and political theory is to criticize tradability if it becomes harmful and dangerous for people and their social relations. The norms that guide the limitation of a market in personal data are necessary if we want to hold on to the idea of a flourishing and well-lived social life.

References

Allen, A. 1988. *Uneasy Access: Privacy for Women in a Free Society*. Lanham: Rowman and Littlefield.

boyd, d. 2014. *It's Complicated: The Social Lives of Networked Teens*. New Haven: Yale University Press.

Celikates, R. and Pollmann, A. 2006. "Baustellen der Vernunft. 25 Jahre Theorie des kommunikativen Handelns. Zur Gegenwart eines Paradigmenwechsels," *WestEnd. Neue Zeitschrift fuer Sozialforschung* 3(2): 97–113.

Cohen, J. E. 2012. *Configuring the Networked Self: Law, Code, and the Play of Everyday Practice*. New Haven: Yale University Press.

2013. "What privacy is for", *Harvard Law Review* 126: 1904–33.

Cooke, M. and Juetten, T. (eds.) 2013. "The theory of communicative action after three decades," *Constellations* 20(4): 516–603.

Craig, T. and Ludloff, M. E. 2011. *Privacy and Big Data*. Sebastopol: O'Reilly Media.

Dworkin, R. 1985. "What Justice Isn't," in Dworkin, R., *A Matter of Principle*, Cambridge, MA: Harvard University Press: pp. 214–20.

Ertman, M. M. and Williams, J. C. (eds.) 2005. *Rethinking Commodification. Cases and Readings in Law and Culture*. New York University Press.

Fuchs, C. *et al*. 2012. *Internet and Surveillance: The Challenges of Web 2.0 and Social Media*. London: Routledge.

Habermas, J. 1987. *The Theory of Communicative Action, Volume 2: Lifeworld and System: A Critique of Functionalist Reason*, translated by T. McCarthy. Cambridge: Polity Press.

Halpern, S. 2013. "Are we puppets in a wired world?" *New York Review of Books*, November 7.

Herzog, L. 2013. "Markets", *Stanford Encyclopedia of Philosophy* (Fall 2013 Edition), edited by Edward N. Zalta. Available at http://plato.stanford.edu/archives/fall2013/entries/markets/.

Honneth, A. 2005. *Reification. A New Look at an Old Idea*. The Berkely Tanner Lectures, edited by M. Jay. Oxford University Press.

Kennett, J. and Matthews, S. 2008. "What's the buzz? Undercover marketing and the corruption of friendship", *Journal of Applied Philosophy* 25(1): 2–18.

Lever, A. 2012. *On Privacy*. New York: Routledge.

Lukes, S. 2004. "*Invasions of the Market*", in Dworkin, R. (ed.), *From Liberal Values to Democratic Transition. Essays in Honour of Janos Kis*. Budapest: Central University Press, pp. 57–78.

Lupton, D. 2013. 'Understanding the human machine', *IEEE Technology and Society Magazine* 32(4): 25–30.

   2014. "Self-tracking Modes: Reflexive Self-Monitoring and Data Practices," Paper for the Imminent Citizenships: Personhood and Identity Politics in the Informatic Age Workshop, 27 August 2014, ANU, Canberra.

Marwick, A. E. 2013. *Status Update. Celebrity, Publicity, and Branding in the Social Media Age*. New Haven: Yale University Press.

   2014. "How your data are being deeply mined", *New York Review of Books*, January 9: 22.

Mayer-Schoenberger, V. and Cukier, K. 2013. *Big Data. A Revolution that Will Transform how We Live, Work, and Think*. London: John Murray.

Millar, J. 2009. Core Privacy: A Problem for Predictive Data Mining, in Steeves, V., Kerr, I. and Lucock, C. (eds.) *Lessons from the Identity Trail: Anonymity, Privacy, and Identity in a Networked Society*. Oxford University Press: pp. 103–20.

Morozov, E. 2014. "Selling Your Bulk Online Data Really Means Selling Your Autonomy. Big tech's war on the meaning of life," *New Republic*, May 13.

Nissenbaum, H. 2010. *Privacy in Context. Technology, Policy, and the Integrity of Social Life*. Stanford University Press.

O'Callaghan, P. 2013. *Refining Privacy in Tort Law*, Heidelberg: Springer.

OECD 2013. Exploring the economics of personal data: A survey of methodologies for measuring monetary value. Retrieved from: http://dx.doi.org/10.1787/5k486qtxldmq-en.

Passig, K. 2012. Unsere Daten, Unser Leben. Internetkolumne, *Merkur. Deutsche Zeitschrift fuer europaeisches Denken* 756: 420–7.

Phillips, A. 2013. *Our Bodies, Whose Property?* Oxford University Press.

Phillips, L. 2014. A Market for Personal Data. Available at: http://hubofallthings.com/market-for-personal-data/. accessed October 17, 2014.

Radin, M. J. 1996. *Contested Commodities*. Cambridge, MA: Harvard University Press.

Radin, M. J. and Sunder, M. 2005. "Introduction: The Subject and Object of Commodification," in Ertman, M. M., Williams, J. C. (eds.), *Rethinking Commodification*. New York University Press, pp. 8–33.

Richards, N. M. 2013. "The dangers of surveillance," *Harvard Law Review* 126: 1934–65.

Roberts, A. 2015. "A republican account of the value of privacy," *European Journal of Political Theory*. DOI: 10.1177/1474885114533262.

Roessler, B. 2005. *The Value of Privacy*. Cambridge: Polity Press.

Sandel, M. 2012, *What Money Can't Buy. The Moral Limits of Markets*. New York: Farrar, Straus and Giroux.

Satz, D. 2010. *Why some Things Should not Be for Sale. The Moral Limits of Markets*. Oxford University Press.

Singer, P. 1973. "Altruism and commerce: a defense of Titmuss against Arrow," *Philosophy and Public Affairs* 2(3) (Spring): 312–20.

Steeves, V. 2015. "Privacy, Sociality and the Failure of Regulation: Lessons Learned from Young Canadians' Online Experiences", in Roessler, B. and Mokrosinska, D. (eds.) *Social Dimensions of Privacy: Interdisciplinary Perspectives*. Cambridge University Press.

Tanner, A. 2014. *What Stays in Vegas*. New York: Public Affairs.

Till, C. 2014. "Exercise as labour: quantified self and the transformation of exercise into labour," *Societies* 4: 446–62; doi:10.3390/soc4030446.

Titmuss, R. 1971. *The Gift Relationship: From Human Blood to Social Policy*. New York: Random House.

Turow, J. 2011. *The Daily You*. New Haven: Yale University Press.

2012. "How companies are 'defining your worth' online." www.npr.org/2012/02/22/147189154/how-companies-are-defining-your-worth-online (accessed October 17, 2014).

Wacks, R. 1989. *Personal Information. Privacy and the Law*. Oxford: Clarendon Press.

2010. *Privacy. A Very Short Introduction*. Oxford University Press.

Walzer, M. 1983. *Spheres of Justice. A Defense of Pluralism and Equality*. New York: Basic Books.

Zuiderveen Borgesius, F. 2014. *Improving Privacy Protection in the Area of Behavioural Targeting*. Ph.D. Thesis, Amsterdam.

Zwick, D. and Dholakia, N. 2001. "Contrasting European and American approaches to privacy in electronic markets: property right versus civil right." *Electronic Markets* 11: 116-20.

9

Privacy, democracy and freedom of expression

ANNABELLE LEVER

Must privacy and freedom of expression conflict? To witness recent debates in Britain, you might think so. Anything other than self-regulation by the press is met by howls of anguish from journalists across the political spectrum, to the effect that efforts to protect people's privacy will threaten press freedom, promote self-censorship and prevent the press from fulfilling its vital function of informing the public and keeping a watchful eye on the activities and antics of the powerful (Brown 2009).[1] Effective protections for privacy, from such a perspective, inevitably pose a threat to democratic government via the constraints that they place on the press.

Such concerns with privacy must be taken seriously by anyone who cares about democratic government, and the freedom, equality and well-being of individuals. But if it is one thing to say that privacy and freedom of expression cannot always be fully protected, it is another to suppose that protections for the one must always come at the expense of the other. After all, the economics of contemporary politics and journalism would seem to be partly responsible for our difficulties in protecting personal privacy while sustaining robust and informative forms of public discourse (Moore 2010: 10–141).[2] Most newspapers are loss-making

Many thanks to Beate Roessler and Dorota Mokrosinska for inviting me to contribute to this volume, and to Dorota and Adam Moore for their very helpful comments on a previous version of this chapter. James Rule's review of my book, *On Privacy*, prodded me to expand the discussion of my methodological approach to privacy, and David Estlund's question to me, at a conference in 2013, had a similarly galvanizing effect on my discussion of 'outing'. I am grateful to them both. Juha Räikkä kindly invited me to a conference, 'Justice: Public and Private', at the University of Turku, Finland, just as I was doing last-minute revisions to this chapter. I am grateful to all the participants there for their suggestions for final changes. Lastly, I am grateful to Routledge for permission to reuse parts of chapter 2 of *On Privacy* in this chapter.

[1] The indifference to privacy by many journalists is noted by Alan Rusbridger (2004) in his review of Rozenberg (2005).
[2] Adam Moore has a helpful – and depressing – discussion of the issue for the USA (Moore 2010: 140, 141). Apparently, at the end of 1945, 80 per cent of US newspapers were

businesses and the need to reduce those losses and, if possible, to turn a profit make investigative journalism an increasingly expensive proposition as compared to both 'comment' and more or less elevated forms of gossip. At the same time, politics has increasingly become the prerogative of a narrow group of people with access to the large sums of money necessary successfully to compete for high office. In those circumstances, the need for critical scrutiny is as important as it is difficult, because the rich and powerful are often able to insulate themselves from scrutiny and criticism, while the poor and powerless suffer from paternalistic, authoritarian and prejudiced rules and regulations.

Revising our ideas about privacy and its protection cannot alone reduce the tensions between freedom of expression and personal privacy typical of our societies, though such revision may be necessary. Moreover, this chapter can only touch on some aspects of the ways in which we need to rethink our interests in privacy, in order adequately to reflect people's diverse interests in freedom of expression, and the important role of a free press to democratic government. Nonetheless, I hope to suggest ways of thinking about people's claims to privacy that can be generalized fairly readily, and that will help to think constructively about the nature, causes and solutions to some important social and political problems, even if, in its nature, philosophical analysis rarely tells us what to do.

More specifically, this chapter argues that people are entitled to keep some true facts about themselves to themselves, should they so wish, as a sign of respect for their moral and political status, and in order to protect themselves from being used as a public example in order to educate or to entertain other people. The 'outing' – or non-consensual public disclosure – of people's health records or status, or their sexual behaviour or orientation, is usually unjustified, even when its consequences seem to be beneficial. Indeed, as this chapter claims, the reasons to reject outing as inconsistent with democratic commitments to freedom and equality, are reasons to insist on the importance of privacy to freedom of expression. While a free press is of the utmost importance to democratic government, it is not identical with the free expression of individuals and, on occasion, the former may have to be constrained in order to protect the latter (Barendt 2007: 231). Hence, this chapter concludes, we should distinguish the claims of individuals to publish reports about their lives – even if this

---

independently owned. By 1982, 50 corporations owned almost all major media outlets in the USA, including newspapers, magazines, radio and television stations, book publishers and movie studios. By 1987, 29 corporations owned them all, and by 1999 they were 9.

necessarily involves revealing the private lives of others – from journalistic claims to publish information about the sex lives of consenting adults. I will start by briefly situating my argument within a democratic approach to privacy, before using the 'outing' of Oliver Sipple to examine people's claims to privacy and their implications for freedom of expression and of the press. I will be assuming that some forms of privacy are legitimate, in order to focus more closely on the question of what information, if any, people may keep to themselves.

We need to democratize our conceptions of privacy for philosophical and other purposes – or so I have argued in previous work (Lever 2011, 2014a).[3] The ideas about privacy we have inherited from the past are marked by beliefs about what is desirable, realistic and possible, which predate democratic government and, in some cases, constitutional government as well. Hence, I have argued, although privacy is an important democratic value, we can only realize that value if we use democratic ideas about self-government, and the freedom, equality, security and rights of individuals to guide our ideas about its nature and value. This chapter, therefore, starts from what I consider to be the central democratic idea: that people are entitled to govern themselves even if they are not distinguished by special virtues, knowledge, resources or interests. People, therefore, do not need to be especially interesting, literate or morally attractive in order to publish their ideas, or to express themselves publicly (Cohen 1993: 207–64, 2009). However, democratic principles also mean that respect for privacy cannot be limited to the meek and self-effacing, nor to the public-spirited and upstanding.

Defining and describing privacy

Before proceeding, however, it may help briefly to clarify some points of terminology and methodology. A great deal of philosophical and legal debate about privacy concerns the best way to define it (Allen 1988: chapter 1; Moore 2010: chapter 2). However, the main reason why it is hard to define privacy – the absence of a set of necessary and sufficient conditions that distinguish privacy from allied concepts – suggests that the fuzziness of our concepts of liberty, equality and rights, rather than some particular obscurity in the concept of privacy itself, likely explains why the boundaries of privacy are hard to fix. No definition of privacy

---

[3] For my articles on privacy, see www.alever.net.

will remove that problem. However, for the purposes of this chapter, we can think of privacy as referring to some combination of seclusion and solitude, anonymity and confidentiality, intimacy and domesticity. Whatever else the word 'privacy' is used to describe, it is used to describe these three groups of words; and whatever else talk of privacy as a moral or political right is meant to illuminate, it is normally meant to illuminate our rights and duties in these.

Democracy

Just as privacy has many meanings, whose merits are controversial, so with most of the other concepts with which we must work, including that of democracy. I will therefore follow standard contemporary usage in referring to democracies as countries whose governments are elected by universal suffrage and where people have an equally weighted vote. I will also assume that democracies require 'one rule for rich and poor' and for governors and governed – that they are constitutional governments. I also assume that democracies enable people to form a variety of associations through which to advance their interests, express their ideas and beliefs, and fulfil their duties as they see them. They are therefore characterized by protection not just for political parties, unions, interest groups and churches, but also by the protections they secure for soccer clubs, scientific societies, families, charities and like-minded people.

Freedom or liberty, equality and rights

Clarifying the way I will be using the word democracy helps to explain the ways I will be using words such as 'freedom' and 'equality'. Completely different things have been taken to epitomize freedom and equality. I therefore suggest that we take whatever forms of liberty are uncontroversially necessary to democratic government as examples of freedom; and we take whatever forms of equality are uncontroversially necessary to democratic government as examples of equality. So, taking some familiar features of democratic government can help us to clarify our ideas about freedom and equality, and can give us a shared reference point for resolving disputes about the relationship of privacy, liberty and equality.

As with freedom and equality, so with rights: we can use standard democratic rights to illustrate people's legal and moral rights, bearing in mind that the precise relationship of the legal and moral is a matter of controversy in most democracies. We can therefore think of the right to

vote as both a moral and a legal right – a right that, in democratic countries, is legally protected partly because people are morally entitled to
participate in forming their government. Problems clarifying the idea of
a right, therefore, can be resolved in the first instance by thinking about
familiar democratic rights – whether legal or moral.

Democracy and methodology

Finally, it will be helpful to clarify what I mean by talking about 'a democratic conception of privacy', and the nature of the argument that I will be
presenting.

By 'a democratic conception of privacy', I mean an interpretation of
the nature and value of privacy, and of its implications for public policy, which is based on democratic principles, ideas and institutions. I do
not assume that there is only one form of democracy.[4] On the contrary,
I imagine that there can be more liberal, republican, socialist, utilitarian and communitarian ways of interpreting central democratic ideas,
rights and values, and of embodying these in customs and institutions.
However, I am concerned with what must be common to any form of
democratic government and society, rather than what might distinguish
them. That is, I assume that democratic moral and political principles
provide the appropriate perspective for determining what rights and
duties to attribute to individuals and, therefore, what forms of privacy,
if any, are to be treated as part of the structure of democratic politics. In
turn, I assume that the claims to privacy – and to political participation,
for that matter – that are necessary for democratic government provide
the appropriate starting point for thinking about the claims of those who
do not live under democratic governments, or who are stateless or not yet
members of any political society at all. This is necessary to ensure that
our reflections on people's moral rights and duties adequately reflect their
legitimate interests in democratic government, whatever their current
circumstances, interests and desires.

The foundational distinction for my approach to privacy, then, concerns the differences between democratic and undemocratic governments, as we best understand them, rather than the differences between
consequentialist and deontological moral theories, or between liberal and
republican political principles (Lever 2014b: 188–90). Given how little

---

[4] Hence my concern with Corey Brettschneider's interesting attempt to justify privacy
rights; see Lever 2015 (forthcoming).

we know about democracy, and the imperfect character even of what we think we know, the analysis of the myriad forms of undemocratic government strikes me as a necessary guide to what democracy requires. As there is nothing inherently democratic about republicanism, liberalism, socialism or utilitarianism, nor of consequentialist and deontological moral theories, none of these seem a particularly helpful starting point if we want to understand the nature and value of privacy on democratic principles. So, while it may be unusual to take the differences between democratic and undemocratic governments as our starting point for moral and political reflection, I believe that it provides our best chance of finding common terrain on which to resolve the competing philosophical, empirical, political and legal debates about privacy and freedom of expression in our different societies.

Oliver Sipple and the ethics of 'outing'

Oliver Sipple was a former US Marine, injured while serving in Vietnam. Sipple lived in San Francisco, and on 22 September 1975 he joined the crowd gathered outside the St Francis Hotel to see President Ford. He was standing beside Sara Jane Moore when she pulled out a gun to shoot the President. Sipple managed to deflect her aim, and to prevent further shots. The police and the secret service immediately commended Sipple for his action at the scene. President Ford thanked him with a letter, and the news media portrayed Sipple as a hero.

Harvey Milk, San Francisco's openly gay City Councillor and a friend of Sipple's, saw this as his chance to strike a blow for gay rights. So, without consulting Sipple, he leaked the fact that Sipple was gay to Herb Caen of the *San Francisco Chronicle*. Caen duly published the news, which was picked up and broadcast around the world.

Although he was known to be gay among members of the gay community in San Francisco, and had even participated in Gay Pride events, Sipple's sexual orientation was a secret from his family, for whom it came as a shock. Outraged, Sipple sued the *Chronicle* for invasion of privacy, but the Superior Court in San Francisco dismissed the suit. Sipple continued his legal battle until May 1984, when a State Court of Appeals rejected his case on the grounds that Sipple had, indeed, become news, and that his sexuality was part of the story. Sipple died in February 1989, aged 47.

Several things seem to be wrong with outing Sipple. The first is that Milk's failure to ask Sipple for permission to talk to the press seems exploitative and contemptuous. Even if one's sexuality were altogether unremarkable, one might object to having it broadcast to all the world; and if it were likely to make one notorious, the subject of hateful abuse and, even, violence, one might well hesitate to have it widely known, even if one felt no shame about it. Second, Sipple's case highlights how easily we can be deceived (or can deceive ourselves) into thinking that we know more about other people's lives and interests than we do. Most cases of outing do not involve one friend outing another, but are motivated by anger at what is, or seems to be, the hypocrisy, injustice or selfishness of someone else. So Sipple's experience suggests that those doing the outing are very likely to underestimate the harm that they inflict on others – both on their immediate victims and on those who care for, or depend upon, them.[5] Hence, outing will often be unjustified on instrumental or consequentialist grounds – because its benefits are uncertain, unpredictable and, such as they are, may be achievable in other ways. By contrast, the harms are usually considerable, unavoidable and the full extent of the damage from outing can be easy to underestimate.

Outing means using someone simply as a means to one's own ends. Strikingly, the Sipple case suggests that this can be morally troubling even when those ends are ones that the victim shares, and has actively endorsed. And this interesting feature of the Sipple case points, I think, to the *political* dimension of *ethical* objections to outing, and to the ways that these differ from a consequentialist weighing of likely benefits and costs, or a Kantian concern with the ways that people can be misused by others. Those are objections to outing that we might have regardless of the society we live in, or our assumptions about the legitimacy of democratic government. By contrast, a political perspective on outing centres on the power that outing involves, and the difficulties of justifying this type of power from a democratic perspective.

Outing involves one person or a group claiming the right to make potentially life-changing decisions for a competent adult, although they have not been authorized to do so, are typically in no position to make amends for any harms their actions cause, and cannot be considered either impartial or expert judges of the claims that they propose to overrule. Such unilateral, unrepresentative and unaccountable power over others is difficult to reconcile with democratic political principles, which limit the extent,

---

[5] An example of this can be seen in Richard Mohr's view that 'To lose a child in a custody case for prejudicial reasons (i.e. because of prejudice against homosexuality) is, to be sure, to suffer an indignity' – which seems like a breathtakingly inadequate description of one potential harm of outing (Mohr 1992: 34).

form and justification of the power we can exercise over others. Moral and political objections to absolute government, therefore, help to explain what is ethically troubling about outing, even when it achieves legitimate objectives, including ones that have the support of its victim.

The Estlund challenge

Of course, to say that 'outing', as usually practised, is at odds with democratic commitments to accountable, representative and participative government is not to say that it is not also at odds with the freedom and equality of individuals. Rather, it is a way of specifying in *what ways and why* outing violates people's freedom and equality, given that at a purely formal level outing pits my claims to freedom and equality against yours, and therefore seems to provide no reasons to condemn – or to favour – outing.

We cannot settle for purely formal conceptions of freedom and equality if we care about democratic government, because attention to how power is distributed and used is essential to creating the conditions in which people can share in the authorization of collectively binding decisions. The importance of this point for the ethics of outing – and for claims to privacy and freedom of expression more generally – becomes apparent once one considers what I will call 'the Estlund challenge' to my analysis of outing. If concerns with a lack of accountability, representation and participation are at the heart of democratic objections to outing, Estlund asked, would not outing be acceptable if settled on as a policy through suitably democratic political procedures, such as majority votes by a government elected by a majority of the electorate?[6]

The Estlund challenge gains its appeal from the fact that legitimate government would be impossible if all error or injustice were forbidden. Democratic legitimacy, therefore, must be consistent with some injustice as well as some error. However, the fact that some unjust decisions are consistent with democratic procedures and legitimacy does not mean that all are, and it is genuinely hard to see how a policy of outing could be reconciled with the idea that governments must protect the legitimate interests of all citizens.

No amount of voting, for instance, will make 'employment at will' a democratic form of employment contract, given the forms of power

---

[6] My discussion here is a response to a question that David Estlund put to me at the conference 'Facts and Norms', 22–23 August 2013, The University of Copenhagen.

involved in the ability to hire and fire workers at will.[7] Likewise – or so I would suggest – no amount of voting will make 'outing' at will consistent with democratic forms of freedom and equality. The reasons for this are at once simple and complex. They are simple, in so far as such unaccountable power over others more closely resembles the power of an absolute monarch over his/her subjects than the powers appropriate to people who see each other as equal and, therefore, owed an explanation for behaviour that harms them. Hence, as I have argued elsewhere (Lever 2011: chapter 3), inadequate protections for the privacy of American workers, consequent on the use of work contracts that entitle employers to fire workers for 'good reasons, bad reasons and no reason at all', illustrate the importance of distinguishing democratic from undemocratic forms of privacy.

But the reasons why outing and employment at will are undemocratic are complex, as well as simple. They are complex, because democratic government is, itself, a complex political ideal and practice and one that can be instantiated in many ways. It is therefore rare for there to be only one democratically acceptable way to organize or distribute power amongst citizens, whether we consider their relations as voters, as producers and consumers, or as family members. Democratic objections to employment at will, I suspect, do not depend on the thought that it is a particular individual – an 'employer' – who is able to fire you, but on the thought that *no one* should be able to have such untrammelled power over something so critical to well-being and social status as the ability to earn a living. On the other hand, the fact that most employment practices put the ability to hire and fire *in the same hands* and, usually, in the hands of those who supervise and regulate our work lives, clearly exacerbates the undemocratic aspects of employment at will. Hence, centralizing the power to 'out at will', or whenever it might lessen prejudice, by granting that power to a corporate body of some kind, rather than to unaffiliated individuals, is unlikely to alleviate democratic concerns about the powers involved in outing and may, indeed, exacerbate them.

Of course, what powers, in practice, are distributed by legal rights to hire and fire at will, or to disclose sensitive information at will, depend on the context in which employment and outing occur. But even under the most favourable circumstances – a developed welfare state, a lack of stigma attached to unemployment – employment at will involves a dramatic ability to disrupt the lives of workers, their relationships to others, their way of life and their sense of themselves. Under less favourable

---

[7] The following paragraphs draw on the work of Matthew W. Finkin and, in particular, on his 1996 Piper Lecture, published in Finkin 1996: 221–69.

circumstances, the results can be devastating.[8] Likewise, what harms one can actually inflict by outing someone depends very much on the extent to which information disclosed in one context can be reused or broadcast in others, and on the sorts of penalties that exist and are enforced for the misuse of information (Anderson 1999: 139–67). Nonetheless, as I have argued, the nature of the power implicit in outing is usually inconsistent with democratic norms of government, even under favourable circumstances in which the information generated by outing cannot be endlessly used, reused and broadcast forever.

Contra Estlund, then, a democratic vote is *insufficient* to render outing legitimate, given the forms of power over others that it usually involves. Nor is a democratic vote *necessary* to the justification of outing in those cases where democratic concerns for freedom and equality might justify it. We do not need a democratic vote to be justified in publicizing evidence of bribery, corruption or serious illness in relation to powerful figures. Serious ill health in a powerful politician, for example, is a matter of legitimate interest for citizens, in so far as it can affect the outcome of important deliberations, the politician's ability to think calmly in crises and their ability to cope with the stresses and exhaustion that politics at the highest levels often involves. Likewise, it seems perfectly fair for journalists and citizens to ask Tony Blair, then UK Prime Minister, whether he had given his children the combined Mumps Measles and Rubella (or 'German Measles') vaccine – the MMR – given anxious debate around its safety at the time, and Blair's public statements of confidence in it. Were it not for the privacy of his children, I would have thought it legitimate for journalists or citizens actively to seek out such information.

Blair's statement of confidence in the MMR vaccine was not really necessary to allay public anxieties at the time, given the overwhelming weight of medical evidence in its favour, and the possibility of disaggregating the triple vaccine into its component parts so that children did not have to have the injections in one go. There was, therefore, no justification for infringing the privacy of Blair's children in order to allay public anxiety, or to substantiate Blair's readiness to fit actions to words. But it is easy to imagine cases where politicians' claims to privacy would seem less powerful – if, say, Blair had been trying to reassure us about the safety of British beef and its freedom from 'mad cow disease',[9] rather than the safety of a vaccine that could be

---

[8] For an example, see Finkin 1997: 1–23.

[9] 'Mad cow disease' is the colloquial designation of Bovine Spongiform Encephalopathy (BSE), and its human form is a version of Creutzfeldt-Jakob disease. More details about BSE and its impact on the UK can be found at http://en.wikipedia.org/wiki/Bovine_spongiform_encephalopathy.

taken in ways that were not controversial at all. A willingness to eat British beef and to feed it to one's children *would* be an appropriate way of substantiating one's claims, as prime minister, to confidence in its safety – perhaps the only way, in the circumstances, to show that one means what one says. It would therefore be appropriate for the press to ask what the prime minister's family were eating, and to try to find out if no answer were forthcoming, whatever the claims to privacy of the PM's family.

Democratic principles, then, mean that individuals and the press must be free to publish true personal information about politicians, in so far as this bears on their willingness to live by rules that they urge on others, or aim to impose on them. These interests in expressive freedom and in democratic government are *constraints* on the ways that governments can regulate privacy, because they mark the boundaries between democratic and undemocratic forms of politics, rather than forming one democratic choice amongst others. It is therefore wrong to suppose that a democratic conception of privacy means that voting is necessary or sufficient to resolve the ethics of outing. Democracy is not reducible to voting, and our interests in privacy include interests in being seen and treated as the equal of others.

Generalizing from the Sipple case: privacy and the ethics of publication

The Sipple case suggests that democratic concerns for freedom, equality and responsibility mean that people ought to have broad, though not absolute, rights over true information about themselves, whether the point of publicizing that information is to enlighten others, to entertain them or to advance a legitimate moral or political cause. Publicizing sensitive personal information, even if it is true, undermines people's privacy, and threatens their social standing and equality with others. It turns some people into instruments for public amusement or edification regardless of the damage that this may do to their self-respect, their ability to command the respect, trust, affection and loyalty of others, and regardless of its impact on third parties.[10]

---

[10] For two recent, egregious cases of public insensitivity to privacy see Laurie Shrage's discussion of the expectation that Caster Semanya's medical results would be publicly released, and the British case of the former boxing promoter Kellie Maloney, who was forced to go public with news of her sex-change operation after threats from a newspaper to 'out' her. See www.theguardian.com/sport/2014/aug/13/kellie-maloney-public-life-woman-newspaper-boxing-promoter and Laurie Shrage 2012: 225–47.

Such publication, we are often told, is justified by the moral failings of the victim, whether those failings involve acts of hypocrisy, ingratitude, sexual infidelity, attention-seeking or, indeed, illegality (Dacre 2008).[11] But while our interests in controlling sensitive information may be self-serving, there is more to our interests in privacy than that. Control of personal information enables us to protect the feelings of other people, as Sipple's case shows, and to respond to their needs and concerns, even when we do not share them. Such control enables us to act with tact, discretion, respect, and out of a sense of duty, whether or not confidentiality protects our own interests. It enables us to distinguish what is owed to those who have cared for us from what is owed to those towards whom we have no special duties. In short our interests in confidentiality are not reducible to interests in avoiding embarrassment, pain, shame or indignity, but include interests in meeting the needs and claims of others for whom, with all their limitations of imagination and sympathy, we may feel love, as well as obligation.

Protection for privacy, therefore, can promote personal as well as political freedom and our ability to form a variety of personal and political ties to others. Whether our expressive interests are artistic, scientific, sexual or religious – and whether our medium of communication is gestures and behaviour or words and pictures – protection for privacy protects our ability to explore the world and our place within it, and to communicate what we have found to others without exaggerating its importance or having to vouch for its truth, beauty or utility. Democratic claims to privacy for expressive and creative activities, as Warren and Brandeis recognized (1890: 193) do not depend on their economic or artistic value, nor on Millian concerns with the conditions necessary for genius to flourish (Mill 1869).[12] Rather, they reflect the claims of even ordinary,

[11] Paul Dacre rightly complains that Britain's libel laws constantly threaten newspapers and journalists with bankruptcy for publishing matters of legitimate public interest. 'Today, newspapers, even wealthy ones like the *Mail*, think long and hard before contesting actions, even if they know they are in the right, for fear of the ruinous financial implications. For the local press, such actions are now out of the question. Instead, they stump up some cash, money they can't afford, to settle as quickly as possible, to avoid court actions – which, if they were to lose, could, in some cases, close them.' However, he also appears to suppose that it is the role of the media to police the nation's morals, and therefore takes it as self-evident that consensual sadomasochistic sex is so evidently 'perverted, depraved, the very abrogation of civilised behaviour' that newspapers ought to be entitled to publish accounts of that behaviour, if they can persuade one of the participants to furnish the salacious details for pay (Dacre 2008).

[12] John Stuart Mill's concern with the need to protect genius in order to ensure social progress underpins his utilitarian justification for protecting the liberty 'of tastes and

unremarkable, individuals freely to develop and exercise their expressive capacities and to do so as the political equals – not the superiors or subordinates – of others.

Rights to privacy are not absolute, however; nor do they invariably trump rights to freedom of expression if, and when, the two conflict. If you are well known and obviously ill, for example, you can expect to be the object of gossip and speculation. But it hardly follows that you should therefore have to anticipate what, now, is almost inevitable: the public broadcasting of such gossip, and its treatment as a means to fame and fortune by strangers. Likewise, if you are well known and seen to be staggering around drunk, or hanging out with people who are notorious, you can expect to be regarded unfavourably by those in the know. As John Stuart Mill emphasized, such knowledge and personal condemnation is the inevitable consequence of social life in a free society (Mill 1869: chapter 4). What is not inevitable, however, is the industrialization of gossip and of its marketing to a mass audience as a form of entertainment, titillation and education. Such industrialized gossip is hard to justify morally, even if we are inclined to think that it should be legal. As Stanley Benn argued, it is wrong to treat an entertainer's life simply as a source of entertainment (Benn 1984: 233). Doing so wrongly treats the entertainer as a person with no feelings that can be hurt, and no aspirations or plans that can be harmed by our intrusive attention. So whatever legitimate purposes the publication of gossip serves can usually be met without humiliating and degrading people, however foolish or complicit they may have been in their humiliation.

Privacy, freedom of expression and the press

It would therefore be wrong to confuse freedom of the press with freedom of expression, or to suppose that privacy and freedom of expression are antagonists, locked in a zero sum game, in which gains to the one can only come at the expense of the other. Our interests in being able to express ourselves freely, and to communicate with others, are varied and not reducible to interests in untrammelled access to other people's ideas and experiences. Protection for people's privacy, therefore, means that

pursuits' in chapter 3 of *On Liberty* (1869). In essence, the privacy claims of ordinary people therefore depend on the conditions necessary for genius to flourish. Brandeis' approach to the protection of privacy is, therefore, consistent with democratic principles in ways that Mill's is not, important though both of their arguments are to any democratic conception of privacy.

it should be legally possible to demand and win damages for wrongful invasions of privacy, and that the press should be regulated in a way that respects people's claims to privacy. Hence we cannot resolve conflicts over the respective claims of privacy and press freedom by assuming that the one is intrinsically more valuable than the other.[13] Instead, we will have to identify and evaluate the expressive and privacy interests at stake when conflict arises, bearing in mind that if the right to publish in a democracy does not depend on literary, moral or political merit, respect for privacy is not just for the virtuous, sensible or the uninteresting. In some cases this means that autobiographical accounts of people's lives will have claims to invade the privacy of other people, which will be lacking in journalistic and biographical accounts of seemingly similar subject matter.

There is, for example, little to recommend the average 'kiss and tell' story, recounting the one-night stand, or lengthy affair of someone who is not famous with someone who is. The format does not lend itself to much variation or reflection, but provides an excellent vehicle for personal grudges, self-justification and self-congratulation. However, citizens must be free publicly to describe their lives and affairs, and to use their lives as art, as science and as an example to others. Because our lives are bound up in the lives of others, it follows that if we are legally entitled to describe and publicize the details of our lives, there is much about the lives of others that we must be legally entitled to publish also, and that we must be able to publish without their permission. Otherwise, most people would find it nearly impossible freely to describe, discuss and publicly to explore the significant events, relationships, constraints and opportunities in their lives. It must therefore be legal to publish stories, autobiographies and reports that are of questionable quality and taste, and that

---

[13] My views on this question fit perfectly with those of Eric Barendt and Adam Moore, who strongly criticize the American constitutional tradition of giving near absolute weight to freedom of expression, and their preference for the European Human Rights approach, which treats privacy and freedom of expression as rights of equal intrinsic importance, whose relative strength must be determined by the facts of a particular case. Thus, Barendt considers that 'the case for detailed, ad hoc balancing may be stronger in privacy cases than it is in libel, because of the infinite variety of ways in which privacy may be infringed' (2007: 244), and Moore (2010: 134) claims that 'The ascendancy of speech protection in the legal realm … is due to an expansive and unjustified view of the value or primacy of free expression' and (2010: 149): 'On my view, speech that is low-value and violates informational privacy rights should be more readily liable to prior restraint and, once broadcast, should expose its publishers to civil and criminal damages. Given that we have no general moral right not to be offended, low-value speech that simply offends would still be protected.'

exhibit moral failings such as selfishness, complacency, insincerity and dishonesty, so long as they are not libellous, defamatory or extortionate.

'Kiss and tell' stories, I would suggest, are an example where the privacy interests of those who wish to avoid publication are unlikely to justify legal constraints on a person's ability to publish 'their story', and to profit financially from the legal freedom to do so. Even if their moral or aesthetic quality, on the whole, is poor, the subject matter of these stories – what it is like to enter a privileged social circle and to be the lover of someone famous when one is oneself unknown – is a legitimate object of personal reflection and public communication in a democracy. It is therefore difficult to see how kiss and tell stories could be made illegal on democratic principles, simply because their first-person narratives are unlikely to meet with the approval of one of the parties to the 'kiss'.

Protection for privacy still has a role in determining other aspects of the publication of 'kiss and tell' stories, even when it is insufficient to prevent publication. For example, it may be desirable to limit how intensely, and how frequently, journalists are allowed to pursue and try to question third parties to such stories, such as children and spouses, even if this makes it more difficult to question the story's author and its main subject. In the UK, for example, the families of those caught up in a media frenzy suffer from press behaviour – packs of journalists and photographers following them around; endless ringing of their doorbells and of their phones; the inability to leave the house without being surrounded by a scrum of journalists – that looks very much like harassment and that is likely to be frightening for children, and even for the adults involved. No one's right to self-expression justifies such behaviour; nor is there any 'right to publish', or to know what people are feeling or thinking, that does so either.

It may be also desirable for newspapers to report the sums they offered and subsequently paid for their 'kiss and tell' stories, to inform their readers whether they were the ones who solicited the story, or merely agreed to publish it, and so on. Were these standard practices, readers would be better placed to judge how far newspapers are being used to carry out a grudge or feud, and how actively they are instigating stories that, under the guise of autobiography, publicly describe and evaluate the private life of well-known figures. Reporting the fees that such stories command may increase their supply for a while, and the invasions of privacy that accompany them. But it is public knowledge that selling one's story of sex with the famous is a way to make money and, even, to launch a career, so there is no reason why newspapers should not disclose the sums involved and the way that they are negotiated. Doing so would promote public understanding

of the economics of a lucrative branch of journalism, and would make it easier to understand the market price, if not the value, of privacy.

However, autobiographical justifications for publishing privacy-invasive
material do not automatically apply to third-person publications, or publications by strangers, whether biographical or journalistic. Where celebrities
do not wish to relinquish their privacy, and have taken steps to secure it, it is
hard to see why journalists should be entitled actively to pursue them, and to
publish stories about their sex lives. Such stories may be entertaining, even
informative, but curiosity about the sex lives of consenting adults cannot
explain why people who are otherwise entitled to privacy should be deprived
of it. Hence, the reasons why it should be legal to publish kiss and tell stories, invasive of people's privacy though they are, do not apply to those cases
where none of the people involved wish to relinquish their privacy.

This is not because autobiography is more important, more expressive or more interesting than biography, nor that it is morally superior to
write about oneself than about other people. Often the reverse is true. Any
democratic conception of freedom of expression will provide significant
protections for journalistic and biographical accounts of people's ideas,
actions and experiences, and the importance of protecting such expression will very likely justify limits on the privacy of politicians and of other
people who hold positions of political power and influence.[14]

In writing your authorized biography, for example, it may be appropriate for me, with your consent, to discuss a formative love affair even if it has
hitherto been secret, and the other partner wishes it to remain so. Whatever
the ethical considerations of a biographer in such circumstances, it should
surely be legal for me, with your consent, publicly to report experiences,
sentiments and beliefs that you are entitled to publish yourself. Likewise
for my unauthorized biography of you: I should be legally entitled to publish, with their consent, intimate information and opinions that others are
entitled to publish as part of the story of their lives.[15] However, when it
comes to stories about the sex lives of celebrities or would-be celebrities, as

---

[14] For a helpful discussion of privacy for politicians and one that pays attention to questions of power and responsibility within different government bodies and administrative
agencies, see Thompson 1987: chapter 5. See also Barendt 2007: 139, 231, 241–4.

[15] For an interesting philosophical discussion of the ethics of biography and, in particular, the ethics of focusing attention on the sex lives of people famous for other things,
see Susan Mendus (2008: 299–314). This is a critique of Thomas Nagel's 'The Central
Question' (2005), a book review of Nicola Lacey's biography of Hart in the *LRB* available
at www.lrb.co.uk/v27/n03/thomas-nagel/the-central-questions. I share Mendus' doubts
about an author's work 'floating free' from their life, as Nagel would have it, and her more
general worries about Nagel's ideas on the public/private distinction. But that does not

I have argued, people have a stronger claim to publish stories about their own lives, even if this means publishing details about the lives of others, than they do to publish stories about people who, however fascinating, have neither the desire nor the obligation to relinquish their privacy.[16]

Conclusion

In this chapter I have argued that people have important personal and political interests in confidentiality, which are intimately related to democratic ideas about the way power should be distributed, used and justified in a society. On that view, ordinary people, with their familiar moral failings and limited, though real, capacities for sensitivity, altruism and wisdom, are entitled to govern themselves and, in so doing, to take responsibility for the lives of others. This suggests that they are not in need of constant hectoring or supervision in order to act well, although they are rightly accountable to appropriate public authorities for their exercise of public powers, their use of public resources and their respect for others' rights. Hence, as we have seen, people's claims to confidentiality do not depend on the usefulness of that confidentiality to others, or on the moral, aesthetic, or even the political and economic worth, of the things that they wish to do with it.

References

Allen, A. 1998. *Uneasy Access: Privacy for Women in a Free Society*. New Jersey: Rowman and Littlefield.

Anderson, D. A. 1999. 'The Failure of American Privacy Law', in Markesinis, B. (ed.) *Protecting Privacy: The Clifford Chance Lectures Vol.4*. Oxford University Press, pp. 139–67.

Barendt, E. 2007. *Freedom of Speech*. Oxford University Press.

Benn, S. 1984. 'Privacy, Freedom and Respect for Persons', in Schoeman, F. D. (ed.) *Philosophical Dimensions of Privacy: An Anthology*. Cambridge University Press, pp. 223–44.

mean Nagel is wrong to worry about the ethics of dwelling on the sex life of someone, like Wittgenstein or Russell, who were our near contemporaries and were entitled, and chose, to keep this aspect of their lives private. It therefore matters that Hart's widow authorized the disclosure of information about Hart's sexuality in ways that Wittgenstein and, seemingly, Russell did not. See Joanna Ryan's letter in response to Nagel's review of Nicola Lacey's biography of Hart in the *London Review of Books* 'Letters', 27.4 (Ryan 2005).

[16] See Davies (2010). On 3 October 2010 the *News of the World* printed an apology to Vanessa Perroncel for invading her private life, and accepted that its claims that she had had an affair with the footballer John Terry were untrue. See also Greenslade (2010).

Brown, M. 2009. 'PCC Chairman Warns of European Threat to Press Freedom', 13 January. Accessed from www.theguardian.com/media/2009/jan/13/pcc-chairman-christopher-meyer-press-freedom.

Cohen, J. 1993. 'Freedom of expression', *Philosophy and Public Affairs* 22 (3): 207–63.

2009. *Philosophy, Politics, Democracy: Selected Essays*. Cambridge, MA: Harvard University Press.

Dacre, P. 2008. 'The Threat to our Press', *Guardian*, 10 November. Accessed from www.theguardian.com/media/2008/nov/10/paul-dacre-press-threats.

Davies, N. 2010. 'Exclusive: Inquiry over Vanessa Perroncel phone-tapping allegations'. Accessed from www.theguardian.com/media/2010/apr/10/newspapers-phone-hacking-inquiry.

Finkin, M. W. 1996. 'Employee privacy, American values and the law', *Chicago-Kent Law Review* 72: 221–69.

1997. 'Discharge and disgrace: a comment on the "urge to treat people as objects"', *Employee Rights and Employment Policy Journal* 1(1): 1–23.

Greenslade, R. 2010. 'Two Newspapers Apologise to Vanessa Perroncel For Breaching Her Privacy', *Guardian Newspaper Media*. Accessed from www.theguardian.com/media/greenslade/2010/oct/07/newsoftheworld-john-terry.

Lever, A. 2011. *On Privacy*. New York: Routledge.

2014a. *A Democratic Conception of Privacy*. London: Authorhouse.

2014b. 'Book review. response to James B Rule', *Law, Culture and Humanities* 10(1): 188–90.

2015. 'Privacy and Democracy: What the Secret Ballot Reveals', *Law, Culture and Humanities* 11(2).

Mendus, S. 2008. "Private Faces in Public Places," in Kramer, M. H., Grant, C., Colburn, B. and Hatzistavrou, A. (eds.) *The Legacy of H.L.A. Hart: Legal, Political and Moral Philosophy*. Oxford University Press, pp. 299–314.

Mill, J. S. 1869. *On Liberty*. London: Longman, Roberts and Green.

Mohr, R., 1992. *Gay Ideas: Outing and Other Controversies*. Boston, MA: Beacon Press.

Moore, A. D. 2010. *Privacy Rights: Moral and Legal Foundations*. Pennsylvania University Press.

Nagel, T. 2005. 'The Central Question', *London Review of Books* 27(3): 12–13. Accessed from www.lrb.co.uk/v27/n03/thomas-nagel/the-central-questions.

Rozenberg, J. 2005. *Privacy and the Press*. Oxford University Press.

Rusbridger, A. 2004. 'The Fame Game', *Guardian*, 27 March, Books. Accessed from www.theguardian.com/books/2004/mar/27/highereducation.news.

Ryan, J. 2005. 'Letters', *London Review of Books* 27(4). Accessed from www.lrb.co.uk/v27/n04/letters.

Shrage, L. 2012. 'Does the government need to know your sex?', *The Journal of Political Philosophy* 20(2): 225–47.

Thompson, D. F. 1987. *Political Ethics and Public Office.* Cambridge, MA: Harvard University Press.

Warren, S. D. and Brandeis, L. D. 1890. 'The right to privacy: (the implicit made explicit)', *Harvard law Review* 4: 193–220.

10

How much privacy for public officials?

DOROTA MOKROSINSKA

Are the private affairs of public officials a matter of public concern? Imagine that a cabinet member in his off-duty capacity makes a discriminatory remark about a minority group. Perhaps he makes a racist joke when at the dinner table with his family. Is the citizenry entitled to know? We do not have to resort to imagined cases. In 1976 the press revealed that President Carter's nominee to the position of Attorney General, Bell Griffin, was a member of private clubs that had a policy of segregated membership excluding blacks, Jews and other minorities. Following that revelation, his nomination became an object of controversy (Thompson 1987: 130). Was the press entitled to reveal Griffin's private club memberships? Was the public entitled to know?

The issue of privacy for office holders has recently come into public focus following the 2014 ruling of the European Union Court of Justice that recognized the "right to be forgotten," stating that search engine companies such as Google or Microsoft "can be made to remove irrelevant or excessive personal information from search engine results." At the time of writing, Google has received over 70,000 takedown requests including requests from (former) politicians (Russon 2014). One concern raised about that ruling is that it will allow politicians to whitewash their records, removing embarrassing information from the public view. From that perspective, the ruling has been subject to severe criticism in the media as a blow against people's right to know: "A politician who was a member of a white supremacist group ... shouldn't be allowed to remove all traces of that information from Google before running for parliament or prime minister" (Keating 2014). Whereas the Court explicitly admitted that, in deciding what to remove, search engines must also have regard to the public interest, the Court provided no guidelines as to what information about politicians' lives is of public interest. In the light of this ruling, the debate over how to draw the line between the private lives of office holders and the public right to know has become pressing.

Academic discussions of the privacy of office holders are few. The prevailing view is that citizens are entitled to know about those personal matters of office holders that are relevant for assessing their (past or likely future) performance in office (Dobel 1998; Thompson 2005). Accessibility of such information is a condition of the political accountability of government officials. On this view, citizens are entitled to know about the racist joke incident if such a remark is relevant for assessing the cabinet member's performance in office.

Is it? There are two issues here. First, does the job description of a cabinet member extend to the remarks he makes at the dinner table with his family? This issue marks a disagreement about what the job of a cabinet member really is. Some think that public offices possess a symbolic dimension that requires office holders to display character traits that align with a set of politically correct values also in their private conduct; others find this conception of public office too demanding (Dobel 1998: 135; Thompson 2005: 237). Second, is there an empirical correlation between making discriminatory remarks during a family dinner and a capacity to carry out policies implementing equality? Do probity or failings in personal life portend probity or failings in office? There is no convincing evidence either way. As Dennis Thompson observed, there are enough examples of government officials who led impeccable private lives and performed poorly in office, and officials whose private lives were the object of public scandals but who did an excellent job in office (Thompson 2005: 236). In the face of these problems, the prevailing view that the scope of public officials' privacy depends on what information is relevant for assessing their job performance does not offer much guidance in political practice.

One radical response to this problem comes from Frederick Schauer (2000). If no correct standards of relevance can be identified, he argues, each view deserves to be taken seriously and, hence, we have reason to disclose all information about office holders that citizens happen to deem relevant. Schauer presents it as a matter of liberal-democratic commitment to equality. The idea that all citizens have an equal say in choosing their representatives commits us, in his view, to giving equal weight to their informational preferences and providing them with information they judge relevant to their voting decisions. Hence a voter who wishes to have information about an office holder's marital fidelity or drinking habits has a right to obtain such information, because "the arguments that militate in favor of the right to vote … are likely to militate as well in favor of an interest in obtaining the information that is relevant to voting" (Schauer 2000: 300–1). The liberal-democratic commitment to freedom offers, in Schauer's view, an additional support for this position: informational preferences that many of us may find irrelevant or morally problematic, he writes, "may, nevertheless, have to be indulged for exactly the same reasons that indulging preferences that some of us find wrong is central to autonomy more generally" (Schauer 2000: 309).

In this chapter I argue, contra Schauer, that the renouncement of the privacy of office holders undermines the liberal-democratic commitments to equality and freedom rather than aligns with them. To pursue this claim, I need to situate the role of privacy in liberal-democratic politics.

Privacy in politics – I

Most defenses of privacy in liberal-democratic politics are of an instrumental character. With regard to the privacy of office holders, the argument is that keeping personal matters of office holders private may contribute to reasoned political discourse. Dennis Thompson and Thomas Nagel argue that the preoccupation with the personal affairs of office holders may detract from policy issues and burden discussions on matters that are the proper object of political regulation with unnecessary disputes. Targeting the extensive media coverage of Bill Clinton's sexual affairs, Thompson emphasized the negative consequences of publicizing the personal lives of office holders:

> Information about private life tends to dominate other forms of information and to lower the overall quality of public discourse and democratic accountability … [T]he Clinton–Lewinsky affair dominated media discussion of not only important new policy proposals on social security, health insurance, and campaign finance reform but also attempts to explain the US position on Iraq in preparation for military action.
>
> (Thompson 2005: 233)

Nagel resorted to similar observations to argue that "[t]he public–private boundary keeps the public domain free of disruptive material" (Nagel 1998: 20). Next to sexual affairs of office holders, disruptive material that the privacy norms are meant to keep out of the political domain, Nagel argued, includes "private racism, sexism, homophobia, religious and ethnic bigotry, sexual puritanism, and other such private pleasures" (Nagel 1998: 30). As he put it:

> There are enough issues that have to be fought out in the public sphere, issues of justice, economics, of security, of defense, of the definition and protection of public goods … The insistence on securing more agreement

in attitudes than we need for these purposes … just raises the social stakes
unnecessarily.

(Nagel 1998: 27, 30)

This instrumental approach to the role of privacy in politics is subject
to two problems. First, it is not clear whether privacy plays this instrumental role in all liberal-democratic societies. Nagel's and Thompson's
arguments are anchored in the historical and cultural contingencies of
specific societies, such as the excessive interest of the American public in
the irregularities in the sexual lives of politicians. To the extent that such
features are characteristic of some societies but not others, these defenses
of privacy are of limited scope. Second, on the instrumental approach, the
political status of privacy is vulnerable. Privacy as a political right does
not stand on its own but only as a way of securing the quality of political
discourse. We could do without privacy if other and better ways to secure
the quality of political discourse were found.

In the liberal-democratic tradition there are approaches to privacy
that move beyond the instrumental approach, such as those of Corey
Brettschneider (2007) and Annabelle Lever (2012; 2015).[1] Privacy, in their
view, is of intrinsic rather than merely instrumental value in that it is
implicated in the foundational value commitments of liberal-democratic
governance, namely freedom and equality. These approaches, however, do not address the privacy of government officials. In what follows,
I investigate the link between privacy on the one hand and, on the other
hand, freedom and equality with the aim of addressing this issue. I place
my argument in the framework of political liberalism. Drawing on previous work (Mokrosinska 2014), I present privacy as constitutive of the
liberal-democratic model of political legitimacy as based on the idea of
public justification. The concept of public justification emphasizes the
significance of disagreement between citizens as regards conceptions of
the good life in determining which moral principles are appropriate for
governing the political domain. The concept of public justification refers
to principles that are neutral between the different moral views about the
good life that divide citizens. My argument links the concept of privacy to
the concept of public justification as understood in this way. I employ this
argument to fix the boundaries of the domain of privacy that is internal to
liberal politics, and to distinguish between those personal affairs of government officials that are a matter of public concern and those that are not.

---

[1] Moore offers another non-instrumental account of privacy (Moore 2000). Given that his
approach does not fit the political liberalism framework, I do not address it here.

In investigating the place of privacy in political liberalism, my aim is not to defend political liberalism. It should prove interesting to see, however, that this prominent political theory is committed to acknowledging privacy as an internal element of political life and to investigate the implications of the liberal account of privacy for the privacy of office holders.

Public justification

Much of political sociology views the political domain as a domain of power relations (see Lukes 1978). However, while descriptively correct, this account is incomplete. To the extent that political relations are relations of power, power is exercised in the name of a collective, which implies that there are reasons that justify the exercise of power in the eyes of its subjects. To admit such reasons into an account of political relations is to say that political relations are not merely relations of power, but relations in which the exercise of power enjoys public justification.

Public justification is at the core of the liberal concept of political relations. The idea that "the social order must be one that can be justified to the people who live under it" is among the theoretical foundations of liberal political thought (Waldron 1993: 57–8; Rawls 1996: 137). The lack of public justification deprives an association of political legitimacy and, indeed, of a political character because, for liberals, the lack of public justification characterizes the non-political condition of a state of nature: "The moral flaw of the state of nature ... is that we act without [public] justification" (Gaus 1996: 182).

There are a number of competing accounts of public justification in liberal thought (Gaus 2003). For my purposes, it will suffice to identify its most frequently recurring features. First, public justification does not refer to just any set of beliefs supporting government action that may prevail among individuals in a given historical period. Public justification is a response to the disappearance of such widely shared beliefs and a way to bypass disagreement between individuals who hold competing views of the good life. As Charles Larmore puts it, public justification refers to "principles of association which individuals have reason to affirm together despite deep substantial disagreements setting them apart" (Larmore 2003: 380). Exactly which issues of mutual concern should be decided by an appeal to principles that all can reasonably accept is a matter of controversy between liberals. On the classic Rawlsian approach, the requirement of public justification is limited to "constitutional essentials and questions of basic justice" (Rawls 1996: 227–30). Others, like Larmore, claim that the rationale for public justification requires applying public justification to issues of daily politics including, for example, issues such as education, housing, city planning and land use, the organization of health care or employment, tax regulations, investment incentives, transportation policy or regulation of the entertainment industry. Given that the point of public justification is to legitimize the use of coercion to those subject to it, almost all state action is in need of public justification, since almost all state action is backed by coercive power (Larmore 1999: 607–8, cited in Quong 2013: 7). Although I cannot discuss this position here, I will endorse it for the remainder of the chapter.

Second, various accounts of public justification converge on the rationale for seeking public justification. Why bypass disagreement? For liberals, disagreement involves two dangers. First, the diversity of private judgments poses a practical challenge to the stability of cooperation between individuals. From this perspective, public justification creates the conditions for peaceful coexistence and stable cooperation between individuals who profoundly disagree. Second, disagreement is a moral problem because it undermines the equal moral status and moral sovereignty of individuals. When there are several competing conceptions of the good in the community, unilateral enforcement by an individual of her favored view is inevitable. However, such a unilateral imposition infringes on the equal freedom of those who hold competing views (Gaus 1996: 182–4). From this perspective, public justification creates relations of equal freedom, moral symmetry and mutual respect between individuals.

I have isolated the concept of public justification as a core concept in organizing the liberal model of political association. By defining the political realm in terms of public justification, liberals construe politics as "the final recourse for people who cannot agree" (Macedo 1991: 53). Does this model commit liberals to grant any special status to privacy in politics?

Privacy in politics – II

For liberals, the political realm is the common ground upon which people, despite deep differences setting them apart, can stand together in a way that enables stable cooperation and equal freedom between them. Not every personal view of the good life, not every lifestyle, commitment or action, and not every piece of personal information has a place in the political realm defined as common ground. Some lifestyles and commitments, for example religious beliefs or sexual morality, concern issues that are objects of irresolvable controversy. Public exposure of contentious issues would drag us into disagreement and destroy rather than establish common ground. Information searches meant to bring such personal commitments under collective attention would have a similar effect. To establish common ground, the material brought under collective attention should allow the people concerned to find principles with which to conduct their lives together and bypass their disagreements. Therefore, the liberal commitment to public justification constrains the material that individuals and groups acting in their political capacity bring to the attention of others. First, this commitment limits the considerations that individuals might wish to employ in deciding matters of mutual concern (e.g. when casting votes in elections or pressing group demands on common resources) to considerations that reasonable others could accept. Second, it requires that individuals engaged in the processes of decision-making that concern the organization of their life together refrain from pressing claims in terms that others could not accept.

Based on the understanding of public justification outlined above, the commitment to public justification in politics rules out certain personal commitments and actions as objects of mutual interference among individuals acting in their political capacity. Similarly, it rules out certain personal information as an object of mutual scrutiny. On pain of endangering politics as a common ground between people who profoundly disagree about matters of worldviews, lifestyles, beliefs and commitments, such material, and the corresponding information, should be withheld or, if known, left unacknowledged. In sorting out which material is appropriate and inappropriate for individuals to introduce into the political forum, public justification sets out rules of concealment and disclosure between individuals acting in their political capacity. Insofar as this requires that individuals withhold certain personal material, I submit, political relations based on public justification involve privacy arrangements. Here I refer to these arrangements as liberal privacy. Insofar as these rules prescribe withholding personal commitments, views of the good life and lifestyle, they are decisional privacy arrangements. Insofar as they prescribe withholding certain personal information, they are informational privacy arrangements.

The depoliticization and privatization of substantive views about which citizens disagree could be taken to suggest that all disagreement is relegated off liberal politics. This is not the case. What is relegated off politics is an appeal to reasons that others cannot accept, and not all cases of disagreement are of that sort. Now it is possible that people disagree but appeal to mutually acceptable reasons. The disagreement arises here from what Rawls called the burdens of judgment: due to the complexity of evidence or the variety of life experiences that bear on judgment, individuals may interpret, apply and rank reasons differently (Rawls 1996: 54–8). Insofar as individuals formulate their conflicting positions in terms of reasons that all sides can accept, reasonable disagreement properly belongs to the political domain. A classic example is the discussion on abortion, in which both pro-life and pro-choice advocates formulate their claims in terms of reasons that their adversaries can accept, namely the value of life and the value of freedom, respectively.

What is private in liberal politics?

I have argued that defining the political realm in terms of public justification as outlined above commits liberals to say that privacy arrangements are internal to liberal politics. What, then, is private in liberal politics?

Certain spheres of activity, such as the sphere of domestic life, have been traditionally marked as private.[2] The realm of privacy I have isolated in liberal politics is not defined in terms of any substantial concerns. The border between the political and the private is constructed out of reasons that people can and cannot reasonably accept as governing their life together; that is, reasons that meet and fail to meet the test of public justification. Public justification sorts out the material that falls in and out of the political realm. Failures to provide reasons that others can reasonably accept therefore identify the material that counts as private from the perspective of liberal politics.

What people can and cannot reasonably accept is a matter of well-known controversy among liberals. However, there is consensus that one fails public justification if one rejects the aim of pressing one's claims on others in terms of reasons that others could accept. Claims that fail public justification in this way are, in the liberal idiom, unreasonable (Rawls 1996: 49). The unreasonable, then, outlines a domain that, on pain of violating the integrity of liberal politics, should be held back from the political forum and, if known, left unacknowledged. Generically, all views that deny the equal status and freedom of some (groups of) individuals fall into this class. Race and gender discrimination, say, are examples of unreasonable commitments and actions. Incapable of organizing the common life, such views

---

[2] Marking the domestic sphere as private has been the subject of feminist critique (MacKinnon 1989; Pateman 1989).

should be confined to private quarters. Appealing to such views in political arguments injects material into the political realm that violates equal freedom and endangers liberal politics as a common ground. The same holds for probing into people's personal affairs with the aim of placing their unreasonable views in the spotlight of collective attention and judgment: when unreasonable views are kept private, the integrity of liberal politics demands that they be left unattended. In this second sense, the privatization of the unreasonable is a version of the liberal tolerance paradox: just as the commitment to equal freedom commits liberals to tolerate the intolerant as long as their intolerant views are kept off the political realm (Rawls 1971: 220), so it requires them to tolerate the unreasonable as long as their unreasonable views are kept off the political realm and do not influence it.

A qualification is in order. I have said that the integrity of liberal politics presupposes a domain of privacy that removes from the collective attention material that is incompatible with the commitment to equal freedom, such as racism or sexism. By removing such commitments from the collective attention, decisional privacy serves liberal politics as a common ground, as does informational privacy, by removing from the public forum corresponding information that is dysfunctional to it. Is this argument not a plea to protect racists, for example, making them free to engage in acts of violence against another racial group? Or to make sexists free to engage in acts of discrimination against women? Does it not commit us to grant privacy protection to environments in which they can engage, undisturbed, in hate speech? In response to this concern, recall that liberals ascribe priority to political rights and duties over other commitments that individuals may have (Larmore 1990: 349–51; Rawls 1996: 30–1). This implies that, whatever private commitments individuals might hold, violation of others' political rights by exercising private commitments is never private. Thus, insofar as adherence to private commitments leads to discrimination in a political sphere, liberals do not divest themselves of the right to interfere (Hartley and Watson 2010: 20). The same holds for cases in which the pursuit of matters classified as private causes harm to others: in the spirit of John Stuart Mill's harm principle, liberals are prepared to allow the state to intrude in order to prevent harm that individuals cause to others. If no harm or rights violation is involved and the unreasonable is kept out of the political realm, however, surveillance or interference is unjustified.

I have argued above that privacy is implicated in the concept of public justification and that privacy is, therefore, internal to liberal politics. The object of privacy is material that is incapable of public justification. One class of material that should be kept private for the sake of the integrity of liberal politics is the unreasonable. However, the scope of failures of public justification is broader than the one sketched here, and so is the scope of privacy in liberal politics.

Beyond the fixed core of liberal privacy

Failures of public justification are not confined to renouncing the aim of justification. One person may strive to justify her claims to others but fail nonetheless. This is the case when the justification one offers appeals to beliefs that others, who adhere to different worldviews, cannot be expected to endorse. For liberals, substantive claims failing public justification in this way should not be invoked in the political decision-making process. Their proper place is in the privacy of personal or associational life, but not in the realm of liberal citizenship. In effect, many substantive beliefs and commitments, important though they are to people's self-understanding, will be depoliticized and set aside as private issues. Exactly what material is depoliticized and set off as private depends on the model of public justification one endorses.

There are two general approaches to public justification (Chambers 2010). On the first approach, public justification is a constraint on the content of reasons to which individuals can appeal in the political domain; it admits only those substantive views upon which all reasonable worldviews could converge (Ackerman 1989). The substantive views that divide individuals fail the public justification test and should be set aside as private:

> When you and I learn that we disagree about one or another dimension
> of the moral truth, we should say nothing at all about this disagreement
> and put the moral ideas that divide us off the conversational agenda of
> the liberal state. In restraining ourselves in this way, we need not lose the
> chance to talk to one another about our deepest moral disagreements in
> countless other, more *private* contexts.

> (Ackerman 1989: 16, emphasis added)

On this content-oriented model of public justification, in a society characterized by pluralism and disagreement religious beliefs or sexual morality are granted the status of privacy: given that they are the object of disagreement, they fail the public justification test. Privacy insulates such matters from public exposure, scrutiny and interference: they should be held back from the political forum and, if known, left unacknowledged.

The same holds for other material about which people, who adhere to different worldviews, can disagree.

On the second approach, public justification, rather than being a restriction on the content of reasons, is a constraint on the process of reasoning whereby citizens arrive at substantive decisions (Chambers 2010). What material is excluded from the political forum depends on the manner in which people engage with each other's arguments and respond to them. As one exponent of this approach argues, what material is let in and out of the political forum depends on (1) whether objections based on public reasons are advanced against appealing to it in political decision-making processes and (2) whether there is any convincing way to answer these objections (Lafont 2009: 132). For example, "citizens can publicly advocate for a ban on same-sex marriage on the basis of religious reasons against homosexuality," provided that they address "any objections against such policy based on the political value of equal treatment. Unless next time around they are willing to accept unequal treatment themselves, they must come up with a convincing explanation of how is it that 'separate but equal' is an acceptable policy as regards this group of citizens but not others" (Lafont 2008). In this procedure-oriented model of public justification, then, citizens cannot determine in advance what material is capable and incapable of justification; that depends on what reasons have survived the scrutiny of public deliberation. Thus, appeals to religious beliefs in advocating a ban on same-sex marriage are depoliticized and set off as private only if citizens advancing religious reasons against homosexuality fail to answer objections that such a policy violates the political value of equal treatment. If no objections are raised, or if the objections are answered convincingly, the political rationale for privatizing these issues is absent and no privacy considerations insulate them from the public gaze (Lafont 2009: 132).

I have argued that the liberal model of political relations relies on a boundary between the private and the political. The boundary tracks the distinction between reasons that can or cannot reasonably be accepted by people who are motivated to justify to one another their claims to power. With respect to the scope of liberal privacy three more comments are in place.

First, the circumstances in which the norms of liberal privacy obtain correspond to the range of application of public justification. Here, following Larmore, I said that the rationale for public justification commits us to say that the requirement of public justification binds in matters of daily politics and not only with respect to the political fundamentals as suggested by Rawls. Adopted for the purposes of my argument, this position implies that the norms of privacy bind in an equally broad political spectrum.

Second, as with public justification, the norms of liberal privacy do not bind individuals in the non-political sphere of what Rawls called the "background culture" of civil society, that is, the culture of "daily life, of its many associations: churches and universities, learned and scientific societies, and clubs and teams" and professional groups (Rawls 1996: 220). As long as individuals act in civil society, unreasonable and comprehensive personal beliefs failing the public justification test need not be kept private (they may be public with respect to the members of a given group or association that share them). Their status in the non-political domain of civil society is not determined by the political account of privacy I outline in this chapter. In that regard, the traditional theories of privacy (for example, those defending privacy in terms of individual autonomy).

Finally, within their domain of application, norms of privacy bind equally on all individuals acting in their political capacities, both citizens and representatives. This is because, following Rawls (Rawls 1996: 220), the requirement of public justification binds on all individuals equally; the norms of privacy implicated in public justification reflect that.[3]

How much privacy for public officials?

Having argued that privacy is internal to liberal politics, I return to the debate surrounding the scope of privacy for public officials. If, as I claim, the rationale for privacy is linked to the demands of political practice, so is the scope of privacy that individuals enjoy when acting in their political capacities. In other words, the scope of privacy due to public officials corresponds to the scope of privacy implicated in the liberal model of politics.

What does that imply regarding the example of a cabinet member making a racist joke when at the dinner table with his family, with which I opened this chapter? Norms of privacy implicated in liberal politics require individuals to bracket their unreasonable views when acting in the political realm. With respect to the material that is so bracketed,

---

[3] Dennis Thompson has a different view on the strength of public justification. He argues that the binding force of public justification applies more strongly to individuals who exercise power over other people and have responsibilities to others on whose behalf they act (Thompson 2004: 2077–9). From this perspective, the strength of the norms of privacy will differ as between citizens and officials. This means that citizens' obligation to leave alone the personal lives of office holders will be less stringent than vice versa.

norms of privacy have others refrain from attending to it. Thus, insofar as the cabinet member's racist beliefs do not show up on the job and do not engage him in practices that discriminate against or harm others, the privacy norms internal to liberal politics would rule against bringing this incident to collective attention.

Similar conclusions hold for revelations concerning those aspects of the personal lives of government officials the controversies over which reflect disagreements about substantive worldviews between individuals. Examples are sexual morality, religious beliefs or matters of lifestyle such as recreational drug use. To the extent that such views are depoliticized and set aside as private in liberal politics, then François Hollande's love affair, Bill Clinton's adultery or cheating at golf, or Barack Obama's past cocaine use are beyond the legitimate business of the public. Irrespective of what the public wants to know about public officials, the integrity of liberal politics imposes constraints on what the public is entitled to know. To insist, like Schauer, that such information may be relevant to citizens' voting decisions is to allow citizens to appeal in their political judgments to material that is dysfunctional to liberal politics. To vote for or against politicians on the grounds of their sexual choices or religious beliefs is to recognize that a particular sexual morality or religion can generate principles capable of governing the common life. This approach to politics violates the liberal commitment to equal liberty.

Compartmentalized lives

On my argument, broader comprehensive views of office holders including their unreasonable beliefs should be set aside as private. On pain of compromising the integrity of liberal politics, such material should be removed from the public gaze and, if known, left unacknowledged. Many, however, are concerned that office holders cannot sufficiently bracket their private views from the performance of their offices, the result being that material failing public justification enters the political realm. This concern is particularly acute with regard to unreasonable beliefs. Some suggest that the unreasonable views of office holders, rather than being relegated to the domain of privacy, should be subject to public censure. As Susan Mendus put it:

> A self-employed furniture restorer may claim that his sexist, racist, or homophobic views are irrelevant to his ability to do his job; a GP or a

police officer ... would have greater difficulty in making the same claim
with the same plausibility ... [P]rivate vices ... are not necessarily private
when discerned in public officials.

(Mendus 2008: 305)

If this objection is right, the racist joke incident featured in my opening
example disqualifies the individual as an office holder because it indicates racist attitudes that inevitably affect his performance in office. I will
devote the remainder of this chapter to discussing this objection.

First, the claim that people cannot separate their public responsibilities from their broader ethical and metaphysical beliefs places one in
opposition to one of the core assumptions of political liberalism. Liberal
citizenship does presuppose that people can distinguish between, and
thereby compartmentalize, different modes of reasoning. In particular,
when deciding fundamental political matters, individuals would accept
the restrictions of public reason, but when deliberating about other matters they need not adhere to such restrictions. Rawls' claim that individuals put aside their comprehensive views when acting in their capacity
as citizens is the first and most influential articulation of the compartmentability thesis (Rawls 1996: 10–13). Insofar as Mendus' objection is
not meant to challenge the liberal framework on this point, it should not
be understood as denying the compartmentability thesis, but rather as
holding that the thesis does not apply to people holding unreasonable
views. It is not clear, however, whether one can press this point on either
empirical or conceptual grounds.

To argue that people holding unreasonable views cannot separate
them from their performance in office, one would have to demonstrate
that there is an empirical correlation between racist, homophobic, sexist and other personal prejudices and the performance of public duties.
It is not clear, however, that such an empirical correlation can be found
(Dobel 1998: 120). While there are undoubtedly cases of politicians acting on their unreasonable beliefs, there is no empirical evidence to warrant a claim that they instantiate a rule. Thompson concedes that "[m]any
people, especially politicians, are quite able of compartmentalizing their
lives in the way this [objection] denies" (Thompson 2005: 236). As Erin
Kelly and Lionel McPherson argue, it is not uncommon for people to
"cabin off" unreasonable views:

Persons are able to compartmentalize even outrageous behaviour ...
Many people, for example, affirm among themselves the superiority of
their own religious or ethnic group, yet might not do this in the public

realm or otherwise in their political behaviour. Ordinarily, we recognize a distinction between our personal interests and those interests it is appropriate to insist upon in the public realm.

(Kelly and McPherson 2001: 45)

The absence of empirical correlation aside, it is not clear that political liberals are prevented, on conceptual grounds, from saying that people holding unreasonable views could compartmentalize them in a way that liberal citizenship requires. In his introduction to the paperback edition of *Political Liberalism*, Rawls distanced himself from his earlier position according to which individuals supporting liberal political principles would also have to be able to endorse them from their broader philosophical views; he recognized that there will inevitably be people who are cooperative in supporting a liberal political regime but who are also illiberal in their comprehensive views (Rawls 1996: xxxix). This claim, as commentators submit, implies that a commitment to liberal political principles is a matter of practical rather than philosophical or epistemic commitment (Kelly and McPherson 2001; Garthoff 2012: 191–2). Loosening the link between the practical commitment to liberal political principles and broader philosophical or epistemic commitments opens up a space for political liberals to argue that holding illiberal commitments and supporting a liberal regime is possible, namely people may hold illiberal views merely as epistemic commitments and refrain from presenting them as authoritative for political purposes (Garthoff 2012: 191). To concede that illiberal comprehensive views need not spill over into the political standpoint is to concede that people whose broader value commitments contain racist, homophobic, sexist and other illiberal ideas can set them aside when acting in their political capacities. Kelly and McPherson endorse just this position to plea for tolerating sexists:

> not all views that are philosophically or morally unreasonable should be counted as politically unreasonable ... Members of private all-male clubs, for instance, may not turn out to be politically unreasonable, though they may hold views about women that fall into the category of the morally or philosophically unreasonable ... [W]e may allow private all-male clubs ... insofar as their members are not attempting politically to pursue the unreasonable philosophical views they might have of women. Since these views have no practical political consequence, they are, in a colloquial sense, merely philosophical.

(Kelly and McPherson 2001: 39, 42)

The concern that people holding unreasonable views are not able to bracket them when acting in an official capacity turns out to have neither strong empirical nor conceptual support. The endorsement of the compartmentability thesis commits liberals to saying that holding unreasonable views does not automatically disqualify individuals from occupying public office: what matters is not whether public officials *hold* certain views, but whether those views *inform* their office performance. To the extent that unreasonable views do *not* inform the job, they are not a matter of public concern. Neither are they the proper object of media reporting.

Preventive screening?

Of course, if unreasonable views *do* show up on the job, this fact *is* a matter of public concern and the proper object of media reporting. The same holds for cases in which holding unreasonable beliefs engages individuals in practices that harm or discriminate against others. What is the proper focus of public inquiry in those cases?

The focus of public inquiry follows the focus of public concern. If the proper object of public concern is not whether public officials hold unreasonable views, but whether unreasonable views show up on the job, then media reporting should be directed not towards the views officials hold, but towards the policies they implement and decisions they take. What, however, if office holders driven by their unreasonable views engage, in their off-duty capacity, in practices that involve harm or discrimination, such as when a cabinet member belongs to a private club that engages in discriminatory practices by supporting private schools denying admission to children of certain minority groups? In such cases, attention to office performance will not do. Is the citizenry entitled to subject their off-duty activities to public screening?

Screening personal lives of public officials with respect to practices that involve discrimination and harm to others' interests does not pose a dilemma for my argument. As I indicated earlier, the pursuit of matters classified as private can become a matter of public concern when it harms others. Thus, personal pursuits involving harm to others are not protected by privacy. Second, the pursuit of matters classified as private can become a matter of public concern when it involves violation of others' political rights or leads to discrimination in the political sphere. One of the most fundamental political rights in liberal-democratic societies is the right to equal moral status. Supporting private schools denying admission to children of certain minority groups violates that right.[4] In violating others'

---

[4] That position is contested. For a critical discussion see Merry 2007.

rights to equal consideration, such personal associations are then not private. As they are not private, no privacy considerations ban their public screening.

I have said that office holders' engagement in practices that involve harm, discrimination and violation of political rights voids the private status of their off-duty pursuits and eliminates an objection against their surveillance. In political practice, screening of the personal lives of public officials or candidates for public office is often undertaken without prior knowledge of misconduct on their part. Indeed, it is undertaken only to establish whether any misconduct has taken place. Whereas some authors defend this policy (Dobel 1998: 129–33), my position does not go all the way toward supporting preventive screening. When screening of the personal lives of public officials or candidates for office is undertaken without prior knowledge of misconduct on their part, we are dealing with cases of surveillance of practices whose private status has not yet been voided. In that case, screening of these domains remains problematic.

One way to deal with this problem is to say that well-grounded suspicions of misconduct are sufficient to void the private status of the otherwise private pursuits of office holders. On this view, well-grounded suspicions of, for example, discrimination against a minority group would eliminate the privacy-based objection against screening. The success of this strategy depends on how the suspicions are supported. First, exactly what counts as well-grounded suspicions should be determined in a way consistent with the nature of liberal politics, namely it should be subject to public justification. Second, it matters how the facts that serve as grounds for suspicions are obtained. Suspicious facts cannot be obtained in the course of surveillance of the personal pursuits of office holders as long as the private status of these pursuits has not been voided. In order to screen the personal whereabouts and doings of public officials, suspicious facts voiding their private status must be available beforehand. This leaves us with two classes of facts that can serve as grounds for suspicion. On the one hand, suspicions could be supported by facts that relate to individuals' public performances, for example previous work experience. Second, suspicions could be supported by facts that relate to individuals' performances in the private domain but are available without intruding into their private pursuits. Examples in point could be an outcome of a legitimate investigation targeting third parties or a report of a criminal act. For example, if, in the course of a legitimate investigation of the school financial administration, the police discover that a private discriminatory club conferred a substantial gift on it, then this fact justifies screening that club's members. In this case, however, the facts that reveal the official's engagement in the discriminatory practices of the club and eliminating an objection against screening his off-duty associations are obtained without first intruding into his associations.[5]

Public scandals and blackmail

I have said that personal affairs of office holders should remain private insofar as they do not inform their performance in office. One could argue, however, that even if private lives do not have a direct effect on their performance in office, they may have an indirect effect. Indirect effects could result from other people's reactions toward the official's private life. Public reaction could undermine confidence in the office, impair its ability to win support for its policies and weaken an official's political position. An argument referring to the possibility of using private information for blackmailing public officials is a version of this argument. The expectations of a negative reaction by the public to revelations concerning their private lives might motivate office holders to submit to the blackmailer. The problem with this argument is that the expected reaction of the public – public scandal – is not always justified in terms of liberal politics. As Thompson puts it: "It is not enough … to point to the public scandal that an official's conduct may cause. The question must always be asked: should the public be scandalized?" (Thompson 1987: 140). In terms of my argument, if material fails public justification and is, thus, relegated to the domain of privacy, public scandal following its revelation

---

[5] A much discussed case regarding screening candidates for high-ranking political office is the confirmation process of Judge Clarence Thomas for the US Supreme Court in 1991. At the moment that Senate hearings of Clarence's confirmation were initially completed, a report of a confidential interview of Anita Hill by the FBI was leaked to the press in which Hill accused Clarence of sexual harassment while he was her supervisor at the US Department of Education and the Equal Employment Opportunity Commission. The hearings were then reopened, and Hill was called to testify in public. The Senate Judiciary Committee challenged and dismissed Hill's accusations of sexual harassment. Thomas insisted on the privacy of his intimate affairs, and the committee generally accepted his claim and did not seek evidence that would involve screening of Thomas' personal life. It refused, for example, to screen Thomas' sexual life or the videos that he rented for his personal use. The commentaries on the committee's refusal to pursue such lines of investigation diverge from critique (Fraser 1992) to qualified approval (Dennis Thompson and Amy Gutmann 1996, 111–14). From the perspective of my argument above, the committee's refusal to screen the personal life of Thomas should be seen as unjustified. Once Hill's accusations were made, the committee had at its disposal reasonable suspicions of legal offence (sex discrimination) that cancelled the privacy and justified the screening of Thomas' personal affairs.

is unjustified in the sense that it is impermissible for citizens to base their decisions and political judgments about the office holder on such information. As such information cannot be used as a valid consideration for judging the public performances of office holders (e.g. it cannot serve as a ground for legal complaint), it cannot properly be used as material for blackmail. To the extent that public reactions are unjustified, they should not count as a reason for exposure and should be disregarded (Thompson 2005: 238).

The normative status of privacy

I have argued that concerns with the integrity of liberal politics set limits to the publicization of personal lives of public officials. I close this discussion by examining what is at stake in respecting the divide between private and public realms in liberal politics.

I have argued that, in advancing the interests of public justification, privacy is a condition of political legitimacy. Political liberals tie the concept of legitimacy to an obligation that falls on individuals as members of political societies. Rawls speaks of a "duty of civility," which is a moral duty to explain how the principles and policies an individual advocates can be supported by reasons that everyone can reasonably accept (Rawls 1996: 217). If, as I have argued, privacy is implicated in public justification, then respect for privacy is an aspect of that duty.

Does this imply anything about enforcement of privacy norms? Public justification is not merely one consideration that individuals, groups and institutions should take into account when acting in the political realm, but it is *the* foundation of the political realm (Wall and Klosko 2003: 10). The constitutive role of public justification in the political order can be seen as an argument in favor of the legal enforcement of those constraints on actions performed in the political domain that public justification entails. If privacy is implicated in public justification, this would also provide an argument in favor of its legal enforcement.

References

Ackerman, B. 1989. "Why dialogue?" *Journal of Philosophy* 86: 5–22.
Brettschneider, C. 2007. *Democratic Rights: The Substance of Self-Government.* Princeton University Press.
Chambers, S. 2010. "Theories of political justification," *Philosophy Compass* 5: 893–903.

Dobel, P. 1998. "Judging the private lives of public officials," *Administration and Society* 30: 115–42.

Fraser, N. 1992. "Sex, lies, and the public sphere: some reflections on the confirmation of Clarence Thomas," *Critical Inquiry* 18: 595–612.

Garthoff, J. 2012. "The idea of an overlapping consensus revisited," *Journal of Value Inquiry* 46: 183–96.

Gaus, G. 1996. *Justificatory Liberalism: An Essay on Epistemology and Political Theory.* New York: Oxford University Press.

2003. *Contemporary Theories of Liberalism: Public Reason as a Post-Enlightenment Project.* London: Sage.

Hartley, Ch. and Watson L. 2010. "Is feminist political liberalism possible?" *Journal of Ethics & Social Philosophy* 5: 1–21.

Keating, J. 2014. "The Problem with the Right to be Forgotten." Accessed September 23, 2014 from www.slate.com/blogs/the_world_/2014/05/13/the_eu_s_misguided_push_for_a_right_to_be_forgotten_on_the_internet.html.

Kelly, K. and McPherson, L. 2001. "On tolerating the unreasonable," *Journal of Political Philosophy* 9: 38–55.

Lafont C. 2008. "Religious citizens & public reasons." *The Immanent Frame.* Accessed September 5, 2014 from http://blogs.ssrc.org/tif/2008/02/08/religious-citizens-public-reasons/.

Lafont, C. 2009. "Religion and the public sphere," *Philosophy and Social Criticism* 35: 127–50.

Larmore, C. 1990. "Political liberalism," *Political Theory* 18: 339–60.

1999. "The Moral Basis of Political Liberalism," *Journal of Philosophy* 96: 599–625.

2003. "Public Reason," in Freeman, S (ed.) *The Cambridge Companion to Rawls.* Cambridge University Press.

Lever, A. 2012. *On Privacy.* New York: Routledge.

2015. "Privacy and democracy: what the secret ballot reveals," *Law, Culture and the Humanities* (forthcoming).

Lukes, S. 1978. "Power and Authority," in Bottomore, T. B. and Nisbet, R. (eds.) *A History of Sociological Analysis.* London: Basic Books, pp. 633–76.

Macedo, S. 1991. *Liberal Virtues: Citizenship, Virtue, and Community in Liberal Constitutionalism.* Oxford: Clarendon Press.

MacKinnon, C. 1989. *Toward a Feminist Theory of the State.* Cambridge, MA: Harvard University Press.

Mendus, S. 2008. "Private Faces in Public Faces," in Kramer, M. H., Grant, C. and Hatzistavrou, A. (eds.) *The Legacy of H.L.A. Hart's Legal, Political, and Moral Philosophy.* Oxford University Press, pp. 299–315.

Merry, M. 2007. *Culture, Identity and Islamic Schooling: A Philosophical Approach.* Basingstoke: Palgrave Macmillan.

Mokrosinska, D. 2014. "Privacy and the integrity of liberal politics: the case of governmental internet searches," *Journal of Social Philosophy* 45: 369–89.

Moore, A. 2000. "Employee monitoring and computer technology: evaluative surveillance v. privacy," *Business Ethics Quarterly* 10: 697–707.

Nagel, T. 1998. "Concealment and exposure," *Philosophy & Public Affairs* 27: 3–30.

Pateman, C. 1989. "Feminist Critiques of the Public/Private Dichotomy," in Pateman, C. *The Disorder of Women: Democracy, Feminism, and Political Theory.* Stanford University Press, pp. 118–40.

Quong, J. 2013. "Public Reason," in Zalta, E. N. (ed.) *The Stanford Encyclopedia of Philosophy.* Accessed September 2014 from http://plato.stanford.edu/archives/sum2013/entries/public-reason.

Rawls, J. 1971. *A Theory of Justice.* Cambridge, MA: Harvard University Press.

1996. *Political Liberalism.* Second revised edition (with a new introduction and the "Reply to Habermas"). New York: Columbia University Press.

Russon, M. 2014. "Google's Right to be Forgotten: 70,000 Politicians, Criminals and Individuals want Offending Content Erased." Accessed September 23, 2014 from www.ibtimes.co.uk/googles-right-be-forgotten-70000-politicians-criminals-individuals-want-offending-content-1456603.

Schauer, F. 2000. "Can public figures have private lives?" *Social Philosophy and Policy* 17: 293–309.

Thompson, D. 1987. *Political Ethics and Public Office.* Cambridge, MA.: Harvard University Press.

2004. "Public reason and precluded reasons," *Fordham Law Review* 73: 2073–88.

2005. *Restoring Responsibility: Ethics in Government, Business, and Healthcare.* Cambridge University Press.

Thompson, D. and Gutmann, A. 1996. *Democracy and Disagreement.* Cambridge, MA: Belknap Press.

Waldron J. 1993. "Theoretical Foundations of Liberalism," in Waldron, J. *Liberal Rights: Collected Papers 1981–1991.* Cambridge University Press, pp. 35–62.

Wall, S. and Klosko, G. 2003. *Perfectionism and Neutrality: Essays in Liberal Theory.* Lanham: Rowman & Littlefield.

11

Privacy, surveillance, and the democratic potential of the social Web

CHRISTOPHER PARSONS, COLIN J. BENNETT,
ADAM MOLNAR

This chapter argues that theories about privacy would benefit from embracing deliberative democratic theory on the grounds that it addresses harms to democracy, and widens our understandings of privacy infringements in social networking environments. We first explore how social networking services (SNS) have evolved through different phases and how they enable political deliberation. Subsequently, we discuss more traditional individualistic and intersubjective theories of privacy in relation to social networking and point out their limitations in identifying and redressing social networking-related harms. We then critique emerging claims concerning the social value of privacy in the context of the social Web. Here we point out how these theories might identify non-individualized harms, yet, at the same time, suffer important challenges in application. We conclude by arguing that deliberative democratic theory can add some critical insights into the privacy harms encountered on the contemporary "social Web" that are only imperfectly understood by individualistic and social conceptions of privacy.

Social networking allows individuals to generate and disseminate user-generated content. The specific mechanisms for such generation and dissemination vary according to the degree of interactivity between publisher and reader, the blurring of "online" and "offline" content and behavior, and the extent to which publishers, participants, and consumers surrender or provide personally identifiable information as a condition for communication. Of course, not all communications are political in nature, nor do all political communications meet basic definitions of deliberation. That being said, social networking can be a significant enabler for public engagement, consultation, and deliberation about political issues (Mergel 2012).

The goal of political deliberation is to arrive at consensus between participants with the aim of reflecting the interests of both the individual and the community simultaneously. Participants should ideally be willing to acknowledge the views of other discursive partners, communicate in a sphere that is not unduly distorted by coercion, and operate in a communicative environment that emphasizes individual freedoms. Further, all those who would be affected by the decisions should be recognized and permitted to participate (Habermas 1998a: 42–4). Such deliberation fosters a sense of commonality among individuals that might unite a political community.

The Web has developed in a way that can facilitate such deliberation, by expanding the range of people who can communicate with one another about issues affecting themselves and their communities, by mitigating the technical barriers to communication, by reducing the costs involved in learning *how* to communicate, and by enhancing the ability for governments to receive or pay attention to the consensus formed by members of the public. What is the role that privacy plays in this process, and what are the potential privacy harms? And how might deliberative democratic theory help us assess and mitigate those harms?

The early Web and its limitations

As envisioned by its creator, Sir Tim Berners-Lee, the Web was designed such that "once someone somewhere made available a document, database, graphic, sound, video, or screen at some stage in an interactive dialogue, it should be accessible (subject to authorization, of course) by anyone, with any type of computer, in any country" (Berners-Lee *et al.* 2000: 37). As standards developed and the technology became mainstream, websites became general information resources through which people requested and received information (Abelson *et al.* 2008: 58). At this early stage, the referentiality of links between different webpages functioned as a primary means of web-based communication; "users" of the Web demonstrated activity merely by choosing *what* to watch and read (Taddicken 2012).

Despite being a predominantly consumption-driven media, early websites did have the capability of fostering intense and reflective discourse between individuals. Though early access to online-promoted speech was limited by access to, and familiarity with, some sophisticated technology (computers, modems, and Internet browsers for consumers, as well as

knowledge of HTML, FTP, and other server-related technologies for producers), individuals could publish content online, and carry on conversations with other similarly experienced computer users (Kies 2010: 42–4).
Content, once distributed on websites, could subsequently be debated in
other channels, such as on listservs or bulletin board systems.

However, Web 1.0 lacked a number of key deliberative features. Despite
the potential for "off-channel" conversations, the technical publishing
system could not incorporate all those involved in the discussion and,
as a result, lacked discursive equality (Kies 2010: 40–2). Consequently,
key features that constitute deliberation itself – reciprocity, reflexivity,
plurality – were only nascent, and were not distributed across the spectrum of web users more generally. With the development of Web 2.0 and
more contemporary web environments, these technical hindrances broke
down to the point where even those speaking different languages could
engage in discourse with one another on a global scale.

Web 2.0 and networked publics

Advancing from Web 1.0, the so-called "Web 2.0" created platforms
where individuals and groups could write, comment on, and edit content using more technically accessible tools. Examples include wiki pages,
blog posts, and early social networking tools. Such platforms function as
"a set of tools that enable group forming networks to emerge quickly. It
includes numerous media, utilities, and applications that empower individual efforts, link individuals together into larger aggregates, intercon-
nect groups, provide metadata about network dynamics, flows, and traffic,
allowing social networks to form, clump, become visible, and be measured, tracked, and interconnected" (Saveri et al. 2005: 22). Essentially,
Web 2.0 services established distinct platforms enabling communication
and collaboration between parties who were geographically distant.

According to boyd (2011: 46), Web 2.0 possesses the following characteristics: *persistence* (online expressions are automatically recorded and
archived); *replicability* (content made out of bits can be duplicated); *scal-
ability* (the content of networked publics is potentially visible); and *search-
ability* (content in networked publics can be accessed through search).
Empirical research suggests that there are some key differences in the
ways that different social media are used for political purposes (Hindman
2009). As noted by Kaye (2011: 224):

> [social network sites] are primarily used for political purposes but with
> a social spin, whereas blogs are used for information and because users

do not like or trust traditional media. For example, [social network site] users are motivated "to be in contact with like minded people," and "to give me something to talk about with others." Blog users, on the other hand, are motivated "for political news analysis," and "for information not found in traditional media.

In effect, while web platforms *can* facilitate communication and collaboration, there is no necessary relationship between participating on such a platform and becoming more involved in political deliberation. However, by reducing the technical challenges and costs of communication, and increasing the availability of Internet-capable devices, the potential for a broader population to debate any issue has arisen. Whereas initial iterations of the Web required some basic HTML coding skills and perhaps familiarity with how to upload the code to a server, Web 2.0 established an online environment where anyone with an email address and web browser could quickly write and disseminate their thoughts online.

Web "3.0" and political deliberation

If Web 2.0 can be characterized as constituting sets of discrete communications platforms, Web 3.0 can be better understood as establishing a social infrastructure, deeply integrated with wireless mobile computing systems. Fuchs (2010) argues that 3.0 systems are characterized by a web of cooperation, wherein service users "read existing texts or create new ones (cognition), they discuss how texts could be changed, appended, and enhanced (communication), and they together produce new content (cooperation)" (Fuchs 2010: 131). Data sources are disparate and extend beyond classic means of interacting with computer systems to include speech recognition, optical character analysis, crowdsourced semantic search engines, and other techniques that extract data from "unstructured" content sources. Mobile devices are key to this iteration of the Web, bringing remote sensing tools (such as picture and video cameras, global positioning, and audio recordings) to the Web through direct sensor-to-Web interfaces.

These features of Web 3.0 facilitate, as never before, a more dispersed, interactive, and potentially deliberative Internet insofar as a range of communications technologies permit a wider number of people to discuss issues across a wide breadth of platforms, including YouTube videos, written blogs, Facebook or Twitter, or forums such as Reddit. And as a result of contemporary "embedding" features, it is possible to weave together different modes of communication into a common space: YouTube videos can function as comments on blogs, Tweets sharing an insight or confrontational position can be embedded in Facebook pages, and so forth. As a result, it is possible that a wide range of individuals from a spectrum of society *can*, though may not, participate in political debate. Moreover, requirements for written literacy are diminished as individuals increasingly take part in debates using rich multimedia formats as well as more traditional means of online communication. And these varied content formats can all be used within the same "thread" of a conversation. Web 3.0 breaks down the geographical and literary barriers insofar as individuals within and outside a geographical community who believe they will be affected by a given issue can participate in the discussion.

At the same time, the use of these devices generates mass amounts of "unstructured" content that facilitate cognition, communication, and cooperation, but also provides enormous potential for surveillance. The monitoring of deliberation between individuals using web-based communications systems becomes much easier as communications take advantage of commercial communications platforms or integrate external software analytics programs. Even without reading or hearing the content of a person's communications, it is possible to map subscribers' circle(s) of friends and associates, communications patterns, the geolocation from where (and when) a person accesses the service, the willingness of individuals to browse "controversial" content and associate with suspected "deviants," and more (Danezis and Clayton 2007; Diffie and Landau 2007; Strandburg 2007). Moreover, such surveillance can begin at a broad level, by capturing data that identifies classes of persons, and then subsequently drill down to focus on specific individuals who are of interest (Solove 2008: 4). Such surveillance has the capacity to shape individuals' willingness to communicate, particularly over politically sensitive subjects (MacKinnon 2012), a central argument underpinning the litigation against the surveillance of bulk telephone records by the US National Security Agency (Electronic Frontier Foundation 2013).

Surveillance online does not just affect individuals, then, but theoretically *all* users (and affiliates of users) of different web communications systems. The surveillance of Web 3.0 therefore stands at odds with its democratic potential. Web 3.0 may increase the range of parties involved in political deliberations, but it also increases exponentially the potential for surveillance and the risks to privacy. How might the privacy literature come to terms with the potentials and harms of the "social Web"?

Privacy boundaries and the social Web

Dominant conceptions of privacy predominantly based upon liberal-democratic foundations attempt to understand privacy through the frameworks of information control, spatial violation, and expressions of individual autonomy and liberty. This privacy paradigm has deep roots in Western liberal political theory, resting on a conception of society comprising relatively autonomous individuals who enjoy a private sphere that is distinct from a public sphere of government and the state. Autonomous individuals are understood as more-or-less rational actors who can separate "public" from "private" behavior, and who require "a modicum of privacy in order to be able to fulfill the various roles of the citizen in a liberal democratic state" (Bennett and Raab 2006: 4). Although expressions of how such separations should be theoretically and practically achieved vary, scholars and practitioners differentiate between places, practices, and the revelation of particular kinds of information when drawing privacy boundaries for ethical, instrumental, and political reasons (Bennett 1992).

A spatial boundary is often implicit when we attach verbs such as "invasion" or "intrusion" to uncomfortable privacy experiences. The classic definition of privacy offered by Samuel Warren and Louis Brandeis ("the right to be let alone") differentiated between what individuals should, and should not, expect to be outside of reasonable public inquiry (Warren and Brandeis 1890). Since their initial proposal, the language of privacy has often adopted an explicit or implicit spatial dimension. Contemporary legal notions of a "reasonable expectation of privacy" are often concerned about the place or space within which the subjective privacy claim is being asserted, and whether society would see that such a claim is justifiable (Austin 2012).

For others, the privacy boundary is drawn in terms of the specific behaviors or actions that should be shielded from intrusion, such as sexual behaviors, medical matters, or similarly "intimate" actions. In John Stuart Mill's (1859) terms, there should be certain "self-regarding" activities of private concern, contrasted with "other-regarding" activities susceptible to community interest and regulation. A related way to think about the boundary is in terms of individual decisions and choices. Per this understanding, privacy is essential for enabling liberty and autonomy, both of which permit individuals to behave as responsible adults in liberal democracies (DeCew 1997: 41). This concept of decisional privacy has been relied upon, especially in American constitutional law, to protect decision-making surrounding abortion, contraception, and the right to rear children in accordance with one's own religious convictions (Allen 1988).

And finally, the boundary can be drawn in terms of information, and particularly between sensitive or non-sensitive forms of information. The former are assumed to be inherently private and worthy of higher levels of protection. Examples in most legal formulations include information on race, sexual orientation, health, and political affiliation. Other scholars and jurists have developed complicated (and often debatably subjective) conceptions of a person's "biographical core" and what facets of this core are more or less deserving of privacy protection (Kerr *et al.* 2008; Millar 2009). However, what is in the biographical core is not necessarily sensitive; and what is sensitive is not necessarily core. These disputes go to the heart of contemporary debates about what is and is not personal data and therefore what can be subject to regulation under data protection law.

A notion of privacy that flows from certain assumptions about the boundary between the self and the other plays an important role within liberal democratic theory because it: prevents the total politicizing of life; promotes freedom of association; shields scholarship and science from unnecessary governmental interference; permits the use of a secret ballot; restrains improper police conduct such as compulsory self-incrimination and unreasonable searches and seizures; and serves to shield institutions, such as the press, that operate to keep government accountable (Westin 1967; Schwartz 1999). This privacy paradigm underpins the passage and implementation of "data protection" or "informational privacy" laws that allow individuals rights to control their information and impose obligations on organizations to treat that information appropriately (Bennett and Raab 2006).

A notion of privacy based on a boundary between the self and the other certainly resonates, but also has limitations when applied to web-based communications platforms and when used to challenge the specific strategies of surveillance that accompany social networking environments. As will be made clear, although boundary-based conceptions of privacy can identify and offer remedy for some of the harms on the social Web, they are less helpful in repulsing the most routine forms of surveillance within this environment.

What lies outside the bounds of boundary concepts?

Most privacy models conceive risks as stemming from personal information about individuals (data subjects) being collected and processed by organizations (data controllers) that cross certain boundaries. The Web 1.0 model tended to reflect this basic relationship between controllers and subjects. However, Web 2.0 confused the boundary, because individuals themselves create data on web platforms and environments, and thus also become data controllers. These platforms and environments are themselves built by private corporations. Consequently, organizations are not necessarily *creating* the content so much as *creating the tools* of content creation; actual content tends to be subscriber-generated.

Privacy or data protection laws impose obligations on data controllers, and grant rights to data subjects. In the context of Web 2.0 services the advisory body of European Data Protection Agencies, charged with overseeing data protection law, defined SNS providers as "data controllers under the Data Protection Directive" on the basis that "these services provide the means for the processing of user data and provide all the 'basic' services related to user management (e.g. registration and deletion of accounts)" (EU Article 29 Working Party 2009). However, even in 2009 these distinctions were becoming problematic because of the growing tendency to use Web 2.0 platforms for public, rather than private or semi-private, communications between friends, family, and colleagues. It is thus difficult sometimes to assert that a privacy boundary was crossed in a web platform or infrastructure. Where an individual is "responsible" for the disclosure, she will often be limited in her ability to assert that a boundary was violated because that individual in question made that information public. These problems are only exacerbated in an era of global data processing, where the Web 2.0 environment spans many organizations and many legal jurisdictions (Bennett *et al.* 2014a).

Boundary problems also arise when certain actions are facilitated by technological design, such as the persistent monitoring of nearby wireless access points or the geolocation of a subscriber relative to other subscribers. What then does it mean to protect certain kinds of sensitive information in one place rather than another? Is it a violation for the mobile phone affiliated with a given web platform to report on the close presence of two subscribers, especially if they do not know that their devices are reporting on their presence to the infrastructure owner? Or does the violation only refer to the recording and reporting on the specific intimate action? Must we differentiate between locations where such intimate actions take place (such as bedrooms or bathrooms, or halls used for union meetings) and the performance of such an action, in such a place? Or do we instead rely on the fact that individuals may have consented to such reporting and, as such, must assume responsibility for the surveillance?

Of course, the protection of space and behavior is arguably both under the "umbrella" of information, and the control of information *across* said boundaries. Yet defining what constitutes "personal" information is a contradictory maze between what privacy regulators ascribe as personally identifiable, what individuals understand as identifiable, and what the companies operating the services themselves perceive as *legally or operationally* deserving of protections (Bennett *et al.* 2014a). Moreover, given that many theories of privacy have been instrumentally established to protect personal information, they are challenged by the increasing capture and processing of metadata – the data about the data, typically including identifiers such as users' IP addresses, their operating systems, and any information gained from cookies. Such information can subsequently be used to identify individuals and their personal browsing habits as well as to track their physical location. In a study of twenty-four SNS, not one identified any element of metadata as personally identifiable information, nor did the SNSes give users any expectation of privacy regarding their metadata. The broader privacy implications associated with the capture and processing of metadata are rarely addressed (Bennett *et al.* 2014b) unless in response to public campaigns (Opsahl 2013).

The strain between traditional privacy frameworks and how Web 2.0 and 3.0 platforms and infrastructure operate becomes clear when examining the services provided. Users of SNS, through the course of their online communication, often encounter other individuals who have not joined the service or who have not even chosen to disclose information on the platform. In such scenarios the individual subscriber *and* the platform or infrastructure owner would be considered controllers. Moreover, there is a question concerning what constitutes genuine spaces, actions, or information that deserve privacy on political grounds, particularly when data provided or collected by web platforms and infrastructures can be recombined to reveal political affiliation, movement patterns, sexual orientation, or other characteristics. When all these patterns may affect how a person might be engaged politically, then what needs protection? Perhaps the attempt to ascertain what types of data need protection is a hopelessly lost effort on the social Web (Mayer-Schönberger and Cukier 2013).

So, instrumentally, a problem has arisen: the companies that operate social networking platforms and environments must grapple with the massive collection and dissemination of their users' personal information. Moreover, companies must ascertain the legal basis for collecting information about individuals *who are not* subscribers to the service or platform in question, but whose information is disclosed *by actual* subscribers. Individuals must, at the same time, struggle to find out if their "biographical core" is being inappropriately revealed in the course of using, or being mentioned on, these platforms. Surveillance scholars often rightly criticize privacy for missing the broader harms and concerns linked to social surveillance for commercial, personal, and state purposes. The belief that privacy creates some kind of space or bubble around an individual that cannot be intruded upon without justification (Stalder 2002) is seen as insufficient to capture how privacy is, today, "compromised by measured efforts to position individuals in contexts where they are apt to exchange various bits of personal data for a host of perks, efficiencies, and other benefits" (Haggerty and Ericson 2006: 12). In response to these deficiencies a rather different framework has developed that focuses on how privacy enables communities and personal development by attending to intersubjective and community bonds.

Intersubjectivity and privacy theory

Responding to the deficiencies surrounding boundary concepts of privacy law and policy, some scholars and jurists have focused on how privacy is needed to strengthen community and facilitate intersubjective bonds needed for democratic action. For these scholars it is not enough to protect distinctly political places, behaviors, and information, but to shield the plurality of actors who are involved in the act of behaving politically. Privacy, then, is as much or more a common right than an individualized one. In what follows, we outline the dimensions of intersubjective concepts of privacy and then explain why these theories also face challenges in the face of Web 2.0 and 3.0 environments.

Approaches to privacy that try to stipulate a boundary tend not to capture the processes through which people engage in social action and become actors capable of social action more generally. Such relationships, in particular their political instantiation, are taken up in Regan's approach to privacy as a social value that is necessary to secure a democratic society's economic and political interests. She recognizes that the value of the term is truly realized upon considering its aggregated societal benefits (Regan 1995: 220–8). More specifically, she posits three interrelated social values to privacy: as a "common value" – something we all have an interest in; as a "public value" – as essential to a democratic system of government; and as a "collective value" – or an indivisible or non-excludable good and one that cannot be allocated through market mechanisms. There are, therefore, *social values* to privacy as, according to Regan, it is "becoming less an attribute of individuals and records and more an attribute of social relationships and information systems or communication systems" (Regan 1995: 230).

Regan is not alone in bringing the social importance of privacy to the fore. Recent efforts have demonstrated that even liberal privacy scholars such as Westin have been mischaracterized in the literature. Steeves, for example, maintains that Westin "argues that some collective benefit is not a sufficient reason to invade privacy … From the start, Westin's full legislative program accordingly questioned whether or not surveillance should be tolerated by the public, based on its effect on social relationships" (Steeves 2009: 195). Indeed, Steeves holds (along with Regan) that privacy cannot merely be "traded off" for other benefits, but needs to be understood as a social construction through which "privacy states" are negotiated. Surveillance, then, is problematic on the grounds that it "objectifies the self, collapses the boundaries between social roles and negates the conditions necessary for inter-subjectivity" (Steeves 2009: 208). Steeves' analysis coheres, broadly, with Schoeman's view that while autonomy is required to be self-expressive and demands certain privacy considerations, the point of autonomy is not to *disengage* from one's relationships but to enhance and form new and deeper relationships (Schoeman 1992). For these scholars privacy is not exclusively focused on individuals who live with boundaries about them, but upon how those same individuals necessarily parse and develop the connections *between and amongst* each another (Etzioni 1999).

For Nissenbaum, a right to privacy is not about the ability to *control* information, but instead reflects "a right to live in a world in which our expectations about the flow of personal information are, for the most part, met; expectations that are shaped not only by force of habit and convention but a general confidence in the mutual support these flows accord to key organizing principles of social life, including moral and political ones" (Nissenbaum 2009: 231). In focusing on social life, Nissenbaum argues that our expectations of privacy must be coherent with the situations in which events, actions, and information are expressed. Behaviors, actions, words, or information might deserve a reasonable expectation of privacy in one context but not in another. Social norms and conventions largely dictate, or help describe, the privacy norms applicable to an individual and their community, and vary on an ongoing basis.

When social norms are in flux, however, as a result of emergent and viral technologies the privacy norms may be disturbed and contested. In her anthropological research, Nippert-Eng found that "[c]hanging technologies, expectations, and the habits that incorporate them mean that the need to attend to the problem of social accessibility is highly likely to persist in the future. The need to personally attend to this aspect of achieving privacy will not go away" (Nippert-Eng 2010: 209). Turkle's (2012) book, *Alone Together*, documents many of the challenges (and failures) for people trying to negotiate these norms among themselves, especially when using social media platforms and infrastructures, suggesting that establishing whether a person has exceeded a privacy norm or expectation remains fraught with difficulty. Furthermore, infringements on individuals' and communities' expectations of privacy are often realized significantly after the fact. The result is that the harms can become internalized realities and, in the context of rapidly changing technologies, possibly engrained as normal operating practices for the contemporary web-based systems. As a result, the practices that generate such harms can be extremely difficult to reverse.

An intersubjective approach to privacy, then, focuses on ensuring that the bonds that form communities and support the development of individuals vis-à-vis their relation within communities are secure from inappropriate monitoring. This approach emphasizes the relations that constitute populations and their collective capacity to engage in politics. When surveillance naturalizes "Othered" identities, and subsequently identifies relationships on this basis, there is a chilling effect upon the willingness of citizens and residents to develop deeper understandings about one another, which, as a result, further weakens social bonds. While such effects may be most felt by individuals who retreat from associating with others on the basis of an individualized fear of being part of a group, what is centrally being chilled is the capacity to engage in relationships and the building of trust within and across communities. Such relationships are the targets of this mode of surveillance when data on individuals are captured as a result of community associations (Strandburg 2007).

Intersubjective approaches to privacy that are principally attentive to the bonds between individuals in communities align in many ways with the character and purpose of social networking. Web 2.0 and 3.0 also confound traditional boundary distinctions. The harms that are experienced are often challenging for any particular individual to recognize and articulate, because they are linked to how the surveillance affects communities as a whole. By focusing on the community-based conditions that enable the flourishing of human dignity, an understanding of privacy that acknowledges the link between private development and community involvement is made richer. However, this approach to privacy still suffers challenges when we begin to consider the emerging and complex risks within the social Web.

Intersubjective privacy on the social Web

Whereas specific risks and harms to individuals can often be identified and acted upon, it can be more difficult to recognize actionable harms to communities. Yet for intersubjective conceptions of privacy to carry weight, they must surely identify some recognized and actionable harms on a community or a social level. But these are the very harms that can be most challenging to both detect and report in the context of Web 2.0 and 3.0, where data collection, dissemination, and analysis can take place without the individual's or the community's knowledge.

Moreover, what defines a community is often unclear. For example, when Google smartphones are used by those traveling to a political protest to report road conditions on Google Maps and shared through Google's Web 3.0 infrastructure, what is the "community" to be understood and protected? Is it all Google smartphone users? Or just localized Google smartphone users? Or users of Google Maps attending the political event in question? Without a clear definition of what constitutes a community, it is challenging to ascertain the specific harms associated with a group. In the context of establishing intersubjective bonds or social privacy norms, it is essential to know *which bonds* between *which people* are being monitored (and influenced by such monitoring) in order to evaluate whether a discriminatory form of surveillance is taking place, and whether the privacy practices being applied to the data are suitably calibrated to the groups' norms.

Further, if people do know that a privacy violation of some sort has taken place on the social Web, how then should they calculate or report that violation? Targeted communities face a choice of either continuing to experience the violation, and communicate and account for that harm on the very platforms and infrastructures believed to be the source of the harms, or else maneuver to alternative (and perceived "safer") communications systems. Network effects operate as powerful disincentives to leaving a network that has coalesced over time.

Even if a population has decided to (and can) remain and account for the normative or empirical harms experienced, there is the challenge of translating that negotiated understanding into actionable policy or law.

In effect, while parties can deliberate to come to a consensus about the harms experienced, their ability to do anything about those harms can be limited when they are associated with a community writ large rather than specific individuals. Historically in the United States and other jurisdictions, experiences of general chilling effects born of suspicions of surveillance have been insufficient for courts to overturn or establish injunctions on either government or corporate practices (Kravets 2010; ACLU 2013). And while some corporations have expanded the uses of encryption to secure the personal communications of their individual subscribers (Gallagher 2013), there has been little appetite by corporations thus far to shield their users, as communities, on the grounds of their associations.

More recently, however, we have seen a broader willingness for courts to question whether corporate and government monitoring of communications coheres with established constitutional laws, indicating that even if individuals cannot *specifically* articulate harm, the harm may still have affected the communities with whom the individuals are affiliated (Feiler 2010). Many civil liberties and rights groups have waged a coordinated effort to articulate principles that would secure *both* individual and communal rights and expectations of privacy (see www.necessaryandproportionate.org). In the wake of the revelations by Edward Snowden, both communal and individual harms are clearly being recognized. While the national security-related revelations of 2013 and 2014 are extremely significant, it remains to be seen whether they will lead to reforms in what legally constitutes inappropriate state and corporate surveillance.

In summary, then, there are deficits in applying the social conceptions of privacy to account for the contemporary uses of web platforms and environments. At one level, as we have suggested, communities and contexts have merged. Therefore, an analysis of privacy as contextual integrity, as proposed by Nissenbaum, provides little guidance when the environment itself fuses contexts and communities, and disrupts norms and expectations. According to Regan's framework, what does it mean to say that privacy has social value on the social Web? How can it be a common value of a community, when violations may be occurring to emergent, and not yet normatively formed or recognized, collectives? Moreover, we are not necessarily dealing with privacy as a collective or indivisible good, when increasingly individuals are being encouraged to "choose" their individual privacy settings and protect more or fewer personal data than their peers; under these assumptions, privacy on the social Web is clearly "divisible."

Perhaps, then, privacy should be seen as a public value, or a good that advances a particular form of community, promoting a public or a common realm – a "community of one's peers" in Hannah Arendt's (1958) philosophy? In conclusion, we suggest that it might be possible to see more clearly the role that privacy might play on the social Web by thinking of privacy in these terms: as a public value, rather than as a common or a collective value. In Regan's terms, "privacy may be essential to a democratic political system because some commonality among individuals is necessary to unite a political community and the development of commonality requires privacy" (Regan 1995: 227). More specifically, we suggest how an integration of deliberative democratic theory might provide an important theoretical foundation, rarely considered in the privacy literature, upon which to promote privacy and respond to the harms made possible by surveillance on the contemporary Web.

Conclusion: deliberative democratic theory and the social value of privacy

While both boundary-based and social theories of privacy operate as helpful means to understanding the significance of surveillance on Web 2.0 and 3.0, deliberative democratic theory provides another useful theoretical foundation from which to critique web surveillance and defend the essential normative freedoms of association and speech. Specifically, by reorienting the very conditions of political analysis away from the harms experienced by either individuals or communities to supporting the deliberative requirements for a flourishing democracy, a more holistic accounting of the implications of surveillance-based harms can be developed.

Deliberative democratic models, such as that of Habermas (1998a, 1998b), take the pluralist character of human subjectivity seriously, insofar as individuals are ethically obligated to consider attitudes and practices that are associated with their own as well as their community's best interests (Young 2001: 672). In the context of political deliberation on the Web, these ethical obligations are practically supported by web-based communications systems that are designed to let persons of different political, cultural, and economic positions, and who are affected by a given issue, to communicate with one another to reach an understanding of a problem and a solution. That the Web tends to retain such discourse for extensive periods of time, if not permanently, means that settled issues can be reopened as new participants enter into the deliberative process.

Thus any consensus is temporary and potentially more inclusive than more transitory discursive processes. Moreover, some communications systems will enable high impact contributions to surface to the top of the discussion, whereas those less useful, or outright malicious, contributions can be suppressed from popular view (though not removed entirely). Given that the social Web functions as a space of individuals working with, and within, communities, the Habermasian model lets us focus on individual and public autonomy and rights simultaneously, instead of prioritizing the individual over community or vice versa.

Habermas emphasizes that individual and public autonomy co-originate, and thus are equally necessary to establish the basic laws of a nation-state that secure individual freedoms. To establish such basic laws in the first place, individuals must be able to exercise their public autonomy as collaborative participants in a political system. In effect, public autonomy, made possible by engaging in public deliberation with other members of the public, presupposes that individuals regard themselves as privately autonomous, and that they can shape their freedoms through exercising their public autonomy (Habermas 1998b). Any theory of privacy that is ontologically premised on either individual or community autonomy and rights as the basis for legal privacy protections misunderstands the ontological genesis of basic law. A theory of privacy attentive to Habermasian theory would, therefore, recognize first the importance of securing both private and public autonomy, and would also lead to laws that ensure both public deliberation and private rights.

This deliberative democratic model allows us to critique surveillance that excludes or otherwise inhibits participation in politics. Stymying expression within a political community undermines the legitimacy of law itself, since equitable assent cannot be acquired from all citizens (Habermas 1996). Where surveillance, discrimination, manipulation, or other coercion manifests on the social Web, a harm is registered regardless of whether it is focused on a specific individual (or small set of isolated individuals), or upon broader established communities, or on emergent communities. In effect, this theoretical foundation advances a social understanding of privacy by promoting the development of both communities *and* individuals. Deliberative democratic theory, then, is consistent with a "holistic" accounting of privacy since it recognizes the equal moral and political weight of individuals along with the integrity of communities.

We are not suggesting, however, that adopting a Habermasian approach to conceptualizing privacy, which is mindful of the individual and the public alike, would force the rewriting of privacy scholarship generally. Rather, under this model, harms that affect large communities in a political association (such as one entire ethnic group) are as significant as harms that affect individuals' private rights. Thus it is possible to rely on deliberative theories of privacy to register the broad social harms associated with community-based surveillance while, at the same time, prospectively affording individual-based tools to redress those harms. This linkage is possible because community-based harms have an associated derivative (and negative) effect on the rights of the individuals involved, just as negative impacts on individuals have a correlative effect on the communities within which they operate. Consequently, where individuals refuse to engage in collective discourse because of illegitimate or coercive surveillance, their communities experience harms, thus affecting the full potential of the group's deliberations.

As noted earlier, one of the greatest boons of the contemporary Web is that it has significantly broken down what counts as a mode of deliberation. Participation is less predicated on access to sophisticated technologies given the widespread adoption of mobile communications devices. Moreover, even reading and writing skills are of diminished importance, with individuals able to share photos, videos, and other multimedia to express their particular positions and engage in debate with others. Whereas text and written literacy was initially a prerequisite for participating in deliberation online, this is less the case given the structure and composition of the contemporary and emerging social Web. Where and if, however, either commercial or state surveillance hinders or diminishes individuals' willingness to communicate, or communities' willingness to knowingly come into being, then the deliberative potentials of the Web are undermined along with the privacy interests of those interested in contributing to deliberations. Thus privacy and the deliberative potential of the Web are inescapably interrelated.

The focus on deliberative theory facilitates a critique of surveillance that has debilitative effects on the political rights of individuals and communities. Because this theoretical approach recognizes community and individual rights as co-original, it reveals a more comprehensive understanding of the sources and effects of privacy harms. Moreover, given that the Web is characterized as a mixed-media communications environment wherein political participation is facilitated between individuals and communities that might not otherwise meet or communicate, it behooves established and emerging democracies alike to protect this environment in a way that identifies and responds to contemporary privacy claims. Traditional individualistic or intersubjective approaches to privacy are part of these response mechanisms, but must be encapsulated within a more holistic model of political participation in order to respond to the routine and accelerating modes of surveillance that all users of the Web now experience. Deliberative democratic theories that focus on the co-originality of individual and public autonomy and, accordingly, the co-emergence of individual and community rights offer a foundation from which critical theories of privacy and surveillance can be based. They also more effectively respond to the realities of communication and deliberation on the social Web.

References

Abelson, H., Ledeen, K. and Lewis, H. R. 2008. *Blown to Bits: Your Life, Liberty, and Happiness After the Digital Explosion*. Boston: Addison-Wesley Professional.

ACLU (American Civil Liberties Union) 2013. "Supreme Court Dismisses ACLU's Challenge to NSA Warrantless Wiretapping Law." Accessed February 26, 2013 from www.aclu.org/national-security/supreme-court-dismisses-ac lus-challenge-nsa-warrantless-wiretapping-law.

Allen, A. 1988. *Uneasy Access: Privacy for Women in a Free Society*. Totowa: Rowman and Littlefield.

Arendt, H. 1958. *The Human Condition*. Chicago University Press.

Austin, L. M. 2012. "Getting past privacy? Surveillance, the Charter and the rule of law," *Canadian Journal of Law and Society* 27(3): 381–98.

Bennett, C. J. 1992. *Regulating Privacy: Data Protection and Public Policy in Europe and the United States*. Ithaca, NY: Cornell University Press.

Bennett, C. J. and Raab, C. D. 2006. *The Governance of Privacy: Policy Instruments in Global Perspective*. Cambridge, MA: MIT Press.

Bennett, C. J. Parsons, C. and Molnar, A. 2014a. "Real and substantial connections: enforcing Canadian privacy laws against American social networking companies," *Journal of Law, Information & Science* 23(1): 1–24.

    2014b. "Forgetting, Non-Forgetting and Quasi-Forgetting in Social Networking: Canadian Policy and Corporate Practice," in Gutwirth, S., Leenes, R., and De Hert, P. (eds.) *Reloading Data Protection: Multidisciplinary Insights and Contemporary Challenges*. New York: Springer, pp. 41–60.

Berners-Lee, T., Fischetti, M. and Michael, L. 2000. *Weaving the Web: The Original Design and Ultimate Destiny of the World Wide Web by Its Inventor*. New York: Harper Business.

boyd, d. 2011. "Social Network Sites as Networked Publics: Affordances, Dynamics, and Implications," in Papacharissi, Z. (ed.) *A Networked Self: Identity,*

Community, and Culture on Social Network Sites. New York: Routledge, pp. 39–58.

Cronin, C. and DeGreiff, P. (eds.) 1998. *The Inclusion of the Other: Studies in Political Theory.* Cambridge, MA: MIT Press.

Danezis, G. and Clayton, R. 2007. "Introducing Traffic Analysis," in Acquisti, A., Gritzalis, S., Lambrinoudakis, C., and Vimercati, S. di (eds.) *Digital Privacy: Theory, Technologies, and Practices.* New York: Auerbach, pp. 95–116.

DeCew, J. Wagner 1997. *In Pursuit of Privacy: Law, Ethics, and the Rise of Technology.* Ithaca, NY: Cornell University Press.

Diffie W. and Landau, S. 2007. *Privacy on the Line: The Politics of Wiretapping and Encryption.* Cambridge, MA: MIT Press.

Electronic Frontier Foundation, 2013. "First Unitarian Church of Los Angeles v. NSA." Accessed from www.eff.org/cases/first-unitarian-church-los-angeles-v-nsa.

Etzioni, A. 1999. *The Limits of Privacy.* New York: Basic Books.

European Union Article 29 Working Party 2009. Opinion 5/2009 on Online Social Networking. 01189/09/enwp163. Adopted on 12 June.

Feiler, L. 2010. "The legality of data retention directive in light of the fundamental rights to privacy and data protection," *European Journal of Law and Technology* 1(3). Accessed from http://ejlt.org/article/view/29/75.

Fuchs, C. 2010. *Internet and Society: Social Theory in the Information Age.* New York: Routledge.

Gallagher, S. 2013. "Googlers say 'f*** you' to NSA, company encrypts internal network," *Ars Technica,* 6 November. Accessed from http://arstechnica.com/information-technology/2013/11/googlers-say-f-you-to-nsa-company-encrypts-internal-network/.

Habermas, J. 1996. *Between Facts and Norms: Contributions to a Discourse Theory of Law and Democracy.* Cambridge, MA: MIT Press.

  1998a. "A Genealogical Analysis of the Cognitive Content of Morality," in Cronin, C. and DeGreiff, P. (eds.) *The Inclusion of the Other: Studies in Political Theory.* Cambridge, MA: MIT Press, pp. 3–46.

  1998b. "Three Normative Models of Democracy," in Cronin, C. and DeGreiff, P. (eds.), *The Inclusion of the Other: Studies in Political Theory* Cambridge, MA: The MIT Press, pp. 239–52.

Haggerty, K. and Ericson, R. (eds.) 2006. *The New Politics of Surveillance and Visibility.* University of Toronto Press.

Hindman, M. 2009. *The Myth of Digital Democracy.* Princeton University Press.

Kaye, B. K. 2011. "Between Barack and a Net Place: Motivations for Using Social Network Sites and Blogs for Political Information," in Papacharissi, Z. (ed.) *A Networked Self: Identity, Community, and Culture on Social Network Sites.* New York: Routledge, pp. 208–31.

Kerr, I., Binnie, M. and Aoki, C. 2008. "Tessling on my brain: the future of lie detection and brain privacy in the criminal justice system," *Canadian Journal of Criminology and Criminal Justice* 50(3): 367–87.

Kies, R. 2010. *Promises and Limits of Web-deliberation*. New York: Palgrave Macmillan.

Kravets, D. 2010. "Judge Tosses NSA Spy Cases," *Wired Online*, January 2010. Accessed from www.wired.com/threatlevel/2010/01/nsa-spy-cases-tossed/.

MacKinnon, R. 2012. *Consent of the Networked: The Worldwide Struggle for Internet Freedom*. New York: Basic Books.

Mayer-Schönberger, V. and Cukier, K. 2013. *Big Data: A Revolution that Will Transform how We Live, Work, and Think*. New York: Houghton-Mifflin-Harcourt.

Mergel, I. 2012. *Social Media in the Public Sector: A Guide to Participation, Collaboration and Transparency in the Networked World*. San Francisco: Jon Wiley & Sons, Inc.

Mill, J. S. 1859. *Three Essays*. Oxford University Press.

Millar, J. 2009. "Core Privacy: A Problem for Predictive Data Mining," in Kerr, I., Lucock, C. and Steeves, V. (eds.) *Lessons from the Identity Trail*. Oxford University Press, pp. 103–20.

Nippert-Eng, C. E. 2010. *Islands of Privacy*. University of Chicago Press.

Nissenbaum, H. 2009. *Privacy in Context: Technology, Policy, and the Integrity of Social Life*. Stanford University Press.

Opsahl, K. 2013. "Why Metadata Matters," *Electronic Frontier Foundation (EFF)*, June 7. Accessed from www.eff.org/deeplinks/2013/06/why-metadata-matters.

Regan, P. M. 1995. *Legislating Privacy: Technology, Social Values and Public Policy*. Chapel Hill: University of North Carolina Press.

Saveri, A., Rheingold, H. and Vian, K. 2005. "Technologies of Cooperation," *Institute for the Future*. Accessed from www.rheingold.com/cooperation/Technology_of_cooperation.pdf.

Schoeman, F. D. 1992. *Privacy and Social Freedom*. Cambridge University Press.

Schwartz, P. M. 1999. "Privacy and democracy in cyberspace," *Vanderbilt Law Review* 52: 1610–702.

Solove, D. J. 2008. *Understanding Privacy*. Cambridge, MA: Harvard University Press.

Stalder, F. 2002. "Privacy is not the antidote to surveillance," *Surveillance and Society* 1(1): 120–4.

Steeves, V. 2009. "Reclaiming the Social Value of Privacy," in Kerr, I., Lucock, C. and Steeves, V. (eds.) *Lessons from the Identity Trail*. Oxford University Press, pp. 191–208.

Strandburg, K. J. 2007. "Surveillance of Emergent Associations: Freedom of Association in a Network Society," in Acquisti, A., Gritzalis, S., Lambrinoudakis, C. and Vimercati, S. di (eds.) *Digital Privacy: Theory, Technologies, and Practices.* New York: Auerbach, pp. 435–58.

Taddicken, M. 2012. "Privacy, Surveillance, and Self-Disclosure in the Social Web: Exploring the User's Perspective via Focus Groups," in Fuchs, C., Boersma, K., Albrechtslund, A. and Sandoval, M. (eds.) *Internet and Surveillance: The Challenges of Web 2.0 and Social Media.* New York: Routledge, pp. 255–72.

Turkle, S. 2012. *Alone Together: Why We Expect More from Technology and Less from Each Other.* New York: Basic Books.

Warren, S. and Brandeis, L. 1890 "The right to privacy," *Harvard Law Review* 4(5): 193–220.

Westin, A. F. 1967. *Privacy and Freedom.* New York: Atheneum.

Young, I. M. 2001. "Activist challenges to deliberative democracy," *Political Theory* 29(5): 670–90.

PART III

Issues in privacy regulation

12

The social value of privacy, the value of privacy to society and human rights discourse

KIRSTY HUGHES

Aligned with the liberal perception of the role of the individual, privacy has traditionally been seen as an individualistic right, as a right that the individual holds in opposition to the interests of society. Priscilla Regan's landmark book *Legislating Privacy* (1995) highlighted the ways in which policy debates concerning privacy were premised on an individualistic notion of privacy and connected this to similar tendencies within the philosophical literature. Whilst scholars touched on these issues in various different forms prior to Regan's book (Gavison 1980; Simitis 1987), Regan's analysis pinpointed limited engagement with this issue and provoked renewed interest under the name of the "social value of privacy" (Cockfield 2007; Solove 2008: 89–98; Steeves 2009; Nissenbaum 2010: 86). Yet the term "social value of privacy" remains puzzling, in part because it is used in several connected and overlapping senses. The first is the idea that *privacy is a common good*, the second is to discuss *the value of privacy to society* and the third is to *reclaim the socializing function of privacy*. All three uses have roots in the richness of Regan's analysis.

The first derives from Regan's argument (1995: 212–43) that privacy is a social value because it is a common value (shared by individuals), it is a public value (of value to the democratic political system) and it is a collective value (technology and market forces make it increasingly difficult for any one person to have privacy unless everyone has a minimum level of privacy). Essentially this means that privacy is something we all value, it is important for the democratic political system and we cannot have it unless we work together. This privacy as a common good mode of reasoning can be seen in Nehf (2003), where it feeds into analysis of why a loss of privacy is a societal problem, in the same way that damage to the environment may be regarded as a societal problem. Others have expressed doubts as to whether we cannot have privacy unless everyone has a minimum level of it (Nissenbaum 2010: 87–8). The second approach, namely the value of privacy to society, is also evident in Regan's analysis (1995: 225–7); when she laments the neglect of the importance of privacy to society, she hones in on one facet of this when she discusses the "public value." Following in this vein, scholars have referred to the social value of privacy when analyzing the higher order social goods that privacy promotes. This can be seen in Solove's work (2008: 91–2) when he argues that "[t]he value of privacy should be assessed on the basis of its contributions to society" and discusses "[u]nderstanding privacy as having a social value – the benefits it confers on society" and "[u]nderstanding the social value of privacy ... requires that we demonstrate the benefits to society of remedying certain harms to individuals." Similarly Nissenbaum (2010: 86) recalls the "voices calling attention to the social value of privacy; that is, the value of privacy to society."

The third use of "the social value" is to "reclaim the socialising function of privacy." This can be seen in Steeves (2009), where she discusses the ways in which privacy scholarship has become focused upon informational control and has been taken out of its social context. This third use connects to the second use (arguments for why privacy is beneficial for society), but it is a broader argument, which extends the scope of privacy and has implications for arguments as to why privacy is beneficial for the individual. Like Hughes (2012) and Roessler and Mokrosinska (2013), Steeves' analysis aims at moving past an informational conception of privacy and providing a richer analysis of privacy in its sociological context. Thus, whilst each of the three uses of the term are connected – indeed the shift between each of them is a subtle one and it is important that we are clear as to what we mean by the "social value" – each is an important question and a vital facet of privacy scholarship in its own right.

This chapter is focused on the second and third uses of the term, namely the ways in which privacy is beneficial to society (one of which is the socializing function). There are at least three ways in which society benefits from privacy. The first is that privacy precludes the dissent into a totalitarian regime. The second is that privacy cultivates the intellectual development of society by providing the emotional and physical space in which ideas can be formed, developed and explored. The third is that privacy fosters social relations by enabling us to form different sorts of relationships with different levels of intimacy. Such relations are important to human well-being and happiness, as well as to social harmony. Each of these values emphasizes the role that privacy plays in contributing to the sort of society to which we aspire: a democratic, reflective and harmonious society. Each has something to offer in determining the interests that are protected under the right to privacy, against whom the right to privacy may be enforced and the balance that is struck between this right and other related interests. If we do not recognize each of these different ways in which society is enriched by privacy, if we conflate these different benefits, then we may continue to undervalue privacy in the same way that we undervalue it when we focus solely on the benefits for the individual. It is thus important that we are clear as to the various ways in which privacy benefits society and it is essential that all three are fully accounted for in human rights scholarship.

Legal analysis continues to lag behind developments in privacy theory. Regan (1995: 27) noted that in philosophical analyses "[w]hen privacy competes with another social value or interest, the social basis of the other interest is explored while the *individual* basis of the privacy interest is examined." Yet whilst theorists may have responded to Regan's call, the jurisprudence of the European Court of Human Rights still largely follows the liberal tradition of privacy scholarship. The second part of this chapter examines the principles and values that the European Court of Human Rights has developed in its jurisprudence and the ways in which the Court has primarily presented privacy as an individualistic right. At first glance it is perhaps unsurprising that the ways in which society is enriched by privacy have a limited role to play in human rights discourse. Civil and political rights such as those protected in the Convention are founded on liberalism. The *raison d'être* of the Convention rights is to remove certain fundamental interests from the risk of being trumped by a utilitarian calculation of majoritarian societal interests and/or political whim. To justify prioritizing these rights of the individual, one would expect, and indeed one needs, a strong argument for why the right is valuable to the individual. Thus it may be thought inevitable that the Court would focus upon the individual in interpreting and applying the right. Yet this is not inevitable. In fact it is in sharp contrast to the way in which the Court presents other civil and political rights such as the rights to freedom of expression, assembly and religion. Examining two key areas of the Court's jurisprudence, namely surveillance and media privacy, reveals that whilst there are occasional references to the importance of privacy to society overall, this area is underdeveloped. The chapter concludes with a reflection upon whether this should give rise to concern, and how the Court's jurisprudence could and should be developed in the future.

The value of privacy to society

As noted above, some analyses conducted under the guise of the social value are concerned with the extent to which privacy is beneficial to society. I prefer to refer to this particular line of inquiry as the "value of privacy to society" rather than "social value" due to the range of issues considered under its remit. There is a second reason for wishing to avoid the use of the term "social value"; this relates to the range of arguments for why privacy is beneficial. As I explain below, there are at least three arguments: the democratic argument; the intellectual development of society argument; and the social interaction argument. As there are a number of arguments, I prefer the term "value of privacy to society" because it clearly refers to the ways in which society benefits, whereas "social value" conjures up the idea of socializing, of being sociable, which is in fact one, but only one of the ways in which society benefits from privacy. This may appear to be an exercise in semantics, but if we use the term social value, then it is difficult to distinguish the latter of the three values (social interaction) from the term for the group of values (the social value). If we fail to clearly identify the multitude of ways in which privacy enriches society, then this could undermine the strength of the argument.[1] Let us now consider each of these arguments in turn.

Central to privacy scholarship is the idea that privacy is a bulwark against totalitarianism, that it is vital for democracy. History and literature suggest that totalitarian dystopias flourish when privacy is diminished; thus it is unsurprising that scholars have argued that privacy is essential to democracy. For example, Spiros Simitis (1987: 732) claims that privacy is a "constitutive element of a democratic society" and Ruth Gavison (1980: 455) writes that privacy is "essential to democratic government because it fosters and encourages the moral autonomy of the citizen, a central requirement of a democracy." She explains that "[p]art of the justification for majority rule and the right to vote is the assumption that individuals should participate in political decisions by forming judgments and expressing preferences. Thus to the extent that privacy is important for autonomy, it is important for democracy as well." Annabelle Lever (2012: 24–8) also argues that the secret ballot box is the paradigm

---

[1] This is also why I do not adopt Benjamin Goold's (2009 and 2010) term "political value." This term is apt for Goold's argument, which focuses upon the problems of state intrusions into privacy, but it does not apply to the full range of ways in which privacy is valuable to society.

example of the relationship between privacy and democracy citizenship, as all individuals are entitled to vote whether or not others approve of their decision. Thus one of the core values of privacy is that it allows individuals to have distance from the state: no democracy can flourish where individuals have no privacy from the state. It is a prerequisite to a non-totalitarian state. Indeed, as Benjamin Goold (2010: 42–3) argues, "it is difficult to imagine, for example, being able to enjoy freedom of expression, freedom of association or freedom of religion without some accompanying right of privacy." Whilst many highlight the democratic need for citizens to have privacy from the state, Gavison (1980: 456) goes further and argues that respecting the privacy of politicians may also be crucial if we are to attract talented persons into public office. Thus the democratic argument may be relevant to media privacy as well as issues such as state surveillance.

Further insight into the societal benefits of privacy derives from analyses of the role of privacy in intellectual development. Privacy fosters autonomous individuals, who have the space and time to develop opinions and ideas. At the heart of these arguments is the sense that society as a whole is better off if it facilitates the development of autonomous individuals; that privacy provides us with the space in which to develop the sorts of ideas and thoughts that are valuable to society. Those opinions and ideas may lead to scientific, artistic, technological or political contributions from which we may all benefit. This type of argument was powerfully made in Virginia Woolf's (2002) classic essay *A Room of One's Own*. Following this line of reasoning, Neil Richards (2008: 389 and 2015) argues that we need to protect private reading, thinking, private spaces and confidential communications, as these are prerequisites to the development of ideas and beliefs. These ideas and beliefs need to be developed "away from the unwanted gaze or interference of others" so that we can confidently develop ideas that are worth expressing. In some senses the intellectual development argument overlaps with the democratic argument for privacy. Clearly we need freedom to develop ideas and opinions for there to be any meaningful form of democracy, but the argument is also relevant to ideas, thoughts and reading not connected to democratic functions. In this sense it is connected to the broader autonomy-based arguments for free speech that overlap with, but are not synonymous with, the democracy-based arguments for free speech. The inclusion of the intellectual development argument has implications for the scope of the right to privacy, as whilst the democratic argument supports a right to privacy from the state, the intellectual development argument supports a broader right to privacy enforceable against commercial organizations and private individuals as well as the state.

If privacy and freedom of expression serve the same function, then the rights are perhaps interchangeable in scenarios in which the two rights clash. It is worth considering then whether privacy offers anything over and above what is offered by freedom of expression. The social relations argument assists here. A broader explanation of the societal value of privacy is that privacy facilitates social interaction and alleviates tensions that could otherwise erupt in chaos, conflict and public disorder. It offers the mental and physical space essential to plurality, tolerance and our interactions with others. I have argued elsewhere (Hughes 2012) that to understand privacy, we need to examine the ways in which privacy is experienced, and that insight can be derived from social interaction scholarship, in particular from the work of Irwin Altman (1975). Altman (1975: 23) argues that "privacy is not solely a 'keep out' or 'let in' process; it involves a synthesis of being in contact with others and being out of contact with others." Building upon this work, I have suggested that the right to privacy is a right to the protection of the different barriers that are employed to restrict others from accessing us and that privacy serves to facilitate social interaction. As discussed above, the social interaction approach is a broader argument, but it has implications for the perceived value of privacy and the extent to which the right to privacy is enforced against other competing rights and interests. It highlights how privacy provides time and space away from others to rest and prepare ourselves for further interaction, and it allows us to form different types of relationships, which allow us to explore different facets of our personalities. By allowing these periods of respite and facilitating multiple spheres of interaction, privacy mediates social interaction. This is not just beneficial for the individual seeking privacy, it is also beneficial for social relations (Steeves 2009; Hughes 2012; Roessler and Mokrosinska 2013). Other scholars have also emphasized the role of privacy in fostering social relations, for example Feldman (1997) Schoeman (1992) and Solove (2008), although they have not connected their analysis to social interaction scholarship.

Analysis of the societal values of privacy reveals that there is a cluster of different and overlapping societal values, all of which are important to the development of the sort of society to which we may aspire. The societal values have implications for the extent to which we protect privacy vis-à-vis other rights and interests, the scope of the right to privacy (the interests that we protect) and against whom the right can be enforced (the state or private actors). It is therefore crucial that they are reflected in privacy laws and privacy policies. Yet to what extent are these arguments shaping human rights discourse?

To what extent are these societal values recognized in the jurisprudence of the European Court of Human Rights?

The Convention on the Protection of Human Rights and Fundamental Freedoms (European Convention on Human Rights or ECHR) CETS No. 005, is the primary human rights instrument in Europe. Individuals bring proceedings against their state before the European Court of Human Rights. The Court then issues judgments: it can find that the state has violated the Convention, and it may require the state to pay non-pecuniary damages and costs under just satisfaction.

The Convention does not contain an express right to privacy. Article 8 ECHR protects the right to respect for private life, family life, home and correspondence. However, as Article 8 was designed to implement Article 12 of the Universal Declaration of Human Rights (which does refer to privacy), it seems to have been intended that it would deal with privacy rights. The Court has also referred to a right to privacy (see, for example, *Armonienė* v. *Lithuania* (2009) and *Mosley* v. *United Kingdom* (2011)) and a number of Parliamentary Assembly resolutions expressly state that Article 8 guarantees a right of privacy (see, for example, Resolution 1165 [1998] of Parliamentary Assembly of the Council of Europe on the Right to Privacy).

The very fact that there is a right indicates that privacy is important. Human rights by their nature protect some interests from incursions by other societal interests. Thus by protecting a right to privacy, the privacy of an individual is protected over and above other societal interests. Moreover, the range of activities protected under the remit of the right to privacy may give an indication of the perceived value of the right. Feldman (1997) rightly points to the array of what he terms "privacy-related rights" protected under Article 8 to demonstrate the social nature of privacy. Feldman is right to highlight the dynamic scope of the right developed under Article 8. The value of privacy to society is also relevant to the ways in which those rights are presented and evaluated. The right to privacy contained in Article 8 is not an absolute right; it is a qualified right, which means that interferences can be justified in certain circumstances when the right clashes with other rights and interests. In these cases the Court has to weigh up the competing right and interests to determine whether the interference with the right is justified. There are two types of scenarios in which this can arise: (1) where there is a competing public interest; and (2) where the right clashes with another Convention right. Given the qualified nature of the right, we need to take a closer look at the principles that the Court has developed in the jurisprudence, and its analysis of the right to privacy vis-à-vis other competing rights and interests.

The Court's general principles

In its judgments the Court sets out a number of "general principles" elaborating on the nature of the right. In doing so it touches upon many of the arguments advanced in privacy scholarship; for example, the Court's references to "physical and psychological integrity," and the "right to identity and personal development" (see for example *Von Hannover* v. *Germany* (2005)) echo arguments made in the academic literature based upon bodily integrity, autonomy, dignity and human flourishing (Rachels 1975; Reiman 1976; Solove 2008). It is implicit in the Court's analysis that protecting these qualities for individuals is beneficial for society. This is not, however, the same as developing a strong sense that privacy has a societal value. It is worth comparing the general principles in Article 8 cases with the general principles that the Court has set out in other qualified rights cases. The other qualified rights protected by the European Convention on Human Rights are Article 9 ECHR, freedom of thought, conscience and religion; Article 10 ECHR, freedom of expression; and Article 11 ECHR freedom of peaceful assembly and association with others. In those cases the Court expressly recognizes the ways in which society benefits from the protection of those rights. For example, the Court stated in *Eweida* v. *United Kingdom* (2013, at [79]) that Article 9 is "one of the foundations of a democratic society," and that "the pluralism indissociable from a democratic society, which has been dearly won over the centuries depends on it." The Court emphasized in *Handyside* v. *United Kingdom* (1976 at [49]) the role of freedom of expression in a "democratic society," declaring that it is "one of the essential foundations for such a society, one of the basic conditions for its progress." Similarly in *Kudrevicius* v. *Lithuania* (2013) the Court asserted "that the right to freedom of assembly is a fundamental right in a democratic society and like the right to freedom of expression is one of the foundations of such a society."

These dicta are all typical of the Court's approach; indeed the Court regularly emphasizes in the Article 9, 10 and 11 ECHR cases the importance of those rights to society, to the progress of society, to a pluralistic and tolerant society and to a democratic society. Conversely, in the Article 8 cases the Court's general principles focus upon the benefits of privacy for the individual. Even where the Court acknowledges that the right includes forming relationships and interaction in a public context, the Court examines this from the perspective of the individual. Thus, at the level of general abstract principles the Court tends to portray privacy as an individualistic right. Does this feed into the Court's analysis when it comes to applying the principles to specific cases?

The Court's application of the principles

The Court's analysis is rather mixed. On the one hand, the Court has expressly addressed society's interest in preserving particular types of confidentiality, especially doctor/patient (*Avilkina v. Russia* (2013)) and lawyer/client confidentiality (*Michaud v. France* (2014)). This relates to core societal interests expressly provided for in the text of the Convention itself, namely public health, political democracy and the rule of law, and in the case of *Michaud* (2014 at [118]) it also has implications for Article 6 ECHR, the right to a fair trial. Thus it is perhaps unsurprising that the Court has emphasized the importance of preserving privacy in these contexts. On the other hand, there are cases in which the Court has not addressed the value of privacy for society at all, even where these cases also have implications for democracy. For reasons of space, discussion is limited here to some brief examples from two important areas: surveillance and media privacy.

Surveillance

Where one would expect the Court to emphasize the connection between privacy and democracy is in the state surveillance cases. Yet the Court's analysis here is limited. Whilst the Court has found that surveillance activities engage, and sometimes violate Article 8, the Court has not systematically referred to the impact on democracy. Indeed, there are some cases where the Court has not addressed this issue at all. Perhaps the clearest recognition of the implications for democracy is to be found in one of the first Article 8 cases, *Klass v. Germany* (1978), in which the Court was asked to consider whether a regime of secret surveillance violated Article 8. In considering whether the regime violated Article 8, the Court noted that fostering democracy could both support and oppose the use of secret surveillance:

> Democratic societies nowadays find themselves threatened by highly sophisticated forms of espionage and by terrorism, with the result that the State must be able, in order effectively to counter such threats, to undertake the secret surveillance of subversive elements operating within its jurisdiction. The Court has therefore to accept that the existence of some legislation granting powers of secret surveillance over the mail, post and telecommunications is, under exceptional conditions, necessary in a democratic society in the interests of national security and/or for the prevention of disorder or crime ...
>
> The Court, being aware of the danger such a law poses of undermining or even destroying democracy on the ground of defending it, affirms that the Contracting States may not, in the name of the struggle against espionage and terrorism, adopt whatever measures they deem appropriate.
>
> *(Klass v. Germany* at [48]–[49])

The Court has also recognized that secret surveillance can destroy democracy in wiretapping cases. In *Malone* v. *United Kingdom* (1985 at [81]) the Court accepted that "the exercise of such powers, because of its inherent secrecy, carries with it a danger of abuse of a kind that is potentially easy in individual cases and could have harmful consequences for democratic society as a whole." Similarly in *Kennedy* v. *United Kingdom* (2011 at [167]) the Court acknowledged that wiretapping "could have harmful consequences for society as a whole." Yet there are other surveillance cases where the Court has not addressed the relationship between privacy and democracy. This is evident if one considers the Court's limited acknowledgment of the value of privacy to society in cases such as *S and Marper* v. *United Kingdom* (2009), *Gillan and Quinton* v. *United Kingdom* (2010) and *Uzun* v. *Germany* (2011). Thus, overall the Court has not developed a strong notion of the role of privacy as a bulwark against totalitarianism comparable to that which has appeared in the academic scholarship.

S and Marper (2009) concerned the compatibility of the UK's DNA database with Article 8. Under domestic law DNA samples of suspected offenders could be retained indefinitely in the database. The Court found that this violated Article 8 because blanket and indiscriminate retention failed the proportionality test under Article 8(2). Given that the case *S and Marper* concerned an extensive police database, one might expect to find a strong statement from the Court regarding the democratic function of privacy. Yet there is only one brief reference in the Court's judgment to "the interests of the data subjects and the *community as a whole* in protecting the personal data" (2009 at [104], emphasis added). One could argue that the limited express discussion of the democratic/anti-totalitarian function of privacy is irrelevant given that the Court held that Article 8 was violated. However, this is premature. The blanket and indiscriminate nature of the database provided the Court with a relatively easy case to consider under the proportionality principles, and it may be much more difficult for the Court in cases where the state has in place a more limited regime. The Court's analysis does not provide a sense that the core issues are being tackled.

Similarly in *Gillan and Quinton* v. *United Kingdom* (2010) the Court, whilst holding that extensive stop and search powers violated Article 8 (as they were not sufficiently circumscribed nor subject to adequate legal safeguards), offered no insight into the societal importance of preserving privacy. The Court acknowledged the potential impact on other rights if the measures were not restricted, namely the possibility of discriminatory action and the impact on those exercising rights to freedom of expression and assembly, but there was no discussion of the role of privacy in a democracy.

Finally there is *Uzun* v. *Germany* (2011). The German state suspected that Uzun was involved in a terrorist organization (the Antiimperialistische Zelle) and consequently the Federal Office for Criminal Investigation, by order of the Federal Public Prosecutor General, built a Global Positioning System (GPS) receiver into a car used by Uzun. The Court held (at [52]) that the use of the GPS tracking device interfered with Uzun's Article 8 right. In determining whether the interference was justified, the Court noted (at [78]) that the authorities had previously sought to use other less intrusive measures but these had not been effective, (at [80]) that the interference was (in its view) only for a short period of time (three months) and that it affected Uzun essentially only at weekends, thus it was not total and comprehensive surveillance. The Court also noted (at [80]) that the investigation concerned very serious crimes. The Court therefore held (at [80]–[81]) that the interference was proportionate. The Court's suggestion that three months is a short period of time to be subject to surveillance is questionable, as is its declaration that GPS surveillance is less intrusive than interception of telephone communications. Yet the Court's judgment never directly addresses the role of privacy in preserving democracy and preventing the demise into a police state. There are a number of references to the potential for abuse of secret surveillance and the need for legal safeguards, but overall the Court appears to downplay the impact of the surveillance, noting for example (at [80]) that GPS surveillance is less intrusive than visual or acoustical surveillance.

The danger of these forms of surveillance is the erosion of democratic freedom and the threat of a creeping totalitarian police state. These issues should be at the forefront of legal and policy analysis. Yet they are not addressed by the Court's analysis. In all three cases there is a sense that the role of privacy in preserving democracy remains under the surface. Unlike other Convention rights cases, there is no declaration that privacy plays a fundamental role in a democracy. Nor does the Court consider the impact that extensive surveillance can have upon a democratic society. This is not to suggest that the Court has not protected privacy. Indeed, the Court found a violation of Article 8 in both *S and Marper* and *Gillan and Quinton*. Yet where the Court has found a violation, it has done so either on the basis that the measures were not sufficiently prescribed by law (see *Malone* v. *United Kingdom* (1985); *Liberty* v. *United Kingdom* (2009)), or that broad sweeping measures were disproportionate (*S and Marper* v. *United Kingdom* (2009); *Gillan and Quinton* v. *United Kingdom* (2010)). It is likely that the Court will face more difficult cases where surveillance is prescribed by domestic law and where the proportionality argument is more complex. In those cases the Court will need a stronger sense of the value of the right at stake. To adequately deal with surveillance one needs to consider the broader impact that such measures can have upon society and the cumulative effect of seemingly justifiable limited erosions of privacy. There is therefore a need for the Court to include in its general principles some express statements of the importance of privacy to democracy, in a manner comparable to those statements used in relation to other rights. Moreover, whilst the Court's analysis of the relationship between surveillance and democracy is highly limited, its analysis of the impact of surveillance on intellectual development or social relations is non-existent.

Media privacy

The situation is more complex where the Court has to balance two Convention rights. The paradigm case is where an individual relies upon the right to privacy and the press invokes the right to freedom of expression. Let us consider first the way that the rights are presented in the jurisprudence. Following the death of Diana, Princess of Wales, the Council of Europe Parliamentary Assembly issued Resolution 1165 (1998) on the right to privacy. One of the aims of the Resolution was to assert that the right to privacy and the right to freedom of expression are of equal importance, yet the manner in which the rights were presented sheds lights on the perceived underpinnings of the two rights:

> The Assembly reaffirms the importance of every person's right to privacy, and of the right to freedom of expression, as fundamental to a democratic society. These rights are neither absolute nor in any hierarchical order, since they are of equal value.
>
> (Resolution 1165 at [11])

The Resolution speaks of the "person's right to privacy" and freedom of expression as "fundamental to a democratic society." A similar picture emerges from the Court's leading Article 8 case on the balance to be struck between the two rights, *Von Hannover* v. *Germany (No. 2)* (2012). Princess Caroline von Hannover has brought a number of proceedings to the European Court of Human Rights. In *Von Hannover* v. *Germany* (2005) she complained about a German magazine publishing photographs of her carrying out everyday activities. The European Court of Human Rights found that Germany had failed to protect her Article 8 right. In *Von Hannover* v. *Germany (No. 2)* (2012) Princess Caroline brought further proceedings. This time she alleged that the German courts' refusal to issue an injunction preventing publication of further photographs violated Article 8. The Grand Chamber found that there was no violation as the domestic courts had carefully balanced the various factors identified by the European Court of Human Rights. The Chamber's analysis offers important insights into the way that the Court perceives the two rights. It commenced its analysis (at [95]–[102]) with a statement of general principles. As in other cases, the right to privacy was presented as a right for the individual to personal identity and development, whereas freedom of expression was presented as a right essential to democracy. The criteria for balancing Articles 8 and 10 were then set out at [108]–[113]. The criteria are as follows: whether the publication contributed to a debate of general interest; how well known is the person and what is the subject of the report; the prior conduct of the person concerned; the content, form and consequences of the publication; and the circumstances in which the photographs were taken. These criteria largely focus upon the particulars of the individual case in hand. The societal value of freedom of expression is perhaps incorporated into the consideration given to the "initial essential criterion," namely concerning "the contribution made by photos or articles in the press to a debate of general interest." There is no equivalent consideration of the societal benefits of protecting privacy, although this could be incorporated into the Court's analysis of the "consequences of publication."

One would be concerned about the way in which the Court presents the principles underpinning the rights if it were not for the fact that the Court tends to disregard these principles when it comes to determining each case. In reality, one is increasingly left with the feeling that these principles are a cut and paste exercise, which pad out the judgment rather than guide the Court's analysis. This is unfortunate, because the principles could shape the Court's analysis if they were properly applied to provide context to the balancing criteria. Instead the Court tends to apply the *Von Hannover (No. 2)* set of criteria in a mechanical fashion rather devoid of context. In its most recent cases it has not even applied the criteria itself, but has simply considered whether the domestic courts have applied the criteria, with no real concern for the outcome of that balancing process, even if this leads to inconsistent results. This is apparent from the opposing results of *Ruusunen* v. *Finland* (2014) and *Lillo-Stenberg and Saether* v. *Norway* (2014). In *Ruusunen* the Court held that the right to privacy justified the use of the criminal justice system to protect details of the private life of its former prime minister, yet in *Lillo-Stenberg* the Court held that there was no violation of Article 8 when newspapers published photographs of the wedding of an actress and a musician.

Given the Court's current mode of analysis, it seems unlikely that the inclusion of the societal benefits of privacy in the Court's stated principles would affect the Court's reasoning. This would render any argument for inclusion academic. Thus, if the societal benefits of privacy are to influence judicial decision-making, we not only need to argue that the Court needs to reconsider how it conceptualizes privacy, but also that it needs to develop this analysis in its reasoning. Let us consider the scope for these developments.

The scope for development

Clearly, from the point of intellectual consistency it would be preferable if the Court included the societal values of privacy in its stated principles. The Court could do this by asserting that privacy constitutes one of the essential foundations of a democratic society, one of the basic conditions for its progress and intellectual development, and is crucial in facilitating harmonious social interaction. This leads us to consider whether it would be difficult for the Court to embrace the societal values of privacy and whether it would make a difference to the Court's analysis. In my opinion it may be relatively easy for the Court to develop this aspect of the jurisprudence, but it is less clear that it would alter the outcome of the Court's reasoning.

The democratic function of privacy is the easiest to accommodate. The history and ethos of the European Convention on Human Rights suggests that democracy is important to the Convention as a whole. The Convention was drafted in the aftermath of the Second World War with the intention of ensuring, as noted in the preamble, the preservation of democracy and the protection of fundamental rights. The Court has often noted the importance of other rights to a democratic society and it would not be difficult to do so in relation to Article 8. Moreover, whilst the Court has not systematically approached privacy from this perspective, there are sufficient strands in the surveillance jurisprudence that could be developed.

There is also scope for incorporating the intellectual development argument. This could be done by analogy with the Court's analysis of the importance of other rights such as freedom of expression to the "progress of society." In the context of the right to privacy the Court has acknowledged the importance of privacy for the development of the individual and his or her identity, and it would be a natural development of that analysis for the Court to recognize the societal values of such development.

The social relations function is the most problematic. Yet there are some aspects of the Court's analysis that suggest that the right is not limited to the conservative notion of privacy as a process of closing oneself off from society. Indeed there are a number of principles in the Court's analysis that suggest that the Court may appreciate the role that privacy plays in fostering social relations; for example, the Court has stated that the right includes a right to establish relationships with other human beings and the outside world and that there is a zone of interaction of a person with others, even in a public context, that may fall within the sphere of "private life" (see *Von Hannover* v. *Germany*). This suggests a broader notion of privacy that could include an understanding of the social value of privacy.

However, whilst the principles remain abstract, such declarations would make little difference. The Court rarely engages with the principles in any depth. There are legitimate reasons for this; indeed, it is difficult to discern what the Court can realistically do to evaluate the impact of a specific intrusion on intangible principles such as democracy, intellectual development and social interaction. Thus one could conclude from the experiences of the Court that theory and principles are simply of limited use. Such a conclusion would be premature; whilst we may need to do more to render philosophical analyses useful in legal decision-making, there are two ways in which such declarations and principles could be useful.

The first is to use this declaration of principles to provide a starting point for the Court's analysis. If the Court commences its analysis from the perspective that privacy is beneficial for society, then it may require more from the state before it will find that an interference with the right is justified. This is the position that Regan argues for when she declares privacy to be "a social value" in the first categorical use of the term social value. This means that it is presumed that privacy is beneficial for society in legal and policy debates, in the same way that it is generally presumed that freedom of expression is beneficial for society. This could prove beneficial in some of the surveillance cases where the Court may be inclined to downplay the significance of some incursions, where the proportionality analysis may become too nuanced, too context-specific and lose sight of the bigger picture. As Solove explains (2008: 100): "the value must be assessed more systematically, not merely by the happenstance of the specific activities involved in any one particular circumstance." A declaration by the Court of the benefits of privacy to society could also feed into policy-making at the domestic level and define the terms upon which those debates are premised.

For the Court to go further with the societal importance of privacy in the balancing or proportionality analysis, it would need to unpack the different ways in which privacy is beneficial for society. This requires more than simply recognizing that privacy may be beneficial for democracy, intellectual development and social interaction. Here the Court could only incorporate such insights in a meaningful way by drawing deeper on philosophical and sociological research. Given the institutional constraints on the Court, this is highly unlikely unless that research is better connected to legal decision-making.

One thing that the Court could do more easily is link the balancing criteria that it has already established back to the overarching principles to give the criteria context and weight. For example, in considering the nature of a sanction in media privacy cases, the Court could consider why a heavy sanction is problematic. One reason is because a heavy sanction could have a chilling effect on free speech, and free speech is important to democracy. The Court could then consider whether protecting privacy in these circumstances may foster democracy, and therefore whether we need to be concerned about sanctions in this case. This cannot exhaust the Court's analysis because democracy is not the only value underpinning these Convention rights; there are other values at play such as autonomy and dignity, values that are equally difficult to unpack. Nevertheless, whilst these cases are never going to be easy to resolve, a stronger notion of underlying principles may lead to more consistent results than a mechanical application of criteria taken out of context.

Conclusion

The Convention rights are essentially rights of individuals. The important role that they play in protecting interests and values fundamental to the individual should not be underestimated. Nor should we lose sight of the fact that their purpose is to protect the interests of the individual over and above the interests of society. It is by recognizing the needs of the individual that we protect the most vulnerable from majoritarian rule. One danger that comes with emphasizing the value of privacy to society is that we may lose sight of the need to protect the individual from being trumped by society. However, the value of privacy to society does not necessarily undermine that task. Indeed, a thorough understanding of the value of privacy can, and should, support arguments for protecting an individual's right to privacy even when there are other compelling societal interests at stake, such as crime and national security.

Most legal analyses of the right to privacy tend to focus upon the value of privacy for the individual. This derives from the way in which privacy is understood as a concept rather than the way in which human rights are understood in a legal context, as there are other human rights that are more readily perceived as beneficial to society. For example, whereas the right to privacy is associated with values such as dignity, autonomy or personhood, the right to freedom of expression is linked to values such as democracy, truth and tolerance. Yet privacy also plays a crucial role in any democratic society, and in fostering discourse and social interaction. It follows that preservation of privacy is important for society, as well as for the individual.

The European Court of Human Rights offers a broad interpretation to the right to privacy and whilst the right is a qualified right, the Court has, on numerous occasions, upheld the right to privacy. The Court has offered significant protection to individuals who were not protected by their domestic regimes, for example in the wiretapping case *Malone*, the DNA database case *S and Marper* and in cases concerned with the intrusive activities of the paparazzi, such as *Von Hannover*. In that context it may perhaps seem petty to criticize the Court for not discussing the societal importance of privacy, particularly given that the focus upon this facet of privacy is a more recent addition to the theoretical scholarship. But we should be cautious about complacency. The manner in which the Court presents the right matters and the focus upon the individual should not be overlooked. To date the Court's surveillance cases have been relatively straightforward, but this will not necessarily be the case in the future. The Court is likely to face tougher calls for deference to national security (which may also be coupled with more limited access to intelligence evidence), and perhaps more difficult proportionality arguments. When faced with such cases, it is imperative that the Court does not lose sight of the bigger picture. Invasions of privacy are often not simply isolated incursions into "aspects relating to personal identity," as significant as that is for the individual, but are in fact an erosion of one of the essential foundations of a democratic society. It appears to be implicit within the Court's analysis that there is a connection between privacy and the broader societal aims, but it would be preferable to see this brought center stage into the Court's general principles (alongside the interests of the individual) in a way that is comparable with the other Convention rights.

In cases in which there is a clash between privacy and free speech, it is important to note the societal benefits of protecting privacy, and in particular the importance of privacy to social interaction. If we consider privacy just as an individualistic right, then it may be difficult to justify protecting privacy against free speech because free speech also has a core role in democracy and human flourishing. By acknowledging the role of privacy in fostering social interaction, we provide a further weight to the privacy argument that can be employed when weighing it up against freedom of expression. This means that we may need to adjust some of the criteria that we use when balancing these two rights. It also means creating a stronger link between the criteria used to evaluate the rights and the principles underpinning the rights. It may also necessitate expanding upon some of the abstract concepts underpinning the societal values of privacy.

Overall though, what is clear is that the Court's jurisprudence is not just limited in terms of the way in which it conceptualizes rights, but also in what it does with those concepts of rights. Whilst it is desirable that the Court acknowledges the full value of privacy, this will be meaningless unless the philosophical concepts also play a greater role in shaping and enriching the Court's analysis.

References

Altman, I. 1975. *The Environment and Social Behaviour: Privacy, Personal Space, Territory and Crowding.* Monterey: Brooks/Cole Publishing Company.

Cockfield, A. 2007. "Protecting the social value of privacy in the context of state investigations using new technologies," *University of British Colombia Law Review* 40(1): 41–68.

Feldman, D. 1997. "Privacy-related Rights: Their Social Value," in Birks, P. (ed.) *Privacy and Loyalty*. Oxford University Press, pp. 15–50.

Gavison, R. 1980. "Privacy and the limits of the law," *Yale Law Journal* 89: 421–71.

Goold, B. 2009. "Surveillance and the political value of privacy," *Amsterdam Law Forum* 1(4): 3–6.

　2010. "How Much Surveillance Is Too Much? Some Thoughts on Surveillance, Democracy and the Political Value of Privacy," in Schartum, D. W. (ed.) *Overvåkning i en rettsstat*. Bergen: Fagbokforlaget, pp. 38–48.

Hughes, K. 2012. "A behavioural understanding of privacy and its implications for privacy law," *Modern Law Review* 75(5): 806–36.

Lever, A. 2012. *On Privacy*. London: Routledge.

Nehf, J. P. 2003. "Recognizing the societal value in information privacy," *Washington Law Review* 78(1): 1–92.

Nissenbaum, H. 2010. *Privacy in Context: Technology, Policy and the Integrity of Social Life*. Stanford University Press.

Rachels, J. 1975. "Why privacy is important," *Philosophy & Public Affairs* 4(4): 323–33.

Regan, P. 1995. *Legislating Privacy*. Chapel Hill: University of North Carolina Press.

Reiman, J. 1976. "Privacy, intimacy and personhood," *Philosophy & Public Affairs* 6(1): 26–44.

Richards, N. 2008. "Intellectual privacy," *Texas Law Review* 87: 387–445.

　2015. *Intellectual Privacy*. Oxford University Press.

Roessler, B. and Mokrosinska, D. 2013. "Privacy and social interaction," *Philosophy and Social Criticism* 39: 771–91.

Schoeman, F. 1992. *Privacy and Social Freedom*. Cambridge University Press.

Simitis, S. 1987. "Reviewing privacy in an information society," *University of Pennsylvania Law Review* 135: 707–46.

Solove, D. J. 2008. *Understanding Privacy*. Cambridge, MA: Harvard University Press.

Steeves, V. 2009. "Reclaiming the Social Value of Privacy," in Kerr, I. R., Steeves, V. and Lucock, C. (eds.) *Lessons from the Identity Trail: Anonymity, Privacy and Identity in a Networked Society*. Oxford University Press, pp. 191–208.

Woolf, Virginia 2002. *A Room of One's Own*. London: Penguin Books.

13

Privacy, sociality and the failure of regulation: lessons learned from young Canadians' online experiences

VALERIE STEEVES

When Canada first considered enacting private sector privacy legislation in the late 1990s, it was primarily in response to the 1995 European Union Directive restricting the flow of personal data to countries that did not have data protection laws in place. Because law reform was seen as a way to avoid the erection of trade barriers between Canadian companies and their European trading partners, privacy was cast as a commercial issue rather than a social or political issue. The desire to comply with European laws also meant that legislators looked to data protection as the regulatory tool of choice (Bennet and Raab 2002). Data protection, it was reasoned, would not only promote harmonization; it would help Canadian companies compete by leveling the playing field and reigning in rogue companies that did not follow the information practices that were generally accepted by the international business community at the time (Industry Canada and Department of Justice 1998). In addition, data protection was an attractive way to build consumer trust in the emerging information economy at home, because it would provide individuals with more control over their personal information (Industry Canada and Department of Justice 1998).

Given the strong international consensus behind data protection in general, and the commercial imperatives behind the Canadian approach to privacy legislation in particular, it is somewhat surprising that young people were, and continue to be, an important part of Canadian privacy policy discourses. However, from the beginning Canadians legislators ascribed young people a key role in their digital privacy strategy. As savvy digital natives, they were presumed to have a "natural" affinity for both technology and innovation (Shade 2011; Bailey 2013; Bailey and Steeves 2013). Because of this, legislators believed that early uptake of networked technologies by youth would help fuel the digital economy and drive wealth creation. Since the absence of strong privacy protections was seen as a barrier to this uptake, data protection for youth was an attractive market intervention because it ostensibly gave them control over the collection, use and disclosure of their personal information without unduly hampering commercial entities that sought to commoditize it.

At the same time, there were competing discourses within the legislative debate that sought to position privacy as a human right and social value. Legislators situated in this perspective argued that a private life is an essential element of human dignity, and lays the foundation that enables us to exercise other rights such as the right to free expression and free association. In addition, privacy enables us to enjoy a degree of autonomy and enter into relationships with others based on trust. They concluded that data protection alone, with its narrow focus on individual forms of redress, cannot fully protect these elements of privacy because it does not interrogate the social and public goods and harms associated with surveillance (Industry Canada and Department of Justice 1998). They called for broad restrictions on surveillance and remedies that would make privacy, especially privacy of networked communications, the default rather than the exception. However, these alternative discourses were marginalized within the legislative debate (Shade 2011; Steeves 2015a); and when the federal government passed the Personal Information Protection and Electronic Documents Act (PIPEDA) in 2001, it positioned the law – which contained a set of ten data protection practices – as a cornerstone of its emerging e-commerce agenda.

Inherent in PIPEDA is the assumption that transparency on the part of data collectors will enable young people (and their parents) to make informed decisions about what they choose to disclose about themselves (Steeves 2015b)[1]. In other words, young people can protect their privacy by choosing to withhold information that they deem "private." This

---

[1] In Canadian law there are no express provisions regarding the age of consent regarding the collection of personal information. Although contract law would suggest that parental consent is required for at least younger minors, PIPEDA is silent on the issue and the legal position of mature minors is unclear. Except for websites specifically targeting young children, most sites do not have a mechanism to ensure that minors participate only with parental consent; and those sites targeting young children typically only ask for parental consent for minors under the age of thirteen, mirroring the requirements of American law. In any event, children typically slip between the cracks, making their own decisions about what information to disclose. Facebook is an excellent example. Even though its terms of use indicate persons under the age of thirteen cannot join the network, our 2013 survey indicated that 32 percent of eleven- and twelve-year-olds have a Facebook account.

assumption is particularly conducive to commercial interests because it legitimizes the ongoing collection and commodification of the information young people do choose to disclose online. It also helps insulate the marketplace from more onerous regulations, such as opt-in consent provisions and blanket restrictions disallowing the collection of information from minors, that may slow innovation and competitiveness in the emerging information economy (MediaSmarts 2014).

Although there has been a continuing debate about the need for stronger regulations that better protect the role that privacy plays in young people's social lives, particularly given the growing commercialization of young people's social spaces enabled by seamless commercial online surveillance (Lawford 2008), the parliamentary committees reviewing PIPEDA have consistently eschewed a broader approach to protecting the social value of privacy and instead have tinkered with parental consent provisions or education to help young people understand the existing law (Standing Committee on Access to Information, Privacy and Ethics 2014). Often the lesson is that children who want to protect their privacy should not post information about themselves on social media. The corollary is that children who do post information have consented to its collection and use by a variety of actors, from corporations and marketers to schools and gaming companies, because they no longer "care" about privacy. Moreover, when risks to children have been identified (e.g. exposure to offensive content, cyberbullying), legislators have typically looked to surveillance as a way to protect young people from harm, further eroding their ability to enjoy private communications (Bailey and Steeves 2013). Either way, protecting the social value of privacy recedes as a policy alternative.

This chapter draws on qualitative and quantitative research on Canadian young people's use of networked technologies to revisit the assumptions behind the current policy framework and test the efficacy of the privacy protections that are currently in place. I start by examining the evidence regarding young people's technical skills, especially in regard to innovation, and their general attitudes to privacy. I then examine how transparent commercial information practices are to Canadian youth, and whether the data protection model – that assumes consent mechanisms will provide opportunities to protect the privacy of information through intentional non-disclosure – resonates with their lived experiences and expectations. Finally, I provide some evidence to measure the level of trust young people have in e-commerce in general and the current regulatory framework in particular.

The evidence does not paint an encouraging picture. I argue that, although Canadian young people have not demonstrated a natural affinity for technological innovation, they have flocked to networked technologies as a way to enrich their social lives. In that context, they have developed a number of social norms around exposure in an attempt to enjoy the benefits of online publicity while still carving out private socio-technical spaces for self-expression and intimate communication. Young people accordingly seek privacy and publicity at the same time and in the same socio-technical space, by carefully crafting networked communications for a variety of contexts and audiences. Accordingly, young Canadians' experiences of privacy are defined by their interaction with others and are not just a feature of individual decisions to disclose or withhold information in networked spaces.

Because of this, the legislative model adopted by Canadian legislators fails to fully capture the ways in which privacy is implicated in young people's lives. Moreover, PIPEDA privileges notions of consent that legitimize commercial practices of mining the social world; this mining in turn has the potential to restructure young people's social relationships and restrict the kinds of identity performances available to them. This constitutes a profound invasion of young people's privacy, by unintentionally creating invasive online spaces and restricting the social norms that enable young people to negotiate the kinds of privacy they need to meet their developmental goals and enjoy networked sociality.

I conclude by suggesting that a social model of privacy more fully captures the richness of both online publicity and online privacy in young people's lives, and better explains the relationship between privacy, identity, sociality and trust. Once privacy is seen as a social negotiation between actors who seek a comfortable boundary between self and others, disclosure of information does not negate a privacy interest; rather, privacy is mutually constructed when the individual seeking privacy has his or her privacy claim respected by others, independent of whether they are aware of the disclosure. In the words of one fourteen-year-old, "just because someone can see something doesn't mean they should look." A failure to respect a privacy claim – to look – erodes trust because it signals that the other does not acknowledge the claimant as a person requiring dignity and respect for boundaries. Since privacy is co-constructed with others, it is also closely linked to both identity and reputation in interlinking ways. A successful presentation of the self requires control over which audience sees which performance, and when audiences cross over boundaries or performances are unsuccessful, disputes can be managed by moving between public and private spaces to enlist others in reputational repair. By conceptualizing privacy as a social construction, we move away from simplistic models that focus on consent and control over the flow of information, and create the space for legislative solutions that more closely align with young people's needs, such as "right to forget" clauses, and restrictions on data mining and behavioral advertising.

Young Canadians' experiences – privacy, performativity and social connection

The Canadian government's early commitment to encouraging young people to adopt networked technologies as tools for learning and innovation has had mixed results. On the one hand, young Canadians are among the most wired in the world. Of children between the ages of nine and seventeen, 99 percent have access to the Internet outside of school, largely through portable devices, (Steeves 2014b: 7), and by age seventeen, 85 percent have their own cell phone (Steeves 2014b: 10). In addition, almost all students have at least basic technical skills across a variety of platforms (Steeves 2014a: 14). On the other hand, there is little evidence that suggests that Canadian youth are particularly savvy or innovative, and most prefer to consume content that has been posted by others. For example, the majority of older students (65 percent) do not know how to use advanced search functions to find information online, and half never look beyond the first page of search results (Steeves 2014a: 15). And although 75 percent of young people rank YouTube as one of their favorite sites, only 4 percent post their own videos with any frequency (Steeves 2014b: 32). One teacher summarized it this way: "I don't think students are all that Internet-savvy. I think they limit themselves to very few tools … They're locked into using it in particular ways and don't think outside the box" (Steeves 2012b: 9).

Although high levels of connectivity have not led to significant gains in learning or innovation, young Canadians have flocked to networked tools that enable them to access entertainment content and communicate with their friends and family (Steeves 2014b: 17). Corporations such as Facebook have often pointed to this activity to argue that young people no longer care about privacy and are content to trade it away for access to websites and apps (Hill 2010). However, Canadian youth have consistently reported a high interest in networked privacy. As early as 2000, qualitative interview participants indicated that they were attracted to online media precisely because they believed them to *be* private. They reasoned that, since most adults at the time were unable to access the Internet, their online activities were largely anonymous, and they enthusiastically used this privacy to experiment with ways of being that were difficult or impossible to experience offline (Media Awareness Network 2001: 17).[2] For example, chat functions enabled them to interact anonymously with others in a public space, to experiment with flirting and to "try on" a variety of identities. As one thirteen-year-old boy in Toronto put it in 2004, "Sometimes I pretend to be a boy looking for a girl. Sometimes I pretend to be a girl looking for a boy. And sometimes I pretend to be a girl looking for another girl" (Media Awareness Network 2004). This kind of interaction provided a unique opportunity to explore the broader social world at little risk to themselves because their actions were shielded by a veil of privacy.

The unrestricted access young people enjoyed in the early years of the Web was increasingly restricted as policymakers raised concerns about offensive content and online predation (Bailey and Steeves 2013); schools introduced highly invasive surveillance mechanisms, such as keystroke capture software (Steeves and Marx 2014), and many parents began to proactively monitor their children's online interactions as a form of care (Steeves 2015b). However, young people have consistently devised strategies to avoid this surveillance and keep their networked communications and activities private. In 2004, for example, interview participants reported that they used instant messaging language that was difficult for adults to understand and deleted their browsing history so they could not be tracked, precisely because it was important to them that their communications – which continued to take place on publicly accessible media and were therefore accessible to those who looked – remained private (Media Awareness Network 2004: 1–16).

This need for private socio-technical spaces where children can participate in social interactions with their peers and experiment with their own identities is closely tied to their developmental need to individuate and explore who they are outside the family (Shade 2011). In effect, this networked social interaction helps them co-produce their subjectivity through their interaction with others, who reflect their performances back to them so they can evaluate them and either incorporate or reject the type of identity they have portrayed into their sense of self (Mead 1934; Goffman 1959; Phillips 2009). Social identities and peer group membership are accordingly reinforced through what Licoppe calls "connected

---

[2] See also Livingstone 2009: 91.

presence," that is the distribution of social interactions across a variety of platforms through which "the (physically) absent party gains presence through the multiplication of mediated communication gestures on both sides, up to the point where copresent interactions and mediated distant exchanges seem woven into a single, seamless web" (Licoppe 2004: 135). This online connectedness is particularly key for adolescents, who construct and display their identities by mapping their social relationships with peer groups and making them visible to others (Livingstone 2009).

Privacy is central to this process because it is what enables them to draw boundaries around their various identities (for example as friend, sibling and student) and manage their social relationships with a variety of audiences, from peers to parents and family to teachers. Privacy is accordingly not sought through selective non-disclosure of personal information that young people consider to be private. Instead, they disclose a great deal of personal information as they perform a variety of identities, and then rely on social norms that govern their interactions with others to maintain the boundaries between their various performances to ensure that some performances are (not) seen by (some) others.

This equal importance of privacy and publicity, and the complex negotiations that enable young people to enjoy both, are perhaps best exemplified by young Canadians' experiences on social media. Given young Canadians' predilection to socialize online, it is unsurprising that the vast majority have incorporated social media into their daily lives. Penetration is highest among older youth: for example, 95 percent of seventeen-year-olds are on Facebook and 63 percent use Twitter. Posting on these and other social media accounts is one of the most frequent activities reported, as is perusing what others had posted on their accounts: almost three-quarters (72 percent) of seventeen-year-olds read or post on friends' social network sites at least once a day or once a week (Steeves 2014b: 28). Social media use also starts early. Almost one-third (32 percent) of younger children (aged nine to eleven) have a Facebook account even though the terms of use on the site forbid children under the age of thirteen from joining the network, and social media supplants playing online games as the most popular online activity by age twelve (Steeves 2014b: 22).

Our interview participants in 2013 indicated that this high degree of connectedness is a way to monitor the "drama" that publicly unfolds among their peer group and to stay in the loop with respect to the latest gossip. In addition, since their social media posts are visible to others in their social circle, they can explicitly step in and out of the online gaze to play pranks on each other, and demonstrate their competence in the online environment. The visibility of social media also provides an opportunity to carefully monitor peer reaction to their own and others' postings, in order to identify online presentations that are successful (and perhaps worth imitating) and those that are not (Steeves 2012a: 6–8).

Peer reactions were particularly important to them, since the ease with which unsuccessful performances (e.g. a bad photo or losing control of a sext) can be seen, copied and forwarded poses significant risks to their social status. Although public display is clearly part of the fun of social media, poor public displays can be devastating and open them up to ridicule and embarrassment. Young people accordingly spend a great deal of time and effort carefully selecting photos that present a positive image, or at least avoid a negative one, before they post them publicly, and take steps to make sure bad photos are kept out of public view. As these fifteen-year-old girls put it:

Diana: I just don't take stupid pictures that I know could ruin my reputation, or something.
Leah: I don't think any of my friends would.
Diana: Exactly. And if I take stupid pictures on a camera, then I delete it, right.

(Steeves 2012a: 33)

Young people also closely monitor the way they are being portrayed in photos taken by others so they can preemptively stop certain kinds of images from being posted publicly. For example, interviewees reported that friends would frequently take snap shots of them goofing around in private. However, as the following discussion illustrates, they routinely go into each other's phones or cameras and proactively delete any they do not want seen by others, in order to manage the way they are viewed publicly on social media:

Emma: Cause … if there's a picture of my goofing off, like making a funny face, you don't want everyone to see that, it's between you and your friends.
Taylor: Yeah, other people, other people probably all make fun of you, and then that'll stay around for a while because that's happened before.
Emma: Yeah, only your friends understand why you're doing it …
Taylor: Yeah, and then everyone else, like, sees it and then they're kind of like, "oh, why are you doing this?"

(Steeves 2012a: 32)

Failing to provide access to photos so they can be pruned is seen as a breach of friendship, and can justify breaking into the friend's phone or social media account without permission to directly delete an embarrassing image. Persisting in posting an unflattering photo without permission signals the end of the friendship. On the other hand, close friends keep potentially embarrassing photos on a private device, such as a smart phone; the fact the image is privately held and will not be distributed is understood to be a sign of intimacy and trust. For example, thirteen-year-old Lya in Toronto pulled out her phone and showed a particularly funny photo to her best friend Allie, who was also in the group. The photo showed Allie making a face. Even though others in the group wanted to see it, Lya refused to show it to them, indicating that is was something only for her and Allie to enjoy.

Friends are also expected to proactively monitor comments and photos posted of friends and, in the event that someone does post something embarrassing or mean, go online and repair the damage to the friend's reputation. This was illustrated when twelve-year-old Emma recounted that one of her schoolmates had posted a bad photo of her on Facebook and people began to post derogatory comments about her appearance. She texted her friends, who immediately responded by posting comments such as: " 'No, Emma looks cool, she's awesome, she's so brave' and stuff, and [Emma] was like, 'I love you guys' " (Steeves 2012a: 32).

Again the distinction between the public and the private spheres is crucial here. Although the public nature of the posts in Emma's case exacerbated the social consequences since they were seen by so many of Emma's peers, that publicity also enabled Emma to privately monitor her online persona and call on her friends to defend her. Emma did not publicly challenge the attack, but instead privately marshalled her social resources in response. Emma's friends then entered the public sphere to repair the harm that had been done to her online reputation.

Our quantitative survey indicated that these kinds of steps are common among the population as a whole. Of the students surveyed, 97 percent reported that they would take steps to protect themselves if someone posted a photo of them online that they did not want others to see. Asking the poster to take the photo down was the most common response (80 percent). "Untagging," as a form of direct action, rose dramatically as children aged, and was especially common for older teens (72 percent). Calling on friends for help was also one of the top three responses for dealing with online conflict for all age groups (Steeves 2014c: 22–3).

These findings suggest that the construction of networked privacy is a highly social activity. Friends rely upon each other to mutually manage their public image by creating boundaries around what is and is not exposed to public view, and keeping certain images private signals intimacy. Friends also privately monitor the ways in which other friends are portrayed online and step into the public sphere to respond to attacks and repair reputational harm.

Interestingly, the teenagers we spoke to in 2013 reported that maintaining boundary control was much more difficult for them because of parental concerns around online safety. Although almost all of them enjoyed connecting with family online, the kinds of surveillance to which many of them are subjected was disheartening, and made it difficult for them to enjoy both private interaction with friends and relationships of trust with family. For their part, the parents we talked to were ambivalent about monitoring their children online. Although most thought monitoring was necessary because they needed to protect their children both from strangers and from the consequence of their own poor judgment, they were also uncomfortable about invading their children's privacy.

The teens we spoke to responded empathetically and acknowledged that parents were only trying to protect them. However, they all took a variety of steps to make sure parents could not access their interactions with their friends. Many used technical controls, such as privacy settings and the routine deletion of histories, to evade "lectures." When one girl from the fifteen to seventeen-year-old age group indicated that "My mom keeps on [posting] me, 'You're on Facebook! Get off! Do your homework!' And I'm like ... de-friend" (Steeves 2012a: 17), the group exploded with similar stories about taking steps to ensure that their interactions with friends remain inaccessible to their parents. Even many of our youngest survey respondents felt that parents should not force their children to friend them on social media sites (56 percent) or read their texts (44 percent), and took steps to avoid being watched. The equivalent percentages among older children were much higher (77 percent and 83 percent, respectively) (Steeves 2014c: 34).

Again, this heightened concern among teenagers is consistent with a developmental need for privacy from parents. A private sphere provides older children with the autonomy they need to explore the "public-private boundaries of the self" (Peter *et al.* 2009: 85) and "renegotiate their familial relationships ... seek to define themselves within a peer group ... [and] venture out into the world without parental supervision" (Draper 2012: 223). One teen in Toronto summarized: "There should be a point where parents will just, like, leave you alone and not have to know every single thing about you. Like, I get, the protection side, but they don't need to know every single thing about you" (Steeves 2012a: 18).

Failure to meet this need for privacy creates tensions within the family and abrogates the reciprocal trust that is at the heart of family life. The teens we spoke to were vituperative about parents and other family members "spying" on them, even though they were aware of the fact that their social media posts are public and can be seen by others. For example, after one teen found out that her cousins "snitched" on her by telling her mother about a photo she had posted on social media, "the same night I go and delete them ... then [my mom] gets mad, she's like 'don't delete your family members.' I'm like, well, tell them to stop stalking me" (Steeves 2012a: 18). Another teen facing the same situation blocked her little brother because "he's like a little spy for my mother" (Steeves 2012a: 18).

This loss of privacy also makes it harder for teens to express themselves online because performances intended for peers can be taken out of context by family members. This in turn disrupts their "ability to disclose private information in appropriate ways and settings" (Peter *et al.* 2009: 83) with both friends and family, and complicates the boundary negotiation between their various roles, because they can be held to account by all their audiences for comments that were intended for one particular group and not another.

To summarize, Canadian young people have accordingly consistently sought ways to protect their privacy from others online, while at the same time embracing online publicity for the purposes of identity construction and social connection. Our participants carefully crafted different personas for their various audiences (family, friends, schoolmates, employers, teachers) and used privacy settings and other strategies to try to keep one performance (e.g. girlfriend) from leaking into another (e.g. daughter). Although the introduction of social media in particular has complicated their efforts to maintain a sense of privacy because social media largely collapse the lines between their various audiences, young people continue to respond to a lack of privacy by developing new techniques to shield themselves from unwanted observers in an attempt to reinsert comfortable boundaries as they continue to disclose parts of themselves to others as a means to social connection and identity experimentation.

Revisiting the regulatory framework

The current regulatory model, with its focus on transparent information practices and informed consent, fails to capture this rich interplay between privacy, performativity and social connection because it assumes that privacy is an individual choice to withhold or disclose information. From this perspective, privacy is best protected when organizations that collect personal information are transparent about their information practices, so individuals can make informed decisions about what they disclose and what they keep private. The corollary follows that young people who voluntarily disclose information about themselves on a technological platform have consented to the terms of use associated with that platform, and have willingly abandoned any further privacy interest in their data. All that is needed after disclosure is to provide rights of access and correction so young people can ensure that the data collected from them are accurate.

For this model to work, corporations must be transparent about their information practices so data subjects can make informed decisions about what they choose to disclose. However, the evidence suggests that young Canadians are not well informed about the informational practices of the corporate platforms they use. For example, 65 percent of youth aged eleven to seventeen report that no one has ever explained a terms of use policy or a privacy policy to them, and 68 percent mistakenly believe that the presence of a privacy policy on a site ensures that the personal information they post will not be shared with anyone. And although 66 percent indicate that they have been taught how companies collect and use personal information, 39 percent believe that companies are not interested in what they say and do online (Steeves 2014c: 38–9). This suggests that there is a significant gap between corporate practices and young people's expectations.

This lack of knowledge could arguably be addressed by additional education and outreach. However, full transparency may not be a complete corrective. Even when young people understand the commercial model behind their favorite sites, many report that they have no choice but to accept the terms of use, because doing so is the only way they can access the socio-technical spaces they increasingly rely on for social connectedness. Two girls in Ottawa put it this way:

> Like, if we had a choice to say no, I would choose no. We can't or else we can't go on the thing for some of them [fifteen-year-old].
>
> Depending on the consequences of saying no cause sometimes if you say no to like download something, it just like can't do anything with it and then it's just, yeah [fourteen-year-old].
>
> (Burkell et al. 2007: 14)

From this perspective, young people are often not given any real choice: children who do not wish to register or consent to the collection of their personal information are simply told not to use the service (Steeves 2006, 2007). Many young people report that, in those circumstances, they just press "click" and accept whatever terms of service are imposed on them, whether they like them or not (Burkell *et al.* 2007: 14).

But the deeper problem with the regulatory model is the assumption that information, once disclosed, cannot attract a privacy interest. Although young Canadians do sometimes choose to withhold information to keep it private, they more typically choose to disclose information and then negotiate their privacy as they interact with others in networked spaces. Their privacy expectations are accordingly driven less by the fact that unintended others may be able to see what they post, and more by strong ideas about who should and should not be looking. Although they are sometimes unable to successfully negotiate a comfortable degree of privacy (especially because of surveillance related to adult concerns about cyber-safety), the privacy they seek is defined by a complex interplay of opening and closing to a variety of social relationships in a variety of social settings where their interactions can be seen by others. Notions of transparency and consent simply cannot help them to protect their privacy because young people do not operate within a binary division between non-disclosure/private and disclosure/public.

Moreover, the bad fit between the regulatory understanding of privacy and young people's lived experiences of privacy has made it difficult for PIPEDA to construct trust in the digital economy. Although young people tend to be most concerned about privacy from people in their social world, they see commercial surveillance as "creepy" and a type of "stalking" (Burkell *et al.* 2007: 15; Steeves 2012a: 25). Attitudes towards the marketing embedded in the socio-technical spaces they inhabit range from ambivalent to distrustful, and a number report that online corporations are trying to "fool" them or "trick" them into releasing information (Steeves, 2012a: 24). Many have little faith in the data protection process, arguing that corporations intentionally write their privacy policies in language that is incomprehensible so they can "Take advantage of the kids ... cause they can't read at university level" (Burkell *et al.* 2007: 15).

The failure of the current regulatory model to devise a privacy-respectful networked environment is perhaps best illustrated by the finding that the vast majority of young Canadians report that neither the corporations that own the platforms (83 percent) nor the marketers who want to advertise to them (95 percent) should be able to even *see* what they post on social media (Steeves 2014c: 34, 36). Again, just because data is disclosed on the Internet does not mean that young people have abandoned their privacy interest in who can watch it. Although 28 percent also paradoxically report that they like it when companies use the information they post to advertise to them, three-quarters say they want more control over what corporations do with the photos and information they post online. Clearly, the existing framework is not providing them with enough control.

Conclusion

The dominant understanding of privacy as informational control cannot fully capture the ways in which privacy is implicated in young people's online social interaction, identity and performativity because it focuses on the flow of information across the boundary between self and other, instead of on the boundary itself (Steeves 2009). By focusing on disclosure, regulators have downloaded the regulatory burden onto the individual children who inhabit networked spaces and typically call upon young people to stop disclosing information about themselves to others. For example, when a photo of a young Canadian girl who had committed suicide after an intimate photo of her was circulated electronically was used in an online dating site advertisement, then Information and Privacy Commissioner of Ontario Ann Cavoukian stated:

> The unfortunate reality is that people give out far too much information about themselves, believing that their information is "private" and they are safe behind their screen. You are not! We all need to take steps to protect ourselves online, especially on social networks. Young people must be especially careful to consider the potential risks, and make it a practice to only post photos that they want everyone to see, including strangers and prospective future employers. If not, don't post it!
>
> (Contenta 2014)

This approach conflicts with the nuanced ways in which children seek to negotiate both publicity and privacy in public spaces and ignores the social norms they have developed to manage the expectations of their various audiences. Instead, regulators need to carve out anonymous spaces where young people can interact without being constantly monitored, and reconsider the use of surveillance as a protective mechanism. This is especially important in schools, where privacy plays an essential role in creating an environment where children can learn, express themselves and not be afraid to make mistakes (Steeves and Marx 2014).

In addition, given the commercial goals behind the regulatory framework, further research is needed to better understand how commercial mining of the social world restructures social relationships and restricts the kinds of identity performances available to young people online. Early findings indicate that the algorithms applied to the data collected sort children into categories for marketing purposes, and these categories often reproduce real-world patterns of discrimination. The detailed individual profiles that result enable marketers to integrate mediatized messages into children's social environment, through behavioral targeting and "natural" or immersive advertising. This encourages children to internalize the identity created for them by the algorithmic sort itself (Bailey and Steeves 2015). From this perspective, commercial surveillance is a profound invasion of young people's privacy, because it uses the data it collects to reshape their social world and steer their social interactions. It also creates a feedback loop that reinforces mainstream stereotypes: information architectures lend themselves to certain kinds of identity performances (e.g. highly sexualized performances of girls), and these architectures combine with social norms to open children up to discrimination (e.g. slut shaming, homophobia). Children co-opt stereotypical performances because they are the cultural capital available to them for identity construction, and this both reinforces discriminatory tropes in children's culture and opens up particular children to harassment based on sexism, racism, homophobia, classism and ableism.

Data protection makes it difficult to question these practices, because a binary notion of consent legitimizes commercial uses and makes it difficult to constrain what happens to the data once consent is given. However, conceptualizing privacy as a social value opens up policy to a broader critique that can interrogate the social impact of commercial surveillance. In addition, a social model of privacy more fully captures the richness of both online publicity and online privacy in young people's online lives, and better explains the relationship between privacy, identity, sociality and trust. It also points to legislative solutions that more closely align with young people's experiences, such as "right to forget" clauses, and restrictions on data mining and behavioral advertising.

References

Bailey, J. 2013. "Cogs in the Wheel of Economic Progress? Claims-Making About Girls and Technology in Canadian Policy Discourse." Shirley E. Greenberg

Chair for Women and the Legal Profession – Speaker Series. University of Ottawa.

Bailey, J. and Steeves, V. 2013. "Will the Real Digital Girl Please Stand Up? Examining the Gap Between Policy Dialogue and Girls' Accounts of Their Digital Existence," in Wise, J. M. and Hille, K. (eds.) *New Visualities, New Technologies: The New Ecstasy of Communication*. London: Ashgate, pp. 41–66.

(eds.) 2015 (forthcoming). *eGirls, eCitizens: Putting Technology Theory and Policy Into Dialogue with Girls' and Young Women's Voices*. University of Ottawa Press.

Bennet, C. and Raab, C. 2002. *The Governance of Privacy: Policy Instruments in Global Perspective*. London: Barnes and Noble.

Burkell, J., Steeves, V. and Micheti, A. 2007. *Broken Doors: Strategies for Drafting Privacy Policies Kids Can Understand*. Ottawa: On the Identity Trail.

Contenta, S. 2014. "Dating website apologizes for using Rehtaeh Parsons's picture," *Toronto Star*, August 30.

Draper, N. 2012. "Is your teen at risk? Discourses of adolescent sexting in the United States," *Journal of Children and Media* 6: 223.

Goffman, E. 1959. *The Presentation of Self in Everyday Life*. New York: Anchor Books.

Hill, K. 2010. "Zuckerberg's Right: Young People Don't Care (As Much) About Privacy," *Forbes*, January 10.

Industry Canada and Department of Justice. Task Force on Electronic Commerce. 1998. *Building Canada's Information Economy and Society: The Protection of Personal Information*. Ottawa: Public Works and Government Services Canada.

Lawford, J. 2008. *All in the Data Family: Children's Privacy Online*. Ottawa: Public Interest and Advocacy Centre.

Licoppe, C. 2004. "'Connected presence': the emergence of a new repertoire for managing social relationships in a changing communication technoscape," *Environment and Planning D: Society and Space* 22: 135–56.

Livingstone, S. 2009. *Children and the Internet*. Cambridge: Polity Press.

Mead, G. H. 1934. *Mind, Self and Society*. University of Chicago Press.

Media Awareness Network. 2001. *Young Canadians in a Wired World: The Students' View*. Ottawa: Media Awareness Network.

Media Awareness Network. 2004. *Young Canadians in a Wired World, Phase II: Focus Groups* Ottawa: Media Awareness Network.

MediaSmarts. 2014. *Youth and Digital Skills Symposium: Preparing Young Canadians to Make Social, Economic and Cultural Contributions*. Ottawa: Information and Communications Technology Council.

Peter, J., Valkenburg, P. and Fluckiger, C. 2009. "Adolescents and Social Network Sites: Identity, Friendships and Privacy," in Livingstone, S. and Haddon,

L. (eds.) *Kids Online: Opportunities and Risks for Children*. Bristol: The Policy Press.

Phillips, D. 2009. "Ubiquitous Computing, Spatiality, and the Construction of Identity: Directions for Policy Response," in Kerr, I., Lucock, C. and Steeves, V. (eds.) *Lessons From the Identity Trail: Anonymity, Privacy and Identity in a Networked Society*. New York: Oxford University Press, pp. 303–18.

Shade, L. R. 2011. "Surveilling the Girl via the Third and Networked Screen," in Kearney, M. C. (ed.) *Mediated Girlhoods: New Explorations of Girls' Media Culture*. New York: Peter Lang, pp. 261–76.

Standing Committee on Access to Information, Privacy and Ethics, House of Commons, Canada. 2014. *Privacy and Social Media in the Age of Big Data*, 1st sess., 41st Parliament.

Steeves, V. 2006. "It's not child's play: the online invasion of children's privacy," *University of Ottawa Law and Technology Journal* 3(1): 169–88.

2007. "The watched child: surveillance in three online playgrounds," *Proceedings of the International Conference on the Rights of the Child*: 119–40.

2009. "Reclaiming the Social Value of Privacy," in Kerr, I., Lucock, C. and Steeves, V. (eds.) *Lessons From the Identity Trail: Anonymity, Privacy and Identity in a Networked Society*. New York: Oxford University Press, pp. 191–208.

2012a. *Young Canadians in a Wired World, Phase III: Talking to Youth and Parents About Life Online*. Ottawa: MediaSmarts.

2012b. *Young Canadians in a Wired World, Phase III: Teachers' Perspectives*. Ottawa: MediaSmarts.

2014a. *Young Canadians in a Wired World, Phase III: Experts or Amateurs? Gauging Young Canadians' Digital Literacy Skills*. Ottawa: MediaSmarts.

2014b. *Young Canadians in a Wired World, Phase III: Life Online*. Ottawa: MediaSmarts.

2014c. *Young Canadians in a Wired World, Phase III: Online Privacy, Online Publicity*. Ottawa: MediaSmarts.

2015a (forthcoming). "Now You See Me: Privacy, Technology and Autonomy in the Digital Age," in DiGiacomo, G. (ed.) *Current Issues and Controversies in Human Rights*. Toronto: Oxford University Press.

2015b (forthcoming). "Swimming in the Fishbowl: Young People, Identity and Surveillance in Networked Spaces," in van der Ploeg, I. and Pridmore, J. (eds.) *Digitizing Identities*. London: Routledge.

Steeves, V. and Marx, G. 2014. "Safe School Initiatives and the Shifting Climate of Trust," in Muschert, G., Henry, S., Bracy N. and Peguero, A. (eds.) *Responding to School Violence: Confronting the Columbine Effect*. Boulder: Lynne Rienner Publishers, pp. 71–88.

14

Compliance-limited health privacy laws

ANITA L. ALLEN

Information privacy laws, also termed "data protection" laws, regulate the collection, use, dissemination and retention of personal information. These laws – which in the United States are products of constitutions, statutes and common law – have the social dimensions I call "compliance" and "impact" limitations. Any sort of law regulating conduct can have compliance and impact limitations; they are not unique to privacy law. Nor are compliance and impact limitations unique to *information* privacy law. Indeed, of special relevance here, laws protecting the *physical* privacy of our bodies no less than the confidentiality and security of our data can have these social dimensions.

To start, what are compliance and impact limitations as they relate to information privacy laws? Impact limitations are the adverse distributive consequences of information privacy laws, whereby some population groups benefit more than or at the expense of others. Indeed, information privacy laws that seem on their face and by design to benefit all population groups more or less equally may, in fact, disadvantage some demographic groups relative to others, by virtue of socio-culturally salient differences. The intended beneficial impact of a body of privacy law can be impaired by the societal condition of race prejudice, for example. Consider, in this respect, an illustration borrowed from Lior Strahilevitz of an impact limitation of US privacy laws restricting access to most criminal history data (Strahilevitz 2013: 2018–20). US laws that treat government-held criminal history information as private are intended to benefit ex-offender job applicants equally, but instead make winners of white job applicants and losers of African Americans. As suggested by Strahilevitz, given the familiar disproportionately high rate of African American incarceration, in the absence of reliable criminal history data to the contrary, employers will use visible race as a proxy for criminality. Employers will presume that an African American male seeking work is more likely to have a serious, violent criminal past than his white counterpart. While one must be skeptical of the implication that African Americans would be better off overall if their criminal histories were detailed in a public registry, the example highlights the possibility that laws with which the public complies as required can have adverse implications for some socially disadvantaged groups (Allen 2013: 245).

A second example of what I am calling "impact" limitations can be borrowed from Strahilevitz, this one relating to consumer credit information (Strahilevitz 2013: 2027). Laws that require keeping consumer credit reports confidential may work to the detriment of low income people with good credit habits and to the benefit of high income people with bad credit habits. While consumer credit information is readily available in the USA to potential lenders, employers and landlords with whom consumers voluntarily seek to establish a relationship, the ability of the law to protect all equally is limited by cultural uses of high income level as a proxy for creditworthiness. Entities without ready access to a consumer's official credit report will make decisions based on a presumption that is not universally true – that poor people are poor credit risks (Strahilevitz 2013: 2027–31).

Laws that are not problematically impact-limited may nonetheless be problematically compliance-limited. Information privacy laws crafted to benefit all population groups more or less equally may fail to do so because individuals and institutions required by law to protect data by concealment and non-disclosure significantly fall down on the job when it comes to the information of certain culturally salient groups. Uneven obedience to privacy law that exposes individuals in particular disadvantaged social categories to harm – racial minority group members, low income group members or women, for instance – constitutes a "compliance" limitation of the law. The laws that protect mental health patients from intimate assault are compliance-limited with respect to women, to the extent that psychotherapists and psychiatrists are more likely to have unethical sexual contact with female patients (Karasu 2013: 35).

The focus of this chapter is compliance-limited health information privacy laws. Health information privacy laws in the United States include federal privacy rules promulgated pursuant to the Health Insurance Portability and Accountability Act (HIPAA) (1996), the Genetic Information Nondiscrimination Act (2010) and state common law or statutes requiring medical confidentiality and special treatment of information relating to HIV/AIDS and pharmacy records (Allen 2011a). The UK and other countries in the EU have analogous laws. Those expected to comply with health privacy laws – and related institutional rules and professional ethics codes – have sometimes failed egregiously to do so in instances where the adversely affected patients are women and girls.

The availability of digital photography and communication technology creates special new perils for female patients' privacy. The lure and consequences of noncompliance with privacy rules are worsened by the ability to upload patient images and information onto the Internet quickly and inexpensively. The popularity of digital media is a new and deep threat to the physical privacy of patients' bodies and the confidentiality of medical encounters. I offer the case of Dr. Nikita Levy to demonstrate serious ethical problems confronting contemporary medical practice – problems far worse than patient-targeted Googling (Baker *et al.* 2014).

Our societies have major privacy and data protection laws. Medical privacy laws merit strict compliance. The laws further important kinds of moral dignity and autonomy, beneficence and justice, along with public health goals (Allen 2011b: 111–20). Privacy law obedience implicates internationally recognized human rights (Allen 2011a). Doing well by women requires, as a normative matter, attention to the causes and cures of compliance limitations. What can be done to maximally deter noncompliance targeting women (Moore *et al.* 2007)? The challenges behind this question merit attention alongside the more general health privacy challenges of our times relating to genomics, neuroscience, electronic medical records, medical data breaches and commercially driven "big data" analytics.

A physician to thousands who did not comply

The extraordinary case of Dr. Nikita Levy illustrates that health practitioners do not always comply with health privacy laws that would otherwise protect their female patients. Dr. Nikita Levy was a popular Jamaican-born specialist in obstetrics and gynecology employed by the Johns Hopkins Hospital. Located in the city of Baltimore, about 40 miles north of Washington DC, the Johns Hopkins Hospital is one of the most respected research hospitals in the United States. Over the years Dr. Levy treated thousands of patients in Johns Hopkins's East Baltimore Clinic. Many of Dr. Levy's patients were low-income African American women and adolescent girls.

On February 4, 2013 one of Dr. Levy's assistants notified the hospital of an alarming discovery: Dr. Levy had photographed patients using camera devices disguised as writing pens (Johns Hopkins University 2013). Johns Hopkins security officers went to Dr. Levy's office the very next day, where they confronted Dr. Levy and confiscated his spy cameras. Johns Hopkins turned over the confiscated cameras to the Baltimore Police Department as evidence of possible criminal wrongdoing. On February 8, 2013 Johns Hopkins terminated Dr. Levy's employment. Within days, Levy was dead in his home. A poignant suicide note left for his wife stated that he did not want to live to "see her suffer with the truth" (Dance *et al.* 2013). The truth is that the doctor was a pornographer. Police who went to Levy's home to further investigate his medical office misconduct found a bank of computers and servers on whose drives resided images of unsuspecting patients undergoing intimate examination.

From an ethical point of view, there can be no question that Dr. Levy's conduct was harmful, wrong and the product of a deeply flawed moral character. For purely selfish reasons, Levy deceived his patients, breached their trust and invaded their privacy by collecting and electronically disclosing personal information and images. From a legal point of view Levy's conduct was also harmful and wrong, since US laws proscribe breaches of medical confidentiality and other invasions of personal privacy. Indeed, Johns Hopkins sent a letter to Dr. Levy's patients asserting that "Dr. Levy had been illegally and without our knowledge, photographing his patients and possibly others with his personal photographic and video equipment and storing those images electronically" (Johns Hopkins University 2013).

Conduct like Levy's can occur anywhere, and would be condemned as unethical and illegal in other countries. For example, in 2014 a young physician, Dr. Suhail Ahmed of Cardiff, was sentenced to 30 months in prison after secretly photographing and assaulting patients at Torbay Hospital in Devon in 2012 (Walker 2014). In officially announcing a decision to increase Ahmed's punishment for "utterly outrageous and invasive behavior," Lord Justice Fulford stated that: "In our view this activity is one of the worst examples of breach of trust that can be contemplated because of the vulnerability of the victims and the importance of maintaining public confidence in those who work within a vital public service" (BBC News 2014).

Dr. Levy failed to comply with privacy laws. His conduct respecting his patients illustrates that health privacy laws applicable to US hospitals and physicians are compliance-limited. Health privacy laws of general application can fail broadly to command compliance as they relate to all groups served. Indeed the Department of Health and Human Services has fined US health care companies millions of dollars in the past several years for systemic failures respecting all their patients, not just specific vulnerable sub-groups and populations. In Levy's case, we are dealing with one doctor who treated thousands of patients over a long career. But suppose all women or women belonging to certain ethnic groups are predictably subjected to serious privacy intrusions by individual health professionals for reasons that directly relate to gender inequality and subordination? Proactively addressing relevant compliance limitations would become a normative ethical requirement of fairness and equality. In societies whose cultures tolerate disrespect for women, pornography and viewing young women and girls as sex objects, egregious privacy abuses are in fact a risk of practices and procedures that give potential offenders control over women's bodies and ready access to technologies of data capture and disclosure.

Surrendering physical privacy to receive care

The delivery of health services typically requires consent. It requires consent to, first, being touched, probed, manipulated, closely observed or recorded; and, second, to sharing personal information received in confidence (Allen 2015). These consent requirements – subject to numerous exceptions for emergencies, public health, education, research and law enforcement – relate to what are commonly thought of as privacy or confidentiality. That consent is an ethical requirement that flows from ideals that include respect for individual autonomy and beneficent concern for the sense of personal security, intimacy and modesty. Health care providers and the institutions in which they work elicit the trust of patients by offering the promise of limited access to persons' bodies and personal information (Rakel 2011). This critical promise is fulfilled by adherence to social norms and institutional and legal requirements that call for discretion in collecting and sharing patient information, permitting access to medical records and the exposing of patient's bodies to observation.

Along with others, American culture has on the whole moved far from customs of centuries past when male physicians were not generally permitted to touch the bare skin of female patients or even to refer explicitly to their health conditions. However, current customs and practices reflect an appreciation for the sensitivity of patient privacy. Because of privacy – even in this era of openness – neither health care providers nor families, friends, employers, researchers and governments can have the free access to patients and patient data that they might desire. Working with some populations may require awareness of special cultural demands of privacy and modesty (McLean *et al.* 2010: 308).

Emergencies aside, patients who must be examined are not required to disrobe completely, and examinations take place underneath gowns and behind curtains and walls. Hospitalized patients are accorded rooms to themselves or with only one or two other patients. Injuries, wounds, medical conditions and medical care are not routinely photographed or recorded without the knowledge and consent of the patient. In the context of women's health, precisely to reduce the risk and fear of inappropriate behavior, physicians often conduct pelvic exams in the presence of third person, such as a partner or nurse. Mammographers and ultrasound technicians are typically women and care is taken to minimize bodily exposure. These practices potentially add to the cost of care, but reflect expectations of privacy in women's health and generate new expectations of privacy by those who come to rely on them (Hawke 1998: 56). Women expect health care providers to act as guardians of their health and health privacy, since women necessarily surrender bodily privacy as a condition of care. It is worth noting, however, that employment discrimination laws restrict the ability of providers to exclude male health care workers. Moreover, patients can harass female physicians in ways that infringe upon their privacy and intimacy (Phillips and Schneider 1993).

Confidentiality and cameras

Confidentiality is a species of privacy. It refers to restricting access to information or data to authorized recipients. The confidentiality of medical information has been a tenet of the Western medical professional since the ancient era of the Hippocratic Oath. Lessons about confidentiality are part of the standard professional training of clinicians and biomedical researchers. The existence of a privileged patient–physician confidential relationship has been preserved in the laws of evidence and procedure. This uniquely confidential relationship is highly valuable to the medical community as breaches of privacy erode patient trust in physicians (Berle 2008: 90). Without trust in the patient–physician relationship, the effectiveness of patient care deteriorates as patients are not as willing to reveal information important for treatment and diagnosis, or may even refuse to seek medical treatment for treatable conditions due to privacy concerns.

Taking and distributing images of others without their consent is one of the oldest recognized forms of privacy invasion and it continues today. Even flattering, fully clothed images made or distributed without consent can raise privacy concerns. Unsurprisingly, then, taking photographs of medical patients is a sensitive business. A woman in the state of Missouri sued in federal court a plastic surgeon who treated her for excess skin and fat removal following massive weight loss, after he gave numerous "before and after" shoulder-to-knee frontal nude photographs of her from her medical records to a local newspaper without her consent. The images were published on the paper's website and also in a print edition of the paper (*Doe* v. *Young*, 2011).

Consent and limits on use and distribution can satisfy the ethical expectations of patients. Patients who believe health care providers have improperly photographed or recorded them describe their injuries as a violation of confidentiality and privacy. Informed consent procedures do well to alert patients when they are consenting to medical photographs or recording, the uses that will be made of the images and the extent to which the images will be shared through various media (Butler 2002). Electronic publishing and the ease of transferring data irretrievably over the Internet require that patients know exactly the consequences of their consent; some have suggested that specific informed consent for electronic publishing should be required (Hood *et al.* 1998).

Health privacy laws reflect shared ethical ideals but have not prevented health care workers from egregiously violating the privacy rights of patients. Neither privacy regulations nor criminal laws prevent people or institutions from acting badly towards others. They can, however, deter and punish. In the Cardiff case, an initial sentence of 18 months in jail for Dr. Ahmed was later increased to 30 months to underscore the seriousness of the crime (Bond 2013).

Contexts of noncompliance

In a Facebook posting in 2013, Dr. Amy Dunbar of Mercy Hospital in St. Louis, Missouri talked freely and with emotion about her disappointments and frustrations in her relationship with an ob/gyn patient who missed an appointment for an induction procedure. Dr. Dunbar did not disclose the patient's name or what the HIPAA medical privacy law regards as personally identifiable health information. She broke no laws. Many people complained about what she posted anyway, and the hospital at which she worked issued a statement that recognized an ethical wrong she committed: "Mercy [Hospital] values the dignity and privacy of all our patients and we are very sorry that this incident occurred. While our privacy compliance staff has confirmed that this physician's comments did not represent a breach of privacy laws, they were inappropriate and not in line with our values of respect and dignity" (ABC News 2013). Doyle Byrnes, the Kansas nursing student who posted a picture of herself on Facebook holding up another woman's placenta, like Dr. Dunbar, was compliant with the law, though not with the highest ethical standards.

Are some patients, because of their gender, more likely to fall prey to noncompliance and privacy invasions than others? Must we think of our health privacy laws as compliance-limited for reasons relating to the social status of women? I believe we should. Compliance limits exists because secret pornography is lucrative and personally satisfying, but not for these reasons alone. When privacy laws ask us to do things that our friendships and family loyalties countermand, we may choose not to comply with the law.

Pornography and assault

Nowadays women commonly pose for nude and partially nude self-portraits and portraits, shared among friends and lovers. Cellphones have made erotic snapshots commonplace. These practices of voluntary self-revelation in no way alter the significance of covert imaging by medical professionals. When a physician purports to examine a woman's body for medical reasons, but is motivated by lust or pornography, the examination is not a medical examination at all. It is an act of the sort Anglo-American common law would classify as battery – harmful or offensive contact. If Dr. Levy asked certain patients to come in for medically unnecessary visits just to capture them on camera, these visits amounted to scheduled battery, planned sexual assaults.

The feminist philosophical concept of objectification is an apt one, among others, to apply to the wrongs Dr. Levy committed (Papadaki 2014). The bodies of the Baltimore women photographed by Dr. Levy were treated without consent as objects for others' erotic pleasure or curiosity. Mere objects have no reasonable expectations of privacy that one is bound to respect. Yet the women of Baltimore were not mere objects. The Johns Hopkins community officially recognized the fact that all of its patients are moral subjects with separate identities and agency. It was no surprise that Dr. Paul B. Rothman, Dean of the Medical Faculty, along with Ronald R. Peterson, President of The Johns Hopkins Hospital and Health System, announced in a February 26, 2013 press release that notwithstanding Levy's horrific actions, "Protecting patients' dignity and privacy is part of the core values that we instill" (Johns Hopkins University 2013).

Since rules prohibited Dr. Levy's conduct, the objectification of his patients must be explained by something other than a lack of rules and policies adopted to deter unethical, tortious and criminal privacy abuses. A personal failure of one man's morals and professional ethics is the most direct explanation. And yet Levy did not act solely for his own benefit and pleasure, as the bank of Internet servers secreted in his home suggested. Indeed there is a vibrant market for "ob/gyn" (obstetrics and gynecology) pornography accessible through Google and similar portals. Is there a market for male urology pornography? To understand why Levy's patients were abused, one has to understand Levy as participating in a (disreputable) social practice against the background of gender subordination and the authority of the white coat. Women are sexualized and objectified, even as medical patients. That women are often perceived as easy and costless targets may mean that even women professionals treat them with less respect than that with which similarly situated men might be treated.

Expedience

Even when health care workers do not go so far as to turn patients into pornography, they can act with surprising disregard for the privacy of female patients. I have very often cited classic American legal cases that reflect norms of bodily privacy surrounding women's sexual and reproductive health, the oldest being the Michigan Supreme Court decision *DeMay* v. *Roberts*, 46 Mich. 160, 9 NW 146 (1881). A Michigan husband and wife successfully sued a physician who brought an "unprofessional, young, unmarried man" to their home and permitted him to help deliver their baby. The Court found that a woman is entitled to the "privacy of her apartment" at such a time as childbirth. A feature of the case is that there were no bad intentions to explain the felt privacy offense. The doctor brought along the young man because he needed help with his medical bag and lantern. But the Court still sided with the woman and her husband against the doctor, whom they blamed for deceit.

A century later a married couple in Maine brought *Knight* v. *Penobscot Bay Medical Center*, 420 A.2d 915 (1980), a similar lawsuit claiming that a hospital violated the couple's privacy by permitting a layperson – the male spouse of a nurse waiting for her shift to end – to observe delivery of their child through a glass partition from a distance of 12 feet. The hospital staff did not think viewing at a distance was a problem, especially since other women had given permission in the past. Neither *DeMay* nor

Knight involved lurid motives; but plaintiffs in both cases believed the wrongdoing in question stemmed from a lack of due respect for a woman qua woman – a woman undergoing the quintessential gendered and intimate medical experiences of labor and childbirth.

Friendships and family

Observing reproductive health encounters against the patient's wishes is a privacy concern, but so is sharing health information. In an interesting case, the disregard shown in a female patient's privacy was related, not to objectification or expedience, but to certain cultural assumptions about privacy that a health care worker well-versed in the law nonetheless held dear (*Bagent* v. *Blessing Care Corp* 2007). Illini Hospital in the state of Illinois hired Misty Young as a phlebotomist in 2001. In February 2003 Young attended the Hospital's mandatory training session regarding the then new federal HIPAA health information privacy rules, which require special protections for individually identifiable patient health information. The law required hospitals to inform patients of their privacy rights and train staff to respect privacy. Illini Hospital staff were taught the motto: "What you see here, and what you hear here, remains here." Following the training, Young signed the hospital's confidentiality policy and a code of professional conduct, acknowledging that she understood and accepted that the only people to whom she could give confidential information were doctors and nurses directly involved with a patient's care. Young went on to violate the rules by telling the twin sister of a patient whose lab results she had seen that the patient was pregnant. Young assumed a superseding bond of confidentiality between sisters and friends. Despite the morally comprehensible rationale for her violation, Young lost her job.

It is not usual for hospital workers to believe that their interpersonal relationships take precedence over professional ethics. A social media case demonstrates the idea that family loyalties, perhaps heightened in an ethnic minority setting, can render privacy laws compliance-limited. In *Yath* v. *Fairview Clinics* (2009) Asian American Candace Yath brought suit against a Minnesota medical facility and members of her husband's family. A female member of Yath's husband's extended family worked at a clinic where Yath was treated. The relative saw Yath at the clinic and, out of curiosity, accessed Yath's electronic medical record. She learned that Yath had been treated for STIs associated with an extramarital affair. News spread throughout the family and reached Yath's husband. From the offices of a business at which a family member worked, someone created a social media page depicting Yath as a vain and unhygienic adulteress: "Rotten Candy." The Court found that the MySpace posting was an invasion of privacy even if the plaintiff could not prove that anyone read it. The felt need to shame an unfaithful relation resulted in the abject failure of the federal health privacy laws to command compliance. None of this is to say that social media cannot be good for patients if it can aid diagnosis or identification of contacts or kin (Ben-Yakov and Snider 2011).

The domain of ethics is rife with tensions and conflicts among treasured values. Health care professionals may assume that friendships and family relationships exempt them from privacy rules. The clash between ordinary ethics and cultural values on the one hand and professional ones on the other can result in significant harm. One can honestly believe that family comes first. One can honestly believe that friendship supersedes professional obligations of the workplace and workplace rules. Our culture allows us to think this way. The social inequality of women makes women safe and attractive targets. We can predict that their privacy will be particularly vulnerable to invasions notwithstanding the law. In light of recording technologies and the Internet, the approach to policymaking, training and education we currently take around health privacy needs to be amended. Amendment should take into account gender inequality and ethical uncertainty arising out of conflicting principles and priorities in personal and work life. Having strong privacy laws to protect medical data is vital, but attention to ethical contexts that compliance-limit privacy rules is a critical ancillary.

Race, class and intersections

Health care providers are prompted to abandon professional ethics and violate privacy on personal grounds – both sympathetic and repulsive – that include family loyalty, friendship, social media communication and criminal sexual preferences. Dr. Levy's several hundred victims were women, and most were low income African American women. Black women in the United States have rarely enjoyed the confidence of secure self-ownership. Historically, they have belonged to masters, husbands, fathers, lovers and the state. Even well-to-do black women patients can reportedly feel that health care providers do not value their bodies as much as they value and fear those of others. Black women suspect their race and class will make compliance limitations more likely. They may be correct, calling for special vigilance.

It is impossible to know for sure whether Levy's own race and ethnicity contributed to his misconduct. Yet what we do know is past abuses suffered in the hands of white physicians is often given by black patients as a reason for seeking and trusting black physicians. Precisely because of his race, Dr. Levy was able to maintain a large, faithful, trusting client population of African American women, their daughters and granddaughters. Had fewer of his patients been African American, one wonders whether Dr. Levy might have taken loyalty less for granted.

Like typical developed and developing nations, the United States has customs, policies and laws that deter and punish medical privacy offenses. Yet how health care workers understand their privacy obligations and whether they are motivated to respect others' privacy determines whether privacy invasions like the ones I describe here occur. Privacy invasions take place because of a widespread but dubious moral truism that what people (or certain people) do not know and are not likely to find out cannot hurt them. Dr. Levy may have presumed knowledge of his patients' values and limitation; he may have felt that what his trusting adult and teenage patients did not know could not hurt them. His suicide spared him direct contact with the rage of a betrayed community.

Compliance-limited rules threaten public health

Turning patients into pornography is both inherently wrong and wrong for its potential impact on public health. Medical photography, video and other imaging is a growing phenomena with clear benefits for patients and physicians in a wide variety of medical settings (Segal and Sacopulos 2010). The use of digital capture has expanded (Terushkin *et al.* 2010; Sinclair 2012) into many areas of medical practice, education and research (Witmer and Lebovitz 2012). This expansion could be met with added skepticism if fears of unauthorized sexualized medical photography are suspected.

Dermatology is an area of clinical medicine where photography is of particular importance (Watson *et al.* 2012). Photographs are useful for clinical detection and documentation of skin lesions over time that may signal melanoma or other skin cancers (Witmer and Lebovitz 2012). Total body photography by dermatologists promises to increase the likelihood of detecting new lesions and changes in old ones. Medical photography is standard in reconstructive and cosmetic plastic surgery practices (DiSaia *et al.* 1998). If a patient is to undergo multiple procedures, photographs can chronicle progress. Physicians' photographs are a useful adjunct to the patient's medical history. "Before" and "after" photos can help patients understand changes relative to their goals and expectations for elective surgeries such as rhinoplasty, facelifts and liposuction. In fields such as psychology, psychiatry and neurology, video documentation of encounters, therapy and movement disorders can be of particular value (Soares and Langkamp 2012). Recording patients with behavioral conditions can be of use even when patients are unaware they are being observed. Covertly filming patients has found a use in diagnosis of dangerous conditions such as Munchausen's Syndrome by Proxy (Thomas 1996).

In addition to use in clinical medicine, medical photography is important for research, education and publication (Katzan and Rudick 2012, West *et al.* 2009). In medical fields that are best served by tracking patient progress through images, photographs or videos provide credibility to the research and publication. The importance of proper resolution, lighting and positioning can be paramount (Archibald *et al.* 2010). Medical photography is in use as educational materials and for training (Ganguli *et al.* 2006). While films are not a substitute for hands-on experience, they can greatly accelerate the educational process. Students learning the basics can observe procedures in lecture settings before seeing them in person. Educational applications extend to experienced doctors who can view the films to learn about new procedures and new advances. Related to educating health professionals is filming doctors for critique and review. In order to provide the best service to patients, doctors are under constant review. In addition to the obvious benefits of peer review of performance, filming doctors has also proven to increase their effectiveness (Makary 2013). The knowledge of being filmed causes doctors to be much more thorough in their procedures due to the psychological effects of the oversight.

In addition to all of the purposes related to the treatment of the patient and the advancement of the medical field, there is the common use of medical photography for malpractice litigation, advertising and television viewing (Moskop *et al.* 2005). The latter uses are frankly commercial in nature. "Before and after" photographs may induce potential clients to undergo an elective procedure.

Medical patients are willing to consent to medical photography. Indeed, an arresting study found that 81 percent of the patients surveyed indicated that they would welcome having a video recording of one of their own medical procedures and most said they would be willing to pay for it (Makary 2013). Studies seeking to isolate factors that contribute to whether medical photography is accepted or rejected by patients indicate that patients prefer specific consent and official-looking institutional equipment rather than a personal-looking device (Moore *et al.*

2007; Lau *et al.* 2010). Patients are significantly more likely to consent to photographs through which they cannot be later identified. The use to which images will be put matters. Patients feel differently about treatment, medical education, publication, patient education and commercial uses.

Medical photography can be useful in the documentation of reportable situations such as abuse, assault, rape and gunshot wounds, although gender issues make some hesitant to extend usage (Brennan 2006). Generally speaking, laws require doctors to report gunshot wounds and many jurisdictions permit or require doctors to report suspected child abuse to the proper agency. Having physical evidence of a patient's suspected physical abuse can facilitate future proceedings that bring criminals to justice.

The perceived legitimacy of medical photography is potentially undermined by the frank distrust that results from unauthorized and inappropriate photography like Dr. Levy's coming to light. If female patients cannot trust their doctors to honor ordinary privacy expectations, they may avoid seeking medical care or conceal pathologies in what they regard as intimate areas of their bodies (such as breasts and uteruses) prone to life-threatening malignancies (Berman *et al.* 2003). Avoiding necessary medical care contributes adversely to public health, and increases the economic cost of treatment and cure when help is eventually sought. Given public health risks associated with sex, pregnancy and childbirth, it is urgent that sexually active women, women of childbearing age and pregnant women take advantage of health resources. On the side of principle, a host of moral and ethical values, including fairness, respect and integrity, are compromised where female gender, minority race and low socioeconomic class, separately or in tandem, add to the privacy risk of utilizing the health care system.

Video surveillance and photography are not always in opposition to public health. Installing video cameras in a Long Island New York Hospital increased compliance with infection control hand-washing rules from 6.5 percent to 81.6 percent; educational methods simply urging compliance failed to secure adequate compliance (Makary 2013). Ironically, medical photography could be employed to monitor health care providers and deter inappropriate and unauthorized clinical conduct. Lawful, authorized cameras in the ob/gyn office might deter unlawful spy cameras and unnecessary medical examinations, though not without a cost to the felt confidentiality of the physician/patient encounter. Openly watching the watchers could have utility in deterring "secret" taping using the most recognizable spying devices. Some patients have photographed or recorded their physicians covertly. Covert taping may turn patients into criminals and do nothing to deter misconduct by clinicians. Federal and state communications privacy laws in the United States treat some forms of non-consensual audio, and possibly video, recording as illegal wiretapping.

Conclusion

Health privacy law is an area of particular growth and importance. Privacy theorists are slowly beginning to utilize empirical and analytic methods to discern and predict who actually benefits from privacy law. The winners and losers can reflect who introduces laws and who votes to enact them; who has the resources and social status to benefit from mandated confidentiality or permissible disclosures; who occupies the voiceless fringes of society (Strahilevitz 2013). Moreover, as I have argued elsewhere, legal privacy is not always a good thing – whether for women, people of color, low income people or lesbian-gay-bisexual-transgender-queer community members (Allen 2011b). However, I believe health privacy law compliance can make winners of women no less than men, women of color no less than better-off population groups. Uncovered through empirical observation and social analysis, the potential for impact and compliance limitations in privacy law has strong normative implications. It bears on the choices that persons of conscience, character and goodwill make respecting the frequency, content and context of data acquisition, data use, data disclosure and data retention. It bears on the choices regarding who has what kind of free, unmonitored access to the bodies of others and in the presence of what types of technology. For the sake of practical ethics and legal justice, theorizing about privacy law and policy must include analysis of the normative implications of both its impact and compliance limitations.

References

ABC News, February 5, 2013. http://abcnews.go.com/blogs/health/2013/02/05/doctors-digital-quip-causes-online-kerfuffle/.

Allen, A. L. 2011a. *Privacy Law and Society*. Minneapolis: West/Thomson Reuters.

 2011b. *Unpopular Privacy: What Must We Hide*. New York: Oxford University Press.

 2015. "Privacy and Medicine," in E. N. Zalta (ed.) *The Stanford Encyclopedia of Philosophy* (Spring 2015 edition, http://plato.stanford.edu/entries/privacy-medicine/.

2013. "Privacy law: positive theory and normative practice," *Harvard Law Review Forum* 136: 241–25.

Archibald, D. J. *et al.* 2010. "Pitfalls of nonstandardized photography," *Facial Plastic Surgery Clinics of North America* 18: 253–66.

Baker, M. J. *et al.* 2014. "Navigating the Google blind spot: an emerging need for professional guidelines to address patient-targeted googling." *Journal of General Internal Medicine* 29: 1–2.

BBC News Devon, January 29, 2014. www.bbc.com/news/uk-england-devon-25952005.

Ben-Yakov, M. and Snider C. 2011. "How Facebook saved our day!" *Academic Emergency Medicine* 18: 1217–19.

Berle, I. 2008. "Clinical photography and patient rights: the need for orthopraxy," *Journal of Medical Ethics* 34: 89–92.

Berman, L. *et al.* 2003. "Seeking help for sexual function complaints: what gynecologists need to know about the female patient's experience," *Fertility and Sterility* 79: 572–6.

Bond, A. 2013. "Doctor jailed after taking intimate pictures of female patients with his mobile phone", *Mirror* (UK), 19:43, 4 October 2013. Available at www.mirror.co.uk/news/uk-news/doctor-suhail-ahmed-jailed-after-2339680.

Brennan, P. A. W. 2006. "The medical and ethical aspects of photography in the sexual assault examination: why does it offend?," *Journal of Clinical Forensic Medicine* 13: 194–202.

Butler, D. J. 2002. "Informed consent and patient videotaping," *Academic Medicine* 77: 181–4.

Dance, S. *et al.* 2013. "Accused Hopkins gynecologist suffocated himself with helium; Police seized multiple hard drives, servers from home of doctor said to have recorded patients; health regulators launch inquiry," *The Baltimore Sun*, February 20, 2013.

DiSaia, J. P. *et al.* 1998. "Digital photography for the plastic surgeon," *Plastic and Reconstructive Surgery* 102: 569–73.

Ganguli, S. *et al.* 2006. "Part I: Preparing first-year radiology residents and assessing their readiness for on-call responsibilities," *Academic Radiology* 13: 764–9.

Hawke, C. 1998. "Nursing a fine line: patient privacy and sex discrimination: sensitive legal issues surround sex-based hiring and assignment for nurses," *Nursing Management* 29: 56–61.

Hood, C. A. *et al.* 1998. "Videos, photographs, and patient consent," *British Medical Journal* 316: 1009–11.

Johns Hopkins University (2013) "Chronology of the Dr. Nikita Levy Case," www.hopkinsmedicine.org/news/Nikita_Levy.html.

Katzan, I. L. and Rudick, R. A. 2012. "Time to Integrate Clinical and Research Informatics," *Science Translational Medicine* 4: 162 [one page].

Karasu, T. B. 2013. "The Ethics of Psychotherapy," in D. A. Sisti *et al.* (eds.) *Applied Ethics in Mental Health Care: An Interdisciplinary Reader.* Cambridge, MA: MIT Press, pp. 35–58.

Lau, C. K. *et al.* 2010. "Patients' perception of medical photography," *Journal of Plastic, Reconstructive & Aesthetic Surgery* 63: 507 [e-publication only].

Makary, M. A. 2013. "The power of video recording," *Journal of the American Medical Association* 309: 1591–92.

McLean, M., Al Ahbabi, S. *et al.* 2010. "Muslim women and medical students in the clinical encounter," *Medical Education* 44: 306–15.

Moore, I. N. *et al.* 2007. "Confidentiality and privacy in health care from the patients' perspective: does HIPAA help?," *Health Matrix* 17: 215–72.

Moskop, J. C. *et al.* 2005. "From Hippocrates to HIPAA: privacy and confidentiality in emergency medicine – Part II: Challenges in the emergency department," *Annals of Emergency Medicine* 45: 60–7.

Papadaki, E. L. 2014. "Feminist Perspectives on Objectification," in. N. Zalta (ed.) *The Stanford Encyclopedia of Philosophy* (Summer 2014 Edition), http://plato.stanford.edu/archives/sum2014/entries/feminism-objectification.

Phillips, S. P. and Schneider, M. S. 1993. "Sexual harassment of female doctors by patients," *New England Journal of Medicine* 329: 1936–9.

Rakel, R. E. 2011. "Establishing Rapport," in R. E. Rakel and D.P. Rakel (eds.) *Textbook of Family Medicine*, 8th edn. Philadelphia: Saunders, pp. 146–65.

Segal, J. and Sacopulos, M. J. 2010. "Photography consent and related legal issues," *Facial Plastic Surgery Clinics of North America* 18: 237–44.

Sinclair, R. 2012. "Skin checks," *Australian Family Physician* 41: 464–9.

Soares, N. S. and Langkamp, D. L. 2012. "Telehealth in developmental-behavioral pediatrics," *Journal of Developmental & Behavioral Pediatrics* 33: 656–65.

Strahilevitz, L. 2013. "Toward a positive theory of privacy law," *Harvard Law Review* 126: 2010–42.

Terushkin, V., Oliveira, S. A., Marghoob, A. A. and Halpern, A. C. 2010. "Use of and beliefs about total body photography and dermatoscopy among US dermatology training programs: an update," *Journal of the American Academy of Dermatology* 62(5): 794–803.

Thomas, T. 1996. "Covert video surveillance – an assessment of the Staffordshire Protocol," *Journal of Medical Ethics* 22: 349–50.

Walker, A. 2014. "Doctor Secretly Photographed Female Patients, Installed Covert Cameras in Toilet," *Breitbart*, April 25, www.breitbart.com/.

Watson, J. J. *et al.* 2012 "Necessities in clinical photography," *Journal of Hand and Microsurgery* 4: 30–1.

West, S. L. *et al.* 2009. "Reflections on the use of electronic health record data for clinical research," *Health Informatics Journal* 15: 108–12.

Witmer, W. K. and Lebovitz, P. J. 2012. "Clinical photography in the dermatology practice," *Seminars in Cutaneous Medicine and Surgery* 31: 191–9.

15

Respect for context as a benchmark for privacy online: what it is and isn't

HELEN NISSENBAUM

Introduction

In February 2012, the Obama White House unveiled a Privacy Bill of Rights, embedded in a comprehensive report, *Consumer Data Privacy in a Networked World: A Framework for Protecting Privacy and Promoting Innovation in the Global Digital Economy* (2012: 9). In addition to the Bill of Rights, the Report's Framework for Protecting Privacy laid out a multi-stakeholder process, articulated foundations for effective enforcement, pledged to draft new privacy legislation, and announced an intention to increase interoperability with international efforts (Civil 2012). The White House report was but one among several governmental studies and reports in the US and elsewhere (e.g. Federal Trade Commission 2012; World Economic Forum 2012) responding to increasingly vocal objections to information practices above and below the radar that were so out of control that in 2010 the *Wall Street Journal*, sentinel of business and commercial interests, launched a landmark investigative series *What They Know*, which doggedly revealed to readers remarkable and chilling activities ranging from ubiquitous online monitoring to license plate tracking and much in between (Angwin and Valentino-Devries 2012; Valentino-Devries and Singer-Vine 2012). The dockets of public interest advocacy organizations were filled with privacy challenges. Courts and regulatory bodies were awash with cases of overreaching standard practices, embarrassing gaffes, and technical loopholes that enabled surreptitious surveillance and the capture, aggregation, use, and dispersion of personal information.

As awareness spread, so did annoyance, outrage, and alarm among ordinary, unsophisticated users of digital and information technologies as they learned of practices such as Web-tracking, behavioral advertising, surveillance of mobile communications, information capture by mobile apps (including location), capture of latent and revealed social network activity, and big data.[1] Most salient to individuals are practices of familiar actors, with which they are directly acquainted, such as Facebook, Google, Amazon, Yelp, and Apple. More informed critics point to information brokers, back-end information services, ad networks, voter profilers, "smart grids," surveillance cameras, and biometric ID systems, to name just a few, which relentlessly monitor and shape lives in ways neither perceptible nor remotely comprehensible to the public of ordinary citizens.

Acknowledging the problem, governmental bodies in the USA have kept citizens' privacy on the active agenda, pursuing cases against specific activities (e.g. *Google Inc.* v. *Joffee et. al.* (2014); *Federal Trade Commission* v. *Wyndham Worldwide Corporation, et al.* (2014);[2]*Re: Netflix Privacy Litigation* (2012)). They have conducted studies, public hearings, and multi-stakeholder deliberations on specific practices, such as commercial uses of facial recognition systems, surreptitious uses of personal information by mobile apps, and applications of big data (US National Telecommunications and Information Administration 2013a). Such initiatives are also underway in Europe in governmental as well as nongovernmental sectors, including, for example, the World Economic Forum, the Organisation for Economic Co-operation (OECD), and the European Commission (World Economic Forum 2012; European Union 2013).

This chapter focuses on the White House Consumer Privacy Bill of Rights and within it, the Principle of Respect for Context. It argues that how this Principle is interpreted is critical to the success of the Privacy Bill of Rights as an engine of change – whether it succeeds in its mission of change or devolves to business as usual.

White House Report and respect for context

Until the Department of Commerce took up its study of privacy, a prelude to the 2012 White House Report, the Federal Trade Commission (FTC) had been the key government agency spearheading important

---

[1] Anxiety over the digital age, and more specifically, big data, is a major theme in mainstream tech and business journalism as of 2013. For more information, see *The New York Times'* special section "Big Data 2013." Available at http://bits.blogs.nytimes.com/category/big-data-2013/.

[2] Accessed from www2.bloomberglaw.com/public/desktop/document/FTC_v_Wyndham_Worldwide_Corp_No_213cv01887ESJAD_2014_BL_94785_DNJ.

privacy initiatives in the commercial arena with rulemaking and legal action. The report signaled direct White House interest in contemporary privacy problems and buoyed hopes that change might be in the air. The Report and Bill of Rights were cautiously endorsed by a range of parties who have disagreed with one another on virtually everything else to do with privacy, including public interest advocacy organizations such as the Electronic Frontier Foundation, the Electronic Privacy Information Center, the Center for Democracy and Technology as well as industry leaders, including Google and Intel.[3]

Of the seven principles proposed in the Consumer Privacy Bill of Rights, six are recognizable as kin of traditional fair information practice principles, embodied, for example, in the OECD Privacy Guidelines (1980). However, the third principle of "Respect for Context" (PRC), the expectation that "companies will collect, use, and disclose personal data in ways that are consistent with the context in which consumers provide the data" (White House Privacy Report 2012: 47), is intriguingly novel and, in part, a reason the Report suggested that something beyond business-as-usual was its aim. How far the rallying cry around respect-for-context will push genuine progress, however, is critically dependent on how this principle is interpreted. Context is a mercilessly ambiguous term with potential to be all things to all people. Its meanings range from the colloquial and general to the theorized and specific, from the banal to the exotic, the abstract to the concrete, and shades in between. If determining the meaning of context were not challenging enough, determining what it means to respect it opens further avenues of ambiguity. Whether the Privacy Bill of Rights fulfills its promise as a watershed for privacy, and whether the principle of respect for context is an active ingredient in the momentum, will depend on which one of these interpretations drives public or private regulators to action.

Meanings of context

Setting aside general and colloquial uses, as well as idiosyncratic ones, this chapter takes its cues from specific meanings and shades of meanings embodied in recorded deliberations leading up to public release of the Report and in action and commentary that has followed it, all clearly influential in shaping the principle. My purpose is to highlight how different meanings imply different policy avenues, some seeming to favor the

---

[3] See Civil 2012; EPIC.org 2012; D. Hoffman 2012; M. Hoffman 2012.

entrenched status quo, others to support progressive if limited improvement. Ultimately, I will argue that the interpretation that opens doors to a genuine advancement in the policy environment is embodied in the theory of contextual integrity; it heeds the call for innovation, recognizes business interests of commercial actors, and at the same time places appropriate constraints on personal information flows for the sake of privacy.

In the subset of interpretations with systematic implications for policy, four are of particular interest because they reflect persistent voices in discussions leading up to and following the White House Report: context as technology platform or system, context as sector or industry, context as business model or practice, and context as social domain. Although within each of the four there are nuances of meaning and subtleties of usage, for purposes of this discussion they have been set aside or, where possible, absorbed into the core. One example of this is *the context of a relationship*, which is more general and abstract than the four listed. In deciding whether this framing warranted a separate analysis, I examined comments from the Online Publishers Association introducing this phrase. Finding that it was referring specifically to the relationship between publishers and their clients (readers, viewers, etc.), I was comfortable in absorbing this understanding of context within that of business practice.

There are many ways context may be relevant to those modeling human behavior. Contextual factors are considered external to a given model but might increase its descriptive or predictive accuracy. In explaining online behavior, for example, contextual factors such as geolocation, time, stage in a series, or a myriad other possibilities may serve to refine a model's performance, helping to explain and predict at finer grain behaviors such as web search, receptiveness to advertising, and even to vulnerability to malevolent overtures, such as phishing attacks (Kiseleva *et al.* 2013a, 2013b). In this manner, contextual factors could be cited in explanations of varying privacy expectations. Thus one may observe that expectations are affected by the context of a promise, a relationship, a conversation, or an event. Place – geospatial or physical location – such as, home, office, café, supermarket, park, corner of Broadway and Bleecker, is a particularly salient contextual refinement (see, e.g. Dwork and Mulligan 2012). Context as place is of natural interest not only because it reflects common English usage, but also because, historically, it has served to qualify privacy expectations, such as in distinguishing the home from public space (US Constitution amendment IV; Selbst 2013).

I have not given independent consideration to context abstractly conceived because I have not seen systematic ties to specific expectations
of privacy. Although place is a significant factor in accounting for privacy expectations, it was not singled out in the White House Report. The
importance of place in affecting privacy expectations is not necessarily
as an independent factor, that is, whether an activity takes place inside
a building or outside, at one particular geolocation or another, but as it
functions in social terms, as, say, a church, home, or hospital – as will be
clarified later in this chapter.

Context as technology system or platform

Many of the privacy issues we are confronting emerge from the realm of
digital networks – the Internet, and the myriad platforms and systems
sitting atop (or below) it, such as mobile systems, email, social networks,
cloud providers, and the Web itself. For most of us these disparate technical
substrates, systems, and platforms are experienced indistinguishably from
one another and, although technical experts give a more rigorous account
of their differences, they are akin from the perspective of user experience
and political economy. We talk of communication and transaction taking place *online* or *in* cyberspace and the privacy problems emerging from
them are associated with these electronically mediated contexts without
a clear sense that they may emerge in different ways because of the different architectures and protocols. They become the problems of online privacy – problems of a distinctive domain requiring a distinctive approach. It
is a short distance to conceive of this technological substrate as a context,
one that makes a difference to privacy; we readily conceive of talking in
the context of, say, a phone call, acting in the context of an online social
network, expressing ourselves in the contexts of Twitter, Facebook, and
Wikipedia, or in the contexts of a mobile app, or location-based services.
In such expressions contexts are defined by the properties of respective
media, systems, or platforms whose distinctive material characteristics
shape – moderate, magnify, enable – the character of the activities, transactions, and interactions they mediate. They also shape the ways information
about us is tracked, gathered, analyzed, and disseminated. If properties
of technical systems and platforms define contexts, then a principle that
supports *respect* for contexts presumably implies that policies should be
heedful of these defining properties of systems and platforms.

The idea of context as technical system or platform is suggested in the
foreword of the White House Report when it states:

Privacy protections are critical to maintaining consumer trust in networked technologies. When consumers provide information about
themselves – whether it is in the context of an online social network that
is open to public view or a transaction involving sensitive personal data –
they reasonably expect companies to use this information in ways that
are consistent with the surrounding context. Many companies live up to
these expectations, but some do not. Neither consumers nor companies
have a clear set of ground rules to apply in the commercial arena. As a
result, it is difficult today for consumers to assess whether a company's
privacy practices warrant their trust.

(White House Privacy Report 2012: i)

Comments by others reflect a similar interpretation. AT&T, for example,
notes that diverse technical platforms generate distinctive challenges
to privacy: "Indeed, the power of Web 2.0 inter-related media is precisely that content can be used in ways that were not expected or understood when they were collected" (Raul *et al.* 2011: 8). Google encourages
enforceable codes of conduct that "reflect changing practices, technologies and shifting consumer expectations" (Chavez 2011: 9); and Intuit
observes that "Collecting information for use in routing a request on the
Internet should have different standards for transparency, acceptable
uses, protection, and retention than the information collected to describe
a patient's visit to a physician" (Lawler 2011: 11). Finally, the idea that
technology defines context is suggested in the framing of the National
Telecommunications and Information Administration (NTIA)'s July
2012 kickoff multi-stakeholder (MSH) process around mobile applications, suggesting that mobile apps define a normative category.[4]

Context as business model or business practice

In the discourse surrounding the Report, the interpretation of context
as prevailing business model or business practice was evident in various
comments, particularly those offered by incumbents in the IT and information industries, for example, "Technology neutral and flexible legislation can actually aid small business growth as it provides a clear set of
'rules of the road' for everyone, while at the same time allowing those
rules to be adapted to each business' unique situation" (Intel 2011: 4). This

---

[4] *Multistakeholder Process to Develop Consumer Data Privacy Code of Conduct Concerning
Mobile Application Transparency.* Symposium conducted at the open meeting of The
National Telecommunications and Information Administration, Washington DC, July,
2012.

comment suggests that technology per se does not define privacy rules of the road, but that these should be guided by the needs of distinctive business models aimed at promoting growth. Similarly, "TRUSTe supports the continued role of industry in defining purpose specifications and use limitations based on the unique needs of a company's business model" (Maier 2010: 8). According to Google, "The fast-paced introduction of new Internet services drives equally rapid shifts in consumer expectations and preferences. An effective privacy regime must allow for realtime reactions to address changes in consumer privacy preferences resulting from the introduction and adoption of new tools and services" (Chavez 2011: 2). Asserting a special privilege for the business practices of online publishers, the Online Publishers Association, with members including *WebMD*, *FoxNews*, and *The New York Times*, claims that "Online publishers share a direct and trusted relationship with visitors to their websites. In the context of this relationship, OPA members sometimes collect and use information to target and deliver the online advertising that subsidizes production of quality digital content" (Horan 2011: 4).

Interpreted as the model or practice of a particular business, context is established according to that business' aims and the means it chooses to achieve these aims. There is nothing surprising about merchants orienting their buying and selling practices around profitability, so we should not be surprised that information service providers orient their models around growth and competitive edge. According to this understanding, contexts are defined by particular business models, in turn shaping respective information flow practices. Taking Google's comment above as a concrete case in point, this interpretation suggests that contexts generated by its business-driven Internet services, for example, shape consumer expectations of privacy, and not the other way around. Similarly, AT&T speculates that the privacy assumptions users hold will bend flexibly to the contours of "marketing purposes," defined as whatever is needed to strengthen a business model (Raul *et al.* 2011: 17).

Context as sector or industry

Endorsing the sectoral approach that the United States has taken to privacy protection, TRUSTe notes that "the regulatory frameworks currently in place in the US reflect this inherently contextual nature of privacy e.g. FCRA/FACTA (information used in 'consumer reports'), Gramm-Leach-Bliley (information sharing between financial institutions and affiliates), HIPAA (transactions involving protected health information by 'covered entities')" (Maier 2010: 2). In a similar vein: "Intuit's experience in multiple sectors has taught us that providers and consumers of information in the health sector, for example, have different requirements and expectations for protection than do those in financial services ... Subject matter experts could help inform the development of appropriately balanced codes" (Lawler 2011: 9).

I have placed "industry" in the same category as "sector," not because they have identical meanings, but because, in practice, these terms are used interchangeably in the commentaries from which I rendered the category. Adopting the interpretation of context as sector or industry, respect for context would amount to adherence to the set of rules or norms developed by, for, and within respective sectors or industries.

Context as social domain

This interpretation, supported by the theory of contextual integrity, presents contexts as social spheres, as constituents of a differentiated social space. As such, they serve as organizing principles for expectations of privacy. Although contextual integrity relies on an intuitive notion of social sphere, covering such instances as education, health care, politics, commerce, religion, family and home life, recreation, marketplace, work, and more, scholarly works in social theory and philosophy have rigorously developed the concept of differentiated social space, though with diverse theoretical underpinnings and terminology (e.g. sphere, domain, institution, field[5]). In intuitive as well as academic accounts, spheres generally comprise a number of constituents, such as characteristic activities and practices, functions (or roles), aims, purposes, institutional structure, values, and action-governing norms. Contextual norms may be explicitly expressed in rules or laws or implicitly embodied in convention, practice, or merely conceptions of "normal" behavior. A common thesis in most accounts is that spheres are characterized by distinctive internal structures, ontologies, teleologies, and norms.

From the landscape of differentiated social spheres the theory of privacy as contextual integrity develops a definition of informational privacy as well as an account of its importance. Taking context to mean social sphere, respect for context would mean respect for social sphere. To explain what *this* means and why it opens new and significant avenues

---

[5] For a further discussion on spheres, see Nissenbaum 2010: 80, 131, 166–9, 198–200, 240–1.

for the proposed White House policy framework requires a brief excursus into the theory of contextual integrity.

A detour: theory of contextual integrity

Other accounts of the profound anxiety over privacy, fuelled by the steep rise in capture, analysis, and dissemination of personal information, point to the loss of control by data subjects and sheer increased exposure. Although these factors are part of the story, the theory of contextual integrity holds the source of this anxiety to be neither in control nor secrecy, but appropriateness. Specifically, technologies, systems, and practices that disturb our sense of privacy are those that have resulted in *inappropriate* flows of personal information. Inappropriate information flows are those that violate context-specific informational norms (from hereon, "informational norms"), a subclass of general norms governing respective social contexts.

Aiming at descriptive accuracy, the theory articulates a model wherein informational norms are defined by three key parameters: information types, actors, and transmission principles. It postulates that whether a particular flow, or transmission of information from one party to another, is appropriate depends on these three parameters, namely, the type of information in question, about whom it is, by whom and to whom it is transmitted, and conditions or constraints under which this transmission takes place. Asserting that informational norms are context-relative, or context-specific, means that within the model of a differentiated social world they cluster around and function according to coherent but distinct social contexts. The parameters, too, range over distinct clusters of variables defined, to a large extent, by respective social contexts.

Actors – subject, sender, recipient – range over context-relevant functions or roles, that is, actors functioning in certain capacities associated with certain contexts. These capacities (or functional roles) include the familiar – physician, nurse, patient, teacher, senator, voter, polling station volunteer, mother, friend, uncle, priest, merchant, customer, congregant, policeman, judge, and, of course, many more. Actors governed by informational norms might also be collectives, including institutions, corporations, or clubs.

The parameter of *information type* likewise ranges over variables derived from the ontologies of specific domains. In health care these could include symptomologies, medical diagnoses, diseases, pharmacological drugs; in education they may include cognitive aptitude, performance measures, learning outcomes; in politics, party affiliations, votes cast, donations; and so forth. There are, in addition, types of information that range across many contexts: to give a few basic examples, name, address, and gender.

Transmission principle, the third parameter, designates the terms, or constraints under which information flows. Think of it as a sluicegate. Imagine that you are applying for a bank mortgage on a new home and have signed a waiver allowing the bank to obtain a copy of your credit report from Equifax. To map this transaction onto the structure of context-specific informational norms: (1) actors: you, the applicant, are the data subject, the bank is the data recipient, and the credit bureau is the sender; (2) information type includes the various fields of information that are provided in a credit report; and (3) transmission principle is "with the information subject's signed waiver." The transmission principle, abstractly conceived, has not been explicitly recognized in scholarly or policy deliberations even though, in practice, its implicit role in social convention, regulation, and law can be pivotal. Isolating the transmission principle as an independent variable also offers a more general account of the dominant view of privacy as a right to control information about ourselves. Through the lens of contextual integrity, this view mistakes one aspect of the right for the whole, since control over information by the information subject is but one among an extensive range of options, including, "in confidence," "with third-party authorization," "as required by law," "bought," "sold," "reciprocal," and "authenticated," among others.

A feature of informational norms that bears emphasizing is that the three parameters – actors, information types, and transmission principles – are independent. None can be reduced to the other two, nor can any one of them carry the full burden of defining privacy expectations. This is why past efforts to reduce privacy to a particular class of information – say "sensitive" information – or to one transmission principle – say, control over information – are doomed to fail and, in my view, for decades have invited ambiguity and confusion, hindering progress in our understanding of privacy and attempts to regulate its protection. Control over information is an important transmission principle, but always with respect to particular actors and particular information types, all specified against the backdrop of a particular social context. Although much could be said about each of the parameters, the scope of this chapter limits us.

Contextual integrity is achieved when actions and practices comport with informational norms. But when actions or practices defy expectations by disrupting entrenched or normative information flows, they violate contextual integrity. As such, informational norms model privacy expectations. When we find people reacting with surprise, annoyance, and indignation, protesting that their privacy has been compromised, the theory would suggest as a likely explanation that informational norms had been contravened, that contextual integrity had been violated. Conversely, informational norms may serve as a diagnostic tool with prima facie explanatory and predictive capacities. From observations of technical systems or practices, which result in novel patterns of information flow according to actors, information types, or transmission principles, the theory would predict that people may react with surprise and possibly annoyance. Contextual integrity provides a more highly calibrated view of factors relevant to privacy than traditional dichotomies such as disclose/not disclose, private/public.

The diagnostic or descriptive role of contextual integrity is not the full story, but before turning to the ethical dimension, two quick implications bear mentioning. One is that when it comes to the nuts and bolts of privacy law, policy, and design, area experts in respective contexts – education, health care, and family and home-life – are crucial to understanding roles, functions, and information types. They, not privacy experts, are best equipped to inform processes of norm discovery, articulation, and formation. A second implication is that though practices in well-circumscribed social institutions may be thickly covered by informational rules, only a fraction of all possible information flows in daily life are likely to be covered by explicit norms. Compare, for example a court of law, a stock exchange, and a hospital with an informal social gathering, a shopping mall, a beauty parlor – picking a few at random. The lens of contextual integrity provides a view of emerging digital (sociotechnical) information systems in terms of radical disruptive information flows, in turn an explanation of contemporary anxiety and acute concern over privacy. But many novel information flows are disruptive not because they contravene explicit norms, but because they open up previously impossible (possibly unimaginable) flows. In these instances, consternation follows because flows are unprecedented, and may or may not expose new vulnerabilities and hazards. How to cope with these puzzling cases, in addition to the ones in which existing norms are violated, is a challenge for the prescriptive dimension of contextual integrity.

Contextual integrity: ethics and policy

Novelty and disruption are not problematic even if they result in direct contraventions of entrenched informational norms. Even a superficial survey reveals many welcome alterations in flows brought about by adoption of information and network technologies; for example, enhanced health indicators, robust and cheap new forms of communication and association, such as through social networks, and information search tools online. In many of these instances novel flows have replaced suboptimal ones that had become entrenched in particular contexts due to the limits of past technologies, media, or social systems. Questions must be addressed, however. How to evaluate disruptive information flows brought about by novel technologies, media, and social systems; how to distinguish those that embody positive opportunities from those that do not; those that violate privacy from those that do not – all important challenges for any theory of privacy. When AT&T asserts, "Consumers approach the Internet with a consistent set of expectations, and they should be able to traverse the Internet having those expectations respected and enforced" (Raul *et al.* 2011: 10), it endorses the normative clout of our privacy expectations. And because we may not agree that *all* expectations deserve to be met, we can reasonably require a theory of privacy to account for the difference between those that do and those that do not. This is the challenge any normative theory privacy should address and it is the challenge for which a normative dimension of contextual integrity was developed.

A fundamental insight of contextual integrity is that because information flows may systematically affect interests and realization of societal values, these can be used as touchstones for normative evaluation. Where novel flows challenge entrenched informational norms, the model calls for a comparative assessment of entrenched flows against novel ones. An assessment in terms of interests and values involves three layers. In the first, it requires a study of how novel flows affect the interests of key affected parties: the benefits they enjoy, the costs and risks they suffer. These may include material costs and benefits as well as those less palpable, including shifts in relative power. Beyond this largely economic analysis, frequently followed in policy circles, the normative analysis directs us to consider general moral, social, and political values. These would include not only costs and benefits but also considerations of fairness, the distribution of these costs and benefits, who enjoys the benefits and who endures the costs. Thus, for example, where new flows involve power shifts, this second layer asks whether the shifts are fair and just. Other core ethical and societal values that have been identified in a deep and extensive privacy literature are democracy, unfair discrimination, informational harm, equal treatment, reputation, and civil liberties. This literature has shone light particularly on the connections between privacy and aspects of individual autonomy including moral autonomy, boundary management, and identity formation.[6]

The third layer introduces a further set of considerations, namely, context-specific values, ends, and purposes. This layer sets contextual integrity apart from many other privacy theories. It offers a systematic approach to resolving conflicts among alternative patterns of information flow, which serve competing interests and values respectively. In a particular context, one pattern of flow might support individual freedom; an alternative, safety and security. The additional analytic layer may resolve the conflict. In some, freedom will trump, in others, security will trump depending on facts on the ground and respective goals and values. Although privacy is often pitted against the interests of business incumbents, or is viewed as conflicting with values such as national security, public safety, and freedom of expression, contextual integrity allows us to unravel and challenge such claims. This layer insists that privacy, as appropriate information flows, serves not merely the interests of individual information subjects, but also context, social ends, and values.

The claim of this chapter is that context, understood as social sphere, is far more likely to yield positive momentum and meaningful progress in privacy law and policy than understood as technology, sector, or business model. With context-specific informational norms establishing the link between context and privacy, *respect for context* amounts to respect for contextual integrity. To flesh out this claim, a fresh look at the White House Privacy Bill of Rights will be instructive.

Respect for context and the Consumer Internet Privacy Bill Of Rights

The White House Privacy Bill of Rights embodies "fair information practice principles" (FIPPS), as have many codes of privacy before it in the USA and internationally. Appendix B of the report accounts for its debt to FIPPS and other codes in a table that lines up respective principles of the Consumer Privacy Bill of Rights (CPBR) alongside respective principles in the OECD Privacy Guidelines, the Department for Homeland Security (DHS) Privacy Policy (2013), and Asia-Pacific Economic Cooperation (APEC) Principles (White House Privacy Report 2012: 59).[7]

---

[6] See Nissenbaum 2010, especially Part II.
[7] "Appendix B: Comparison of the Consumer Privacy Bill of Rights to Other Statements of the Fair Information Practice Principles (FIPPS)," (White House Privacy Report 2012.)

The CPBR principles of Transparency, Security, Access and Accuracy, and Accountability have relatively straightforward counterparts in the other sets of guidelines, each worthy, in its own right, of in-depth critical analysis. Respect for Context, the focus of this chapter, is aligned with Purpose Specification and Use Limitation principles. The White House's CPBR principles of Focused Collection and Individual Control, whose counterparts in the OECD Guidelines are listed as Collection and Use Limitation principles, would therefore also be affected by the interpretation of Context.

Let us zoom in for a closer look at the right of Respect for Context, "a right to expect that companies will collect, use, and disclose personal data in ways that are consistent with the context in which consumers provide the data" (White House Privacy Report 2012: 55). Its close kin are given as (1) Purpose Specification and (2) Use Limitation, which require that (1) "The purposes for which personal data are collected should be specified no later than at the time of data collection and the subsequent use limited to the fulfillment of those purposes or such others as are not incompatible with these purposes and as are specified on each occasion of change of purpose" (White House Privacy Report 2012: 58); and (2) "Personal data should not be disclosed, made available or otherwise used for purposes other than those specified in accordance with Paragraph 9 (i.e. purpose specification) except ... (a) with the consent of the data subject; or (b) by the authority of law" (White House Privacy Report 2012: 58).

Speaking philosophically, we can say that the Purpose Specification and Use Limitation principles have only indexical meaning, emerging in particular, concrete instances of use. Once purposes are specified, uses are also limited accordingly. But what these purposes are, or may be, is not given in the principles themselves. One could admire the adaptability of these principles – a virtue of FIPPS, by some counts. Or point out, as has Fred Cate, that FIPPS themselves do not provide privacy protection, merely procedural guidance whose substantive clout is indeterminate.[8] According to Cate, the FIPPS purpose specification principle offers some traction for privacy protection. He points out, however, that unless constraints are placed on what purposes are legitimate (and why), a purely procedural Purpose Specification principle opens a glaring loophole in FIPPS.[9] This point is crucial for my argument about context.

---

[8] For Cate's cogent analysis, see Cate 2006. See another astute discussion in Rubinstein 2010.
[9] In fairness, others in the policy arena have noted the indeterminacy of the linchpin Purpose Specification and Use Limitation principles and are attempting to set substantive

Use Limitation, in turn, is compromised by the wild-card character of Purpose Specification, as is the principle of Collection Limitation (often called Data Minimization), which restricts information collection to that which is necessary for specified purposes. Talk about a vicious circle! Other principles that may seem to be inoculated against this indexicality are also affected, albeit indirectly. Take Security and Data Quality requirements. Although no explicit mention is made of purpose in these principles, they are implied, as what counts as reasonable standards for both is surely a function of the purposes for which information is gathered and for which it is earmarked – for example whether the information in question is being collected for purposes of national security versus consumer marketing. The meaning of these principles is dependent on purpose, and purpose may be specified by the data collector, at will. Unless and until purposes are shaped by substantive requirements, FIPPS constitutes a mere shell, formally defining relationships among the principles and laying out procedural steps to guide information flows. Given the centrality of FIPPS in virtually all privacy (or data protection) policies throughout the world, it is surprising to find that privacy is elusive, and even that fairness itself can be questioned in the contemporary regimes of privacy policies (Nissenbaum 2011).

A question of interpretation

The rhetoric surrounding NTIA's release of the Consumer Privacy Bill of Rights was of a new page, ambitious and optimistic. The principle of Respect for Context offered a salient departure from FIPPS' Purpose Specification and Use Limitation principles. Herein lay the promise of something materially different, something better. But whether the promise can be fulfilled and not devolve to business as usual will depend on how we interpret context. In the previous section, we saw that the interpretation of Respect for Context is important not only in its own right, but is pivotal, too, for fixing meanings for other key principles, including, Access and Accuracy, Focused Collection, and Security. Fixing meanings *correctly*, that is in a way that the innovation embodied in Respect for Context materially advances the state of privacy protection in the USA, is, therefore, critical. Below I will explain why, among the four alternatives, context understood as social domain is the most viable basis for progress.

standards. For example, the EU Article 29 Working Party in Opinion 03/201d on purpose limitation and aspects of the problem discussed in Rauhofer 2013.

Consider context as business model or practice. Under this interpret-ation, context would be determined by the exigencies of a particular busi-ness and communicated to individuals via general terms of service. In the context of an online purchase of physical goods, for example, it is reason-able for a merchant to require a consumer's address and valid payment information. But if business purpose is a blank check, we are in trouble. Even in this simple illustration, questions remain: what happens to the information after delivery is completed? With whom can this informa-tion be shared, and under what terms? For how long, and who is respon-sible if harm follows its unintended leakage, or theft by criminals? With the ever-growing thirst for data, questions such as these have multiplied by orders of magnitude and while our intuitions are robust when it comes to merchants of physical goods, reasonable purpose for businesses *in* the information business is murkier still.

If business model and practice define context, political economy would shape the relationship between the information collector and informa-tion subject, allowing no recourse to standards beyond business expe-dience (except in the few sectors where privacy legislation exists). By definition, each business entity determines what is and is not expedi-ent. Other standards, such as security, use limitation, collection mini-mization, and access, which all are defined in terms of purpose, will be defined accordingly. Defining context as business model leaves the door wide open to anything reasonably conceived as profitable for respective businesses – buying up information resources, extracting information resources from transactions, and using them in any manner (limited only by positive law and regulation). This is not to say that business models are irrelevant to context and informational norms, only that the promise of change will not be fulfilled if business interests are the sole arbiters of context (Friedman 1970). Although business needs are an important con-sideration, they do not form a sound basis for privacy's moral imperative.

What about context as technology platform or system? First, con-sider what this means. It is quite sensible to refer to a Facebook profile, a Bing search, a Fitbit group, the Web, an email exchange, and a Google+ Hangout as contexts. The question here, however, is not whether it is *sens-ible* to use the term context in these ways but whether these ways can form the reference point for Respect for Context. Answering affirmatively means technological affordance would determine moral imperative; it means accepting that whatever information flows happen to be afforded by a social network, a Web search engine, health-tracking device, and so forth, not only determine what *can* happen but what *ought* to happen. In these stark terms, the thesis may seem absurdly counterintuitive, yet it is embodied in familiar practices and reasoning. Take, for example, controversies surrounding online tracking. After conceding there was strong support for providing individuals the means to delete third-party cookies, various workarounds emerged, such as flash cookies and browser fingerprinting that reinstated cross-site tracking functionality. If technological affordance defines moral imperative, there are no grounds for critiquing the workarounds. Similarly, when Mark Zuckerberg stated that Facebook had altered norms because the system had altered actual flows, he was right, by definition, because whatever flows are enabled by platforms simply *are* the flows that context legitimates.

Denying that technological affordance defines respect for context does not mean it is irrelevant to it. Practices are changed and sometimes they pull norms and standards along with them. The explosive growth of (socio) technical information systems, the source of much consternation over privacy, is responsible for radical disruptions in information-gathering, analysis, and distribution, in the types of information that is accessed, analyzed, and distributed, the actors sending and receiving information, and in the constraints or conditions under which it flows. These disruptions not only divert information flows from one path to another and one recipient to another, or others, but also may reconfigure ontologies, yield new categories of information, and new types of actors and modes of dissemination. Such changes may call for the reconsideration of entrenched norms and development of norms where none previously may have existed.

The "old" technologies of the telephone, for example, introduced novel parameters of voice dissemination including new classes of actors, such as telecommunications companies, human operators, mechanical and electronic switches. Existing norms of flow governing communications and, say, eavesdropping, may provide initial models for new conditions afforded by the telephone. As novel systems cause increasing divergence from pre-existing affordances, novel challenges demand deeper examination of what is at stake in a social world, conversations, and relationships that have been reconfigured by telephonic media. A pair of famous US Supreme Court cases, roughly forty years apart, reveal this progression: *Olmstead* v. *United States*, 277 US 438 (1928) and *Katz* v. *United States*, 389 US 347 (1967). Landmark Fourth Amendment cases involving a historical reversal of law, these cases have been endlessly analyzed and taught. The common lesson drawn from them, which I have no cause to challenge, is that the 1967 Court finally "got it right." Shifting attention from the foreground of what counts as a legitimate expectation of privacy, to the background of how the world had changed, we note that as telephones became normalized, phone-mediated conversations became integral to social life. In my view, this is key to explaining *why* the Court "got it right" in the *Katz* case. The ascent of telecommunication in social, political, and economic life also meant addressing head-on the status of newly emerging actors, forms of information, and constraints on flow. To this day (underscored by the Snowden revelations) we are living with the consequences of legislation that attempted to define duties of phone companies, and the varied access they (and others) would have to new forms of data, from pen register data to content of phone calls.[10]

Technical systems and platforms shape human activity by constraining and affording what we can do and say; in this sense, they are rightly conceived as contexts and deserve to be objects of attention and regulation. Allowing that people act and transact in contexts shaped by technical systems, does not mean, however, that these systems fully account for the meaning of Respect for Context. So doing allows material design to define ethical and political precepts; it allows the powers that shape the technical platforms of our mediated lives not only to affect our moral and political experiences through built constraints and affordances, but further, to place them beyond the pale of normative judgment.

The practical implications of this distinction can be seen in relation to the first NTIA multistakeholder process. No fool's errand, its mission was to establish a code of conduct for mobile applications developers. The NTIA process, which (1) identified a new class of actors, including mobile app developers, among others and (2) articulated baseline constraints on appropriate behaviors in the ecologies of mobile information services, concluded with a set of guidelines (US National Telecommunications and Information Administration 2013b). In my view, respect for context, should not stop with these. Beyond the baseline, it would require

---

[10] 18 USC § 2511(2)(a)(i) 2011, accessed from www.gpo.gov/fdsys/granule/USCODE-2011-title18/USCODE-2011-title18-partI-chap119-sec2511/content-detail.html: "It shall not be unlawful under this chapter for an operator of a switchboard, or an officer, employee, or agent of a provider of wire or electronic communication service, whose facilities are used in the transmission of a wire or electronic communication, to intercept, disclose, or use that communication in the normal course of his employment while engaged in any activity which is a necessary incident to the rendition of his service or to the protection of the rights or property of the provider of that service, except that a provider of wire communication service to the public shall not utilize service observing or random monitoring except for mechanical or service quality control checks." Thanks to Chris Hoofnagle for calling attention to this crucial point.

that distinct sets of informational norms be fleshed out for mobile app developers according to the social meaning, or function, of their specific apps. Although developers of, say, Yelp, Google Maps, Foursquare, Fitbit, and Uber should fulfill these baseline obligations in their collection, use, and disclosure of personal information, their obligations do not stop with these. One could reasonably expect Fitbit to treat the information it gathers differently from, say Uber, or Foursquare. Mobile app developers do not escape additional obligations of social context any more than physicians are relieved of duties of confidentiality when information is shared with them over the phone rather than during an office visit. Where technical platforms mediate multiple spheres of life, the need to distinguish technological affordance from moral imperative is acute. Doubtless technologies shape contexts, and may even constitute them, but where Respect for Context is a bellwether for privacy, it is a mistake to confuse technological contexts with those that define legitimate privacy expectations.

Interpreting context as sector or industry overcomes some of the drawbacks of context as business model, because instead of devolving to the self-serving policies of individual businesses, norms of information flow could be guided by a common mission of the collective – ideally, collective best practice. This interpretation also aligns with the US sectoral approach to privacy regulation and legislation, which, at its best, allows for the generation of rules that are sensitive to the distinctive contours of each sector. Extracting a Principle of Respect for Context, carrying moral weight, from a descriptive notion of sector requires a bridge. One is to recognize explicitly that sectors include more than industries, which range over a limited set of, primarily, business sectors. Existing practice in the USA goes partway in this direction, in talk of education and health care, for example, as sectors. Extending the range to politics, family, or religion could deepen the appreciation of appropriate informational rules even further. Expanding and qualifying the scope of sectors in these ways, however, brings them close to the construct of social spheres around which the theory of contextual integrity is oriented.

Interpreting the Principle of Respect for Context as respect for contextual integrity means first, that any significant disruption in information flows triggers a call for analysis and evaluation in terms of types of information, actors, and transmission principles. Because shifts and changes characteristic of these disruptions may correspond to shifts and changes in the balance of interests as well as achievement and abatement of values, identifying them is a crucial first step. Second, an evaluation of disruptive flows extends beyond conventional measures of stakeholder interests and even beyond general moral and political values. It brings to the fore context-specific functions, purposes, and values. Context is crucial to privacy, not only as a passive backdrop against which the interests of affected parties are measured, balanced, and traded off; rather, it contributes independent, substantive landmarks for *how* to take these interests and values into account. It makes the integrity of the contexts *themselves* the arbiter of privacy practices – vibrant marketplace, effective health care, sound education, truly democratic governance, and strong, trusting families and friendships.

Summary of argument

For the Consumer Privacy Bill of Rights to advance privacy protection beyond its present state, a great deal hangs on how the Principle of Respect for Context is interpreted. Acknowledging the pivotal place context holds in the White House vision, commentaries have converged around four primary contenders: business model, technology, sector, and social domain. I have argued that respecting context as *business model* offers no prospect of advancement beyond the present state of affairs.

Respecting context as *sector* (or industry) fares slightly better as it offers a framework beyond the needs of individual businesses for establishing standards and norms. How well this approach meaningfully advances privacy protection beyond the present state depends on how sectors are defined. This problem is particularly acute where the sector or industry in question is the "information sector," where the proverbial fox would be guarding the henhouse. Further, if industry dominates the construction of sectors, the influence of sectors such as health care, education, religion, and politics will be diminished, or the commercial aspects of these industries may play a disproportionate role. Correcting for these distortions brings sector-as-context closer to context-as-social domain. Understanding context in purely *technological* terms implies that legitimate expectations should be adjusted to reflect technical affordances and constraints, but in so doing drains respect for context of moral legitimacy, getting things exactly backwards. Our morally legitimate expectations, shaped by context and other factors, should drive design and define the responsibilities of developers, not the other way around.

Interpreting context as *social domain*, as characterized in the theory of contextual integrity, avoids many of the problems associated with the other three options. To respect context under this interpretation means to respect contextual integrity, and, in turn, to respect informational norms that promote general ethical and political values, as well as context-specific ends, purposes, and values. The ultimate contribution of contextual integrity does not rest with the concept of context per se, but with two fundamental ideas behind it: one is the idea that privacy (or informational) norms require all relevant parameters to be specified including actors (functioning in roles), information types, and transmission principles. Omitting any one of these yields rules that are partial and ambiguous. The second fundamental idea is of context-specific ends, purposes, and values, which extend the significance of privacy beyond the balancing of interests, harms, and benefits. Contextual integrity reveals the systematic dependencies of social values on appropriate information flows, once and for all challenging the fallacy of privacy as valuable for individuals alone.

Conclusion: implications for practice

I have argued that how context is interpreted in Respect for Context makes more than a semantic difference. To demonstrate the significance of this difference, let us consider how it might play out in practice by returning to 18 USC Section 2511 (2)(a)(i), which, as we saw, prohibits telecommunications providers from intercepting, disclosing, or using the content of communications except, in limited circumstances, which include rendering service or protecting their property with further exceptions for legitimate needs of law enforcement and national security. For the sake of argument, assume that no such legislation existed and, based on the Principle of Respect for Context, regulation for this slender part of the landscape must be newly designed. What difference does interpretation make?

According to contextual integrity, interpreting context as social domain would focus attention on the role of telecommunications providers as communications' mediators. In this light, the tailored access rights devised by 18 USC Section 2511 (2)(a)(i), allowing surveillance of conversations for the express purpose of assuring quality of service and protection of property was a brilliant compromise. Laxer policies, as supported by the other interpretations, may discourage intimate or political conversation, as well as other sensitive conversations, such as strategic business planning or path-breaking scientific collaborations, creating disadvantage for those needing to communicate or benefitting from it. But beyond these impacts on various parties, they would reduce the utility of communications networks to individuals as well as their service of respective contextual ends, purposes, and values. Context as social domain draws attention to these higher order considerations, also reflected in the drafting of 18 USC Section 2511 (2)(a)(i).

Contexts are shaped by technology, business practice, and industry sector. They may also be constituted by geographic location, relationship, place, space, agreement, culture, religion, and era, and much more besides. In individual cases, any of these factors could qualify and shape peoples' expectations of how information about us is gathered, used, and disseminated. No one of them, however, provides the right level of analysis, or carries the same moral and political weight as social domain. This is the thesis I have defended here. In light of it, I offer an amendment to the Consumer Privacy Bill of Right's Principle of Respect for Context:

> *Respect for Context means consumers have a right to expect that companies will collect, use, and disclose personal data in ways that are consistent with the [social] context in which consumers provide the data.*

Acknowledgments

An early version of this chapter was presented at the Privacy Law Scholars Conference 2013 where James Rule, Mike Hinze, and other participants provided excellent commentary. I have benefitted from deep insights of many colleagues and from opportunities to present the work at the Amsterdam Privacy Conference, University of Washington, Fondation Télécom Seminar on The Futures of Privacy, and the EU JRC Ispra Workshop on Emerging ICT for Citizens' Veillance. Funding from the NSF – CNS-1355398 and DGE-0966187 – and Intel Science and Technology Center for Social Computing provided crucial support for this work. Thanks to Solon Barocas for assembling key materials and sharpening central ideas and to Emily Goldsher-Diamond for outstanding and invaluable research assistance.

References

Angwin, J. and Valentino-Devries, J. 2012. "New tracking frontier: your license plates," *The Wall Street Journal*, September 29. Accessed June 12, 2013 from http://on.wsj.com/1w2G8gB.

Cate, F. 2006. "The failure of Fair Information Practice Principles," *Consumer Protection in the Age of the Information Economy*, July 8. Accessed July 1, 2013 from http://papers.ssrn.com/sol3/papers.cfm?abstract_id=1156972.

Chavez, P. L. 2011. Comments of Google Inc. to US Department of Commerce. Electronic filing, January 28. Accessed June 11, 2013 from www. ntia.doc.gov/files/ntia/comments/101214614-0614-01/attachments/ FINALCommentsonDepartmentofCommercePrivacyGreenPaper%20 %283%29.pdf.

Civil, C. 2012. "President Obama's Privacy Bill of Rights: Encouraging a Collaborative Process for Digital Privacy Reform," in *Berkeley Technology Law Journal*, March 12. Accessed June 11, 2013 from http://btlj.org/?p=1712.

Department of Homeland Security 2013. Website Privacy Policy. Accessed June 12, 2013 from www.dhs.gov/privacy-policy.

Dwork, C. and Mulligan, D. K. 2012. "Aligning Classification Systems with Social Values through Design," *The 5th Annual Privacy Law Scholars Conference*. The George Washington University Law School, Washington DC. June 8.

EPIC.org 2012. "White House Sets Out Consumer Privacy Bill of Rights," Electroning Privacy Information Center. 23 February. Accessed from https://epic.org/2012/02/white-house-sets-out-consumer-.html.

European Union 2013. Committee on Civil Liberties, Justice and Home Affairs. *On the Proposal for a Regulation of the European Parliament and of the Council on the Protection of Individuals with Regard to the Processing of Personal Data and on the Free Movement of Such Data (General Data Protection Regulation).* By Albrecht, J. P. Vol. (COM(2012)0011–C7-0025/2012–2012/0011(COD)). 22 November.

Federal Trade Commission 2012. *Protecting Consumer Privacy in an Era of Rapid Change: Recommendations for Businesses and Policymakers.* FTC Report, March. Accessed June 11, 2013 from www.ftc.gov/ os/2012/03/120326privacyreport.pdf.

Friedman, M. 1970. "The Social Responsibility of Business is to Increase its Profits," *The New York Times Magazine*, September 13. Accessed June 11, 2013 from www.colorado.edu/studentgroups/libertarians/issues/ friedman-soc-resp-business.html.

Hoffman, D. 2012. White House Releases Framework for Protecting Privacy in a Networked World. Post on Policy@Intel blog, February 23. Accessed June 12, 2013 from http://blogs.intel.com/policy/2012/02/23/ white-house-privacy.

Hoffman, M. 2012. Obama Administration Unveils Promising Consumer Privacy Plan, But the Devil Will Be in the Details. Electronic Frontier Foundation, February 23. Accessed June, 12 2013 from www.eff.org/deeplinks/2012/02/ obama-administration-unveils-promising-consumer-privacy-p lan-devil-details.

Horan, P. 2011. Online Publishers Association Re: FTC Preliminary Staff Report on "Protecting Consumer Privacy in an Era of Rapid Change: A Proposed Framework for Businesses and Policymakers" – File No. P095416. Electronic filing, February 17. Accessed June 11, 2013 from www.ftc.gov/policy/public-comments/comment-00315-0.

Intel 2011. RE: FTC Staff Preliminary Report on Protecting Consumer Privacy. Intel Comments to FTC, January 26. Accessed June 11, 2013 from www.ftc.gov/os/comments/privacyreportframework/00246-57451.pdf.

Kiseleva, J., Thanh Lam, H. T., Pechenizkiy, M. and Calders, T. 2013a. "Discovering Temporal Hidden Contexts in Web Sessions for User Trail Prediction," in *Proceedings of the 22nd International Conference on World Wide Web Companion*. Geneva: International World Wide Web Conferences Steering Committee, pp. 1067–74.

2013b. "Predicting Current User Intent with Contextual Markov Models," in *Data Mining Workshops (ICDMW), 2013 IEEE 13th International Conference*. Los Alamitos: IEEE, pp. 391–8.

Lawler, B. 2011. Request for Comments: Information Privacy and Innovation in the Internet Economy. Intuit Comments before the Department of Commerce, Office of the Secretary National Telecommunications and Information Administration, January 28. Accessed June 11, 2013 from www.ntia.doc.gov/files/ntia/comments/101214614-0614-01/attachments/Intuit.pdf.

Maier, F. 2010. TRUSTe's Comments in Response to the Department of Commerce's Green Paper – Commercial Data Privacy & Innovation in the Internet Economy: A Dynamic Policy Framework. Electronic filing, January 28. Accessed June 11, 2013 from www.docstoc.com/docs/150372462/For-body-font-Preferably-Arial_-11-sized-font–which-is-what-most-of.

National Telecommunications and Information Administration 2012. Multistakeholder Process to Develop Consumer Data Privacy Code of Conduct Concerning Mobile Application Transparency. Notice of meeting published by Federal Register, June 28. Accessed June 11, 2013 from https://federalregister.gov/a/2012-15767.

Nissenbaum, H. 2010. *Privacy in Context: Technology, Policy and the Integrity of Social Life*. Stanford University Press.

2011. "A Contextual Approach to Privacy Online," *Daedalus* 140(4): 32–48.

OECD Guidelines on the Protection of Privacy and Transborder Flows of Personal Data. September 23, 1980. Accessed June 11, 2013 from www.oecd.org/internet/ieconomy/oecdguidelinesontheprotectionofprivacyandtransborderflowsofpersonaldata.htm.

Rauhofer, J. 2013. "One step forward, two steps back: critical observations on the proposed reform of the EU Data Protection Framework," *Journal of Law and Economic Regulation* 6(1): 57–84.

Raul, A., McNicholas, E. R., Brown, C. T., Adams, J. P., Mancini, P. K., Krom, K. M. and Kingsley, T. R. 2011. Comments of AT&T Inc. before the Federal Trade Commission in the Matter of the Protecting Consumer Privacy in an Era of

Rapid Change: A Proposed Framework for Businesses and Policymakers. Electronic filing, February 18. Accessed June 11, 2013 from www.ftc .gov/sites/default/files/documents/public_comments/preliminary-ftc-staff-report-protecting-consumer-privacy-era-rapid-change-proposed-framework/00420-58059.pdf.

Rubinstein, I. S. 2010. "Privacy and regulatory innovation: moving beyond voluntary codes," *I/S: a Journal of Law and Policy for the Information Society* 6(3): 356–423.

Selbst, A. D. 2013. "Contextual expectations of privacy," *Cardozo Law Review* 35: 643–897.

US National Telecommunications and Information Administration 2013a. Privacy Multistakeholder Process: Mobile Application Transparency – Background. Accessed from https://federalregister.gov/a/2013-19304.

US National Telecommunications and Information Administration 2013b. Short Form Notice Code of Conduct to Promote Transparency in Mobile App Practices. Washington DC. Accessed from www.ntia.doc.gov/files/ntia/publications/july_25_code_draft.pdf.

Valentino-Devries, J. and Singer-Vine, J. 2012. "They Know What You're Shopping For," *The Wall Street Journal*, December 7, 2012. Accessed from http://on.wsj .com/1w3xdLZ.

White House Privacy Report 2012. *Consumer Data Privacy in a Networked World: A Framework for Protecting Privacy and Promoting Innovation in the Global Digital Economy*. February 23. Accessed June 11, 2013 from www.whitehouse.gov/sites/default/files/privacy-final.pdf.

World Economic Forum 2012. *Rethinking Personal Data: Strengthening Trust.* Report, May. Accessed June 11, 2013 from www3.weforum.org/docs/WEF_IT_RethinkingPersonalData_Report_2012.pdf.

16

Privacy, technology, and regulation: why one size is unlikely to fit all

ANDREAS BUSCH

Introduction

The debate about privacy as a topic of political regulation has been in the headlines and in public discourse a lot recently, prompted not least by the revelations of Edward Snowden. From the summer of 2013 onwards, Snowden – a former National Security Agency (NSA) contractor turned whistleblower – published secret documents revealing comprehensive snooping operations by intelligence services such as the United States' NSA, the UK's Government Communications Headquarters (GCHQ), the German Bundesnachrichtendienst (BND) and others, under programs like PRISM, Tempora or Muscular.[1] In addition, these documents made public a hitherto unknown level of cooperation and data-sharing from dragnet operations among these agencies, thus raising questions about the effectiveness of parliamentary control of the executive in many countries.

As a consequence, calls for more and/or better regulation have been made in public discussion and policy debates in practically all established liberal democracies around the globe. If at times these debates have been quite intense, this is probably because today the protection of personal data affects literally almost everyone, while two or three decades back it was very much only an expert concern.

Over time, a strong link can be shown to exist between such debates about the protection of privacy and the development of technologies endangering privacy, and this chapter starts by tracing it with a special

The author would like to thank Marie-Aude Boulier and Madeline Kaupert for research assistance; he is also grateful to the participants of the authors' workshop at the Netherlands Institute for Advanced Studies (NIAS) for their input and constructive criticism. And he would like to recognize the editors' helpful suggestions as well as their patience.

[1] For a German-language chronology of events up to January 2014, see www.sz.de/1.1807106 (last accessed 2 July 2014).

emphasis on recent developments. The spread of access to the Internet, the proliferation of mobile technology, and the massive use of databases to store personal information ranging from address or credit card details and geographical movements to DNA samples has led to a situation where we are surrounded by what has been called "ubiquitous computing" (Weiser 1991). The more we are permanently surrounded by data processing, the more important the regulation of storage, access to, and use of personal data becomes. But, as will be shown in detail below, significant tensions exist between the values that individuals profess in opinion polls and their actual behavior with regard to protecting personal data. How can these tensions be understood and analyzed both on the individual level and that of whole societies? And what follows from the fact that privacy regulations are empirically found to differ substantially, both between different technologies and between countries?

Acknowledging Nissenbaum's arguments about "context-sensitivity" of informational norms, the chapter interprets such variations as expressions of preference for regulation by "local informational norms" rather than globally harmonized rules and goes on to discuss the tension between such local preferences and the ideals of a global information sphere that were at the root of both the ideational and technological development leading to today's information society.

Privacy and technology: the link in public debates

Debates about privacy – or more precisely, what the rank afforded to privacy shall be in modern society – have been a recurrent theme since the late nineteenth century. While it is generally recognized that these debates undergo cycles of attention with peaks and troughs over the decades, there is far less awareness of the fact that a close and stable link exists between these debates and recent innovations in technological development. Recognition of that fact, however, greatly helps us to understand those debates, and to put them into an appropriate context (see Table 16.1).

A foundation stone in the legal and political debate about "The right to privacy" is a famous article written in 1890 by two eminent US lawyers and published in the *Harvard Law Review* (Warren and Brandeis 1890). This essay is often credited with starting the debate about legal and constitutional foundations of privacy, and with popularizing the phrase the "right to be let alone." What is far less known is that the circumstances triggering this treatise were related to a new technological development

Table 16.1 *Technological developments as initiators of
public debates about privacy*

Time	Privacy-related technology
1890s	Hand-held photography
1920s	Government wiretaps
1960s	Computer-based database of all citizens
1990s	Internet / CCTV / Encryption
2000s	Mobile ("ubiquitous") computing

and changing business practices, namely the spread of handheld cameras and the use newspapers (especially the yellow press) were making of them for commercial profit.

Several decades later, in the 1920s, the tapping of telephone lines began to be employed by state authorities in the United States to help with law enforcement. In a famous legal case (*Olmstead* v. *United States*), a bootlegger was convicted of violating the National Prohibition Act 1919 by unlawfully possessing, transporting, and selling intoxicating liquors. That conviction was based on wiretapped private telephone conversations that had been collected for several months. The US Supreme Court ruled that electronic eavesdropping did not violate constitutional protections against illegal search, arguing that it did not involve physical entry. The Court majority found that Olmstead had, in effect, broadcast his conversations to the general public whenever he spoke on the phone, and that wiretapping "did not amount to a search or seizure within the meaning of the Fourth Amendment" (*Olmstead* v. *US*, 277 US 438 (1928)).

However, the dissenting opinion to that ruling, delivered by Justice Brandeis, became more influential over time than the reasoning of the Court majority (Gormley 1992: 1360–8; Nelson 2004: 261–2) and contributed to the strict regulations for wiretapping that were enacted several decades later when Congress brought wiretapping under court-order and operating-safeguards legislation with the Omnibus Crime Control and Safe Streets Act 1968 (Westin 2003: 437). A privacy concept based on physical property, Brandeis had argued already in 1928, was misguided; legal protection should be afforded to individual security instead, and telephone lines thus enjoy the same guarantee of privacy already extended to sealed letters to ensure one's "right to be let alone."

The next wave of debate about privacy emerged in the 1960s. It was triggered in the early 1960s by a proposal from the US Social Science Research Council (SSRC) to establish a "Federal Data Center" serving to centralize the collection, coordination, and access to government statistical information. Privacy now no longer seemed of concern only to select individuals – the rich and famous or people breaking the law – but suddenly threatened to become a mass issue that could potentially concern everybody in the new era of electronic computers. Popular books started to discuss the issue and its consequences, diagnosing "a naked society" in which "modern world forces ... threaten to annihilate everybody's privacy" (Packard 1964: 4). Hearings were conducted in the US House of Representatives by the Special Subcommittee on Invasion of Privacy by Computers in April 1965, and the SSRC's plans were shelved. But the debates had demonstrated a principal divergence in the policy interests of public administrations and the individual:

> The primary policy tension in the area of privacy and data collection has been between the privacy rights of individuals – defined as the rights of individuals to control information about themselves – and the needs of organizations to conduct their administrative functions and to make timely and accurate decisions about people.
>
> (Regan 1995: 70)

Intense discussions about policy in this area were followed in most liberal democracies, and they resulted in the institutionalization of "information commissioners" and "data protection offices" in many countries during the 1970s and 1980s. In the 1980s the advent of the "Orwell year" 1984 prompted fresh fears and debates (most prominently perhaps in the protests against the planned West German census), and in the 1990s groundbreaking new developments such as the spread in the use of CCTV and – above all – the Internet (facilitated by the public launch of the World Wide Web in 1991, allowing easy access to linked computers) triggered new discussions. A wave of books discussed "the end of privacy" (Sykes 1999) resulting from a "database nation" (Garfinkel 2000) that held and kept everything on record and in which there was consequentially "no place to hide" (O'Harrow 2006). When encryption of electronic communication was promoted by civil rights activists and computer scientists as a means to keep electronic communication private, a conflict ensued with state interests to outlaw such technology and keep email and other communication accessible for (inter alia) the purposes of law enforcement (Diffie and Landau 1998).

The massive spread of mobile phones (with some Internet access) and smartphones (which are actually small computers in disguise) from the early 2000s onwards led to a new situation of "computing anywhere" (or ubiquitous computing) and both multiplied and globalized the number of users. At the same time, an explosion of e-commerce meant that as ever more goods and services were booked and bought online, ever more people left constant traces of their activities as well as their physical whereabouts in electronic form for their service providers to store and use. Services such as search, email, photo storage, and so on were offered for free, but effectively in exchange for obtaining users' personal data. Debates about the privacy consequences of these developments became both more sophisticated and moved from being conducted primarily between experts into the policy mainstream, where they covered both private and public sector behavior. Large-scale hearings in parliaments as well as the establishment of special committees resulted from it in several countries (e.g. Deutscher Bundestag 2013; House of Lords. Select Committee on the Constitution 2009).

New challenges

Public discourse about the balance between privacy and security intensified even further when – in the summer of 2013 – ex-NSA contractor Edward Snowden started to publish confidential material from secret services such as the US NSA, the British GCHQ, the German BND, and others. This material indicated that these services had conducted intense and indiscriminate surveillance of users of electronic communication, allegedly as a means to combat terrorist activities. It also transpired that the services cooperated in ways that were apparently designed to circumvent constitutional limitations on spying against their own country's citizens. As a consequence, in many countries political resolutions were passed, campaigns conducted, and open letters published to demand that these activities be curtailed.

But concern about violations of privacy, so loudly proclaimed in the Snowden case, is not universal or consistent. On the one hand, it varies across policy domains: in contrast to the heated debate triggered by the Snowden revelations, public discourse is far less concerned about other issues that are no less privacy-relevant – such as the use of genetic information to track criminal offenders, the spread of visual surveillance in public spaces (CCTV) or the use of radio frequency identification (RFID) chips in commercial products. Rather than arousing much passion in public debate, discussions in these areas remain largely confined to the policy discourse between experts. And on the other hand, we find substantial variation if we look at the degree of politicization in debates about privacy regulation by country: while in some countries, for example, the use of identification technology in passports and ID cards is hotly debated, in others the same issue arouses no controversy. However, in another issue area – say CCTV cameras in public space – the pattern may be exactly the reverse. A comparative study of the United States, Germany, the United Kingdom, and Sweden has recently demonstrated that substantial differences exist with respect to the mode of regulating privacy-related technologies, the content of that regulation, and the political dynamics driving both (Busch 2011a).

What we find ourselves with is, therefore, a situation in which it is more or less impossible to make generalizing statements about the regulation of privacy. In addition, the present situation is different from that in the past, when worries focused (at least mainly, if not exclusively) on privacy breaches through surveillance by public authorities. Now, however, with the spread of the Internet, the increase in Internet use and the advent of "ubiquitous computing," surveillance on a large scale has also become an area in which big private enterprises (such as Google, Facebook, Apple, Cisco, and others) play an important role. This shifting balance between the public and the private sector puts the issue of privacy into a different perspective.

What drives these developments?

In order to understand these challenges better, the following section will focus on two specific areas to help organize the argument and illustrate it through appropriate examples. We take up central developments and discuss them under the labels of "securitization" and "convenience."

Securitization

Securitization has been a main feature in state development, especially since the terrorist attacks of 9/11/2001, although technology-related transformations in this area started much earlier. Indeed, this is an area that defies the general trend towards the state taking a more "hands-off" approach through privatization and delegation by displaying substantial growth if measured by indicators such as manpower, legislation, or budgets (Busch 2015). Information and communication technology (ICT) had already played an important role at least since the early 1990s, for example in the management of border controls and the increasing volume of air traffic. The progress of economic and political integration above all in Europe, but also later in other parts of the world, had let national borders become a focal point in which growing amounts of person-related data from such different sources as visa application systems, entry–exit systems, criminal watch lists, or passenger name records (PNRs) came together and had to be managed.

Since fulfilling their citizens' desire for security has always been seen as a classical task for, as well as a justification of, their existence, states (in line with an ever broader definition of what constituted security, as reflected in the academic debate about "securitization," see e.g. Balzacq 2011) developed more and more tools to help them obtain information about the persons in their territory. Governments as well as the parties running them found this a topic that appealed to their electorates; bureaucracies manning the administrations thought the increased budgets at their disposal appealing.

Some countries started to collect DNA from criminals in order to help identify them, thus obtaining highly personal information from their citizens that is often stored permanently. The United Kingdom, for example, leads the field with seven million subject profiles – or one in nine inhabitants – on file in its National DNA Database as of March 2012 (Home Office 2013); in other countries the ratio is lower, but also considerable (Nuffield Council on Bioethics 2007: 9). To record the movement of citizens in their territory, some countries have taken to linking existing cameras observing streets and traffic to computers; mobility patterns can thus be obtained, which can be both stored or immediately used to detect violations of tax or insurance rules, or which can help in the arrest of criminals. In the United Kingdom, this technology of "automatic number plate recognition" or ANPR has led to the establishment of a National ANPR Data Centre, which was planned to have the capacity to read 50 million number plates per day and store them for up to five years – without any evidence of wrongdoing (Busch 2010).

Some of the measures taken have proved to be politically contested (such as the United States Real ID Act of 2005; see Ni and Ho 2008) or were declared unconstitutional by the respective courts (such as the German Air Security Bill of 2005, which authorized the shooting down of passenger airplanes if they were used as attack weapons). But overall it is safe to say that under the rubric of "security" an enormous build-up of state capacities to obtain, store, and process their and other citizens' personal data has taken place over the last two decades, which has had highly negative effects on the protection of privacy. The fight against terrorism has served as the motive and the justification for this, as former British

Prime Minister Tony Blair put it in the parliamentary debate about the Prevention of Terrorism Act 2005:

> I think that the civil liberties of the subject are extremely important, but I think that there is one basic civil liberty, which is the right to life. I think that freedom from terrorism is the most important consideration, which must be uppermost in our minds.

(Hansard March 2005, col. 1513)

Not contradicting this general trend is the recognition that institutional, political, and constitutional factors have a significant influence on the degree to which state action has interfered with citizens' fundamental rights, or governments have succeeded in implementing desired measures (Haubrich 2003; Crenshaw 2010).

Thus the existence or not of written constitutions as well as effective protection of human or citizens' rights in a country (e.g. through strong constitutional courts that can invalidate measures that void fundamental rights) affect the degree to which governments can infringe on civil liberties considerably. Another factor is the degree of scrutiny of executive actions, which is linked to the willingness and capability of parliamentary oversight – both vary considerably across liberal democracies. Historical experience with terrorism also plays a role as countries draw specific lessons from the past on how to deal with the phenomenon – and what reactions are considered acceptable (Katzenstein 2003); in addition, previously existing legislation exerts effects of path dependence on new legislation, further contributing to differing outcomes (Wiegand 2011). We can thus conclude that while securitization is a general trend, the specific characteristics it engenders vary substantially across countries – even if we only take liberal democracies into account, as is the case in this chapter.

Convenience

Turning from the aggregate level of statehood to that of the individual, it can be said that protection of personal data has been dear to consumers around the globe for a long time. This is demonstrated by a wealth of survey data that goes back for decades. However, these data also indicate that consumers have been worried for quite some time that their privacy is increasingly under threat.

- In the United States, the share of respondents who were "very" or "somewhat" concerned about their personal privacy rose from 80% in

1990 to 94% in 1999; in 2002, 34% of respondents felt "basically safe" about their right to privacy, and 65% thought it was either "under serious threat" or had "already been lost"; by 2005, the respective numbers had dropped to 16% and risen to 82% (National Research Council 2008: 288, 290).

- In the European Union, concern about data privacy varies considerably between countries, with a mean of 64% being "very" or "fairly" concerned about data privacy (with variations ranging from 32% in the Netherlands to 86% in Germany and Austria); over the past decade, concern has clearly been on the increase, with particularly strong increases in countries where citizens had already been highly concerned about the issue before (Gallup Europe and European Commission 2008: 7–9).

Drawing on this information, one could have expected the trend towards more securitization outlined in the previous section to have met with substantial resistance, and furthermore one might expect that people were highly conscientious in their own actions, aiming to minimize the risk emanating from new technologies (ranging from Internet use to the installation and use of apps on their smartphones). Neither of the two, however, is the case if one looks at available empirical evidence.

Focusing on the latter aspect, it is clear that there has been tremendous growth in people's "connectedness" in recent years. In 2013, around 85% of citizens in advanced countries used the Internet (US: 84%; France: 82%; Japan: 86%; UK: 90%; Germany: 84%) while the global number stands at 40%, a sixfold increase over the year 2000 (ITU database www.itu.int). This means that more than an estimated 2.7 billion people around the globe access and use the Internet (International Telecommunication Union 2013: 1).

The dynamism resulting from this development has certainly been a source of economic growth over the last two decades, and especially over the last decade in which "ubiquitous computing" has become a reality. Economic opportunities have given rise to what the Organisation for Economic Co-operation and Development (OECD) has called "the app economy" (OECD 2013b). These applications that mostly run on mobile platforms are characterized by online delivery and have seen a meteoric rise in availability: in only four years after the launch of the first app stores in 2008 and March 2013 (Apple's iTunes App Store and Google's Android Market), it is estimated that there are some 830,000 apps available in the former and 670,000 in the latter. Overall, there may be some two million apps available, and the number of downloads in 2010 is estimated at ten billion

(OECD 2013b: 8–9). Most of these apps are available free of charge, which is the same price point that many online services such as search engines, email services, and so on occupy. They are thus highly attractive for consumers.

But even though their producers charge no money for them, they have to cover their costs and are interested in turning a profit. The producers must therefore get that income from another source, and the obvious one is their customers' personal data, which they use in many ways. As European Consumer Commissioner Meglena Kuneva put it in March 2009: "Personal data is the new oil of the Internet and the new currency of the digital world" (World Economic Forum 2011: 5).

Studies have shown that "free" apps demand more private information from their users than those one has to pay for. While 50 percent of the former demand personal information (which includes such items as the user's location, access to their browser history, their contact data, etc.), none of the paid apps demands such information (OECD 2013b: 37–42). Such personal information can then be sold to information brokers, who pass it on to advertising agencies for tailoring their advertisements more precisely to certain demographic groups, or they can be used for the purpose of price discrimination – what in economics is termed "extracting the consumer rent", that is making more affluent customers pay more for the same service or good than less wealthy ones in order to maximize profit. Successfully predicting tastes and spending habits can thus result in a substantial profit margin. The travel website Orbitz (www.orbitz.com), for example, experimented with price discrimination based on the type of computer used to access it. As a result, users of Apple Macintosh computers (who are considered to be wealthier and spend as much as 30 percent more a night on hotels) are steered to different (and often costlier) travel options than are users of Microsoft Windows-based PCs.[2] But such discrimination can also happen offline and with the full knowledge of the consumer. An example is car insurance, which lowers tariffs in exchange for the installation of a GPS device in the car to monitor the routes taken and the speed of travel.[3]

---

[2] See http://online.wsj.com/article/SB10001424052702304458604577488822667325882
     .html?mod=e2stor (last accessed 2 July 2014).
[3] See as an example the Austrian insurance company UNIQA and its "Safeline"
     car insurance tariff: www.uniqa.at/uniqaat/cms/privatkunden/kfzversicherung/
     SafeLine_Kfz-Versicherung.de.xhtml (last accessed 31 May 2014). On a side note it is
     interesting that the initial focus on the lowered tariff has now given way to an emphasis on
     the GPS device being helpful in case of theft or a car crash.

To sum the argument up: according to opinion polls consumers value privacy and data protection highly. However, their aggregate actual behavior is substantially at variance with such preferences: rather than being circumspect in their behavior – both offline and online – they elect to leave traces of personal data that firms can use for their profit. It thus seems appropriate to conclude that consumers value the convenience afforded to them by such services and apps more highly than their desire for privacy and data protection.[4]

Professed and revealed preferences: a conflict – or not?

As has been demonstrated in the section on convenience, on the individual level, a substantial tension can be diagnosed between preferences given in surveys about the value of privacy and their desire for data protection on the one hand (which is generally substantial and positive), and actual consumer behavior (which shows few traces of behaving according to these preferences). How can we make sense of that tension?

For a long time, economic theory has dealt with questions of privacy and data protection only tangentially. It was not before the early 1960s that economists like George J. Stigler (1961) began to analyze the "economics of information" in a more formal manner.[5] But while the importance of information as a factor in economics was soon recognized in the field more broadly – triggering for example fruitful analyses of the consequences of information asymmetries in economic transactions – questions of privacy were still disregarded. Only in the early 1980s did economic analysis begin to inquire about the effects of privacy regulations – after these had started to emerge in the 1970s and had become a regulatory challenge. The position taken by authors such as Stigler (1980) and Posner (1981), however, was one emphasizing the importance of information for the proper functioning of markets, and thus one interpreting demands for privacy as an attempt to restrict access to valuable information or to

---

[4] To be precise, one has to restrict this to the (present) situation of these goods and services being a "lumpy" good that can only be accepted or rejected as it is. If there were conveniently usable systems for micropayments that would allow users to actually pay for the services they make use of, different behavior could ensue (even if experimental evidence in this respect is not necessarily encouraging for that view; see OECD 2013a, and the discussion in the next section).

[5] It should be noted, however, that Friedrich August von Hayek had already pointed out the importance of "knowledge" almost two decades earlier and demonstrated the working of the price system as a decentralized information device.

hide negative reputation. Interest in the withholding of information was linked to delinquency and fraud, and the authors professed to be puzzled about rising demand for privacy in a time when – living in large cities instead of small towns and working in large organizations – "the average citizen has more privacy ... than ever before" (Stigler 1980: 623). In exclusively equating a reduction in the availability of information with reduced market efficiency and interpreting "privacy legislation [as] redistributive" (Posner 1981: 408), this position was very one-sided. But it was not until the emergence of Internet commerce in the late 1990s that this position began to be challenged. While not denying that there are economic benefits to the full disclosure of information, authors such as Murphy (1996: 2383) pointed out that "the skepticism in the economic literature [with respect to privacy] is overstated" and argued that privacy and data protection in economic transactions had benefits too – which might even justify changing the default rules in favor of privacy protection. With Internet commerce booming, economists have had clear incentives to analyze the effect of using private information in economic transactions in great detail (Acquisti and Varian 2005).

However, what monetary value should be attributed to personal information is ultimately an empirical question, and one that still puzzles researchers. Such valuations can be arrived at in different ways – either through measuring market valuation or through measuring the value individuals attach to it. But it seems that very little is firmly known in this area. Microeconomic experimental studies demonstrate (much to the confusion of the authors) "an unwillingness to pay for privacy" (Beresford, Kübler and Preibusch 2010: 6); and a broad survey of available evidence conducted by an international organization concludes that different metrics for the valuation of personal data arrive at wildly varying results, depending on whether one looks at implicit valuations through stock prices, market values of legitimate sales of personal data, insurance premiums protecting against data loss, or the results of economic experiments with individuals (OECD 2013a).

Attempts to rationalize the divergence between professed and revealed preferences – and thus to solve the apparent contradiction – can draw on two lines of argument, one relatively new and one more dated. On the one hand, they can draw on the insights of the experimental economics literature and argue that it is unrealistic to expect full rationality in individual decision situations where psychological effects (such as self-control bias, or the desire for convenience or for immediate gratification) may distort individual choices: "The conclusions we have reached suggest that individuals may not be trusted to make decisions in their best interests when it comes to privacy" (Acquisti 2004: 27). On the other hand, the mismatch can be attributed to the "tyranny of small decisions" (Kahn 1966) where – largely due to differences in time perspectives – " 'large' changes are effected by a cumulation of 'small' decisions [and thus] consumers never get an opportunity to vote with their dollars on the large changes as such; and if they were given the opportunity, they might not approve what they have wrought." (Kahn 1966: 45).[6] Both arguments would lead one to conclude that it is inappropriate to infer from revealed preferences that consumers do not really hold their professed preferences. After all, "the question ... 'do consumers care?' is a different question from 'does privacy matter?' " (Acquisti 2004: 27). However, it follows from this that we must treat the differences in revealed preferences with respect to the variations in privacy regulation as serious expressions of will, too. And, as will be argued in the next section, this has consequences for the expectations of achieving common standards in the field of privacy regulation at the supranational and international level.

The social context of privacy regulation

While the desire for privacy can be considered an anthropological constant and a basic human need, the precise amount of privacy a society requires has varied historically, as studies have shown (see Westin 1967; Moore 1984). The argument for taking such differences into account when looking at privacy has recently been made particularly forcefully in the writings of Helen Nissenbaum (2004; 2010). Nissenbaum argues that when looking at privacy, context needs to be taken into account, and in particular she stresses the need for the regard of "context-relative informational norms." Only if such norms are respected can "contextual integrity" be maintained – which is what she proposes "as a benchmark for privacy" (2010: 140). Nissenbaum argues that the framework of contextual integrity can serve as a "decision heuristic," allowing us to understand more fully when and why some of the fast alterations that new socio-technical systems and practices bring to the flow of information in societies "provoke legitimate anxiety, protest and resistance" (2010: 148).

Empirical evidence indicates clearly that we find considerable variation in the desire to protect privacy today, both in terms of differences between

---

[6] I am grateful to James Rule for pointing out Kahn's article and the "tyranny of small decisions" to me when discussing my argument.

technologies that are a threat to privacy and with regard to preferences across countries and communities. Studies have shown that concern about the potential violation of privacy preferences varies substantially, and that it does so across both dimensions: comparing Germany, Sweden, the UK, and the USA with a view to the regulation of recent privacy-related technologies – closed-circuit television (CCTV), radio frequency identification chips (RFID), and machine-readable ID cards and passports – Busch (2011a) finds that preferences for protecting privacy vary both between different technologies in the same country and between different countries for the same technology. Looking at an even broader sample of eight countries from North and South America, Europe, and Asia, Zureik *et al.* (2010) similarly report varying levels of concern about privacy and link them to preferences about collectivism and individualism, institutional factors, legal regulations, and historical experience. And Zwick and Dholakia (2001) relate these differences to a different understanding of the rights involved.

Differences are also evident on two levels that can be regarded as related to these attitudinal differences: On the level of civil society, a detailed study by Bennett (2008) shows that the degree of privacy activism varies greatly across countries in the Americas, Europe, and Australia, and explains this with the differences in issues that triggered the individual conflicts and protests in each of them.[7] Whether protests crystallized around the issue of a census (as in the Netherlands in the 1970s and Germany in the 1980s), the introduction of ID cards (as in Australia in the 1980s or the UK in the 2000s) or the legality of cryptography (as in the USA in the 1990s) makes a difference for both the structure and the strategy of the movement, and hence its political influence. On the level of the state, comparative studies of privacy and data protection agencies have long shown substantial differences in scope, age of existence, and regulatory capacity (Bennett 1992). Thus the respective agencies' manpower and budget varies considerably, as does their power to influence legislation, shape public discourse, or enforce regulations. Voters' preferences and business interests are two important factors that shape these variations; as a consequence, similar problems have led to different solutions (Newman 2008).

Nation states – through common historical experience as well as jointly developed systems of collective opinion and majority-building – are plausible units for the formation of collective preferences that can be regarded

---

[7] It should be noted here that Nissenbaum (2010: 140) counts protests as an indicator of violation of context-relative informational norms and hence contextual integrity.

as (drawing on Nissenbaum) "local informational norms." Looking at the issue of privacy regulation, we can thus say that context-relativity seems to have been realized to a considerable degree within these nation states.[8] Evidently, differences in the perception of the problems linked with the issue of technology and privacy have resulted in different regulatory solutions that we can regard as mirroring the variation in preferences in the communities concerned. If Americans are skeptical about state interference in this area, they can choose not to have a privacy commissioner. If Germans are more worried, they can elect to have privacy commissioners at the federal level plus one in each of their sixteen constituent states or *Länder*. If Britons think having the world's largest database of DNA samples from their citizens helps to fight crime – then that is their choice. If Iceland decides to implement the 1995 EU Data Protection Directive, even though the country is not an EU member, it can do so.

Countries thus obviously pursue their own specific, socially contextual preferences with regard to the regulation of privacy. Implementing these preferences, however, comes at a cost, for it creates a tension with another policy goal for which strong arguments can be put forward, and that is the harmonization of regulatory standards at the international level. Given the link between the protection of privacy and technological developments in what has fast become an (almost) global information society, there are clear benefits to be derived from having the same regulatory standards apply in all countries that choose to participate in that endeavor. The benefits range from lowered compliance costs for firms (which now have to adapt their products to a myriad of different national regulations) and clarity for users of information technology worldwide as to which standards apply and what protection they enjoy to the creation of a homogenous area across which information can flow freely.

Within the European Union substantial steps towards harmonizing data protection regulations were taken in the 1990s to complement the establishment of the Single European Market in 1992.[9] As a supranational regulation binding for one of the biggest markets worldwide, directive

---

[8] This is not to deny that the world can be divided in many ways and that therefore collectives can also be formed and analyzed in other ways, such as social class, age cohort, etc. But nation states (or their governments, to be more precise) are also relevant actors in the negotiations about the design and content of global regulatory compacts. Both preference formation within and their role in international negotiations are good reasons for using them as units of observation here.

[9] On the process leading up to the decision about the directive see Newman (2008: chapter 4). For an overview of international sources of privacy regulation see Busch (2011b).

95/46/EC became very influential also outside the area of the European Union, as it stipulated that personal data could only leave the EU if there was "an adequate level of protection" in the target area as well. To compete for IT business from the EU, countries had to adapt their own privacy regulations to those of the directive if they wished to obtain the adequacy confirmation from the European Commission. This resulted in a number of conflicts (most prominently with the US, see Heisenberg 2005 and Busch 2012), but also saw privacy standards being ratcheted up in some countries.[10] Since EU data protection standards can be considered comparatively advanced, as they offer a high level of protection, this can be seen as a positive development from a position keen on the protection of privacy. But on the other hand one has to acknowledge that in such a process the "context-relative informational norms" discussed above are being replaced by other norms through a substitution process emanating from international negotiations and market considerations. While this brings with it the benefits discussed in the previous section, there is no denying that local social preferences may be overruled as a consequence.

Conclusion

The preceding section has argued that in the field of privacy regulation a tension exists between two policy goals, namely the respect for "local informational norms" and the wish to agree on global informational norms. Good arguments can be advanced for both goals; yet we argue here that the tension between both is ultimately irreconcilable.

The case for the importance of adhering to "local informational norms" has been made eloquently by Nissenbaum. Nissenbaum herself sums it up as "a right to live in a world in which our expectations about the flow of personal information are, for the most part, met" (2010: 231). While there is probably widespread agreement regarding the value of "contextual integrity, achieved through the harmonious balance of social rules, or norms, with both local and general values, ends and purposes" (2010: 231), we have argued here that from a public policy point of view substantial doubts must be raised about its practicability and achievability. The reason is that a domination of context-relative norms means that the regulatory rules about privacy will be shaped by different – and

---

[10] For an example of the influence of the EU directive on privacy legislation in countries such as Australia and Canada, see Westin (2003). The challenges arising from international competition in this area are discussed in Busch (2011b).

perhaps contradictory – preferences, and vary from one geographic and technological domain to the next. But the result of this is a world that is fractured by different sets of effective regulatory rules, especially in the field of information – a world, in other words, that is in conflict with the idea of free and open exchange of information across the globe. A world in line with those ideals – a world free of regulatory borders – would also facilitate exchange and thus help economic development and growth; but this is only a second order consideration in the line of argument presented here.

Looking at the substantial, empirically recognizable variation in privacy regulation across the two dimensions that were discussed in the preceding section of this chapter, we can thus argue that "context-relative norms" seem to be of great importance for societies. Evidently these societies prefer having local control to the promise of globally harmonized rules in this area – even if that means foregoing economic welfare gains. It is from this viewpoint then that we can make sense of the ongoing inability to agree on global norms that has puzzled (and enraged) so many observers. Seen through this lens the absence of harmonization in privacy regulation need no longer be merely seen as the result of absence of an international organization sufficiently strong to bridge the differences in national approaches (as argued by Bygrave 2008) or owed to the problems of legal transplantation (see Reidenberg 2000); it can also be regarded as a "revealed preference" for "local informational norms" at the national level, which acts as a hindrance to the harmonization of regulation at the international level.

Since the chapter started with a reference to the Snowden revelations, I would like to end with some informed speculation on the question of whether the situation just described is likely to change as a consequence. After all, the leaks about extensive electronic surveillance by secret service agencies in a substantial number of countries were regarded as a major political scandal by many commentators. But considerable variation in the assessment of the leaks was also evident, ranging from loud public protests and a parliamentary investigation in Germany to substantial support for the criminal prosecution of Snowden in the USA. These differences, too, can be linked to different "local" (i.e. national) informational norms – although other factors (such as a country's conception of its role in the international power hierarchy and the means acceptable for furthering its own position) will also have played a role here.

Is it likely that Snowden's disclosures will change this in the future and lead to convergence in attitudes and policies, as some activists hope? The scholarly literature has always held it to be unlikely that a critical politi-cization of the issue of privacy regulation would lead it to become decisive in electoral behavior (Lyon 2001: 135; Bennett 2008: 200), and there is little reason to believe that this has changed. Too varied are the interests related to the issue, and too little organizational heft exists around it. In add-ition, any major politicization is likely to impede rather than help speed up agreement at the international level. For the more politicized an issue is, the more it is in the public eye, the less room there is for the political exchange and compromise necessary to alter the status quo. For support-ers of international standards in this field the best hope is thus for "low voltage politics" and bureaucratic piecemeal engineering. Supporters of the status quo, in turn, have the considerable inertia of such processes in their favor, a situation that is likely to be dominant for some more time.

References

Acquisti, A. 2004. "Privacy in electronic commerce and the economics of immedi-ate gratification," in J. Breese, J. Feigenbaum and M. Seltzer (eds.), *EC '04*, pp. 21–29. doi: 10.1145/988772.988777.

Acquisti, A. and Varian, H. R. 2005. "Conditioning prices on purchase history," *Marketing Science* 24(3): 367–81. doi: 10.1287/mksc.1040.0103.

Balzacq, T. (ed.) 2011. *Securitization Theory: How Security Problems Emerge and Dissolve*. London: Routledge.

Bennett, C. J. 1992. *Regulating Privacy: Data Protection and Public Policy in Europe and the United States*. Ithaca: Cornell University Press.

2008. *The Privacy Advocates: Resisting the Spread of Surveillance*. Cambridge, MA: MIT Press.

Beresford, A. R., Kübler, D. and Preibusch, S. 2010. *Unwillingness to Pay for Privacy: A Field Experiment*. Bonn: Forschungsinstitut zur Zukunft der Arbeit.

Busch, A. 2010. "Politik, Prävention, Privatheit: Orwell und die britische Gegenwart," in S. Seubert and P. Niesen (eds.), *Die Grenzen des Privaten*. Baden-Baden: Nomos, pp. 145–64.

2011a. "Die Regulierung von Privatheit: Technische Innovation als Herausforderung von Datenschutzregimes," *dms – Der Moderne Staat – Zeitschrift für Public Policy, Recht und Management* 4(2): 403–22.

2011b. "The Regulation of Privacy," in D. Levi-Faur (ed.), *Handbook on the Politics of Regulation*. Cheltenham and Northampton, MA: Edward Elgar, pp. 227–40.

2012. "The regulation of transborder data traffic: disputes across the Atlantic," *Security and Human Rights* 23(4): 313–30.

2015. "The Changing Architecture of the National Security State," in S. Leibfried, E. Huber, F. Nullmeier, M. Lange, J. Levy and J. Stephens (eds.), *The Oxford Handbook of Transformations of the State*. Oxford University Press, pp. 536–53.

Bygrave, L. A. 2008. "International Agreements to Protect Personal Data," in J. B. Rule and G. Greenleaf (eds.), *Global Privacy Protection*. Northampton, MA: Edward Elgar, pp. 15–49.

Crenshaw, M. (ed.) 2010. *The Consequences of Counterterrorism*. New York: Russell Sage Foundation.

Deutscher Bundestag 2013. *Schlussbericht der Enquête-Kommission Internet und digitale Gesellschaft: Drucksache 17/12550, 5.4.2013*. Berlin: Deutscher Bundestag.

Diffie, W. and Landau, S. E. 1998. *Privacy on the Line: The Politics of Wiretapping and Encryption*. Cambridge, MA and London: MIT Press.

Gallup Europe and European Commission 2008. *Data Protection in the European Union: Citizens' Perceptions: Analytical Report*. Brussels.

Garfinkel, S. 2000. *Database Nation: The Death of Privacy in the 21st Century*. Beijing and Cambridge: O'Reilly.

Gormley, K. 1992. "One hundred years of privacy," *Wisconsin Law Review* 5, 1335–442.

Haubrich, D. 2003. "September 11, anti-terror laws and civil liberties: Britain, France and Germany compared," *Government & Opposition* 38(1): 3–28.

Heisenberg, D. 2005. *Negotiating Privacy: The European Union, the United States, and Personal Data Protection*. Boulder: Lynne Rienner Publishers.

Home Office 2013. *The National DNA Database Annual Report 2011–2012*. London.

House of Lords. Select Committee on the Constitution (ed.). 2009. *Surveillance: Citizens and the State: 2nd Report Of Session 2008–09*. London: The Stationery Office.

International Telecommunication Union 2013. *Measuring the Information Society: 2013*. Geneva.

Kahn, A. E. 1966. "The tyranny of small decisions: market failures, imperfections, and the limits of economics," *Kyklos* 19(1): 23–47. doi: 10.1111/j.1467-6435.1966.tb02491.x.

Katzenstein, P. J. 2003. "Same war – different views: Germany, Japan, and counter-terrorism," *International Organization* 57(4): 731–60.

Lyon, D. 2001. *Surveillance Society: Monitoring Everyday Life*. Buckingham: Open University Press.

Moore, B. J. 1984. *Privacy: Studies in Social and Cultural History*. Armonk and London: M. E. Sharpe.

Murphy, R. S. 1996. "Property rights in personal information: an economic defence of privacy," *Georgetown Law Journal* 84: 2381–417.

National Research Council (ed.) 2008. *Protecting Individual Privacy in the Struggle against Terrorists: A Framework for Program Assessment*. Washington DC: National Academies Press.

Nelson, L. 2004. "Privacy and technology: reconsidering a crucial public policy debate in the post-September 11 era," *Public Administration Review* 64(3): 259–69.

Newman, A. L. 2008. *Protectors of Privacy: Regulating Personal Data in the Global Economy*. Ithaca: Cornell University Press.

Ni, A. Y. and Ho, A. T.-K. 2008. "A quiet revolution or a flashy blip? The real ID Act and U.S. national identification system reform," *Public Administration Review* 68(5): 1063–78.

Nissenbaum, H. 2004. "Privacy as contextual integrity," *Washington Law Review* 79(1): 119–57.

　2010. *Privacy in Context: Technology, Policy, and the Integrity of Social Life*. Stanford Law Books.

Nuffield Council on Bioethics 2007. *The Forensic Use of Bioinformation: Ethical Issues*. London.

OECD 2013a. *Exploring the economics of personal data: A survey of methodologies for measuring monetary value*. Retrieved from: http://dx.doi.org/10.1787/5k486qtxldmq-en.

OECD 2013b. "The app economy." doi: 10.1787/5k3ttftlv95k-en.

O'Harrow, R. 2006. *No Place to Hide: Behind the Scenes of our Emerging Surveillance Society*. New York: Free Press.

Packard, V. O. 1964. *The Naked Society*. London: Longmans.

Posner, R. A. 1981. "The economics of privacy," *The American Economic Review* 71(2): 405–9.

Regan, P. M. 1995. *Legislating Privacy: Technology, Social Values, and Public Policy*. Chapel Hill and London: University of North Carolina Press.

Reidenberg, J. R. 2000. "Resolving conflicting international data privacy rules in cyberspace," *Stanford Law Review* 52: 1315–71.

Stigler, G. J. 1961. "The economics of information," *Journal of Political Economy* 69(3): 213–25.

　1980. "An introduction to privacy in economics and politics," *Journal of Legal Studies* 9(4): 623–44.

Sykes, C. J. 1999. *The End of Privacy*. New York: St. Martin's Press.

Warren, S. D. and Brandeis, L. D. 1890. "The right to privacy," *Harvard Law Review*, 4(5): 193–220.

Weiser, M. 1991. "The computer for the 21st century," *Scientific American* 3: 94–104.

Westin, A. F. 1967. *Privacy and Freedom*. New York: Atheneum.

　2003. "Social and political dimensions of privacy," *Journal of Social Issues* 59(2): 431–53.

Wiegand, I. 2011. "Towards convergence? National counter-terrorism measures in Western Europe: A comparison of counter-terrorist legislation in France, Germany, Italy, the Netherlands, Spain, and the United Kingdom after 9/11," unpublished Ph.D. thesis, Bremen International Graduate School of Social Sciences, Bremen.

World Economic Forum 2011. *Personal Data: The Emergence of a New Asset Class*. Geneva. retrieved from: www3.weforum.org/docs/WEF_ITTC_ PersonalDataNewAsset_Report_2011.pdf.

Zureik, E., Harling Stalker, L. L., Smith, E., Lyon, D. and Chan, Y. E. (eds.) 2010. *Surveillance, Privacy, and the Globalization of Personal Information: International Comparisons*. Montreal and Quebec: McGill-Queen's University Press.

Zwick, D. and Dholakia, N. 2001. "Contrasting European and American approaches to privacy in electronic markets: property right versus civil right," *Electronic Markets* 11(2): 116–20.

17

The value of privacy federalism

PAUL M. SCHWARTZ

Introduction

The United States features a dual system of federal and state sectoral law. In the absence of an omnibus privacy statute, the key question is how these laws interact with each other. When Congress enacts privacy law, it generally allows the states space for further action. The federal lawmaker typically does so through laws that set only a floor, that is, a minimum of safeguards, but that allow the states to exceed their privacy protections. This model has involved a wide range of institutional actors in the regulation of privacy. State legislatures and courts interpret state laws. Congress acts to preempt state law in enacting sectoral legislation, as needed, and federal judges interpret state legislation, including subsequent amendments to existing state law or new laws, to decide if they conflict with federal law.

This existing US model is under pressure, however, because the federal government is largely inactive. The risk is that a new generation of state privacy legislation, such as breach notification laws, will not be consolidated and improved through the federal legislative process. Gridlock in Washington DC has suspended the normal process of privacy federalism.

In the European Union, the situation is different. At present, the Data Protection Directive requires member states to enact legislation that is "harmonized" around its rules for information privacy. In the resulting legal system, the focus remains on the member states, which are left with a "margin for maneuver" that permits national differences in the resulting statutes. The result has not been viewed as satisfactory due to a fragmentation of data protection in the EU. Under the Proposed Data Protection Regulation, however, there will be different concerns regarding the relationship between the member states and Community. The Proposed Regulation will be directly binding on member states and largely replace national data protection law. It will also shift power at the institutional level to the Commission and away from the member states. There is a danger that this approach will stifle innovation and heighten the democratic deficit in the EU.

Thus this chapter will analyze two widely different kinds of privacy federalism. In the USA, there is a diffuse system in which the chief risk currently is that of too little consolidation of privacy law at the federal level. In contrast, in the EU, under the Proposed Data Protection Regulation, the chief danger appears to be from the future centralization of power in the institutions of the Union.

"Privacy federalism" is a combined term and both elements of it should be introduced at this juncture. By "privacy," this chapter generally means the legal rules for regulating the processing of personal information by organizations in the public and private sector. In the United States, this area of regulation is called "information privacy law." The similar term in the European Union and, indeed, in the rest of the world, is "data protection law." By "federalism," this chapter indicates a legal granting of partial autonomy in regulatory decision-making or specific areas of governance to geographically defined smaller units (Feeley and Rubin 2008: 22). This definition is of applicability both to the kinds of shared authority in the United States among the federal government and states, and in the European Union between the institutions of Brussels and those of the member states. Putting these terms together, this chapter uses "privacy federalism" as a reference to the different ways that legal authority for information privacy law or data protection law can be distributed among different levels of regulatory authorities, whether national or state in the United States, or European Union and member states in Europe.

US privacy federalism

This section examines the model of privacy in the sectoral system of the United States. It will analyze the laws as well as the different institutional entities involved in shaping privacy law.

Privacy federalism in a sectoral system

A patchwork of information privacy law exists in the United States. While nations in the EU have long enacted omnibus information privacy laws, the United States has promulgated only sectoral laws. An omnibus privacy law typically extends to government and private companies alike. Examples of such national laws are Germany's Federal Data Protection Act (1977) and France's Law on Information Technology, Data Files and

Civil Liberties (1978). There is no similar kind of national omnibus privacy law in the United States.

In Europe, moreover, national lawmakers typically supplement their omnibus laws with sectoral statutes. In Germany, for example, the Telecommunications Act (2004), among its other provisions, specifically regulates the collection and use of personal data in telecommunications. It has specific rules for "location-based data" (*Standortdaten*), including rules that distinguish between the use of such information for "self-location" (*Eigenortung*) and "external-location" (*Fremdortung*). The Telecommunication Act's specific provisions (2004: §§ 91–107) take precedent over the general rules in the Federal Data Protection Act. Where a specific provision is not present or there is ambiguity regarding it, the requirements of the national omnibus law are applicable.

In contrast to an omnibus law, a sectoral law regulates only a specific context of information use. Information privacy law in the USA takes precisely this approach. As examples, the Fair Credit Reporting Act (1970) contains rules for the use of credit reports, and the Video Privacy Protection Act (1988) establishes rules concerning the use of video rental information. As Daniel Solove and Woodrow Hartzog summarize: "By and large, it is fair to say that US privacy law regulates only specific types of data when collected and used by specific types of entities" (Solove and Hartzog 2014: 586). Due to the absence of an omnibus statute, the legal system in the United States contains gaps in its coverage. As a further matter, in the absence of the safety net that an omnibus law provides, one of the most critical issues for information privacy law concerns a threshold question: the applicability of any specific law. The answer to questions such as the definition of "credit reporting" in the context of the Fair Credit Reporting Act, or "financial institution" under the Gramm-Leach-Bliley Act of 1999, can determine whether any statute at all will apply to the use of personal data.

There is a further important dimension to privacy law in the United States, and it relates to federalism. In the USA, there is a dual federal–state system of lawmaking. Legislative power is shared between the federal government and the fifty states. In particular, state law has played a historically important leadership role in privacy law. This state role goes back to the common law tort of privacy, which has long been the province of state law and state courts (Solove and Schwartz 2009).

In the realm of statutory law, states have also made significant contributions to information privacy law. Perhaps the best recent examples of such innovations at the state level are data breach notification statutes and data disposal laws (Schwartz and Janger 2007: 915). California enacted the first data breach notification law in 2002; forty-six other states have followed it. With the enactment of the Health Information Technology for Economic and Clinical Health (HITECH) Act in 2009, the federal government now has a limited data breach notification obligation in place for health care information covered by federal health privacy law.

Data disposal laws are another recent state innovation. Twenty-six states have enacted such statutes. These laws typically require a business to engage in proper destruction of files with personal information. Other innovative state approaches include laws that restrict the use of social security numbers, provide consumers who are victims of identity theft with the ability to place freezes on their credit reports, and require businesses to supply these victims with the relevant records of transactions associated with their stolen identity. Finally, some states are developing substantive requirements for data security. These set requirements for personal data handling. Massachusetts is regarded as having the most detailed as well as strictest such standards (National Conference of Legislators n.d.).

The continuing lack of omnibus legislation

Certain aspects of the structure of US information privacy law can best be understood through reference to American federalism. One classic distinction is between express preemption, where Congress has in explicit terms declared its intention to preclude state regulation in a given area and implied preemption, where Congress, through the structure or objectives of federal law, has impliedly precluded state regulation in the area. Preemption can also take the form of either field preemption or conflict preemption. Field preemption occurs when Congress intended to occupy an entire field of regulation. Conflict preemption takes place where Congress did not necessarily intend complete exclusion of state regulation in a given area, but to block it where a particular state law conflicts directly with federal law, or interferes with the accomplishment of federal objectives (Epstein and Greve 2007: 1–5).

As this chapter has noted, there is no omnibus federal law in the United States. Even were one enacted, it would not be likely to explicitly preempt all state sectoral privacy law. The result of such a statute would be regulatory chaos as several hundred, perhaps even thousands, of state laws would be invalidated as courts decided how to apply the necessarily general provisions of a federal omnibus law to specific situations. Omnibus field preemption is also unlikely. Information privacy law necessarily regulates many contexts in which entities use personal information, and a single law is unlikely to substitute for all the statutes already in place. Moreover, the federal interest in the regulation of information privacy is not so compelling as to displace all state concerns and state laws on the subject. Its interest can be contrasted in this regard with more typical areas for field preemption, such as nuclear safety or alien registration (*Pac. Gas & Elec. Co.* v. *State Energy Res. Conservation & Dev. Comm'n* (1983); *Hines* v. *Davidowitz* (1941)).

Under conflict preemption, as noted above, federal law blocks any state statute that frustrates its ends. A federal omnibus privacy law might cap or otherwise shape damages for statutory violations. It might regulate other general privacy issues such as rights of action. The merits of such a law would likely be mixed. An omnibus statute with conflict preemption would likely limit future experimentation by sectoral laws at both the federal and state levels. It would also run the risk of ossification.

The example of the Privacy Act of 1974 is illustrative in this regard. The Privacy Act is a sectoral statute, of course, but one that is far-reaching for the American system. It regulates how federal agencies collect, use, and transfer personal information. Yet the Privacy Act's flaws have remained intact for decades, including its problematic definition of "system of records" and its restriction of its protection to citizens and permanent residents. The bipartisan Privacy Protection Study Commission pointed to these and other problems in the statute as early as 1977 (Privacy Protection Study Commission 1977: 491). More recently, the White House's White Paper on "big data" called for broadening the statute's protections to non-citizens (Executive Office of the President 2014: 51–3). Instead, inaction remains the norm and the Privacy Act still has not been amended to make this change.

An omnibus law for the United States would prove even more difficult to amend than the Privacy Act. It would raise complex issues across many dimensions. The legislative issue of deciding appropriate kinds of preemption alone would lead to a legislative logjam of colossal proportions. Where should states be allowed enforcement powers? Which existing state laws should be grandfathered and permitted continuing existence? Should new sectoral state laws be permitted? Should only stricter sectoral state laws be permitted?

At any rate, the current system of sectoral privacy law is firmly entrenched. An omnibus privacy statute does not appear to be on the

Congressional horizon. The current model is also one in which federal sector privacy statutes typically are based on conflict preemption and establish standards that states are permitted to exceed.

Conflict preemption in sectoral laws: floors not ceilings

The federal government's inaction regarding new sectoral privacy law has largely left the creation of new laws to regulate new problem areas to the states. An example of such federal inaction causing a regulatory opening at the state level is data breach notification. Where the federal government has acted in the past, it typically enacts privacy statutes that preempt state law. These federal laws generally block only state laws that conflict with their statutory objectives. At the same time, these federal laws also permit greater privacy protection. In other words, the federal law sets a protective floor and not a ceiling.

The exception to this general rule is the Fair Credit Reporting Act (FCRA) of 1970 (15 USC § 1681a[d]). Both in its original enactment and its important amendment through the Fair and Accurate Credit Transactions Act (FACTA) of 2003, FCRA is an outlier to privacy federalism. This statute, one of the earliest information privacy laws in the United States, regulates how "consumer reporting agencies" furnish "consumer reports." FCRA preempts state law relatively broadly and does so by reserving a large number of subjects for federal law. These include the pre-screening of consumer reports, procedures, and requirements relating to the duties of a person who takes any adverse action with respect to a consumer, and procedures and requirements regarding the information contained in consumer reports. These are examples of subject matter preemption; the federal law occupies the regulatory area.

In 2003 FACTA amended FCRA, not only through subject matter preemptions but also through narrower restrictions targeted to mandated behavior. As an example, FACTA requires consumer-reporting agencies to place fraud alerts on consumer credit files under certain circumstances. In so doing, it streamlines an area of industry procedures while, at the same time, permitting states to engage in further regulation regarding the larger subject area, which is identity theft. The approach of FCRA and FACTA, which is to favor federal preemption that limits stronger state protections, is, however, not typical of privacy preemption in the USA.

To illustrate the more typical approach, we can consider the Video Privacy Protection Act (VPPA) of 1988, the Cable Communications

Policy Act of 1984, the Gramm-Leach-Bliley Act (GLBA) of 1999, the Children's Online Privacy Protection Act of 1998 (COPPA), and the Health Insurance Portability and Accountability Act (HIPAA) of 1996. These laws all permit states to enact statutes that are more protective of privacy.

To begin with the VPPA, its core purpose is to restrict disclosure of video rental information. Regarding preemption, and as the VPPA states, it preempts "only the provisions of State or local law that requires disclosure prohibited" by the VPPA. In a similar fashion, the Cable Communications Policy Act permits a state franchising authority, a state, or a municipality to develop stronger privacy protections than found in this federal law (47 USC § 555[d][2]). These entities have traditionally played an important part in regulating cable companies, and the Cable Communications Policy Act recognizes this historic role. As another example, and one we will explore in more detail below, the GLBA states that its privacy protections "shall not be construed as superseding, altering, or affecting any statute, regulation, order, or interpretation in any State ... except to the extent that [the state law] is inconsistent" with the GLBA (15 USC § 6807[a]). The GLBA adds that preemption will occur "only to the extent of the inconsistency." The GLBA explicitly provides that a state law is not inconsistent with it when the state law provides a safeguard to "any person" that "is greater than the protection" under the GLBA (15 USC § 6807[b]).

Finally, HIPAA, like GLBA, permits greater privacy protections but forbids inconsistent state laws. The most important regulation under HIPAA for preemption purposes is the Privacy Rule, as amended most recently in 2013 by the final omnibus HIPAA Rule. HIPAA's Subtitle F contains a general preemption of any "contrary" provision of state law followed by exemptions for public health and health regulatory reporting. It also permits the Secretary of the Department of Health and Human Services to grant exceptions for state laws that are "necessary" for certain enumerated purposes or relate to controlled substances. Finally, it provides a specific exception for state laws that are "more stringent" than the HIPAA standards.

These privacy statutes open up a world of interpretative possibilities. The key issue is whether a state law is more protective of privacy or inconsistent with the federal law. The line can prove difficult to locate and involves both the judiciary and regulators in a process of identifying why aspects of state statutes are either inconsistent with a federal privacy statute or more protective of privacy.

The GLBA offers an initial example of the necessary interpretative work. Courts have evaluated the issue of whether a state law provision is more protective of privacy than the GLBA or is inconsistent with it. One issue concerns the GLBA's provision that permits companies to share the information of their customers with affiliated entities without permission of the affected person (Janger and Schwartz 2002: 1226–7). In other words, customers of financial institutions are not given the ability under the GLBA to block the sharing of their information with affiliated entities. Courts have upheld state laws that require consumer permission, or an opt-in, before financial institutions may share information with affiliated entities. The GLBA also sets an opt-out before sharing of information with unaffiliated entities (Janger and Schwartz 2002: 1226–7). Vermont law requires an opt-in instead of an opt-out before a financial institution may share information with an unaffiliated entity (Vermont Admin. Code 4-3-42: 2). This law has also been upheld as more protective, but not inconsistent with the GLBA.

Regulators have also been involved in the necessary interpretive work. The GLBA grants the Federal Trade Commission (FTC) regulatory authority, and the agency has acted pursuant to it. In response to inquiries from four states, the FTC found that the state's financial privacy laws provided greater consumer protection than the GLBA and, therefore, were not preempted by it. These states were Connecticut, Illinois, North Dakota, and Vermont. In its opinion letters, the FTC found that compliance with the state financial privacy opt-in laws was possible without frustrating the purposes of the GLBA (Federal Trade Commission 2001). As a result, these laws are not inconsistent with the GLBA and are not preempted by it.

HIPAA has also seen a similarly strong role by a regulatory entity. The key entity is the Office for Civil Rights (OCR) of the Department of Health and Human Services. The most important regulation under HIPAA for preemption purposes is the Privacy Rule, as amended most recently in 2013 by the final omnibus HIPAA Rule. HIPAA's Subtitle F contains a general preemption of any "contrary" provision of state law followed by exemptions for public health and health regulatory reporting. It also permits the granting of exceptions for state laws that are "necessary" for certain enumerated purposes or relate to controlled substances. A further exception is provided for state laws that are "more stringent" than the HIPAA standards. There has been considerable litigation about the HIPAA Privacy Rules and whether a law is contrary to HIPAA or more stringent than it.

Different institutional actors

A large part of privacy preemption in the United States is shaped through institutional choices and behavior. Roderick Hills has argued that federalism is a matter of "how the federal and state governments interact, not in how they act in isolation from each other" (Hills 2007: 4). As these entities interact, the question of institutional design becomes a critical one. The GLBA and HIPAA grant the FTC and the Department of Health and Human Service's OCR, respectively, important roles in developing their respective statutory terms. Under the Cable Communications Policy Act, a state franchising authority, a state, or a municipality may develop stronger privacy protections than this federal law. Moreover, the judiciary, federal and state, is involved in deciding when state privacy law is inconsistent with a federal statute and when it is merely stricter.

The legislatures, federal and state, also play an important role in shaping preemption. By permitting preemption for stricter but not inconsistent laws, Congress has provided a roadmap for further state activity to promote privacy. As a more subtle way of promoting state legislative activity, Congress sometimes grandfathers in states with existing sectoral privacy legislation. For example, FACTA provides exceptions for some of its preemptive ceilings for California and Massachusetts (15 USC § 1681t[b][1][F]). These were the states that beat Congress to the regulatory punch and enacted state protections regarding identity theft before Congress took action through FACTA.

A final important institutional choice concerns enforcement of federal privacy law. Numerous federal privacy statutes permit enforcement by state attorney generals. These include the Controlling the Assault of Non-Solicited Pornography and Marketing (CAN-SPAM) Act 2003, COPPA, FCRA, HIPAA, and the Telephone Consumer Protection Act 1991. One of the benefits of this approach is to reinforce the efforts of other federal enforcement agencies, such as the FTC. After all, the FTC includes privacy as only one of its many regulatory tasks, along with a role in antitrust, mergers, and consumer protection issues other than privacy. Moreover, state attorney generals are generally elected officials. Privacy is a popular issue, and one that is likely to be an attractive area for policy entrepreneurship, which is demonstrated by the COPPA actions brought by the state attorney generals in Texas and New Jersey, and the HIPAA actions of state attorney generals in Connecticut, Massachusetts, Minnesota, and Vermont.

The value of privacy federalism in a sectoral system

The United States features a dual system of federal and state sectoral regulations. This creates an opening for the states to experiment through legislation. Any of the fifty states can act first. This approach allows an opportunity for simultaneous experiments with different policies as well as consolidation of lessons learned.

Another benefit of privacy federalism is the decentralization of enforcement power. The Federal Trade Commission, the Department of Health and Human Services' OCR, state attorney generals, state and local cable franchise boards, and other entities all play a role in deciding when and how to enforce – and thereby develop – privacy laws. This decentralization allows decisions to be made at different levels of government and to reflect pluralistic policy concerns.

There is a final benefit of privacy federalism in the sectoral system of the USA. In the traditional model of federalism, a state law is followed by federal consolidation. The response to state action by a regulated entity is frequently to seek regulatory relief in Washington DC. This pressure for federal legislation can open opportunity for all policy stakeholders once the lawmaking process is open.

Today, however, there is considerable gridlock in Congress. Indeed, the current Congress is the least productive one since comprehensive statistics on federal legislative activity began to be kept in 1947. In short, the federal legislative process for privacy appears broken. It is a victim of the larger dysfunction in the Capitol.

In contrast, the state legislative process for privacy continues unabated. In 2013 the online newsletter of the International Association of Privacy Professionals spoke of a "tidal wave" of new privacy legislation from California (Finch 2013). That same year, *The New York Times* observed: "State legislatures around the country, facing growing public concern about the collection and trade of personal data, have rushed to propose a series of privacy laws" (Sengupta 2013). Legislation and legislative proposals continue unabated in 2014. In California alone, a dozen privacy bills were pending in June 2014 (State of California, Office of the Attorney General 2014).

Ideally, federal consolidation of state legislation provides benefits by avoiding inconsistent regulations, especially in areas with high cost and little positive results. Such a need currently exists for data breach notification legislation, where forty-seven different state statutes raise compliance costs for companies. The first such data breach notification statute, that of California, was enacted in 2002, and the area is ripe for federal consolidation. For the White House, it is even a top priority (Executive Office of the President 2014: 51). Yet Congress does not appear to feel a sense of urgency concerning the enactment of such legislation.

There is a current absence of federal consolidation of state experimentation in privacy and security lawmaking. Regarding states-as-laboratories for policy innovations, Malcolm Feeley and Edward Rubin find such experiments "desirable, presumably ... not because of an abiding national commitment to pure research but because the variations may ultimately provide information about a range of alternative government policies and enable the nation to choose the most desirable one" (Feeley and Rubin 2008: 26). Congressional gridlock leaves the nation without consolidation of privacy experimentation. Statutory variations, such as in state data breach notification statutes, can increase compliance costs without adding commensurate policy benefits for individual privacy.

On a positive note, however, the social value of privacy federalism – its decentralization and development of pluralistic policy concerns – may have enduring power even in the age of gridlock and the absence of federal consolidation of state experimentation. In particular, information privacy norms do not exist a priori, but must be developed by individuals, social organizations, political entities, non-governmental organizations, and regulators. These entities define and elaborate a response, sometimes including regulations, to new kinds of technologies and social forms. Privacy federalism ensures diversity and competition in the resulting responses.

The diversity and competition in resulting state regulation will result from the different mix of intermediate interests, including citizen groups and lobbyists, with different kinds of power in various states. In contrast to other kinds of federalism battles in the United States, however, responses to privacy issues do not typically reflect a Democratic or Republican perspective and "flesh out nationwide controversies" at the state level (Bulman-Pozen 2014: 1946).

EU privacy federalism

As an initial matter, one can only speak of EU "federalism" on its own terms – it is not the equivalent of this legal concept in the United States. There are too many differences in the law and organization of the EU and USA for that to be possible. To single out an initial difference, one can point to the EU concept of "indirect administration." From the early days of the European Community, this intergovernmental association has rested on "indirect administration," which means that the power to implement the law of the Community rests primarily with the member states. In the United States, however, federal power is expressed not only through legislation, but also the implementation of laws through the executive branch. We now consider how member states and EU institutions have shared regulatory power under the Data Protection Directive and then discuss the Draft Data Protection Regulation.

The Data Protection Directive and changes in the EU

The 1995 Data Protection Directive is a "harmonizing" instrument. This term means that it is not directly binding, but relies on member states to enact legislation that reflects its common rules for information privacy among EU member states. In the analysis of Spiros Simitis, the Directive is a "patchwork" that corrects and modifies elements of then existing national data protection law (Simitis 1997: 61–3).

Post-Directive, the focus of EU data protection law still remains at the level of the Member State. The Directive left the national lawmaker a "margin for maneuver," that is, to express national differences in their respective statutes. It also left national data protection authorities and courts with the responsibility of enforcing national legislation. The result has generally been viewed as unsatisfactory. Significant regulatory disparities exist among different nations' privacy law. As a result, international companies face twenty-eight different regulatory regimes when seeking to comply with EU privacy law. In summing up this sense of dissatisfaction, the Proposed Data Protection Regulation states: "Heavy criticism has been expressed regarding the current fragmentation of personal data protection in the Union, in particular by economic stakeholders who asked for increased legal certainty and harmonization of the rules on the protection of personal data" (European Commission 2012: 4).

At the same time, other events have shifted power in the EU away from the member states and to EU institutions. One of these milestones was the Lisbon Treaty of 2007,[1] which increases the role of the so-called "federal" institutions, the Commission, European Parliament, and Court of Justice. It also makes the Charter of Fundamental Rights binding on EU institutions and on member states when implementing EU

---

[1] O.J. [C 306], 2007. Accessed from http://eur-lex.europa.eu/legal-content/EN/ALL/?uri=OJ:C:2007:306:TOC.

law. As a further matter, the Lisbon Treaty provides that the Union is to accede to the Charter of Fundamental Rights of the European Union (CFR). The CFR protects information privacy in its Article 8. In its Article 16(1), the Lisbon Treaty itself provides for a right to the protection of personal data.

Subsequent to the enactment of the Directive, EU courts have acted to protect privacy and to develop EU case law in this area. The European Court of Justice has issued important decisions concerning websites (*Lindqvist*, C-101/01 [Nov. 6, 2003]), the independence of data protection authorities (*Commission* v. *Germany*, C-518/07 [Mar. 9, 2010]), the European Data Retention Directive (*Ireland* v. *Parliament and Council*, C-301/06 [Feb. 10, 2009]), and, most recently, a "right to deletion" vis-à-vis search engines (*Google* v. *Gonzalez*, C-131/12 [May 13, 2014]). In June 2014, moreover, the High Court of Ireland issued an opinion asking the European Court of Justice to decide if the Irish data protection commissioner is "absolutely bound" by the EU's finding in 2000 that the Safe Harbor Agreement provides "adequate" data protection (*Maximillian Schrems* v. *Data Protection Comm'r* (2013)). High Court Judge Gerard Hogan wrote: "There is, perhaps, much to be said for the argument that the safe harbour regime has been overtaken by events" (*Maximillian Schrems* (2013): 32). The opinion cautiously added that the leaks about spying by Edward Snowden might be seen as exposing "gaping holes" in US data protection practices (*Maximillian Schrems* (2013): 32).

As for the European Court of Human Rights, it has ruled in numerous cases involving data protection (Press Unit 2014). These include cases concerning combatting terrorism (*Klaas and Others* v. *Germany* (1978)), the interception of correspondence of detained person (*Pisk-Piskowski* v. *Poland* (2005)), the electronic surveillance of communications (*Taylor-Sabori* v. *the United Kingdom* (2002)), the bugging of a residence (*P.G. and J.H.* v. *the United Kingdom* (2001)), the access to governmental databases about a person (*Brunet* v. *France* (2014)), rights in personal medical information (*Peruzzo and Martens* v. *Germany* (2013)), and the necessary safeguards for personal data in the employment context (*Copland* v. *the United Kingdom* (2007)). With reference to these opinions and the European data protection rights on which they rest, Kai von Lewinski has observed: "In data protection law, Europe no longer speaks German or French: it speaks European" (von Lewinski 2012: 217). This development of fundamental European rights to safeguard data protection helped set the stage for the Proposed Data Protection Regulation.

The road ahead: the proposed Data Protection Regulation

In January 2012 the EU released its Proposed General Data Protection Regulation. This document marks an important policy shift from directives to regulations. In EU law, as has been noted, a directive requires harmonizing legislation from the member states. In contrast, a regulation establishes directly enforceable standards. Christopher Kuner has explained the significance of this change: "a regulation leads to a greater degree of harmonization, since it immediately becomes part of a national legal system, without the need for adoption of separate national legislation; has legal effect independent of national law; and overrides contrary national law" (Kuner 2012: 217). In March 2014 the EU Parliament overwhelmingly voted to adopt the Regulation. The next stage will involve the Council agreeing on the text. Negotiations will then take place among the Parliament, the Council, and the Commission.

In the USA, the privacy community has focused on the Proposed Regulation's expression of individual rights. These protections begin by reaffirming the bedrock EU concept of forbidding any processing of personal information in the absence of a legal basis for the activity. The Proposed Regulation also strengthens existing requirements for data minimization; establishes privacy interests for children, defined as those under 13 years old, and creates an interest in portability of data. Beyond these safeguards, it develops a controversial "right to erasure" (COM 2012) and elaborates stricter requirements before consent can be used as a justification for data processing (COM 2012, Art. 7: 45). It also puts emphasis on the EU concept of protection from automated processing, which the Proposed Regulation combines with limitations on "profiling" (COM 2012, Art. 2: 40–41). It also restricts the use of sensitive data (COM 2012, Art. 43: 71–73).

Beyond these enhancements of privacy rights, the Proposed Regulation contains measures that destabilize the organizational status quo among the law and institutions of European privacy law. The result centralizes data protection decision-making in the Commission. As Niko Härting observes, the Draft Regulation placed the Commission at the top of the institutional pyramid for controlling data protection in Europe (Härting 2012: 460). The critical steps in this regard concern the Proposed Regulation's "consistency mechanism" (COM 2012, Art. 57: 82) and the power that it grants to the Commission to create a wide range of "delegated" and "implementing" acts (COM 2012, Art. 86: recital 37–38).

The first such action that shifts power to Brussels is the Proposed Regulation's "consistency mechanism." The Proposed Regulation creates a new institution, the European Data Protection Board (EDPB) (COM 2012, Arts. 64–72; Arts. 86–89). In so doing, it upgrades the status of the Article 29 Working Party, the panel of national supervisory authorities (COM 2012, Art. 64, 86). The EDPB provides a useful forum in which national supervisory authorities can reach a consensus about important issues. Governmental officials in individual countries with data protection legislation, in particular France, Germany, and the United Kingdom, played a central role throughout the 1980s and 1990s in the creation of supranational privacy protection in Europe (Newman 2008: 88–9). The EDPB offers a new institutional framework for drawing on these important ties. While the EDPB permits each national data protection commission to make final regulatory choices, it requires a draft proposal to be filed with it and the European Commission before a commission can adopt a measure relating to certain kinds of matters. The pre-filing requirement extends to matters affecting information processing in several member states, international data transfers, and a variety of other topics. The EDPB's subsequent recommendations will be valuable to the process of developing consensus about important transnational privacy issues among all member states. The EDPB would offer an opinion on the matter by simple majority.

More controversially, the Proposed Regulation grants significant new power to the Commission. It assigns the Commission the authority under the consistency process to issue opinions to "ensure correct and consistent application" of the Regulation. At an initial stage, the national data protection authority must "take utmost account of the Commission's opinion" (COM 2012, Art. 59[2]: 84). Additionally, the Commission may require national data protection authorities "to suspend the adoption" of a contested draft measure (COM 2012, Art. 60[1]: 84). Thus, through the consistency process, the Proposed Regulation grants the Commission the final word on a wide range of matters concerning the interpretation and application of the Proposed Regulation throughout the EU and beyond.

The Proposed Regulation also assigns the Commission the power to adopt "implementing acts" and "delegated acts" under a wide range of circumstances. Implementing acts enact procedures to put legislation into effect, and delegated acts supplement or amend nonessential elements of EU legislation. The Proposed Regulation contains numerous grants of power to adopt both kinds of acts, plus a general grant in Article 62(1) to issue implementing acts to decide "on the correct application" of the Regulation under almost limitless circumstances (COM 2012, Art. 62[1]: 85). One analysis of the Proposed Regulation has found that it identifies forty-five different areas that can be regulated through such acts (Dix 2012: 321). As Kuner concludes, the result is "a substantial shifting of power regarding data protection policymaking from the EU member states and the [data protection authorities] to the Commission" (Kuner 2012: 227).

The EU's turn away from privacy federalism

There has been considerable controversy in Europe about the Proposed Data Protection Regulation. In Germany, the Bundesrat, or Federal Council, which represents the sixteen states of Germany in the federal legislative process, issued a resolution objecting to the Proposed Regulation (*Bundesrat Drucksachen*). It declared that the Proposed Regulation engages in an "almost complete displacement of the data protection rules in member states" (*Bundesrat Drucksachen* n.d.: 3). In France, the National Commission on Information Technology and Liberties (CNIL) objected to the regulation as "a centralization of the regulation of private life for the benefit of a limited number of authorities, and equally for the benefit of the Commission, which will gain an important normative power" (CNIL 2012). It also pointed to aspects of the Regulation that reinforce the "bureaucratic and distant image of community institutions" and reduce the status of data protection commissioners to that of a "mailbox" for passing on complaints to other authorities (CNIL 2012).

There has also been an outcry against the reliance in the Proposed Regulation on delegated and implementing acts. The resistance is demonstrated by leaked comments dated July 18, 2012 from member states to the Council of the EU (Note from Gen. Secretariat 2012). The national delegations of France, Germany, Italy, Luxembourg, Norway, Sweden, Poland, and the United Kingdom all objected to this aspect of the Proposed Regulation. As the objection from Poland noted, for example, the Proposed Regulation constituted a "rather general basis for the future shape of the future data protection system instead of coherent, seamless and in particular transparent regulation" (Note from Gen. Secretariat 2012: 101). One problem was that certain delegated acts were too broad, such as the authority of the European Commission to define "legitimate interests" of the data controller in specific data processing situations and in specific sectors.

Commentators have also wondered whether the Regulation violates "subsidiarity," a key tenet of EU law. Alexander Dix, the Berlin Data Protection Commissioner, argues that "the powers that the Commission grants itself in this process go far beyond the permissible" (2012: 321). A long-standing advocate of the "modernization" of EU data protection, Alexander Roßnagel finds the Proposed Regulation to represent the wrong kind of reform. He criticizes it as a "highly radical solution" that is based on a "centralized and monopolized regulation" (Roßnagel 2012: 553). Roßnagel calls for a "fully harmonized" Regulation "only where it was truly necessary for reasons of business competition" and a requirement in all other areas of merely a minimum standard with room for experimentation by member states (Roßnagel 2012: 555).

Relatedly, commentators have also found that the Proposed Regulation violates the EU principle of proportionality, which is a means-end test (Ronellenfitsch 2012: 562; Schild and Tinnefeld 2012: 316). Johannes Masing, a Justice of the German Federal Constitutional Court, has emerged as an important critic of the Regulation. In advocating for federalism and its benefits, he argues against the Proposed Regulation's high degree of centralization of power in European institutions. In his view, "the power of every federal structure lies in its diversity" (Masing 2012: 2310). He feels the lesson that the Proposed Regulation largely ignores is that a federal system benefits from an ability to draw on "a living laboratory for the discovery and testing of new sectoral and differentiated solutions" (Masing 2012: 2311).

Without a doubt, the Proposed Data Protection Regulation represents a decisive shift in institutional power – and one away from the member states. To be sure, the Proposed Data Protection Regulations reserves some matters for the member states. These include laws concerning national security, the media and freedom of opinion, health, "professional secrecy," telecommunications law, and church and religious associations law. Nonetheless, the Proposed Regulation occupies a large field and will make data protection overwhelmingly a matter of EU law.

In interpreting this new EU law of privacy, the final and most important judicial decision-makers will be the European Court of Justice and the European Court of Human Rights. National courts will still have a role in deciding issues of data protection law, but they will largely be interpreting and applying the Regulation rather than their respective national omnibus statutes. This development will curtail the development of national data protection traditions.

There will likely also be a lack of resources for the most important European courts with the responsibility for resolving important privacy matters. In the estimation of Masing, the European Court of Human Rights currently faces more than 170,000 pending cases to be decided by its 47 judges (Masing 2011: 10). More broadly, the development of national privacy traditions, linked to local concerns and traditions, has been a source of strength for European privacy law. In the past, the EU has acknowledged this need for relative discretion to be left to member states to interpret the European Convention on Human Rights based on factors such as their different histories and cultural backgrounds. An example of a resulting strong national tradition has been the German Federal Constitutional Court's development of its Basic Law, the post-war German constitution, to articulate first a right of informational self-determination (BVerfG Decision 65, 1, 43, 1983) and, more recently, a right to integrity and confidentiality in communication systems (BVerfG Decision 120, 274 Online-Searches, 2008).

The Regulation also enshrines the Commission as the critical decision-maker through the power given to issue delegated and implementing acts. As an initial example, a delegated act is to set out the circumstances in which notification of a data breach will be provided (Art. 32[5]). The experience with state data breach notification laws in the USA has shown that these issues, including the precise trigger for notification, are critical issues for which a wide range of policy choices are available. Moreover, another delegated act is to provide details regarding the balancing under Article 6(5) of the Regulation between the legitimate interests of the data controller and the interests or fundamental rights of data subject. A processing of personal data will only be permissible when the balance favors the data controller, which makes the elements of this balancing test one of the most important open issues under the Regulation.

In evaluating the impact of these delegating and implementing acts, one also confronts the likelihood of post-enactment difficulties for companies in the face of regulatory indeterminacy. In the period after enactment of the Regulation but before the Commission issues the most important delegated and implementing acts, there will be many open issues – and without national law to fill in the gaps. Here, too, questions of resources are likely to be paramount. In noting the large number of delegating and implementing acts, under the Regulation, Kuner (2012) has questioned the ability of the Commission to generate the delegated and implementing acts within any reasonable time frame. He writes: "the complexity of the issues involved, together with political forces, likely will lead to a delay in adoption of many of them" (Kuner 2012: 14). Kuner notes that, according to one estimate, it may take *fifteen years* for all delegated and implemented acts to be enacted.

Thus the Proposed Regulation's break with privacy federalism raises, at a minimum, new risks. There are also steps that can be taken to protect federalism in EU privacy law. For example, Masing (2011) calls for development of a politically responsible Data Protection Commissioner, whom the Parliament would elect. This is a valuable proposal to help overcome any democratic deficit in EU data protection. The Proposed Regulation currently grants the Commission a problematic power over the national data protection authorities through the consistency process.

Finally, there is the impact of this power of the Commission on the larger democracy deficit in the EU. Here, Masing (2011) proposes creation of a new body, the EU Data Protection Authority. This new entity is to be located within the EU Parliament, which is the sole elected branch of the EU government. In this proposal, the EU Data Protection Authority would consist of representatives from the Parliament; the European Data Protection Board, which is the Proposed Regulation's forum of national data protection commissioners; and the already existing European Data Protection Supervisor, an independent EU office. This institution would further the establishment of checks and balances by dividing the ultimate power of the controversial new consistency process.

Other proposals are possible. For example, the EU might reduce the scope of the Proposed Regulation. The Proposed Regulation creates binding law for member states in a way that occupies too many areas, sweeps too broadly, and leaves too little room for future policy experiments. As a further matter, a revised regulation should respect subsidiarity by reducing the scope for implementing and delegated acts. Such acts should be limited to the topics of a more modest, revised regulation and concentrate on field definitions and the workings of the EU Data Protection Commission. This step will leave adequate room for further policy experiments at the national level.

This chapter has argued that privacy federalism in the United States helps to develop pluralistic policies. It safeguards diversity and competition in the responses and regulations to new technologies and social developments. This diversity and competition in regulation result from the differing mix of intermediate interests in the fifty states. The promise of privacy federalism is at once different and similar in the EU. The account of the positive value of privacy federalism in the United States did not rest on separate state political identities. Indeed, there is no political culture on privacy issues that radically divides regions or states. Through the caldron of state identity, such as it may exist, California, New York, or Arkansas have not developed a strong sense of normative answers for privacy questions.

Here, privacy federalism may serve a different role in the EU, and one that cautions against too strong a suppression of national norms in favor of Brussels. In particular, there are (still) vivid national identities in European member states as well as political cultures that are strongly national in character. Moreover, and specific to this context, the weight of the past has shaped national responses to informational privacy questions in Europe. To pick only two examples, and at the risk of simplifying matters, the United Kingdom's data protection law reflects free speech concerns while Germany's law reflects its experience with oppressive native regimes on its own soil. These kinds of differences recommend at least some autonomy in the member states to develop different answers to the risks and challenges of personal information processing.

The similar promise of privacy federalism in the USA and EU alike concerns the general merit of diversity and competition in responses. As noted, a different mix of political power among constituents, legislatures, executives, and lobbyists will exist in the various fifty states in the USA. A similar landscape will exist in the member states of the EU. To the extent that the resulting divergent results and guarantee of "regulatory friction" for the regulated entities is seen as a benefit, privacy federalism guarantees a condition of ongoing joint regulation. At first view, at least, the Regulation seems to have gone too far in the other direction.

Conclusion

This chapter has drawn a contrast between the legal structures for information privacy in the USA and EU. The USA faces the risk of increasing fragmentation as individual states continue to enact privacy statutes and the federal lawmaker remains silent. There will be many regulatory "inputs" from the states with too little consolidation at the federal level. The EU faces a risk of too few future "inputs" from the member states and too much power consolidated at the Commission. In the USA, the challenge consists of revitalizing federal legislative involvement in the field of information privacy. In the EU, the goal should be creation of data protection law that is attentive to checks and balances in the Community. Here, the Lisbon Treaty is illustrative. Jean-Claude Piris, the Legal Counsel of the Council of the EU, views the Lisbon Treaty as following in the tradition of "successive modifications of the founding Treaties" in demonstrating a decision "not to establish any single EU institution as politically too powerful" (Piris 2010: 237). Moreover, as Anne-Marie Slaughter points out, power in the transgovernmental realm should reflect "the guarantee of continual limitation of power through competition and overlapping jurisdiction" (Slaughter 2004: 259). The resulting balance of power should distribute privacy policymaking power among different EU and international institutions. The current Proposed Regulation falls short in this regard.

References

Bulman-Pozen, J. 2014. "From sovereignty and process to administration and politics," *Yale Law Journal* 123: 1920–56.

Bundesrat Drucksachen [BR] 52/1/12 (Germany).

COM 2012. *Proposal for a Regulation of the European Parliament and of the Council on the Protection of Individuals with Regard to the Processing of Personal Data and on the Free Movement of Such Data (General Data Protection Regulation), final*, January 25, 2012.

CNIL (Commission Nationale de l'informatique et des Libertés) 2012. *Projet de règlement européen: la défense de la vie privée s'éloigne du citoyen [Proposed European Regulation: Defense of Private Life Moves Away from Citizens]*, January 26, 2012.

Dix, A. 2012. "Datenschutzaufsicht im Bundesstaat – ein Vorbild für Europa," [*Data Protection Oversight in the Federal State – A Model for Europe*] *Datenschutz und Datensicherheit* 36: 318–21.

Epstein, R. A. and Greve, M. S. 2007. "Introduction: Preemption in Context," in Epstein, R. A. and Greve, M. S. (eds.) *Federal Preemption: States' Powers, National Interests*. Washington DC: AEI Press, pp. 1–5.

European Commission 2012. *Proposal for a Regulation of the European Parliament and of the Council on the protection of individuals with regard to the processing of personal data and on the free movement of such data (General Data Protection Regulation)*.

Executive Office of the President 2014. Big Data, Seizing Opportunities, Preserving Values. Washington DC.

Federal Trade Commission 2001. *North Dakota Privacy Law is Not Preempted*, 2001 WL 729771.

Feeley, M. M. and Rubin, E. 2008. *Federalism: Political Identity and Tragic Compromise*. University of Michigan Press.

Finch, K. 2013. "Straight From the Pacific Ocean: A Tidal Wave of California Privacy Laws," *The Privacy Advisor*, November 6, 2013.

Härting, N. 2012. "Starke Behörden, schwaches Recht –der neue EU-Datenschutzentwurf," [Strong Authorities, Weak Law – the new EU Data Protection Draft] *Betriebs-Berater* 8: 459–66.

Hills, R. M. Jr. 2007. "Against preemption," *New York University Law Review* 82: 1–68.

Janger, E. J. and Schwartz, P. M. 2002. "The Gramm-Leach-Bliley Act, information privacy, and the limits of default rules," *Minnesota Law Review* 86: 1219–61.

Kuner, C. 2012. "The European Commission's Proposed Data Protection Regulation: a Copernican revolution in European data protection law," *Privacy & Security Law Report* 11: 215–30.

Masing, J. 2011 "Ein Abschied von den Grundrechten," [A Farewell to Fundamental Rights] *Sueddeutsche Zeitung*, January 9, p. 10.

Masing, J. 2012. "Herausforderungen des Datenschutzes," [Challenges for Data Protection] *Neue Juristische Wochenschrift*: 2305–11.

National Conference of State Legislatures, n.d. *State Security Breach Notification Laws.*

Newman, A. L. 2008. *Protectors of Privacy.* Ithaca: Cornell University Press.

Note from Gen. Secretariat to Working Grp. on Info. Exch. & Data Prot. 2012. *Proposal for a Regulation of the European Parliament and of the Council on the Protection of Individuals with Regard to the Processing of Personal Data and on the Free Movement of Such Data (General Data Protection Regulation)* (July 18, 2012).

Piris, J.-C. 2010. *The Lisbon Treaty: A Legal and Political Analysis.* Cambridge University Press.

Press Unit, European Court of Human Rights 2014. *Factsheet: Data Protection* (September 2014).

Privacy Protection Study Commission 1977. *Personal Privacy in an Information Society.* Washington DC.

Roßnagel, A. 2012. "Editorial: Datenschutzgesetzgebung: Monopol oder Vielfalt?," [Data Protection Legislation: Monopoly or Diversity?] *Datenschutz und Datensicherheit* 36: 553–5.

Ronellenfitsch, M. 2012. "Fortentwicklung des Datenschutzes: Die Pläne der Europäischen Kommission," [Further Development of Data Protection: The Plans of the European Commission] *Datenschutz und Datensicherheit* 36: 561–3.

Schild, H.-H. and Tinnefeld, M.-T. 2012. "Datenschutz in der Union – gelungene oder missglückte Gesetzentwürfe?" [Data Protection in the Union: Successful or Unsuccessful Bill?] *Datenschutz und Datensicherheit* 36: 312–17.

Schwartz, P. M. and Janger, E. J. 2007. "Notification of data security breaches," *Michigan Law Review* 105: 913–84.

Sengupta, S. 2013. "No U.S. Action, So States Move on Privacy Law," *The New York Times*, October 30.

Simitis, S. 1997. "Einleitung in die EG-Datenschutzrichtlinie" in Dammann, U. and Simitis, S. (eds.) *EG Datenschutzrichtlinie – Kommentar*. Baden-Baden: Nomos.

Slaughter, A.-M. 2004. *A New World Order*. Princeton University Press.

Solove, D. J. and Hartzog, W. 2014. "The FTC And The New Common Law Of Privacy," *Columbia Law Review* 114: 583–676.

Solove, D. J. and Schwartz, P. M. (eds.) 2009. *Information Privacy Law*, Third Edition. New York: Aspen Publishers.

State of California, Office of the Attorney General 2014. *Privacy Legislation Pending in 2014*.

von Lewinski, K. 2012. "Europäisierung des Datenschutzrechts, Umsetzungsspielraum des deutschen Gesetzgebers und Entscheidungskompetenz des BVerfG," *Datenschutz und Datensicherheit* 8: 564–70.

INDEX

Lightning Source UK Ltd.
Milton Keynes UK
UKOW01n0908101217

314206UK00012B/149/P